D1109628

Global Development and the Environment Series

Series Editors
Richard M. Auty and Robert B. Potter

Microfinance and Poverty Alleviation

Titles previously published in the Global Development and the Environment series, under the Mansell imprint:
Economic Development and the Environment
Agricultural Change, Environment and Economy
Economic Development and Industrial Policy
Water and the Quest for Sustainable Development in the Ganges Valley

Under the Pinter imprint:
Land Degradation in the Tropics
Approaches to Sustainable Development

Microfinance and Poverty Alleviation

Case Studies from Asia and the Pacific

Edited by
Joe Remenyi and
Benjamin Quiñones, Jr.

PINTER
London and New York

Pinter
A Continuum imprint
Wellington House, 125 Strand, London WC2R 0BB
370 Lexington Avenue, New York, NY 10017-6550

First published 2000
© Asia-Pacific Development Council 2000

British Library Cataloguing in Publication Data
A catalogue record for this book is available from the British Library.
ISBN 1-85567-642-7 (hardback)
     1-85567-643-5 (paperback)

Typeset by BookEns Limited, Royston, Herts.
Printed and bound in Great Britain by CPD Wales, Ebbw Vale.

Contents

Foreword

The MicroCredit Summit of February 1997 set the goal of reaching 100 million of the world's poorest families, particularly the women, with microcredit for self-employment by the year 2005. This is a practitioners' goal, not one made by any government agency or international organization for the benefit of donors. Microfinance practitioners have set this goal because they know they can do it and they want to achieve it. The practitioners of Asia-Pacific have a shared excitement of going into this big venture. When the practitioners gathered in Kuala Lumpur, Malaysia in December 1996 on the occasion of the Bank Poor '96 regional meeting at the Asian and Pacific Development Centre (APDC), they dared to say: 'We accept the goal set for Asia-Pacific and will strive to bring microfinance services to a further 70 million of the poorest families here in our region by 2005.' As the global region with both the greatest absolute number of poor families and the longest and most intense experience with microfinance for the poor, this is a most apposite and worthy development goal to set for Asia-Pacific at the dawn of a new millennium.

One hundred million of the poorest families is no more than half the number of the poorest in the world today, but it is still a goal that some will say is too ambitious. Yet, if you apply this goal across countries, it translates as half the number of the poorest in each country and the task can be seen to be highly achievable. Take Malaysia, for example. Official statistics show that in 1996 there were 79,000 households below the poverty line. More than half this number, 43,000, are already clients of the Grameen replication in Malaysia, locally known as Amanah Ikhtiar Malaysia (AIM). So, instead of worrying about 100 million as a big number, we must look into our own countries and see what our microfinance institutions have done and what they can do further to scale up their outreach significantly. We know where we want to be. It is we, the practitioners, who will do the job. We will get started and not wait for other things to happen. We will achieve our goal whether the rest of the world comes to our aid or not. We can persuade others to come to our aid, but if we don't succeed in getting them along the path, our work will not stop. We will continue.

When I began, I did not know anything about microcredit or banking. That was not my job. But I started. I started with only $27, giving loans to 42 people. I was excited about it because of the excitement it created among the

42 people. I never realized you can bring so much happiness to so many people with such a tiny amount of money. To discover that was my greatest excitement.

On that day in 1976, if I stood up in a press conference and said: 'I will be giving two billion dollars as microcredit to two million people in the next twenty years', people would have said, 'You are crazy.' They would have said: 'You know what two billion or million is? How can you reach two million people within only twenty years?' I never had any idea I would get involved with it in a serious way. But that is what exactly happened twenty years later; we now have 2 million families as regular clients of Grameen Bank. Now with the world having so much rich experience, getting to 100 million households should be very much easier.

I did not know whether credit to the poorest would work or not. I went ahead with hesitation, but when it worked the excitement was beyond me. Bankers told me it can work in one village but not in two because it will fall apart. I did it in two villages and it worked! I was again told that two villages and one village is actually the same thing. So I did it over five villages and it worked! That was not a good number for the doubters and disbelievers. I did it over 10 villages, 20 villages, 50 villages, and 100 villages. Still that did not persuade them. They said: 'Well, this is not big enough.' I was challenged to do it over a whole district. I left my job as a professor of a University in Dhaka and went to the district where they said I must do it because success was expected to be much easier in the district where I was teaching. I thought that if I took up the challenge and did it in the district where they said I should do it, maybe they would be convinced. So I went there and did it. They were still not convinced. They asked me to do it over five districts in five different corners of Bangladesh. I did that. But they did not persuade them either. That is when I set up a separate bank, the Grameen Bank.

Doubters and disbelievers will have other doubts as you break new ground, and they will express and continue to express their doubts no matter how far you have gone in achieving your goal. They will say: 'Why do you only give credit, you must also give other things like skills training and everything; otherwise it cannot be done.' Or, 'Why focus on women as clients? Men are the ones who really need a job, not women.' Or, 'Well, maybe yes, your clients are paying back, but we know why they pay back. It is because you are twisting their arms everyday. Your staff has a long stick and they beat the heads of your clients to get your money back. That is the real reason why they pay back.' Or, 'Yes, you can get back your money but you will be permanently at the donor's mercy because you can never be self-sufficient and self-reliant.' And they will say: 'Maybe you give little credit, but that is not development. Development is something big'.

These are not the only discouragements we will face in what we are doing. I am not saying that the constraints and problems you might be encountering now are not real, but the most subtle and dangerous obstacle to your goal is when your confidence is eroded by the taunts of doubters and disbelievers. Many more issues will confront us as we continue to work. One of the most important issues is capacity building. We know how to handle 500 borrowers, but how do we go from 500 to 5,000 clients? Where to start? How do we train our staff? Where will the resources come from? These are real questions that will have to be answered as we do our work. It is these questions with which the authors of the various chapters in this book struggle. The lessons they seek to highlight, however, are not couched in the armchair theories of those who do but look and watch. Rather, the lessons set down here are based on the real world experiences of practitioners, our colleagues in the field. The authors themselves come to this task with a wealth of experience in microfinance in the Asia-Pacific region.

I commend the APDC for bringing out this book because it provides some of the answers for which we have been looking. We cannot break new ground unless we look at our weaknesses realistically and deal with them with courage and perseverance. But sometimes, when we look into our own mirror, we secretly wish the mirror would tell us that we are the fairest of them all. This book is not such a mirror. Rather, it presents a picture that is grounded in the real world of microfinance practice and impact. It shows what we have done so far to reach the poorest with microfinance in the Asia-Pacific region. It discusses the crucial issues related to our performance, taking a close look at the problems, weaknesses and constraints faced by all the major and many of the minor microfinance providers in Asia-Pacific. But most importantly, the book gives some practical wisdom distilled from the experience of microfinance practitioners themselves on how the constraints they face in significantly up-scaling their outreach to the poor might be overcome and what various stakeholders in microfinance, including policy-makers, banking institutions, donors, advocates and microfinance practi-tioners, can contribute to overcome these constraints.

This book has established a very important thing: i.e. the microfinance practitioners have successfully challenged the widely held opinion that the poor are not creditworthy. The experience of microfinance providers is creating a completely new generation of microfinance experts who know better and have observed at first hand why we all must recognize that credit is a powerful tool for self-help-based poverty reduction, as an essential human right.

Some day, people will take what we are doing today and put it in the Smithsonian Institution, the way they did with the Wright Brothers' plane. The Wright Brothers' plane flew for only some 60 feet or so, but that plane is now hanging from the ceiling of the Smithsonian Institution. In the same room, a few feet further, there is a rock, again displayed and getting a lot of attention. That is the rock from the moon. In the early years of the century, people were struggling to fly, yet within the same century, in the living memory of people who are still alive today, humans went to the moon to pick up that rock. This is the speed at which things change in this world. Today, whatever excitement we get out of the work we do in bringing microfinance to the poor, we need to utilize this excitement and enthusiasm to create better methodology and bring state of the art technology to transform the Wright Brothers' plane to the Boeings and Concorde to reach all the poor faster and serve them better. We too have to get to our 'moon' — the poverty-free world.

To do that we must learn from each other, we must pool all our experiences to lead us to new experiences, better experiences.

This book is a step along that path.

Professor Muhammad Yunus
Managing Director
Grameen Bank

Preface

Despite robust economic growth in the last decade, poverty continues to be a major problem in many parts of Asia-Pacific. World Bank and corroborating sources indicate that there are still around 800 million people who are 'absolutely poor'. Recent reversals in the economic growth record of key ASEAN and other Asian economies may well herald an increase in both the head count index and the absolute number of households in poverty. Poverty does not stand still. It will spread further if we do nothing to contain and eradicate it. Continuing effort to reduce population increases in poor and populous countries like China, India, Indonesia, Bangladesh and Pakistan will help stem the rate of growth in the absolute number of poor, but without the creation of sustainable livelihoods that will enable poor households to rise above the poverty line and stay above it, the number of poor households in the world will multiply inexorably. Microfinance is an essential key to the creation of sustainable livelihoods that are productive enough to afford poor households an escape route from poverty based on self-help and mutual support for self-reliance.

If poverty is to be eradicated, sustainable livelihood avenues must be created at a rate much faster than poor people reproduce themselves. It is almost impossible to achieve this goal on a widespread scale without involving the poor themselves in identifying and creating livelihoods that are consistent with the material circumstances and cultural milieux in which they live. Governments and well-meaning voluntary agencies have failed in attempting to eradicate poverty by doing everything for the poor. But we now have a winning strategy that enables the poor to identify their own livelihood projects, create sustainable sources of income, and provide self-employment not only for themselves but also for their children. Our winning strategy is based on extending access by the poor, especially the poorest of the poor, to microfinance.

Poverty can be overcome if the poor have access to microfinance services that enable them to acquire productive assets for self-employment. Microfinance practitioners have proved that the poor are indeed credit-worthy, capable of utilizing scarce capital efficiently in viable income-generating projects, and able to pay back their loans. The APDC, an intergovernmental organization supported by 21 governments and states of the region, has adopted *Microfinance for the Poor* as a leading strategy in its poverty eradication programme. In supporting institutions committed to the poor, we learnt that the poor not only have the desire but also the capacity to improve their situation. If they cannot find wage work, they create work by capitalizing on their survival skills. They are also good borrowers and eager to succeed. They use credit to start new activities or expand existing livelihood projects and pay back their loans on time.

In more recent years, many new initiatives in microfinance have emerged in Asia and the Pacific, inspired as they were by the success of Grameen Bank, the Bangladesh Rural Advancement Committee (BRAC), the Association for Social Advancement (ASA), the SEWA Bank, and many other institutions working with the poor. This book has pieced together the experiences and views of microfinance practitioners in eleven countries of Asia-Pacific to describe the present state of the art of microfinance in the region. It represents an experience grounded in insight into what we have learnt from the past and what we know today about *Microfinance for the Poor*. The APDC is pleased to have played its part in bringing this book to an international audience.

Dr Harka Gurung
Director, 1993–1998
Asian and Pacific Development Centre
Kuala Lumpur

Acknowledgements

The number of contributors to the case studies that make up Parts II and III of this book, which are based on data assembled for the regional meeting on microfinance in Asia and the Pacific, called Bank Poor '96, could fill several pages. The authors are grateful to all of them for their contributions. Special mention must be made of the chief executives and key officers of microfinance programmes, without whose willing response to the many interviews and requests for data the case studies could not have been completed. The authors and our collaborators take pleasure in expressing our deepest appreciation for the co-operation extended. Where our research teams were given access to audited financial statements the resulting case study allowed the authors to arrive at more realistic pictures of the performance of individual institutions, and thence to build up a firm basis on which to identify defensible generalizations. Those that had no audited statements to share with us were patient enough to bear with the additional probing and data requests specified by the researchers.

Most chapters in the book, but especially those in Parts II and III, are the result of the collaborative efforts of colleagues who have toiled long and hard to produce what is presented here. In order to reflect the spirit of co-operation and interchange that has characterized the process of data gathering, literature research, analysis, revision and final writing, authorship of each chapter is given in alphabetical order. This is consistent with the fact that individual contributors took the lead at different times in the preparation of each chapter. In a very real sense the authors have been peer reviewers to one another and to the national consultants with whom they have collaborated. The authors are grateful for the comments and suggestions made on successive drafts of the country case studies by all concerned. We are also, however, pleased to acknowledge the deep debt we owe to the national consultants commissioned by the APDC to do the in-country data gathering and literature research needed to produce the country case studies reported herein. It is as a result of their solid contribution and persistence in the difficult task of 'quality' data gathering that we have been able to arrive at a coherent assessment of (1) the capacity for outreach to poor households by microfinance providers in each country examined, (2) the constraints that must be addressed if that capacity is to be significantly increased, and (3) the capacity-building needs in which added investment will be essential in each country studied if access to financial services is to be brought to most if not all poor households in the Asia-Pacific region. However, the cited authors of each chapter take responsibility for any errors or omissions that may remain, and the views expressed are theirs alone and not necessarily those of the institutions with which they or the national consultants with whom they have collaborated are affiliated.

It is to be regretted that the case studies included in this volume could not be extended to cover all countries in the Asia-Pacific region, especially the 'transition economies' of China, Vietnam, Cambodia and Mongolia. Some initial research was undertaken on China and Vietnam, but time, resource constraints and other problems encountered prevented us from overcoming the data constraints and literature lacunae that besets anyone trying to study microfinance in these countries. It is likely that the transition economies require separate and special treatment in another book.

Initial drafts of individual chapters were received in a wide variety of formats using a remarkable range of word processing software. The staff of the Poverty Alleviation and Employment programme of the APDC did a remarkable job in bringing these drafts into conformity with a reasonably consistent and homogenous format from which to work. The authors and our collaborating contributors are grateful for their efforts. Whatever errors or inconsistencies remain is entirely the responsibility of the authors.

A book such as this cannot come together without significant financial support. In this respect we are most grateful to the poverty programme of the UNDP and UNOPS offices in Kuala Lumpur for assistance with the preparation and printing of early drafts of each chapter. This facilitated circulation among colleagues and contributors alike, and in soliciting comments from nominated readers. Special thanks are also due to our publisher, Cassell, and especially to their commissioning editor, Ms Petra Recter. Her insightful comments and patience have contributed significantly to the structure of the book and our objectivity in the process of drafting final revisions to the text.

A task such as the preparation of this book is in many respects a labour of love. Absence from home, long hours before a computer screen and distracted attention when present are but a few of the 'costs' that those close and dear to us pay. Yet, without the support and encouragement of our partners and other family members we would not have been able to meet the many deadlines that have been our taskmasters in bringing this book to fruition. Our heartfelt thanks to our families is gratefully acknowledged.

Joe Remenyi
Ben Quiñones

Acronyms

ADB	Asian Development Bank
ADBMCP	Asian Development Bank Micro Credit Program
ADBN	Agricultural Development Bank, Nepal
ACPC	Agricultural Credit Policy Council
AIDAB	Association of International Development Agencies in Bangladesh
AIM	Amanah Ikhtiar Malaysia
ANZ	Australia & New Zealand Bank
APDC	Asian and Pacific Development Centre
APRACA	Asia Pacific Rural and Agricultural Credit Association
ARTI	Agrarian Research and Training Institute
ASA	Association for Social Advancement
ASEAN	Association of South East Asian Nations
ASHI	Ahon Sa Hirap, Inc.
ASKI	Alalay sa Kaunlaran sa Gitnang Luzon, Inc.
ASLS	Association Special Loan Scheme
AusAID	Australian Agency for International Development
BAFIA	Banking and Financial Institution Act
BARD	Bangladesh Academy of Rural Development
BBMB	Bank Bumiputra Malaysia Berhad
BEST	Business Enterprise Support Team
BIDS	Bangladesh Institute of Development Studies
BIMB	Bank Islam Malaysia Berhad
BKD	Badan Kredit Desa
BKK	Badan Kredit Kecematan
BKPD	Bank Karya Produksi Desa
BNI	Bank Negara Indonesia
BNM	Bank Negara Malaysia
BoB	Bank of Baroda
BODA	British ODA
BoH	Bank of Hawaii
BoK	Bank of Kiribati
BoT	Bank of Tonga
BP	Banking with the Poor
BPD	Bank Purba Danarta

BPM	Bank Pertanian Malaysia
BPR	Bank Perkreditan Rakyat
BPWCMP	Bougainville Provincial Women's Microfinance Project
BRAC	Bangladesh Rural Advancement Committee
BRDB	Bangladesh Rural Development Board
BRI	Bank Rakyat Indonesia
BSD	Bank Shinta Daya
BSP	Bangko Sentral ng Pilipinas
BURO-Tangail	Bangladesh Unemployed Rehabilitation Organization, Tangail
BWS	Bank of Western Samoa
CARD	Centre for Agriculture and Rural Development
CARE	Cooperative for American Relief Everywhere
CASHPOR	Credit and Savings for the Hardcore Poor
CBRS	Community Based Rehabilitation Scheme
CCSLA	Canefarmers Cooperative Savings and Loan Association
CDF	Credit and Development Forum
CEO	Chief Executive Officer
CGAP	Consultative Group to Assist the Poorest
CGC	Credit Guarantee Corporation
CIDA	Canadian International Development Agency
CIDB	Cook Island Development Bank
CIDBRF	Cook Island Development Bank Revolving Fund
CISB	Cook Island Savings Bank
CRB	Co-operative Rural Bank
CRBLI	Co-operative Rural Bank of Laguna, Inc.
CRR	Cash Reserve Ratio
CUs	Credit Unions
CUCO	Credit Union Co-ordinating Office
CUFA	Credit Union Foundation of Australia
DBK	Development Bank of Kiribati
DBSBL	Development Bank Small Business Loans
DBSI	Development Bank of Solomon Islands
DBT	Development Bank of Tuvalu
DBTSBL	Development Bank of Tuvalu Small Business Loans
DBV	Development Bank of Vanuatu
DBWS	Development Bank of Western Samoa
DCS	Dango Credit Scheme in Simbu Province
DWCRA	Development of Women and Children in Rural Areas
EIU	Economist's Intelligence Unit
ESCAP	Economic and Social Commission for Asia and the Pacific
EU	European Union

FCUL	Fiji Credit Union League
FDB	Fiji Development Bank
FDBRWLS	Fiji Development Bank Rural Women's Loan Scheme
FDBSLS	Fiji Development Bank Special Loan Scheme
FDBAL	Fiji Development Bank Agriculture Loans
FDC	Foundation for Development Co-operation
FELDA	Federal Land Development Authority
FES	Friedrich Ebert Stiftung
FIP	Financial Institutions Project
FFW	Food For Work
FOA	Farmers Organisation Authority
FSP	Food Stamp Programme
FTCCS	Federation of Thrift and Credit Co-operative Societies
FWWB	Friends of Women's World Banking
GDP	Gross Domestic Product
GGS	General Guarantee Scheme
GNP	Gross National Product
GoF	Government of Fiji
GoPNG	Government of PNG
GoSI	Government of Solomon Islands
GPEP	Grains Production Enhancement Programme
GPU	Gami Pubuduwa Unit
GRF-BH	Gerry Roxas Foundation-Bangko Hublag
GRT	Group Recognition Test
GTZ	Deutsche Gessellschaft fur Technische Zusammenarbeit
HAF	Help Age Fiji
HB	Habib Bank
HDI	Human Development Index
HDFC	Housing Development Finance Corporation
HIID	Harvard Institute for International Development
HNB	Hatton National Bank
HPTLS	Hawkers and Petty Traders Loan Scheme
HRDF	Human Resources Development Foundation
HSF	Hanns Seidel Foundation
HUDCO	Housing and Urban Development Corporation
IADP	Integrated Area Development Programme
IBP	Intensive Banking Programme
IDS	Institute for Development Studies
IDT	*Inpres Desa Tertinggal*
IFAD	International Fund for Agricultural Development
ILO	International Labour Organisation
ILS	Ikhtiar Loan Scheme
IMF	International Monetary Fund
IRDP	Integrated Rural Development Programme

ISACPA	Independent South Asian Committee on Poverty Alleviation
JSP	Janasaviya Programme
JTF	Janasaviya Trust Fund
KKR	Koperasi Kredit Rakyat
KPP	Kaunlarang Pangkabuhayan Project
KREP	Kenya Rural Enterprise Programme
KURK	Kredit Usaha Rakyat Kecil
LDAT	Liklik Dinau Abitore Trust
LDC	less developed country
LDKP	Lembaga Dana dan Kredit Pedesaan
LDS	Lutheran Development Service
LFHPT	Loan Fund for Hawkers and Petty Traders
LKP	Lembaga Kredit Pedesaan
LPD	Lembaga Perkreditan Desa
LPK	Lembaga Perkreditan Kecematan
LPN	Lumbung Pitih Negari
MBFG	Malaysian Berhad Finance Group
MBI	Member Based Institution
MCPW	Micro Credit Project for Women
MCS	Microcredit Scheme
MFIs	microfinance institutions
MFI/Ps	microfinance institutions/programmes
MKEJ	Mitra Karya East Java
MSFSCIP	Marginal and Small Farm Systems Crop Intensification Project
MYRADA	Mysore Resettlement and Development Agency
NABARD	National Bank for Agricultural and Rural Development
NBF	National Bank of Fiji
NBFC	non-banking finance company
NBS	National Bank of Samoa
NBSI	National Bank of Solomon Islands
NBT	National Bank of Tuvalu
NBV	National Bank of Vanuatu
NCW	National Council of Women
NDTF	National Development Trust Fund
NEDA	National Economic Development Authority
NEP	New Economic Policy
NGO	non-governmental organization
NKRF	Nukuroa Revolving Fund
NLSF	National Livelihood Support Fund
NOVIB	Netherlands Organization for International Development Cooperation
NRB	Nepal Rastra Bank

NSRDP	North Simbu Rural Development Project
NWFTF-PD	Negros Women for Tomorrow Foundation-Project Dungganon
NZODA	New Zealand Bilateral Overseas Development Agency
ODA	Overseas Development Assistance
OICP	Outer-Islands Credit Project
OIDP	Outer Island Development Plan
P4K	Proyek Pembinaan Peningkatan Pendapatan Petani Kecil
PACS	primary agricultural co-operative society
PBSI	Peoples Bank of Solomon Islands
PBSP	Philippine Business for Social Progress
PCB	Pacific Commercial Bank
PCFC	People's Credit and Finance Corporation
PCFP	Presidential Commission to Fight Poverty
PCRW	Production Credit for Rural Women
PD	Project Dungganon
PHBK	Proyek Hubungan Bank dengan Kelompok Swadaya Masyarakat
PIDS	Philippine Institute for Development Studies
PIEs	Pacific Island Economies
PGS	Principal Guarantee Scheme
PKSF	Palli Karma Sahayak Foundation
PNGBC	PNG Banking Corporation
PNGWCP	PNG Women's Credit Project
PNKP	Putim Na Kisim Project
POKMAS	Kelompok Masyarakat
PRADAN	Professional Assistance for Development Action
PRDA	People's Rural Development Association
PTCCS	Primary Thrift and Credit Co-operative Society
PUGBB	Purbanchal Grameen Bikas Bank
PVTCW	Port Vila Town Council of Women
RASS	Rayalseema Seva Samithi
RBI	Reserve Bank of India
RBPNG	Reserve Bank of PNG
RCCF	Rural Credit Co-operative Foundation
RDC	Rural Development Corporation
RDP-12	Rural Development Project-12, Bangladesh
RDRS	Rangpur Dinajpur Rural Service
RDT	Rural Development Trust
RFEP	Rural Finance Experimental Project
RFSP	Rural Financial Services Project
RGVN	Rashtriya Gramin Vikas Nidhi
RMK	Rastriya Mahila Kosh
RMP	Rural Maintenance Programme

RoSCA	rotating savings and credit association
RRB	regional rural bank
RSF	Rural Self-Reliance Fund
RRDB	Regional Rural Development Bank
RTCLS	Rural Training Centre Loan Scheme
RWCS	Rural Women's Committees for Savings
S&LC	Saving and Loans Clubs
SANASA	'reformed' or 'reawakened' credit co-operative/union movement, Sri Lanka
SBP	Sustainable Banking for the Poor
SCB	State Co-operative Bank
SCF	Save the Children Fund
SDC	Swiss Development Co-operation
SEPMEC	Self-Employment Promotion through Micro Enterprise Credit
SEWA	Self-Employed Women's Association
SEWA Bank	Sri Mahila SEWA Sahakari Bank
SFCL	Small Farmers Co-operative Ltd
SFDP	Small Farmer Development Programme
SHARE	Society for Helping and Awakening Rural Poor through Education
SHG	self-help group
SICUL	Solomon Islands Credit Union League
SIDBI	Small Industries Development Bank of India
SLNSB	Sri Lanka National Savings Bank
SLR	Statutory Liquidity Ratio
SLS	Special Loan Scheme
SP	Samurdhi Programme
SPC	South Pacific Commission
SPFS	South Pacific Forum Secretariat
SPO	Sub-project office
SPMS	Sri Padmavathy Mahila Abyudaya Sangam
TCCS	Thrift and Credit Co-operative Society
TCUL	Tonga Credit Union League
TDB	Tonga Development Bank
TIDRF	Tuvalu Islands Development Revolving Fund
TNYCS	Tonga National Youth Credit Scheme
TRYSEM	Training of Rural Youth for Self-Employment
TSPI	Tulay Sa Pag-unlad, Inc.
UDA	Urban Development Authority
UN-ESCAP	United Nations Economic and Social Commission for Asia and the Pacific
UNDP	United Nations Development Programme
UNOPS	United Nations Office for Project Services

USAID	United States Agency for International Development
USPC	United States Peace Corps
VB	Village Banks
VCUL	Vanuatu Credit Union League
VDC	Village Development Committee
VGD	Vulnerable Group Development
WASLS	Women's Affairs Small Loans Scheme
WBC	Westpac Banking Corporation
WBF	Women in Business Foundation
WCP	Women's Credit Project
WESAP	Women's Economic and Social Advancement Program
WMLS	Women's Mini Loan Scheme
WOSED	Women's Social and Economic Development Programme
WWF	Working Women's Forum, also known as Co-operative Network for Women
YMLS	Youth Mini Loan Scheme
YPEIM	Yayasan Pembangunan Ekonomi Islam Malaysia
YUM	Yayasan Usaha Maju

Contributors

Professor Ruth Callanta
  President, Centre for Community Transformation, City of Mandaluyong, Philippines

Professor Siwar Chamhuri
  University Kebangsaan Malaysia, Malaysia

Harihar Dev-Pant
  Chairman, Nirdhan, Nepal

Dipak Dhungel
  Independent Consultant, Kathmandu, Nepal

Sunimal Fernando
  Executive Director, IRED International, Colombo, Sri Lanka

Edgardo Garcia
  Executive Director, Centre for Community Transformation, City of Pasig, Philippines

Pofessor Mike Getubig
  Xavier University, Philippines

Professor David S. Gibbons
  Managing Director, CASHPOR Technical Services (M), Malaysia

Iftekhar Hossain
  Manager, Acnabin & Co., Dhaka, Bangladesh

Gilberto M. Llanto
  Senior Research Fellow, Philippines Institute for Development Studies, Manila, Philippines

Urben Parhusip
  Independent Consultant, APRACA Consultancy Services, Jakarta, Indonesia
Benjamin R. Quiñones
  Programme Coordinator, Asian and Pacific Development Centre, Kuala Lumpur, Malaysia

Professor Joe Remenyi
  Director, International and Community Development, Deakin University, Australia

Stuart Rutherford
  Independent Consultant, Dhaka, Bangladesh

Javed K. Sakhawat
  Executive Director, Associates for Development Initiatives Ltd, Dhaka, Bangladesh

John Samuel
  President, Bodhigram India, Centre for Social Justice and Development, Puna, India

Professor H. Dieter Seibel
  Head of Development Research Centre, University of Cologne, Germany

Sanjay Sinha
  Executive Director, EDA Rural Systems, New Delhi, India

Introduction

This is a book by practitioners that is addressed to students of microfinance, practitioners of microfinance and development assistance administrators. The readers of this book will be people who want to understand microfinance and are challenged in their professional endeavours to increase the level and quality of support given to microfinance projects and programmes, including resources for microcredit and microenterprise development. As such, the book is organized into four distinct but related parts.

Part I of the book can be considered as the authors' 'desk-study', consisting of two chapters that set the scene for the rest of the work. In Chapter 1 the wealth of information and debate that had to be sifted and reconciled in the finalization of the case studies has been brought together and used to paint a canvas with a broad brush. It is here that we explore why and how the global community of microfinance practitioners believes that it is essential for sustained poverty reduction that financially viable intermediation services (covering savings, credit, insurance and money management), be brought to a substantially expanded number of the poorest of the poor. In Chapter 2 the received wisdom on microfinance is considered in the light of relevant academic literature and other publications commonly available in the public domain. An attempt is made here to identify the principal tenets that make up the current 'state of the art' in microfinance. Attention is drawn in the chapter to areas of agreement and disagreement in the literature, and to examine the passage of ideas and contemporary thinking on 'best practice' in the role of microfinance in poverty reduction. The chapter is based on an extensive study of the literature on microfinance and related topics, but the results reveal a dearth of literature grounded on solid objective data detailing the impact, whether short-term or long-term, of microfinance on the incidence of poverty, the persistence of poverty, and the quality of life in poor households. Until this lacunae is addressed it is likely that the under-investment in microfinance that has characterized the approach to poverty alleviation in decades past will persist. The case studies in this book represent our effort to help fill this gap.

Parts II and III are the core of the book in which four key themes are explored in each of seven country case studies and one regional study. These case studies represent a unique assessment of the capacity for delivery of microfinance services and the constraints to be overcome in the Asia-Pacific region if microfinance services are to be brought to all poor households. The case studies were originally prepared as a resource for Bank Poor '96, the UNDP-APDC regional meeting of microfinance practitioners held at the APDC in Kuala Lumpur in December 1996. BankPoor '96 was an independent forum of practitioners, propitiously timed a few months before the global MicroCredit Summit in Washington, DC in February 1997. Subsequently, the case studies were revised for this book, with the benefit of further research, comments from readers and our peers, plus additional information garnered from the 300 + participants at Bank Poor '96, (including 200 + microfinance practitioners and 100 + government officials, financial sector regulators, bankers and donors involved in microfinance programmes), from virtually every part of the Asia-Pacific region. All the contributors to the case study chapters have themselves been active in microfinance, in one capacity or another, for many years.

Four key themes are addressed in each of the case studies from the unique perspective of the practitioner, covering what must be described as 'the burning issue' in microfinance for the poor — i.e. the challenge of greatly expanded outreach. The four themes are: (1) Capacity of Microfinance Providers for Outreach to the Poor; (2) Microfinance Provider Financial Viability; (3) Resource Mobilization for Expanded Outreach to the Poor; and (4) Policy Framework and Regulatory Environment to Support Greatly Expanded Outreach to the Poor. In addressing these themes, the case studies present an assessment of the capacity of the main microfinance providers in eleven countries in the Asia-Pacific region to bring financial services to the poor. This is the first endeavour of its kind for countries in the Asia-Pacific region. The case studies show that results achieved to date in bringing access to microfinance to poor households are encouraging, but more than 90 per cent of poor households still struggle without the assistance of financial intermediation services. This represents a major obstacle to the success with which poor households can escape poverty through their own endeavours. The difficulties that will have to be overcome before microfinance services can be extended to all poor households in the Asia-Pacific region are not trivial. The urgency with which the global development assistance community must take up the challenge of microfinance has been made all the more critical by the unfolding Asian financial crisis.

Part II of the book is devoted to country case studies from South Asia. Here there are four chapters covering Bangladesh, the cradle of microfinance, India, Nepal and Sri Lanka. Pakistan is also an important focus for microfinance, but it was excluded from the countries studied because of budgetary and logistical constraints. Interested readers will find a selected set of sources on microfinance in Pakistan in the Further Reading section of the Bibliography to this volume. Part III covers three important East Asian countries in which microfinance has become particularly important (i.e. Indonesia, Malaysia and the Philippines), and a regional chapter covering the

Pacific Islands, with special attention given to Papua New Guinea, Fiji, Solomon Islands and Tonga. The authors are conscious that some countries have been excluded form the study, notably China, Vietnam and Thailand, even though the level of interest in microfinance is gaining in importance in the national poverty reduction strategies in these countries. Case studies were begun in China, Thailand and Vietnam, but data and logistical problems intervened to frustrate our efforts. It is our view that a separate volume devoted to microfinance in the transition economies, especially China, Vietnam, Cambodia and Mongolia, is needed. As with Pakistan, a select set of further reading on microfinance in these countries is included in the Bibliography to this volume.

Part IV offers the reader the conclusions that we have drawn from the extensive amount of data gathering and fieldwork that has gone into the preparation of the country case studies and literature reviews undertaken for this book. In so doing the authors have had both students of microfinance and practitioners in mind. Part IV can be read independently of the country case studies, but we would urge readers who choose to so do, to then return to the case studies and the introductory chapters. An important part of the book is the extensive bibliography presented in Part IV. This bibliography is not intended to be all-inclusive, but it is our firm hope that the seminal literature available in the public domain is noted there for readers to consult at their convenience.

Joe Remenyi

I

Microfinance: From Theory to Practice

1

Financing a Revolution: An Overview of the Microfinance Challenge in Asia-Pacific

Mike Getubig, David Gibbons and Joe Remenyi

Introduction

Prior to the Asian financial meltdown of 1997–8 and the deepening political and economic crisis that befell Indonesia following the collapse of international confidence in the Indonesian Rupiah, the World Bank estimated that there were 800 million people in absolute poverty in the Asia-Pacific region, more than two-thirds of them women or girls. Chronic balance of payments problems in the Asian Tiger-economies in the latter years of the 1990s, especially in Indonesia and South Korea, and to lesser extent in the Philippines, Thailand, Taiwan and Malaysia, has seen the Asian miracle come unstuck. In Indonesia, where the crisis was more severe than elsewhere, the collapse of the Rupiah saw three-quarters of the GDP wiped out almost overnight. Inevitably, the human tragedy of these events deepened as people who had worked hard to achieve livelihoods well above the poverty line again found themselves in the poverty mire. The incidence of poverty spread as the crisis deepened. For those people robbed of their wealth and livelihoods by these events, access to locally administered and managed microfinance services are more crucial than ever if they are to rebuild their lives and reclaim the standards of life that the world now acknowledges as a basic human right.

To describe the Asian meltdown as a regional crisis of unparalleled proportions does not overstate the case. If the number of people dispossessed of what they had worked so hard to achieve was the result of a natural disaster or a war, the world would have rushed to assist and mobilize the impressive global phalanx of relief services that now exists to help the victims of natural disasters. However, because this crisis was wrought by policymakers and bankers, no such response has been forthcoming. This too is a tragedy. At no time in recent decades has the need for financial assistance to the poor of Asia been more apposite a response to a situation over which the poor had no control or warning. As economic victims they need help to recover and there is no more effective way to deliver this help than through a dramatic scaling-up of access by poor people to microfinance services.

Microfinance in general and microfinance for the poor in particular are relatively new fields without a body of established theory to guide us. Only fifty or so microfinance institutions in the Asia-Pacific region account for more than three-quarters of all microfinance activity in the region, and not one of these institutions was in existence prior to 1970. Most microfinance providers have been operating for ten years or less. In this brief time the accomplishments of the leading microfinance providers have defied extant theory on banking; in particular concerning the necessity of securing loans with collateral, the ability of the poor to repay their loans in full and on time, and the efficacy of concentrating on female clients. In so doing, the poor, and especially poor women, have defied logic in becoming good clients for sustainable microfinance and sustained rural poverty reduction.

Poverty existed in all countries in the Asia-Pacific region prior to the Asian meltdown of 1997–8, including those countries which experienced the most rapid and impressive economic growth during the years since 1985. The UNDP Human Development Report for 1997 indicates that at least one-fifth of the population of Asia and the Pacific remains below the poverty line. But, this is an incidence that is a substantial improvement on the individual country rates of poverty which, in many Asian economies, exceeded 50 per cent of households only a generation ago. Following the Asian financial meltdown, the incidence of poverty has deteriorated yet again and may have increased three- or four-fold in Indonesia, the worst-affected economy. Economic ground gained in the course of the past two decades of consumption growth and economic development must now be regained, and microfinance will have an important role to play.

The spread of poverty does not rob the people only of their wealth, but also of their dignity. Poverty is the leading cause of death, especially among children. It is a lamentably neglected source of tension in poor households and renders ordinary people vulnerable to exploitation because of their inability to resist duress. Poverty is also a gender issue. Poverty afflicts women much more than men. Worldwide, women and girls comprise 70 per cent of the poor and two-thirds of the world's illiterate. The economic and social burden of structural adjustment is carried disproportionately by the female population and their babies, exacerbated by the persistence of rapid population increases, especially in some of the poorest economies, including Bangladesh, China, India, Indonesia, Papua New Guinea, the Philippines and Thailand. Unless the creation of sustainable livelihoods proceeds at rates that exceed growth in the absolute number of people below the poverty line, the incidence of poverty will remain at unacceptably high levels and will not be reduced. Microfinance providers are excelling in addressing this problem because nearly all have learnt that if one's objective is poverty reduction through the provision of financial services to the poor, women are their best clients.

If sustainable livelihoods are to be created at a much faster rate than past growth in numbers of absolute poor, it is essential to involve the poor themselves. The poor need the respect and dignity that flows from identifying and creating their own livelihood sources. Success in self-help is a powerful motivator and builder of social capital, the web of local and social assistance networks that distinguishes one cultural community from another. It is social capital that substitutes for the absence of broad-based social 'safety-net' systems in poor economies. Sustainable poverty reductions must be firmly based on the social capital and institutional structures that characterize the communities where poor households predominate. Too often history records that government and well-meaning voluntary agencies have failed in attempting to eradicate poverty by doing everything for the poor. This only succeeds in replacing one set of dependencies with another. Success in self-help, on the other hand, leads to self-reliance and growth in the sort of household-level robustness that poor members of poor communities need to weather the storms of misfortune that so often is part of the normal timbre of life below the poverty line.

In this book the contributors record the results of an extensive study of the activities of 44 microfinance providers in eleven countries in the Asia-Pacific region, including today's microfinance leaders and pioneers in the field from Bangladesh, Indonesia, Malaysia and the Philippines. The case studies and the analysis of the data presented are a solid foundation for the belief that *Microfinance for the Poor* offers a proven alternative strategy to the paternalism of government welfare or private charity. Microfinance gives poor people access to resources in ways that enables them to identify their own livelihood projects, create sustainable sources of income and provide self-employment for themselves and their children, and mobilizes under-employed local resources for the sustained benefit of even the poorest microfinance participants and local residents. It is to be lamented, therefore, that so few poor households – less than 3 per cent in the Asia-Pacific region – have access to user-friendly banking services. Not until the footprint of microfinance providers on the landscape of poverty in developing countries is substantially enlarged will the impact of microfinance on the reduction of poverty in the region realize its potential.

Although not a panacea, the microfinance case studies presented in this book support the conclusion that poverty can be overcome if the poor have access to microfinance services that enable them to acquire productive assets for self-employment. The overwhelming experience of microfinance institutions is that the poor are indeed creditworthy, capable of utilizing scarce capital efficiently in viable income-generating projects, and they do pay back their loans, with interest and on time. The dilemma is that too few poor people are being reached by existing microfinance institutions and programmes. The constraints that prevent these microfinance providers from rapidly and significantly expanding their outreach to poor people in the Asia-Pacific region are the primary focus of this book. The results are encouraging, because they show that the task of outreach is achievable and the way ahead is known. Moreover, the scale of the resources needed to bring microfinance services to a majority of poor people is well within the ability of the international community to achieve within a decade, provided it is in collaboration with regional governments and poor people themselves.

The will to bring microfinance services to all poor households cannot be realized unless it is directed at relieving or removing the four crucial constraints to outreach examined in the case studies reported here: (1) institutional capacity for outreach; (2) financial viability of microfinance provider enterprises; (3) resource mobilization for scaling-up of microfinance delivery by existing and proposed microfinance providers; and (4) the policy and regulatory environment needed to facilitate a dramatic expansion of access by the poorest households to microfinance services.

The case studies, which cover the major microfinance providers in Asia-Pacific, clearly show that the success of Grameen Bank in Bangladesh can be replicated, as was done in Malaysia with the establishment of Amanah Ikhtiar Malaysia (AIM) in 1986, and similar replications in at least six other countries in Asia-Pacific since then. But the case studies also show that the approach by Grameen Bank is not the only successful approach to microfinance. Other models, involving self-help groups, co-operatives, friendly societies and many other variations of these institutional forms, have been used to bring credit and other financial services to the poor in the Asia-Pacific region, cultural diversity notwithstanding. The lesson we take from this rich lode of experience is that in supporting institutions committed to the poor, we learn that the poor, when given the opportunity, not only have the desire but also have the capacity to improve their situation. If they cannot find wage work, they create work by capitalizing on their survival skills. Too often this potential for self-help is frustrated by the lack of access that poor people have to the financial services they need to pull themselves up by the bootstraps.

Constraints to Microfinance Outreach to the Poor

Microfinance is the provision of financial intermediation through the distribution of small loans, acceptance of small savings and provision of other financial products and services to the poor. Central to the concept of microfinance is the idea that poverty can be effectively and permanently reduced or eliminated within a reasonable period of time by providing the poor with access to such financial services. In Asia, perhaps more so than elsewhere, a number of institutions have emerged that have helped fuel the interest in microfinance as an instrument for poverty reduction. The most notable microfinance providers have come from Bangladesh, a country with one of the highest incidence of poverty, afflicting tens of millions of people. Foremost among these are Grameen Bank, the BRAC and the ASA, each of which has been hugely successful in reaching out and alleviating poverty for millions of poor 'customers'.

While the case for microfinance as a tool for poverty reduction may seem simple and straightforward, it is beset with many complex issues that have yet to be resolved and which continue to be the subject of vigorous debate. Among these issues, one of the most urgent is the importance that should be attached to the several 'core' constraints to expanded programmes of outreach of microfinance to the poor. The case studies presented in the chapters that follow throw important light on these constraints and the lessons that need to be taken from the experiences of the pioneering microfinance providers across the Asia-Pacific region. In this overview we begin by examining the four 'core' constraints to scaling-up the outreach of microfinance servicing of poor households – i.e. capacity to expand, financial viability for expansion, resources needed to expand significantly and the policy environment needed to nurture the healthy growth microfinance for the poorest. Our aim is to clarify what each of these four means and highlight the consensus of views that exists on them.

Capacity for Outreach to the Poor

Outreach to the poor refers to the extent to which Microfinance institutions (MFIs) are able to expand their client base to provide an ever-greater number of genuinely poor beneficiaries, especially women, with microfinance services. The temptation to grow by attracting new clients who are among the 'near-poor' or the 'not-poor' is difficult to resist. One can always seek to justify an increase in business with such clients by claiming that the trickle-down of benefits to the lowest strata of income earners is more likely because the near-poor are themselves active in the same market places for goods, services and factors of production as the poorest households in their society. Alternatively, one might argue that the inclusion of clients who are not poor in the growth plans of the programme would allow cross-subsidization to the benefit of the poor. However, one should not accept either argument. More genuinely poor people will be assisted to find their way above the poverty line though the targeting of microfinance services at the genuinely poor than through any amount of cross-subsidization or second-round trickle-down effects of microfinance. Why is this so? The answer is based on more than our personal biases and experiences in the field, or from what we have observed as programme evaluators, though these are important sources of our 'learning'.

The capacity to reach out to the poor must include the existence of effective mechanisms to identify and then deliver appropriately designed financial services to poor households. The absence of these leads to inefficiency in the utilization of resources meant for poor people. In the chapters that follow, half of the case studies reported that they seek to serve both poor and non-poor households. The contrast in outreach record between the microfinance providers that target the poor exclusively and those that do not is telling and supports the view that serving the not-poor drains off scarce resources, both financial and human, that could have been used to increase outreach to the poor. On average the institutions that target the poor reach more than nine times the number of poor households than those that have not practised targeting. All of the giants in microfinance – i.e. Grameen Bank, the BRAC, the ASA and P4K – attempt to work exclusively with the poor. They have not become giants because they have eschewed this essential focus on poor households, but exactly the opposite.

The case studies reported in Chapters 4 to 11 show that most microfinance providers do not give sufficient attention to the targeting of genuinely poor households in their search for new clients. Hence, given that reasonably priced financial services are a very scarce commodity at the village level, it is likely that current practices of those microfinance providers that do not target new business at the poorest households experience considerable leakage of resources to the non-poor and the near-poor. The data shows that in the absence of effective targeting procedures, as many as one-half of all new clients in a given year may come from households that are above the poverty line.

Leakage to the not-poor can happen for any one of several reasons: (1) when a microfinance provider either has no definition of 'the poor' (perhaps assuming that all people living in a poor village are themselves poor); or (2) when a conceptual definition is not adequately operationalized so as to be easily and accurately used by the field staff (e.g. definitions of poverty based on per-capita income or calorie consumption levels); or (3) when the fieldstaff have not been given adequate training in targeting and/or motivating the poor. Leakage to the not poor is 'easier', because the not-poor are easier to motivate than the poor. The poor are suspicious and cautious. Experience has taught them to be thus. Fieldstaff trying hard to meet stiff quotas for group formation, for example, may be tempted to include not-poor households who are ready to join, rather than to take more time to motivate genuinely poor women to participate. To minimize the number of staff who succumb to this temptation, a microfinance provider must have adequate quality control of its targeting.

Much of the resistance to poverty targeting in new business expansion is a response to the fact that conventional methods of identifying truly poor households, such as the use of per capita household income or calorie intake, have been found to be impractical and/or costly. Other approaches, such as the self-targeting approach (i.e. restrict loan sizes to below the amounts that would attract the non-poor), or by asking local people to identify who are the poor in the community, are subject to serious errors and biases because of the lack of correspondence between optimal loan sizes and loans small enough not to attract the interest of the not-poor, the presence of political pressures to favour certain persons or groups, and peer-group influences through the normal play of local social mores. The potentially high cost of accurately targeting the poor on the ground has resulted in a discrediting of the effort itself. Fortunately, cost-effective methodologies for identifying and targeting the poor have been developed and tested by successful microfinance programmes in Bangladesh, Malaysia and other places. However, these methods are not as widely known as they deserve to be. Consider, for example, the following:

The field workers of Grameen Bank use a simple set of asset or wealth indicators to identify poor households at village level. The poor are those with less than half an acre of agricultural land and with total household (including agricultural land) assets of less value than one acre of average quality agricultural land in their community. This simple operational definition of the poor has served Grameen Bank well, as evidenced by the findings of all independent evaluation studies so far that at least 90 per cent of the Bank's borrowers are (or were) in the poverty group. Although the Bank's operational definition of the poor requires an interview with the household to identify and value its assets, it is still cost-effective because the interview is very short and is conducted only among prospective clients whose housing condition indicates that they are poor. Moreover, it does not take long to enumerate the few assets of the poor. Checking the validity of answers is also easy and quick, as most neighbours at the village level tend to know the asset holdings of each other.

Specific indicators for identifying the poor have to be valid in the context in which they are used. Grameen Bank's half acre of agricultural land would not be valid in the dry, rocky, single cropped areas of the Indian Deccan nor in the dry, upland single-crop areas in Java or central China. In such places, even two or three acres of agricultural land may be insufficient to produce an income above the poverty line. But simple, context-specific indicators of the poor can be developed for such areas as well. Ownership of farm animals is a good one in such contexts, with the poor households being those without a large farm animal, such as a cow or buffalo, and without more than one or two small farm animals, like goats, sheep or pigs.

In general throughout most of rural Asia CASHPOR Inc., the network of Grameen Bank replicators in six countries, in continuing efforts to improve the cost-effectiveness of member targeting, has discovered that housing conditions or quality are a good first-instance indicator of poverty, as most people will improve their housing if they have any surplus income. CASHPOR has developed a Housing Index that has been validated as a means of identifying rural poor households in India, China, Vietnam, the Philippines, Indonesia and Nepal. As described in the Draft Training Manual on Targeting for Credit and Savings programmes for the Poor (2nd revised edition, Cashpor, 1996), the Housing Index consists of only three indicators of housing quality: size, physical condition and roofing material(s). These three can be observed and assessed by field staff from the roadside, without an interview with the household, making it highly cost-effective as a targeting tool. On average a house can be indexed in five minutes, and about 80 per cent of the rural poor can be so identified with context-specific component items added and varying cut-off points on the Housing Index applied to different socio-economic, cultural and geographic environments.

The experience of CASHPOR Inc. members in using the Housing Index indicates that if a rural house has a permanent roof (i.e. one of concrete, local tile or galvanized iron), this seems to define a reasonably reliable dividing line between the poor and the poorest in many rural Asian communities. Thatched roofs invariably leak after a few years and are time-consuming to repair. Moreover, they attract rodents and snakes that prey on rodents. Rural households tend to replace them with more permanent roofing materials as soon as they have some surplus income; that is, as soon as they move from being very poor to moderately poor. So, if a microfinance provider wants to identify and concentrate on the poorest of the poor in an Asian rural area, it will not go far wrong by working with those households with thatched roofs – after, of course, dealing with those that have no permanent housing at all. However, we acknowledge that housing quality is at best a crude indicator of household poverty status, as many other factors can come into play. As a cost-effective first step in identifying the rural poor, the Housing Index needs to be confirmed by recourse to a household asset test where borderline and appeal cases are concerned. In addition, microfinance providers may choose to emulate the Grameen Bank and to ensure quality control over poverty targeting by using the Group Recognition Test (GRT), which is conducted by a more senior officer not directly involved in initial group formation. The GRT is an oral examination of each potential group and group member, to gauge their understanding of and agreement with the objectives, procedures and rules of the microfinance programme. All group members must pass the test individually before the group can be 'recognized' and admitted to a village-based Centre for receiving financial services. Before a decision is given on group recognition, the officer visits the home of each potential member as a check on their poverty status. Without this or a functionally-equivalent step, management could not be confident of the effectiveness of targeting and would be running a serious risk of allowing an ongoing leakage to not-poor clients of scarce outreach resources intended for the poor.

In 1996, existing microfinance providers in Asia-Pacific were servicing not more than 5 per cent of the 200 million absolutely poor people in the region. If we exclude Bangladesh, the proportion served falls to below 1 per cent. Scaling-up to reach just one-fifth of the 200 million will require a quantum leap on what has been achieved so far. However, if the experience of Bangladesh is any guide, scaling-up by a factor of four or five over the coming decade is a very realistic goal. One key ingredient to so doing is effective targeting, but this is not enough. Also essential is the ability to provide poor households with the right range of financial services. Clients from poor households want credit, but they also want savings products, and as established clients mature and succeed in making more productive use of their savings and their borrowings, they will seek a more sophisticated range of financial products and services. For example, it has often been observed that one of the very first investments poor households make as they experience the joy of an improved capacity to save is in upgrading the quality of their living accommodation. Over time, therefore, microfinance providers do find that there is increasing pressure to offer housing loan services as well as short-term 'production' loans.

A much neglected but critical determinant of capacity for outreach comes from the confidence with which the management and leadership of a microfinance institution sets and pursues its vision and corporate growth goals. Excessive conservatism on the part of senior staff and boards of management can sap the programme of the motivation that staff must have to push the boundaries of market penetration beyond the natural resistance that the poorest households have to change and be innovative in money matters. It is self-defeating to argue that there are clients in the market for microfinance who are 'too poor to work with'!

An abiding constraint on capacity for outreach is the need for microfinance providers to invest in the training of staff for this work. This is exceedingly difficult to do in the absence of external donor support for training. It is unreasonable to expect microfinance programmes to generate sufficient resources from their lending and other revenue-generating activities to fund the level of human resource development that will be essential if a large proportion of poor households are to be reached by microfinance providers. Donors have a critical role here that is suited to their comparative advantage as providers of assistance when no other source is available. Moreover, to the extent that such training has spillover effects and social benefits, there is justification for increased public sector and donor support for investment in training of staff for the delivery of microfinance services to the poor.

Microfinance Provider Viability

The alleviation of poverty through microfinance services requires sustained effort. One round of loans or assistance with money management is not enough to ensure that poor households will lift themselves above the poverty line and remain above it. However, if microfinance providers are to be there to service their clients over the long haul, they themselves must become as financially viable as the projects they finance, i.e. the microenterprises and income generation projects of poor households. Making a profit is important to enable the microfinance provider to build up equity, attract investment capital, service loans taken up for on-lending to poor clients, and instil a philosophy into programme implementation staff that is consistent with what they themselves expect of their poor clients who similarly seek to scale-up their enterprises. Earning a profit, in turn, requires that their income, which largely comes from the interest they charge on loans dispersed, must be able to cover all operating costs (including depreciation on assets), a reasonable loan loss provision, and the costs of funds (including protection of the loan fund from depletion by inflation), and still leave an adequate surplus to build up equity. These are the building blocks of financial viability.

The case studies presented in succeeding chapters show that most microfinance providers have not achieved financial viability. Not more than one in five microfinance providers function on a basis that covers all their operating costs. The remaining four in five are dependent on continuing access to donor grants and/or subsidized loans to remain in operation. This situation may be defensible for microfinance providers whose goal is to 'work themselves out of a job' and eventually exit from the field. However, none of the microfinance providers examined for this study are in this category. The focus in these case studies is on microfinance providers whose intention is to be active into the long term and typically, achieve the status of a people's or village bank of one sort or another. It is disturbing, therefore, to find that after more than five years of active business on the part of most providers studied, two-thirds of them, including many of the biggest and most well-known in Asia-Pacific, were not covering operating costs in 1995.

Full financial self-sufficiency has been attained by only the rare few microfinance providers. This is in part because inadequate attention has been given to realizing a critical mass of clients. Less than 80 per cent of microfinance providers have achieved a client base of 20,000 or more beneficiaries at the start of 1996, yet this is the number that practitioners accept as the minimum required for a microfinance provider to have any chance of realizing full financial viability. Of those that have achieved the lesser goal of operational self-sufficiency, the average return on loans outstanding is a very modest profit of only 1.6 per cent, while the 80 per cent plus of microfinance providers who have yet to reach operational financial self-sufficiency averaged losses on loans outstanding of 24 per cent per annum. While losses of this order are not sustainable without ongoing grants and subsidies from the donor community, one can celebrate the fact that the statistics tend towards lower losses on average, and higher positive returns for those that have already achieved operational financial viability. Nonetheless, it is to be regretted that so few microfinance providers have launched their operations without a commitment to be financially viable from the outset. As a result most microfinance providers remain in the comfort zone of donor dependence, earning unsustainable losses year in and year out.

Financial viability is a choice and there are well-known strategies for achieving it. However, two broad categories of operations policy and management can be identified as both necessary and sufficient. These are:

1. Microfinance providers must adopt pricing policies that are consistent with a return on funds employed that at least match the opportunity cost of those funds. This means charging interest rates that cover costs and providing services on a cost-recovery basis. Pricing strategies that distribute loan funds at below cost are not consistent with the goal of creating microfinance providers that are able to service their clients, independent of external financial support, on a sustained basis.
2. Cost control is critical. Data from the case studies show that there is considerable scope for reducing the unit cost of providing microfinance services. The average operating cost per unit of loan outstanding varies widely between the least-cost and the highest-cost operators. Typically, the minority of microfinance providers that have achieved operational financial self-sufficiency have operating costs per unit of loan outstanding that are only one-third the average of all other microfinance providers studied.

The lower cost base of those microfinance providers with the highest levels of financial self-sufficiency is indicative of the significant economies of scale that characterize the finance sector, but it is also reflective of the fall in cost of funds that comes with savings mobilization and tight programme management to ensure that on-time repayment rates are kept near-perfect. Nonetheless, it is true to say that the current population of microfinance providers in Asia-Pacific are simply not reaching enough poor households to be financially viable. As a result they are caught in a 'Catch-22' situation: i.e. they cannot get the funds to become financially sustainable because they are not financially viable!

Resource Mobilization for Expanded Outreach to the Poor

What basis is there for arguing that added resources directed at microfinance provision will result in greater outreach to the poor? The answer to this question is crucial. It must first be noted that there is a shortage of funds for financing programme deficits until a break-even scale of operation is reached. Most chief executives of the 44 microfinance providers consulted for the case studies examined in this book were unequivocal in their view that they could and would increase outreach to the poor if more funds for building their institutional capacity became available. There is no reticence from that quarter. The case studies data is no less clear and is along similar lines. It is telling that the handful of truly large microfinance providers in Asia-Pacific that have reached large numbers of poor households have not had much difficulty raising the large amounts of funds they needed to get where they are. This is particularly so with respect to the institution-building funds that could not be had from internally generated profits. For example, the Grameen Bank was able to raise US$100 million, mostly in grants, from its consortium of bilateral donors to finance its impressive expansion from 500,000 poor households in 1989 to over 2 million by end 1994. The second largest microfinance provider in the region, the BRAC, also raised a large amount of grants, mainly from bilateral donors, over the same period. Interestingly, the ASA, Bangladesh, probably the fastest-growing microfinance provider in the region during the period 1990–5, has had to raise most of its expansion funds as soft loans. That it has been able to do so, however, is due to the existence of the not-yet-well-known Palli Karma Shahayak Foundation (PSKF) in Bangladesh, an autonomous body set up by government using World Bank money to lend funds to non-governmental organizations (NGOs) for microfinance.

Most other microfinance providers in the region that have reached relatively large numbers of poor households or which have experienced high annual growth rates have been funded by government and by donors. P4K of Indonesia, for example, which was reaching almost 500,000 poor households by the end of 1995, has been funded by the government and the IFAD. Similarly, the AIM in peninsular Malaysia (40,000 clients, representing 40 per cent of the hardcore poor), Grameen Bank Biratnagar, Nepal (30,000 clients), and Grameen Bikas Bank Danghadi, Nepal (10,000 clients), have also been primarily government-funded.

There are a few large microfinance providers that have reached substantial numbers of poor women without government funding, notably India's Sri Mahila SEWA Sahakari Bank (SEWA Bank), and the Indian Co-operative Network for Women (also known as the Working Women's Forum or the WWF), both of which had close to 60,000 clients each by the end of 1995. The SEWA Bank has emphasized savings over loans right from its beginning in 1974, and still today has more than twice as many savers than borrowers, with the latter numbering only 20,840. The SEWA Bank is fully financially self-sufficient. The WWF on the other hand has emphasized credit over savings, with twice as many borrowers as savers (three times as many borrowers as the SEWA Bank), but the WWF has had to be much more dependent upon donor money than the SEWA Bank to finance its growth. As donor funds have dried up so too has the WWF's growth rate plummeted, from 18 per cent in the early 1990s to only 4 per cent per annum in recent years.

If we consider the foregoing facts, it is not difficult to see why microfinance practitioners point to the availability of funds as a key constraint to more rapid and extensive outreach to poor households. There is considerable justification for believing that if more money was directed at funding microfinance outreach, more poor households would gain access to the resources they need to invest in their own escape from poverty.

Microfinance providers source their funding for on-lending and service provision in a combination of the following ways:

a. External donor resource transfers in the form of:
   − grant funds from foreign or local donors;
   − subsidized technical assistance;
   − goods in kind;
   − soft loans;
b. Internally generated resources, in the form of:
   − savings gathered from borrowers and other programme participants;
   − profits on loan business done and financial services delivered;
   − cash donations from programme participants and/or collaborating agencies and enterprises;
   − client-donated goods in kind;
   − assistance from volunteers, including programme clients;
c. Commercial borrowing.

Microfinance providers can be classified according to which of these three sources is the dominant resource provider for outreach and programme growth. So doing places microfinance providers into a continuum that can similarly be described as identifying three Stages of Funds Mobilization for expanded outreach and growth. These stages have the following characteristics:

Stage 1. Dependence on Donor Funding
− financial self-sufficiency has yet to be achieved;
− grants and soft loans are the primary source of programme funds;
− most microfinance institutions are still in this stage and if nothing is done to ensure that future achievements exceed those represented by trends set in the 1990s, then the great majority of microfinance providers will remain in this stage until well into the next millennium;
− all of the largest microfinance institutions − Grameen Bank, the ASA, the BRAC and P4K − funded their initial clientele expansion with funds from bilateral donors, but the majority of the more recently established institutions do not have access to similarly large amounts of funds from these sources;

- significant scaling-up of outreach implies that a majority of microfinance providers will need to graduate from Stage 1 into Stage 2 or Stage 3.

Stage 2. Savings-Driven Outreach Growth

- only one-quarter of the case study microfinance providers had reached this stage of development by the close of 1995;
- microfinance providers in this stage of development typically have reached a level of financial self-sufficiency that is twice that of the average in Stage 1;
- long-term financial viability of microfinance providers demands that an increasing proportion of lending activity is funded from savings mobilized;
- the importance of donor grants and soft loans shifts from funds for on-lending to favour funds for training, infrastructure, and other programme components;
- the average client savings level of microfinance providers in this stage of development for case study microfinance providers was $US26 per person as at the close of 1995. If microfinance services can be brought to a further 100 million poor people by the year 2005, and if all these new clients can bring their average savings deposit up to $US26, this will generate a further $US2.6 billion for outreach. There is every reason to believe that this level of savings mobilization is achievable. By the close of 1996, the average savings deposit per borrower had reached $US39 for Grameen Bank, $US41 for the SEWA Bank, $US87 for the RCCF in China, and $US136 for Bank Shinta Daya of Indonesia. In planning future growth in outreach to poor households, microfinance providers have typically been too conservative and seriously underestimated the contribution that savings mobilization could and should make to the growth of their 'business'.

Stage 3. Borrowing from Commercial Markets

- less than a quarter of microfinance providers have reached this stage;
- financial self-sufficiency averages above 80 per cent;
- as the outreach of microfinance providers to poor households increases to cover most if not all poor households, all microfinance providers will need to access a rising proportion of their funds for on-lending and growth from commercial sources.

Of the case studies examined in the chapters below, half are in Stage 1, another third are in Stage 2 and the remaining four (the ASA and Grameen Bank in Bangladesh, the WWF in India and the PRDA in Sri Lanka), are in Stage 3. However, some microfinance providers began operations from Stage 2, such as the SEWA Bank, while some of the outreach programmes of commercial banks can be said to begin from Stage 3, but most started out from Stage 1 and then worked their way towards Stage 3.

Data from the case studies show that, Grameen Bank excepted, microfinance providers typically access less than 5 per cent of their programme funds from commercial lending agencies. More than 60 per cent of these funds currently comes from members' savings and the balance from donor grants, donations of goods in kind or soft loans. However, if microfinance programmes are ever to reach truly large numbers of poor households in a sustainable way, they will not be able to do it in reasonable time by depending solely on savings mobilization and/or grants and soft loans. This is because the amount of funds needed to service the microfinance needs of a significant proportion of poor households in Asia-Pacific is too large to be covered from these sources. To reach large numbers of poor in a sustainable way, microfinance providers will have to enter Stage 3 in their development, and borrow on commercial terms the added funds required. The higher the savings mobilization of a provider, both in absolute amounts and in relation to their on-lending requirements, the easier it will be to tap commercial finance markets. Hence, it is likely that most microfinance providers will have to go through Stage 2 before entering Stage 3.

Movement from Stage 1 to Stage 3 will be dependent on the success with which microfinance providers are able to overcome the constraints that work to keep them where they are. In particular, the absorptive capacity of most microfinance providers remains limited and will be treated with suspicion so long as their balance sheets show low levels of equity and little or no internally generated funds to back up substantial levels of borrowing from external sources. Attention to these factors of enterprise and programme growth implies investment in the upgrading of management, especially in strategic thinking, enterprise accounting, risk management and related financial fields. However, there is a dilemma here, for lack of funds for dramatic scaling-up of outreach to truly large numbers of poor households in a financially-sustainable way will itself require substantial prior investments. Donors and conventional bankers make an important point when they say that the real, underlying obstacle to expanded outreach is lack of absorptive capacity on the part of microfinance providers in general and lack of expertise in financial and cost management in particular. These gaps in expertise and technical management capacity do add to problems of moral hazard and efficient cost control that contribute to the potential high risks to the savings deposits of the poor if these are entrusted to small, inadequately-capitalized, inexperienced, loss-making, informal financial institutions that are unregulated. Eventually, one cannot avoid the conclusion that the solution is tied to the gross shortage of funds available to microfinance providers for management training, equity capitalization, client motivation-education and product development.

Most microfinance providers began 'business' out of NGO activity. This history is important to appreciate, because efficient and effective NGOs, at least until recently, have been able to attract a lot of grant funding; programme financial viability was not a donor priority. Instead, donors expressly preferred programmes that could 'move funds' out to poor people, with the result that the more expensive credit-plus development programmes flourished. Credit-only or even credit-first approaches were the norm and saving mobilization was not an issue. As donors' grant funds began to dry up, many NGOs were left with relatively expensive, financially unsustainable programmes, and this result is reflected in the case study institutions. Painfully their management began to think about soft loans, when the emphasis of cash-short donors was shifting to full organizational financial sustainability. The lesson of history is clear: *charity and the hand-out mentality are not sustainable development strategies.*

Apart from the fact that there never will be enough hand-outs to go around, the ability of microfinance providers to meet the financial services needs of their clients indefinitely needs 'equity'. Financial sustainability comes with the ability to earn a reasonable profit on equity while at the same time maximizing outreach and financial services to the poor. Financial institutions that only cover their current costs cannot build up equity, as they have no profits to offer shareholders as dividends to maintain and attract their investment, or to salt away as retained earnings. Without significant growth in equity, a financial institution cannot be strong and provide adequate protection to a large number of depositors. Ultimately, it is the equity of a financial institution that protects its depositors.

History is instructive and hindsight shows that prudent financial management would have dictated different expansion strategies for most microfinance providers. Few programmes have paid enough attention to ensuring branch-level financial viability before making a commitment of organizational resources into horizontal expansion, chasing clients and establishing as many branches as possible and the head office capacity required to support/supervise them adequately. A 'financial viability first' strategy would have seen microfinance providers choose vertical expansion of one branch until it became financially sustainable with a modest head office capacity. In addition, more emphasis could have been given to savings mobilization in order to maximize self-reliance. Then formal financial institutions could have been approached to fund the establishment of more financially viable branches, and horizontal expansion could have taken place. This option is still open to newer and smaller microfinance institutions and is the way forward for sustainable outreach.

Policy Framework and Regulatory Environment for Outreach to the Poor

Most microfinance providers are not banks and cannot offer their clients the protection that flows to banks as a consequence of the clearly stated rights and duties that are attached to having a legal identity. In response, microfinance providers that have wanted to expand and grow have sought registration as friendly societies, not-for-profit enterprises, credit unions, trusts of various kinds, member associations and affiliated programmes of existing private or public sector institutions. A majority of respondents consulted in preparing the case studies pointed to the lack of legal sanction for microfinance institutions in their countries as a significant constraint on their ability to mobilize savings, manage risk, seek legal redress when necessary, or tap into commercial sources of funds for expansion.

Less than half of the 44 microfinance providers studied for this book are licensed to provide financial services. Most of them do so informally and without any protection for their depositors. In most cases this is because the central bank or monetary authority does not have the legal authority to license them, as most microfinance providers do not meet the criteria for registration of a formal financial institution. In many countries in the Asia-Pacific region, therefore, there is a need for legal and regulatory innovations that recognize the importance, uniqueness and legitimacy of microfinance providers as formal financial institutions that are like banks but essentially different.

One might argue that a microfinance provider does not need to be registered as a bank, albeit a bank with strictly limited licence, because it can register as an NGO or a credit union or some similar institution. This is in fact so, but experience also shows that these options have not proved attractive to most microfinance providers. There are likely to be situation-specific reasons for this, but the most common is that the strict focus on poor households is problematic under any of these non-bank options. It is also more difficult to tap the commercial market for funds under any of these non-bank guises. But the biggest drawback remains the confidence and legality with which an aggressive savings mobilization programme can be implemented when the microfinance provider is either not registered to operate in this area or even acting illegally if it does so.

Central bank regulation that is directed at the formal banking sector can be inappropriate to the circumstances of microfinance institutions and deleterious to their growth into financially viable vehicles for delivering banking services to poor households. Repressive interest rate ceilings that prevent the lender from following full-cost recovery pricing policies, high liquidity requirements that unnecessarily limits outreach to the poor, inappropriate debt-to-equity ratio rules that exclude collaboration with commercial lenders, or regulations that mandate collateralized lending to the exclusion of collateral substitutes are but a few examples.

Additionally, governments sometimes implement fiscal measures or direct interventions in the economy through line agencies or government-owned institutions with little or no thought to the possibility that policy decisions in these areas could be detrimental to the development of microfinance providers serving the poor. Even before the coming of reforms to correct for the mismanagement of crony-capitalism, inappropriately set exchange rates, credit rationing to favoured clients, or gross corruption, government regulation and policy did little to foster the work of microfinance providers or their clients in poor households. With the introduction of structural adjustment reforms, little appears to have changed. The poor and the vulnerable continue to be overlooked. Governments that deliberately incorporate provisions that protect the poorest from the human burden of structural adjustment are few and far between. Yet, in circumstances where structural adjustment policies are being implemented, governments need to be encouraged to see and use microfinance providers as an apt and effective mechanism for lightening the burden of structural adjustment on poor households.

It would be preferable if hard data could be quoted to show that microfinance institutions have been able to insulate their poorest clients against the worst side-effects of structural-adjustment-based policy reforms. However, to our knowledge no such hard data exists. Although this is an argument for the support of research in this area, the lack does not diminish the a priori belief in the likelihood that microfinance institutions could have a powerful role in this area. Nonetheless, a word of caution is needed. The financial crisis that is unfolding in Asia in the late 1990s has left many poor households at almost every stage in the continuum that exists between the rescue operations needed by those requiring 'relief' to survive, and those still able to invest in their own self-help. It is also likely that microfinance institutions are no better suited to delivering welfare-style relief to poor households than they are to ensuring that poor households realize the investments in self-help that structural adjustment reforms or the spread of the economic crisis is frustrating them from undertaking.

A Way Forward

The MicroCredit Summit held in Washington, DC, in February 1997 adopted an outreach target of an additional 100 million of the world's poorest families to receive credit for self-employment and other financial and business services by the year 2005. This lofty goal is worthy of pursuit, but how might it be attained? From where might funds of adequate amount come to finance such a venture?

The MicroCredit Summit secretariat has prepared a document that suggested an order of magnitude needed for the task ($US21.6 billions) and identified possible sources, by type of provider, from which the funding might be forthcoming. These details are summarized in Table 1.1.

Table 1.1   MicroCredit Summit Estimate of Funds Needed for Expansion of Microfinance
Outreach

Sources of funds:	Amount (US$ billions)	Percentage (%) of total
1. Commercial Markets	8.0	37.0
2. Bilateral Donor Agencies	4.0	18.5
3. International & Regional Financial Institution	3.0	13.9
4. Private Sector (Practitioners, Service Clubs, Religious Organizations etc.)	2.5	11.6
5. Deposits of Microcredit Borrowers	2.0	9.3
6. National and Local Governments	1.6	7.4
7. United Nations' Organizations	0.5	2.3
Total	21.6	100.0

Source: MicroCredit Summit Secretariat, 1996, Washington, DC.

Results from the case studies bear on the estimates in Table 1.1 in important ways. In particular, the past growth record of microfinance providers suggests that greater attention needs to be given to savings mobilization as a potential source of outreach finance. Also, if the indicated role of commercial sources is to be realized this will represent a significant break with past experience. Never before has the private commercial sector been willing to stand financier for anything approaching 37 per cent of growth funding of MFIs, not even for the most successful and financially viable microfinance providers. The case studies indicate that if past trends are repeated, savings of poor households will supply not less than a third of microfinance programme funds for on-lending and possibly as much as two-thirds. This justifies far more attention to the problems of preparing for greater savings mobilization than is being considered by interested stakeholders in the public and private sectors or among donors in general.

Some microfinance providers studied have been extremely successful in gathering savings from borrowers and other programme participants. The average savings mobilized for all case study programmes was a striking 64 per cent of loans outstanding at the close of 1995. However, this figure is misleading because the average is artificially inflated by five cases for which the ratio of savings to loans outstanding exceeds 1.0. These five are the GPU of the Hatton National Bank, Sri Lanka (5.08); the SEWA Bank, India (2.12); the Bank Purba Danarta (BPD), Indonesia (2.02); the RRDB, Kalutara, Sri Lanka (1.06); and Bank Shinta Daya (BSD), Indonesia (1.04). If these five are excluded the average falls to 36 per cent of $US320 million in loans outstanding, with Grameen Bank at 30 per cent. Overall, in 1995 savings mobilization was the single most important source of funds for growth in the loan portfolio of all case study institutions combined.

How have the leading savings mobilizers performed on outreach to the poor? Is it possible in practice to give strong emphasis to both loan disbursement and savings mobilization? In theory, of course, strong emphasis on savings mobilization could provide a large amount of funds for on-lending to the poor at a relatively cheap cost (the interest rate paid on deposits is always lower than that of funds on the commercial money market). In practice, however, only one of the five leading microfinance savings mobilizers, Bank Shinta Daya, Indonesia, has used their mobilized savings primarily for on-lending to the poor. Neither the Bank Purba Danarta of Indonesia, the leading savings mobilizer per client of all cases studied, at US$1,212, nor the GPU of the Hatton National Bank of Sri Lanka, a close second with an average savings of US$1,083 per borrower, is using a significant proportion of its savings mobilized for on-lending to the poor. The BPD has only 262 poor borrowers. Loans outstanding to these 262 borrowers account for less than 1 per cent of the balance of deposits. Similarly the GPU has only 500 poor borrowers, with total loans outstanding to them accounting for only 6.6 per cent of the balance of deposits. Neither the BPD nor the GPU support the 'savings first' argument. Could they be exceptions? This is possible, but the experience appears to carry with it the warning that savings, once mobilized, may not in fact be used for on-lending to the poor. This is consistent with the experience that has characterized national savings mobilization initiatives in developing countries ever since the 1960s. There is little reason to believe that the temptation of cheap money, which is how governments or other elite groups tend to see savings mobilized from the rural poor, as any less attractive for their own purposes today than they have been in the past. It does suggest, however, that unless a tight link is forged between savings mobilized from the poor and loan disbursements to the poor, there will be a leakage to uses that favour the not-poor, including governments and sectional interests.

An approach that gives more or less equal emphasis to savings mobilization and loan disbursement among the poor may, in practice, be a strategy that is easier to keep focused on the needs of the poor. BSD of Indonesia, which has a savings:loans outstanding ratio marginally above 1.0, is a case in point. BSD is one of the case study microfinance providers that are reaching reasonably large numbers of poor families (almost 9,000 in 1995) in a financially sustainable way. However, only one-fifth of its balance of deposits is accounted for by loans outstanding to poor borrowers, whereas they have provided almost a third of those deposits. Hence, even BSD has not been able to prevent a leakage of savings mobilized from the stream of funds recycled into poor households. Nonetheless, BSD is serving a sizeable number of poor clients and this result does appear to be tied to the fact that BSD does not over-emphasize savings mobilization. It mobilizes enough savings to cover its loans outstanding, but does not emphasize savings mobilization to the point at which it becomes 'the tail that wags the dog', as appears to be the case at the BPD, the GPU, the SEWA Bank and other microfinance providers where the value of the savings portfolio exceeds the value of the loan portfolio.

A vexed issue among microfinance practitioners is the strategy of using compulsory savings as a mechanism for risk management and savings promotion. In point of fact the issue of voluntary versus compulsory savings deserves less attention than the impact on savings behaviour of the loan programme. A much neglected but crucial aspect of savings mobilization is the extent to which the savings habit is linked to loan dispersal. When a poor person borrows but is unable to use those funds to generate additional or sufficient income to meet scheduled repayments, the latter are often made from existing cashflow. This may require self-denial and/or postponed gratification in ways not normally associated with personal savings. In effect the offer of credit and savings services nurtures savings habits both through loans dispersed and deposits collected. Consider, for example, loans made for the fattening of a farm animal. Until the animal has been fattened and sold, the borrower must make repayments from cashflow not generated by the loan itself. If this kind of savings were added to the amounts mobilized by more conventional means, then the grand total of savings mobilized by microfinance providers working among the poor would be much greater than their recorded deposits received.

A relatively recent innovation in Bangladesh has pioneered a new role for government and multilateral agencies in ensuring that microfinance providers can get access to the funds they need to build institutional capacity and to scale-up to reach truly large numbers of poor households. The ASA has used this innovation to scale-up rapidly in only a few years, to become financially self-sufficient without depending solely on grant funds and to rival Grameen Bank and the BRAC in size. The ASA has had access to soft loans from the PKSF, a national-level autonomous company limited by guarantee, deliberately established and sanctioned by the government of Bangladesh for financing NGOs that provide financial services to the poor. The PKSF was established in 1993 with a grant of $US10 million from the government. This amount was then added to the facility of a $US100 million soft loan from the World Bank. In 1995 alone the ASA borrowed some $US1.3 million from the PKSF for up-scaling its lending to the poor. This amount was almost one-quarter of the funds the ASA mobilized in that year. It is conceivable that similar politically-insulated revolving MicroCredit funds can be established in other countries of the region. The UNDP MicroStart programme, launched in 1997, is an example, albeit an under-funded one. Under MicroStart revolving funds of $US 1 million will be established in each of 20 to 25 countries around the world, to finance start-ups and scaling-up of microfinance providers working with the poor. We must wait on history to tell if it is a successful venture, but in the meantime there is reason for other governments to follow the lead of Bangladesh and set up their own PKSF.

Concluding Observations

Microfinance may not be a panacea for persistent and systemic poverty, but the experience of microfinance providers is that poor people, and especially poor women, gain a real boost in their efforts to escape poverty as a result of gaining access to microfinance services.

Bringing microfinance services to a greatly increased number of poor households is a worthy challenge to accept as the global community prepares to enter a new millennium. Microfinance must be a prominent item on the agenda of development for the coming generation. We should celebrate the fact that we move forward armed with the knowledge that poverty can be overcome and that the institutions that will help keep poverty at bay can be established on financially viable foundations.

Experience has been a good teacher and we confidently expect that microfinance providers will open an avenue of escape from poverty to many millions more poor households in the decade ahead. Moreover, in offering support for microfinance providers, the international development assistance community does not have to be shackled to chronic institutional dependence as the price of meaningful and sustained poverty reduction. Financial viability is a management choice.

When donors and other members of the international development community insist that the microfinance providers they support will adopt financially sustainable practices, they simultaneously are choosing an 'option for the poor'.

Acknowledgement

The authors gratefully acknowledge comments received from many colleagues on earlier drafts, especially Iftekhar Hossain, Mohini Malhotra, Ben Quiñones, Petra Recter, Stuart Rutherford, Hans Dieter Seibel and Helen Todd. The views expressed are those of the authors alone.

2

Is there a 'State of the Art' in Microfinance?

Joe Remenyi

Introduction

In February of 1997 an international meeting of development professionals met in Washington, DC, for the MicroCredit Summit. This meeting drew together more than two thousand grass-roots-level practitioners and development professionals from every area of development. The purpose of the Summit was to promote a significant increase in commitment from practitioners, governments, donors and other development professionals to microfinance as a strategy for sustainable poverty-reducing development. In seeking to replicate on a massive scale what microfinance has done for a small proportion of the world's poor, the Summit was a celebration of the achievements of pioneering microfinance institutions in reducing poverty and improving the quality of life of the poor. Only a decade ago it was widely believed that it was impossible to successfully sustain a poverty alleviation strategy based on financially viable banking with the poor.

In this chapter we examine the 'conventional wisdom' on microfinance, otherwise also known as 'banking with the poor'. The chapter is a combination of views expressed by practitioners, knowledge and opinions recorded in the fast-growing academic literature on microfinance and its role in poverty reduction, and some personal observations on the theoretical foundations of the link between growth of household income, employment generation, and the delivery of microfinance services to the households that make up the poverty pyramid in the economies of countries in the Asia-Pacific region. In so doing the chapter examines the importance that must be given to the fact that the community of the poor is not homogenous. There is a poverty pyramid and microfinance institutions must decide whether they will target those at the bottom in preference to those with incomes that are closer to the poverty line. In order to do this we must begin with an agreed definition of microfinance and come to understand what have come to be the stock responses of conventional wisdom in the field.

The chapter also seeks to highlight those issues that remain the subject of debate among writers on microfinance. In some areas there is a distinct gap between what practitioners reveal as their 'received wisdom' and what is reflected in the literature. Nowhere is this starker than in the topic of poverty targeting and the identification of the appropriate client groups for microfinance. The argument is put that it is not enough to say that the clients of microfinance are 'the poor', whom the World Bank has 'familiarly' identified as persons whose survival is dependent on incomes that are a dollar a day or less. In this chapter we explore why this definition is not enough as a guide to the design of microfinance outreach, and why the advocates of microfinance are convinced that the persistence of poverty and the failure of so many poor people to escape from poverty is linked to the absence of microfinance services better suited to the circumstances and needs of the poor. The answers to these questions bears on why microfinance is more than a transitory 'fad' in contemporary development thinking and practice. On one issue the literature is clear: i.e. financial intermediation is the lubricant that oils the wheels of economic activity in the 'poverty economy' just as much as it performs this role in the 'modern economy'. However, the literature is also clear on the view that microfinance is not a panacea for persistent poverty. The conventional wisdom has matured to the point where microfinance is accepted as an important and necessary component of what is needed if poor households are to succeed in their efforts to climb above the poverty line and remain there.

We begin by defining microfinance and the 'products' microfinance providers seek to bring to their clients.

What is Microfinance?

A feature of 'development' in the decades since the close of the Second World War has been the spread of the money economy. No longer is subsistence production in a rural setting the norm. A consequence of this 'global' change has been an increase in the need for banking services, especially credit and savings. When banks provide these services, we describe what they do as 'intermediation'; that is the bringing together of the independent acts of savers and borrowers to facilitate one another's goals. Microfinance is no different except that its market consists of poor households and very small enterprises (microenterprises) in the rural and informal sectors of developing countries. The formal banking system that serves this intermediation role for larger enterprises and wealthier clients in the modern sector of poor economies has typically found it impossible to service this market of poor households using traditional banking practices.

The reasons for the failure of modern banking to meet the needs of the poor for financial intermediation services are many, but essentially the obstacles have been built on prejudice, misconception, lack of motivation, institutional rigidity, and ignorance. In essence, poor people were perceived in banking and finance circles as a poor market, offering few if any opportunities for 'investment', with the implication that there is little opportunity for entrepreneurs in banking and finance to make a profit from 'banking with the poor'. Moreover, in the conventional wisdom of banking circles, poor people were characterized as lacking collateral against which to borrow, and the financial 'products' sought by poor people (small loans for short periods of time, regular deposits of small amounts saved for specific purposes, etc.) involve very high transactions costs and risks that are difficult to manage using the 'technology' of modern banking. In other words, it was generally felt that the poor do not participate in banking because they are too poor to do so. Not only can conventional banks not afford to offer poor people financial services at a loss, but also poor people cannot afford to pay the cost of delivering these services at the profit rates that commercial modern sector banks need to operate and sustain their financial viability. Consequently, the conventional wisdom has always favoured the view that banking with the poor cannot be undertaken unless it is heavily subsidized. Microfinance, which is about profitable banking with the poor, challenges this view. Subsidized credit and subsidized banking with the poor are inimical to 'best practice' in microfinance.

Microfinance institutions succeed where modern banks have failed because they have learnt six key lessons:

- How to accommodate collateral substitutes as an effective basis for client selection.
- How to use self-interest to manage risk and maintain near-perfect on-time repayment rates.
- How to minimize the cash costs of making small loans and collecting small savings.
- How to mobilize peer pressure and social mores to enforce contractual obligations.
- How to design and deliver finance 'products and services' that meet the needs of the poor.
- How to segment the market to keep focused on the poor, yet target the well motivated.

On the basis of these lessons microfinance providers have come to understand that banking with the poor can be profitable, but only if costs are contained, risks are managed and clients treated as active partners in the conduct of the business of the enterprise. This is fast becoming the 'new' conventional wisdom, though there remains a significant group of academics and finance professionals who are sceptical.

MFIs, whether a bank, a co-operative, a credit union, an NGO, a self-help group (SHG) or some other form of non-bank financial intermediary, seek to provide clients from poor households with a range of money management and banking services. These services can be grouped into five basic 'product' types:

- *Credit*, especially a reliable source of working capital, dispersed against 'collateral substitutes' such as standing in the community, group guarantees or compulsory savings;
- *Deposit services*, designed to offer poor households alternative savings options to the hoarding of cash or other stores of value that do not generate an income stream or involve greater risk and lower returns;
- *Insurance products*, including insurance against loan default due to misadventure, illness, death, natural disasters or unanticipated economic crisis, plus targeted savings products that provide a form of 'insurance' designed to meet anticipated life-cycle-related obligations, such as weddings, funerals or other socio-cultural events;
- *Financial advisory services*, specific to money management and household-level financial planning; and
- *Advocacy services*, whereby the views and needs of the poor are given a voice and brought to the attention of policymakers, regulators and those with the authority to influence the environment in which poor households and informal sector institutions, especially microenterprises, have to operate.

The experiences of microfinance practitioners have proven to be a rich source of stories and lessons for development professionals active in poverty reduction projects and programmes. Global interest in what these practitioners have to say has fuelled a publication boom on topics related to microfinance and poverty alleviation. In 1996 alone, at least nine new books were published on the topic.[1] Many times this number of articles and research reports appeared in the mainstream learned journals and research publications of larger development agencies, such as the World Bank and the United Nations development agencies. In recent years the great bulk of this literature has been directed at the success or otherwise of particular microfinance institutions or the practices that these institutions have tested. The overall impression one gains from this literature is that:

- there is now a consensus view on the determinants of success in microfinance;
- there are important differences between informal sector MFIs and their formal-sector counterparts that give MFIs a comparative advantage in 'banking for the poor'; and
- the market for microfinance is characterized by under-investment and excess demand.

In other words, microfinance has much yet to contribute to rural development and poverty reduction, though there remain differences of opinion on implementation strategies, priorities and policies.[2] Some of these differences are explored in what follows.

From Rural Credit to Microfinance

The intellectual foundations of the literature explosion on microfinance reach back many decades, especially into the seminal writings on rural finance as a key missing link in the search for sustained agricultural development, rural modernization and institutional innovation.[3] Much of this earlier literature was very critical of the rural credit programmes instituted in the late 1950s through to the 1970s because it failed, contrary to firmly held expectations, to ignite the fires of sustained rural economic growth and improvements in agricultural productivity. The basic strategy of these early programmes was to displace traditional rural informal moneylenders (characterized as exploitative, monopolistic and inefficient), with benevolent and right-thinking government-sponsored development finance institutions or delivery programmes. Typically these programmes involved subsidized rural credit, delivered through a specially created rural financial institution or as a programme of a rural co-operative, farmer's association or similar legal entity. Often the credit programme was integrated into a broader 'community development' initiative of macroeconomic scale. Disbursement of funds and administration of the rural credit repayment and monitoring processes were given into the hands of bureaucrats, in collaboration with local leading individuals identified as 'exemplars' of modernity.[4]

Almost without exception these early attempts to bring rural finance into the mainstreams of rural and community development in developing countries failed. They failed to help the poor; failed to ignite the fires of sustained agricultural development; failed to mobilize rural resources to the modernization effort; failed to avoid mass defaults on loan repayments; failed to bridge the gap between rich and poor; failed to avoid gross leakage of scarce poverty reduction resources to non-target groups; and failed to avoid the pitfalls of corruption and moral hazard.[5] The consequence of this litany of failures was disillusionment with government-funded and -operated rural credit programmes or institutions, and a new-found romanticism in the efficacy of traditional informal rural financial services providers, especially among adherents of a world view of microfinance that Hulme and Mosley (1996) have described as the 'Ohio Orthodoxy'.[6]

The Importance of Anecdotes and Case Studies

As we explore the avenues of the microfinance literature to distil what we know about bringing financial services to poor clients effectively and efficiently, we find that (1) contrary points of view persist in many areas, (2) the objective 'quantitative' basis on which one ought to form views is lamentably thin, and (3) intuition, fuelled by the insights and anecdotes of practitioners, remains an essential but powerful tool of analysis.

In the contemporary market of ideas on development strategies, there does appear to be a consensus among the 'practitioners'. This is evidenced by the fact that in the contemporary development environment every bilateral donor and NGO seems to believe that it too must be involved in microfinance if it is to retain credibility as a development agency with an option for the poor. Among development researchers and academics, however, a similar clear consensus does not exist, even though the greater number of writers are sympathetic to the call by practitioners for a significant expansion in the level of resources devoted to microfinance for poverty reduction.[7] The disquiet of some researchers is in part the product of the thinness of the knowledge base about how the pioneers in microfinance have achieved their success and its sustainability. Much of what is known remains 'story-book' in character, reflective of the 'missionary zeal' that seems to infect all converts to the microfinance field of development, whether as researchers or practitioners. The accounts written by many of these converts resemble 'ripping good yarns' or awe-inspiring biographical treatises that fill the reader with 'hope and a vision splendid' of the harvest waiting to be taken in.[8]

There is a great deal of value in these inspirational but anecdotal writings because they are not trivial contributions to the literature. The data they present supports the view that microfinance is an important 'log in the jam' of persistent poverty. However, if this log is to be freed and the potential harvest gathered in, far more quantitative information is needed on the success with which competing strategies have been applied by different MFIs to meet the unique needs of the markets they have set out to serve. This data base is improving and has received a fillip from the recent appearance of a number of statistically based reports and publications that go beyond individual case studies.[9]

It is a brave person who can generalize with confidence from a mass of anecdotal information and incomplete case studies. However, there is one generalization about microfinance that does appear to receive universal support. It is that the track record of contemporary MFIs unequivocally shows the importance in this particular market place of adaptation by the MFI to the unique social, cultural and political environment in which the target groups to be served conduct their economic activities. Willingness to learn from experience is essential in any replication exercise, the model being followed notwithstanding. Hulme and Mosley (1996) have gone so far as to suggest that the spread of microfinance into new socio-cultural and political environments will be all the more successful if outreach is based on the results of an initial 'action-research' pilot project.[10] The nature of the process of adaptation to the web of 'social capital' that distinguishes one society from another is a core concern in much of the literature on microfinance and microenterprise development.

Who are the Clients of MFIs?

The target clients of MFIs are the poor. The World Bank (1996a) numbers these at around one billion persons (200 million households) and describes them familiarly as those people who have access to not more than a 'dollar a day' to meet their essential basic needs (i.e. for food, clothing, transport, health, education, housing, social obligations and other requirements). Women and children make up the greatest proportion of these one billion people. The MicroCredit Summit set 100 million 'new' clients as the outreach target for MFIs between 1997 and the year 2005, which, if achieved, will bring financial services to one-quarter of the poor people in the developing world. Of these new clients 70 million will be from the Asia-Pacific region and, if the past is any guide, the vast majority will be female.

Much has been written about the measurement of poverty, the appropriateness or otherwise of income-based poverty lines, and effective targeting of the poor.[11] These important topics have also been considered in Chapter 1 above so here we will limit ourselves to four very important points that cannot be overstressed. (1) There is more diversity among the poor than there is homogeneity. (2) Poverty is multifaceted and involves more than economics. (3) As MFIs succeed in lifting their clients above the poverty line, the share of their business devoted to clients who are not poor will increase with repeat business. (4) If an MFI is to remain true to its commitment to target the poor, it must have cost-effective ways of separating the poor from the not-poor in a poor village. Knowing what the poverty line is is not enough. Before proceeding we deal with each of these issues in turn, so as to consider the nature of the poverty economy wherein MFIs must operate. This is in keeping with the practical adage that success in any entrepreneurial venture is dependent on only three things: know your market, know your market, and know your market!

Diversity in Poverty

All successful MFIs, without exception, recognize that 'the poor' are not a homogeneous market, but a highly heterogeneous collection of groups of consumers, producers, savers, investors, innovators and risk-averse economic actors. In order to serve each of these different categories of clients, the MFI must deliver services that are tailored to each market. In many instances the MFI will find itself needing to have a range of microfinance products if it is to offer different groups of poor households the financial intermediation services they need to finance their escape from poverty.

The Poverty Pyramid

Elsewhere Remenyi (1991, 1993, 1994a and 1995), has characterized the diversity of 'the poor' as forming a 'poverty pyramid' of households. Each level of the poverty pyramid constitutes a unique market for microfinance services, needing tailored financial products and intermediation assistance. The poverty pyramid has the following features:

- At the bottom of the pyramid are the poorest of the poor, the vulnerable poor, including pregnant women, old people, children and the infirm. (Lipton and van der Gaag, 1993, called these people the 'ultra' poor.) Their vulnerability is directly tied to the fact that the contribution they make to household income is not sufficient for their own survival. They are vulnerable because their survival is dependent on the economic activity of others. Access to microfinance services by the vulnerable poor can create the means by which their physical productivity is boosted and the value of their economic activities within the home or the village is lifted so that their vulnerability is lessened.

- Above the vulnerable poor are the labouring poor, whose main source of income is the sale of their labour, either in the market place or to themselves in the course of subsistence production. Rural credit programmes of the past were essentially targeted at the agricultural activities of this stratum. MFIs also serve the needs of poor and subsistence farmers, but there is a deliberate attempt to concentrate the finance provided on activities that diversify the sources of income of poor farm households beyond staple crop production. An important source of this diversity is support for entry by members of the labouring poor into economic activities that 'add value' to existing economic activities though improved quality, greater productivity, simple proces- sing or the addition of new products into the present range of household outputs. Finance to enable poor households to realize the benefits of greater economic diversity can propel poor households up the poverty pyramid into more productive opportunities in self-employment and entrepreneurial activity.

- The next highest stratum of poor persons are the self-employed poor. Here individuals are not engaged in subsistence activity but in producing for the market, often on a part-time basis. The self-employed poor need working capital and are fully integrated into the cash economy when working as self-employed persons, even though they may not have given up waged labour or subsistence activity entirely. MFIs can enable members of the vulnerable and labouring poor to migrate into this higher stratum by funding their involvement in cash-income-generating activ- ities, many of which will be part-time and home-based self-employment options. What distinguishes members of the 'self-employed' poor from those on lower strata is that they are dependent on the market for their 'reward'. Typically, this reward is at a higher level of income than the opportunity cost of subsistence activity or contract labouring, though this is not always so. Poor people are rational and will choose self-employment only when the opportunity cost is less than the own wage earned from their self-employment. Because the opportunity cost of self-employment is seasonal, the demand for microfinance for self-employment will also tend to be seasonal.

- At the apex of the poverty pyramid are the microenterprise operators, whom we call the 'entrepreneurial poor'. These persons are distinguished by the fact that they employ others, possible family members on a part-time basis, to assist them in the conduct of their business. Typically the microenterprises of the entrepreneurial poor will be directed at value-adding to goods or services that can be described as 'wage goods' produced for and purchased by poor households in the rural and urban informal sectors of developing economies – i.e. food, clothing, household items, transport, health services, etc. Working capital is often the critical constraint that prevents the entrepreneurial poor from expanding their businesses beyond a part-time activity. Only if these microenterprises can be assisted to grow can they become the means by which the entrepreneurial poor, their families and their employees can migrate to income levels above the poverty line.

More than lip service is required if the diversity of microfinance products demanded by potential clients in each level of the poverty pyramid are to be met by the MFI. This observation has become one of the most important conventions of microfinance 'best practice'.[12]

Going Beyond Economics to Address the 'Causes' of Poverty

The focus in this chapter is on the monetary aspects of microfinance. This does not mean that the wide range of non-monetary activities of many MFIs is regarded poorly or with scepticism. On the contrary, the conventional wisdom strongly recognizes that poverty is multifaceted, not just about economic deprivation. There is widespread support for the need by some MFIs to embrace activities that are directed at the alleviation of the non-economic dimensions of poverty in order to ensure that the microfinance services provided can have a sustained impact on the incomes of the poor. Circumstance dictates for which MFIs it is essential to go beyond the delivery of economic services in order to address the root causes of poverty in the communities where they work. Where an important root cause is the absence of an efficient finance market, specialization in microfinance may be sufficient. But, where the root causes of poverty are institutionalized by other factors, concentration on the delivery of financial services is unlikely to be enough for sustained poverty reduction. In these instances, the MFI may not be able to ignore the need to do something about:

- gender bias;
- abuse of human rights;
- denial of access to justice and the due processes of the law;
- side-effects of economic activities that endanger health and quality of life;
- chronic illiteracy;
- absence of avenues for the needs of the poor to be brought before appropriate authorities; or
- other factors that institutionalize poverty.

If the systemic causes of poverty go beyond economics and include the powerlessness that flows from the persistence of gross injustice and unfair practices, then it will be difficult for the MFI to make headway in its poverty reduction efforts unless it addresses these matters. In many instances it is only by confronting these non-economic dimensions of poverty that the systemic nature of chronic poverty can be effectively overcome and the probability of permanent escape from poverty significantly increased.[13]

Many MFIs have a heritage that comes directly from the social-welfare-oriented NGO sector, at times retaining close links with NGOs as a form of strategic alliance. In other instances, the MFI will deliberately devote significant resources to activities that are not directly related or contributing to their 'banking' functions because their members judge it important also to address the non-economic dimensions of poverty. The SEWA in India and the Indonesian Welfare Foundation in Java are quintessential examples of MFIs for which this is the case. Friedmann (1992) has depicted the activities of NGOs, MFIs included, directed at non-economic dimensions of poverty as 'empowerment' activities intended to raise awareness among the poor to the base causes of poverty and to mobilize group action to overcome the problem(s). Whether these 'empowerment' activities complement or compete with the business of being a successful microfinance provider is an issue that is actively debated in microfinance circles. In the literature and in practice economists tend to advocate a minimalist and tightly focused approach to microfinance for the poor, reaping the benefits of specialization. Writers from other disciplines, however, tend to favour more holistic strategies as the most effective way of tackling the causes of persistent poverty directly.[14]

The Dilemma of Repeat Business

If MFIs are successful in helping their poor clients escape from poverty, they will have a rising number of clients who have graduated to levels of income above the poverty line. It is not the intention of all MFIs that they should lose these, their best clients, to regular banks or other mainstream financial institutions once they achieve a level of economic well-being that is above the poverty line. There are MFIs that do plan to graduate their success cases into the modern banking sector or other formal non-bank financial institutions. These are identified as 'linkage-programme' MFIs, which have been the primary focus of the APRACA (1983), the FDC (1992), and others.[15] These linkage-programme MFIs have an important place as 'transition facilitators' in the development of financial markets serving poor households. However, there are many other MFIs that do not see themselves as 'working themselves out of a job' once their clients achieve incomes that are above the poverty line. These MFIs, which includes prominent players such as ACCION, the AIM, the ASA, BRI, the BRAC, Grameen Bank, P4K, SANASA, TSPI and many others, see themselves as permanent entities. Their successful clients are to them an asset to be retained and nurtured, not passed on to the competition in the formal financial sector. However, this fact poses a dilemma for these MFIs; a dilemma that is not well understood in the academic literature on the extent to which MFIs succeed in targeting the poor.

As the number of their successful clients grows, so too does the pressure on the MFI to divert more and more of its resources to serve the needs of these established clients for repeat business. By responding to this pressure, MFIs inevitably divert resources from outreach to poor households who have yet to benefit from access to the services on offer. This dilemma is not easily resolved and there is unlikely to be a unique correct response. Each MFI must determine its own optimal balance of old and new clients, based on local priorities and policy pressures. However, the more that an MFI serves the demand from existing clients for repeat business instead of reaching out to new clients still languishing below the poverty line, the less does the MFI appear to be serving the poor or successfully reaching out to the poorest of the poor. Much of the literature that claims that MFIs are not reaching the poorest of the poor in favour of the not-so-poor or the near-poor, has not appreciated the pervasiveness and importance of this dilemma.[16]

Identifying the Poor

It is a simple statistical exercise for deskbound researchers to identify the poor according to a designated poverty line, but in the village or urban slum it is not so simple to apply this income standard because households are reluctant to divulge details of their income. Depending upon what they perceive as your purpose in seeking such information, they can be expected to tell you what they think you want to hear. (See Todd, 1996b.) This may understate or overstate true household income. Hence, for the MFI staff member in the field there is always the challenge of accurately identifying who are the genuinely poor in a village in order to concentrate their efforts on recruiting the poor and not the 'near-poor' or 'not-poor' into their pool of beneficiaries. Many strategies have been tried to achieve this goal, and over time several cost-effective and reliable 'proxies' for income have been identified.

Some comment has already been made on this topic in Chapter 1 above, to the effect that proxies for household income normally rely on the fact that poor people are asset-poor and will almost invariably live in the worst housing situations. Hence, even a cursory examination of the house of a potential client and the most general enquiries as to what animals are owned is often enough to separate the poorest households from the least poor in the village. In other instances it is possible to rely on the fact that the village people themselves know which households in their village are the poorest and which the richest. Typically they are able to rank a list of their neighbours on an economic scale from highest to lowest, and such lists (presented as a set of cards, one for each household in the village) are readily assembled in private by each household member and the results then collated into a 'consensus view' of which households in a village are at the bottom of the poverty pyramid. This consensus view is rarely far from the truth. It is also these households that are the target of MFIs committed to recruiting new beneficiaries from the poorest households. Such information is, therefore, essential if the MFI is to concentrate its recruiting of new clients among the ranks of the poorest and prevent leakage of benefits to those already above the poverty line.[17]

The Simple Economics of Microfinance and Poverty Reduction

Poor people remain poor for many reasons. The advocates of microfinance are convinced that an important contributor to the apparent inability of poor households to escape from poverty and retain a place in the economic spectrum above the poverty line is their lack of access to microfinance. Persistent poverty cannot be overcome unless investment by the poor in the poor is increased. Investment by the poor is low not because poor people do not save, nor is it because they have few investment opportunities, are lazy or know no better. Investment levels by poor households are lower than they would be if the markets that facilitate financial intermediation existed, or where they exist functioned more efficiently. Increased investment by poor households in self-improvement, the accumulation of productive assets, or in the establishment and expansion of microenterprises is facilitated by MFIs that:

- meet the needs of the poor for working capital;
- offer relevant investment advice;
- present productive savings options to compete with asset hoarding;
- offer insurance for risk management or life-cycle savings;
- respond rapidly and flexibly to unplanned changed circumstances or misadventure; and
- provide advice on flexible money management tailored to the circumstances of poor households.

Access to microfinance can lead to higher disposable incomes for the poor by bringing into play one or more of the following five, well-understood, economic mechanisms specific to investment and savings activities of poor households:

1. increased income as a result of reduced unemployment at existing wage rates;
2. higher wage rates as a result of productivity improvements in existing and new employment;
3. investment in upgrading existing productive assets or acquisition of additional productive assets;
4. higher returns for goods and services marketed as a result of access to new or higher valued markets;
5. lower household, livelihood and enterprise production costs as a result of technology transfer, lower cost loans, or access to cheaper basic needs, or intermediate goods and services.

Each of the above five mechanisms for raising household income is dependent on added investment in people, equipment, inventory, infrastructure (especially safe water, sanitation, schools, transport and communications), or social capital (including community institutions and governance systems that oversee the network of obligations and entitlements contained in the customs and cultural mores that are so essential to the survival of the poorest of the poor and to society as a means of handling crises and structural change). Inevitably, therefore, if poverty-reducing development is measured by rising levels of household income, then the process of development must involve increasing rates of investment in all of these areas.

The poverty 'trap' is characterized by a situation wherein poor people invest very little and have little to invest. The non-availability of microfinance is one important reason why this trap persists.[18] When all goes well, microfinance facilitates investment, the fruits of which are:

- increased household income,
- an expanding household and community asset base, and
- greater household-level capacity to save.

There is no mystery or disagreement here! There is universal consensus on this observation about best practice microfinance.

The market for microfinance can be presented as consisting of demand factors on one side and supply factors on the other. MFIs are the intermediaries between the two, and interest rates the measure of whether demand is being met or not. If interest rates are rising, then demand exceeds supply and if they are falling, the opposite is the case. However, demand will be determined by a wide set of factors, including the number of profitable investment opportunities that exist at any one moment in time. This number is always far less than the number of not-so-profitable investment opportunities, so that as the interest rate rises the number of investment opportunities that will be profitable at the new higher interest rate is also less. In this way interest rates, which are in effect the price of money, act as a rationing mechanism by which scarce loanable funds are allocated first to those investments that are expected to be most profitable. Clearly, if anything happens to cause the expected profitability of investments to increase, possibly because of the influence of technology transfer or some factor that causes costs to fall while prices remain unchanged, then demand for funds to invest will increase, putting pressure on interest rates to rise. This process can be represented diagrammatically, as is done in Remenyi, 1991.

The other side of the market for investments is the finance constraint or the supply of loanable funds (savings and credit). If a householder sees an investment opportunity and wants to take it up but does not have sufficient personal savings to finance the venture, the only alternatives are to borrow or to let the opportunity pass. Advocates of microfinance for poverty reduction believe that poverty persists in part because too many poor people fail to qualify to borrow from existing formal sector financial institutions and so must let the opportunity pass. MFIs loosen this finance constraint by bringing within reach of poor households additional sources of loanable funds at costs that are well below those that one must pay to private money lenders in the informal or the formal finance sector. As supply of loanable funds increases, whether as a result of an inflow of 'new' money received as a grant, moneys borrowed by the MFI for the purposes of on-lending, or as a result of an effective savings mobilization programme that reduces the level of unproductive hoarding, the interest rate is forced down and the number of investment opportunities that can be profitably taken up increases.[19]

The relationship between investment and income is positive if the investment is profitable. Hence, a given level of investment is expected to lead to an increase in income. However, the amount by which income increases is not so easily determined. Technology can be defined as that amount of a given product or service that can be produced as a consequence of a given level of investment. This is simply the investment:output ratio, where labour-using technologies typically have lower investment:output ratios than labour-displacing technologies. However, while it is relatively simple to define these technological relationships, it does not follow that an increase in output will lead to an increase in income. If many producers invest in a new process or in expanding their output, the increase in supply could cause market prices to collapse, in which case the increase in output is likely to result in a fall in income. Clearly, therefore, the impact of added investment on the income of a borrower will depend on market conditions for the product or service in question. If the market remains buoyant, the increase in output can be expected to result in a rise in income, costs of production and all other factors accepted as given and unchanged.

Income can also increase as a result of added investment if increased employment is needed for output to increase. In this instance it is the income of the employee that is in question, not just the income of the person doing the investing. Here too, if the investment is labour-using rather than labour-saving, the impact of the increase in investment will be a rise in employment and an increase in disposable income as the level of unemployment falls, wages remaining unchanged or rising. As a consequence of the increase in disposable income, the capacity to save by poor households can also be expected to rise. When savings do rise, these further enhance the supply of funds for investment, initiating another sequence of exchanges as the supply and demand for loanable funds are again brought into equality through the aegis of the intermediation role of financial institutions. In the end, the increase in investment prompted by a loosening of the finance constraint has what economists call a 'multiplier' effect on income and savings, which in turn generates a momentum for further increases, much like a stone thrown into a pool generates not one ripple but many, each pushing out further and further from the initial point of impact.

The foregoing represents an attempt to use the simplest of economic concepts to define a domain for microfinance services providers and, thereby, provide an insight into the theoretical foundations that link microfinance, poverty reduction and development. The better MFIs do their job of intermediation between savers and those who would use available savings and other sources of loanable funds 'productively' (whether for investment or consumption purposes), the greater will be the income and asset accumulation 'dividends' to poor households. This intermediation role is not restricted to the disbursement of credit, but also includes the provision of appropriately designed savings services, information dissemination that enables clients to make better financial decisions, and, at times, skills development to facilitate more efficient and productive investing, saving and money management by all members of poor households.

Types of MFI Providers

The evolution of MFIs is a direct response to the failure of past attempts by government- and donor-funded rural credit programmes to reach poor farmers or poor landless households in the rural areas. The first MFIs appeared in South Asia almost twenty years ago, but they have since spread to Latin America, Southeast Asia and, more recently, Africa, China, the South Pacific and the economies of the former Soviet bloc. The most famous of the MFIs and possibly the most successful are Grameen Bank and the Bangladesh Rural Advancement Committee (BRAC), both established in the late 1970s as pilot projects and then formalized in the early 1980s, in the case of Grameen Bank as a private sector bank with a limited licence, and in the case of the BRAC as an NGO. These two institutions have had a global influence and there have been many successful attempts at replication in other developing countries. (See Todd, 1996a.)

The Grameen Bank 'model' has six key features:

- Grameen Bank is a licensed bank and as such can present itself as part of the legally recognized network of financial institutions able to access the due processes of the law to protect depositors and its other 'clients'.
- Banking operations are built on loans given on the strength of collateral substitutes through 'peer group' procedures for client selection, risk management and loan repayment enforcement. Small groups of not more than five members meet regularly and take responsibility for mutual assistance and collection of small amounts of money on a frequent schedule.
- Loans are made almost exclusively to poor women from households that own no farmland or other significant assets.
- The programme is 'minimalist', specializing in the delivery of small loans for short duration at a rate of interest that is above the inflation rate and the cost of capital. Client training, deposit and loan repayment collections and participant motivation work is 'externalized' onto groups and group leaders. Group formation and group activities are crucial to the Grameen Bank model, but the cost of these is largely borne by the group members themselves.
- All borrowers must make a commitment to a compulsory saving regime, which acts as a form of loan default insurance programme.
- All potential clients must make a commitment to a set of sixteen key 'decisions' that relate to acceptance of Grameen Bank principles of good citizenship, social goals and personal wellbeing. (See Gibbons, 1994.)

The BRAC model (common to many NGOs that support a microfinance programme) shares many of the features of the Grameen Bank model, but it also includes 'social welfare' components that minimalist micro-credit programmes do not hold essential to the exercise of their brief. There are only two unique elements to the BRAC-NGO model:

- Microfinance is part of a broader strategy of 'holistic development', that may or may not use the group approach to deliver and regulate the services offered.
- Opportunistic tailoring of activities to meet local circumstances and complement the non-microfinance aspects of the programme designed to help poor households help themselves.

Some of the larger NGOs, such as OXFAM, Save the Children, World Vision, CARE and CONCERN, follow implementation and funding strategies that lend their individual microfinance programmes characteristics that are genuinely unique. Many NGOs see their involvement in microfinance as a necessary but temporary activity, which they are happy to abandon once the target households graduate into the mainstream financial system. (See Lovell, 1992.)

The Co-operative Model relies on a revival of the credit co-operative or the credit union in a significant number of developing countries, especially Sri Lanka and the South Pacific. This model is based on:

- Owner-managed firms, where all members have an equity interest in the health of the MFI.
- Distribution of benefits through lower cost member services and higher returns on member deposits.
- Membership targeted at all households who cannot access financial services from the banking sector, many of whom will be households from below the poverty line.
- Special attention to savings mobilization.

The co-operative or credit union may offer members complementary community or personal development programmes, but normally MFIs based on the co-operative model specialize in being a financial intermediary. In some countries the credit-union type of MFI is also known as a 'thrift and credit' society, some of which had their genesis as informal savings clubs or a rotating savings and credit association (RoSCA). (See Huppi and Feder, 1990; and Hospes, 1992.)

The Village Bank model, such as the Unit Desa of Bank Rakyat Indonesia (BRI) and the BPRs ('Bank Perkreditan Rakyat', or rural banks) of Indonesia, is more like Grameen Bank than a BRAC. This model:

- Features the legal status of a 'limited bank' serving a specified market.
- Eschews the physical infrastructure of a formal-sector bank.
- Offers flexible service delivery as its hallmark, often involving part-time service facilities out of rented accommodation.

Indonesia has led the world in experimenting with village banks, offering rural communities the opportunity to access banking through banks that are 'mobile', operate on a schedule that does not require it to open every business day all day, and specialize in the recycling of rural savings through small loans to rural households and microenterprises. (See Binhadi, 1995; and World Bank, 1990b).

There is no accurate estimate of the number of MFIs that currently exist in developing countries. The World Bank's Sustainable Banking for the Poor (SBP) programme has identified around 1000 MFIs worldwide, that have at least 1000 clients and have been operating for not less than three years, two-thirds of which were established since 1980. Across the 101 developing countries represented in the SBP survey, in September 1995, MFIs held a total of 46 million active savings deposit accounts and 14 million active loans. If these numbers included every NGO that has a loan programme or sponsors a savings club or RoSCA, no matter how small, the total number of active MFIs would increase many-fold, but the absolute level of savings mobilization and credit dispersal would not increase very much beyond these totals.

The most rapid growth of MFI activity has been in Asia, followed by Latin America and Africa. Asia has the advantage of having started first, and has achieved significant independence from donor funding. The SBP-World Bank survey of MFIs for 1995 found that 59 per cent of MFI funding came from donors, compared to 55 per cent in Latin America and 47 per cent in Asia. Government funding provided a further 3–4 per cent, commercial loans around 12 per cent, deposit growth another 25 per cent and the balance of about 12 per cent came from earnings on microfinance activity. As a profile of a business sector these figures would be cause for disquiet but for the fact that they also reflect a trend towards financial viability. Nonetheless, the current reality is that the MFI sector in developing economies is an infant industry in which very few individual programmes are fully financially self-sufficient. At the close of 1995, none of the MFIs reporting to the SBP programme at the World Bank or those reporting to the APDC Bank Poor '96 programme for Asia-Pacific, were making net profits.

Because there are so few MFIs that can boast client numbers in excess of 100,000, across the whole of the developing world there is a core of less than 100 MFI entities that dominate the microfinance scene. Consider the data in Table 2.1, which summarizes the figures provided to the APDC's Bank Poor '96 Programme for the Asia-Pacific region.

Table 2.1   MFIs in Selected Asia-Pacific Countries by Number of Clients and Activity, 1996

Country	No. of MFIs*	No. of Clients (millions)	Total Value of Loan Portfolio (US$ million)	Average Size of Loans Made (US$)	Average Size of Members' Savings (US $)
Bangladesh	10	5.74	218.23	38.0	10.1
China	5	0.08	0.93	11.2	0.2
India	15	2.49	6.87	2.8	2.9
Indonesia	3	16.75**	2.03	612.0	180.0
Malaysia	6	0.08	11.80	149.7	85.0
Nepal	9	0.06	1.80	31.0	4.8
Pakistan	6	0.34	6.20	18.3	24.4
Philippines	16	0.04	7.98	191.6	30.7
Sri Lanka	7	0.33	4.90	14.8	10.3
Thailand	3	0.30	2.25	7.4	0.6
South Pacific	3	0.01	0.35	46.7	53.3
All Asia-Pacific	92	26.28	269.17	28.0***	9.0***

* Includes only those reporting to Bank Poor '96.
** Composed of 2.3 million 'credit' accounts and 14.5 million 'deposit' accounts.
*** Excludes Indonesia. Including Indonesia the figures are US$ 225.3 and US$ 112.3 respectively.
Source: Getubig, Remenyi and Quiñones, 1997, Table 6, pp. 44–5, supplemented with data supplied to APDC by BRI for Indonesia.

The SBP figures show that in 1995 around 80 per cent of MFI activity in developing countries was in Asia, 15 per cent in Latin America and the balance of 5 per cent in Africa. Hence, what Table 2.1 tells us is that most microfinance providers are small in terms of numbers of clients being served. If one excludes Grameen Bank in Bangladesh and BRI in Indonesia, the average MFI in Asia has less than 3000 clients. This is so because the typical MFI is NGO-based, area-specific in focus, and sees the simple dispersal of very small loans for microenterprise development or income generation as their primary interest in microfinance.

The Conventional Wisdom on Key Microfinance Issues

> No one tears a piece off a new coat to patch up an old coat. If one does, one will have torn the new coat and the piece of new cloth will not match the old. (Luke 5:36)

Begin Small and be Prepared to Learn

Much has been learnt about the successful delivery of microfinance services since the earliest studies of finance and rural development.[20] The most profound of these lessons is the importance of allowing every MFI to adapt to its socio-cultural environment and not to slavishly replicate a particular model that has succeeded in the land of its origins. Hulme and Mosley (1996) argue that the initial establishment phase of any new MFI or MFI outreach programme must resemble an 'action research' pilot programme that is responsive to local conditions and local constraints. The pilot project should enable MFI management to learn from experience and then to direct the evolution of their MFI to match the needs of their target market and the policy environment in which they have to operate. One might think that there is nothing particularly profound about this observation, but such a strategy is in marked contrast to the replication efforts that characterized the community development movement of a generation ago, and that still typifies the approach to microfinance by many social welfare NGOs seeking to enter the field.

Characteristics of the Market for Microfinance

Modern sector banks and financial institutions have failed spectacularly to meet the finance needs of poor households in developing countries. The reasons for this failure are not a mystery. They are directly related to the inappropriateness of conventional banking practices to the needs of the poor. In one way or another the literature published on microfinance addresses this 'fact' in one or more of the following seven contexts:

1. Formal-sector lenders are reluctant to lend to poor households because they assess risks to be significantly higher when lending to a client about whom they know very little, who is unlikely to have a business plan, rarely maintains financial records of any sort, is probably illiterate and may not even have a fixed address.
2. The transaction costs of providing very small loans, collecting even smaller regular repayments, or handling very small savings deposits and withdrawals are prohibitively high as a proportion of the amount loaned or deposited using conventional banking procedures.
3. The practical avenues for the enforcement of contractual financial obligations is costly, far exceeding the value of loans made, while informal means for enforcing loan repayments are notoriously difficult to exercise in the absence of close personal knowledge of the borrower and an ongoing relationship with the community from which borrowers hail.
4. Chronic poverty robs borrowers of the capacity to offer lenders acceptable title to tradable collateral assets against which lenders might spread the risk of loan repayment default.
5. Less is known about the markets in which the 'economics of survival' is played out than formal sector financial service providers need to confidently assess loan requests, or design financial products and services that meet the unique microfinance needs of poor households.
6. There is an institutional and official bias against informal-sector poor households and their economic activities, that finds expression in official harassment and attempts to impose unaffordable and excessive regulation. Bouman (1989) was moved to comment in this regard: 'Discussion about informal money lenders in Asia are usually charged with emotion ... Negative views about informal financial intermediaries, pushing ignorant and helpless farmers into debt in order to grab their lands are widespread ... Informal credit is conceived as exploitative and excessively dear; it is believed to encourage (conspicuous) consumption rather than productive investment ... Most Asian policymakers are convinced of the moral and technical superiority of the formal financial sector over the informal one for supplying credit as an instrument of rural development' (p. 6).
7. There is also a 'popular' bias against the poor, whether held consciously or unconsciously, that undermines trust, integrity and honesty accorded to poor householders by private-sector finance workers. Suspicion of the poor is fuelled by misinformation, fear of poverty, and the popular image promulgated in the media that associates poverty with the unscrupulous, the unreliable and the hopeless 'basket case'. The popular perception is also that the world of the poor is an environment of chronic uncertainty, vulnerability to violence, widespread exploitation, an ardent readiness to succumb to opportunities of moral hazard, and fear born of rampant corruption and crime.

Sources of the Comparative Advantage of MFIs

The staff of MFIs are not saints or any less subject to the influences of the media and peer group biases against the poor that permeate every layer of most societies, rich or poor. Nonetheless, the track record of MFIs has given us a clearer understanding of the sources of their comparative advantage as providers of financial services to the poor. In considering these it is as well to begin by dispelling a myth. MFIs are not dependent for their success on the existence of a charismatic 'great man'. While it is a clear advantage to have a Professor Yunus as the programme director, the successful replication of the Grameen Bank model in many countries in Asia and the Pacific, including Indonesia, Malaysia, Nepal, Philippines, Sri Lanka, Vietnam and Papua New Guinea, is clear evidence that the 'great man' theory does not apply. What is relevant is the importance of having a committed team, good management and shared goals.[21] Ironically, an important source of the comparative advantage of MFIs is the fact that they are largely unregulated. This enables the MFI to be highly flexible and to adapt to meet market needs, without the official binds that formal financial sector institutions must observe. This same freedom ought also to free the MFI to adopt pricing strategies for the sale of its services and financial products that cover costs and make a profit, but few MFIs have been bold enough to take this step. Instead, many MFIs self-regulate, placing on-lending rates at a ceiling related to those imposed by the government in the formal banking system.[22]

On a competitive level, MFIs have the advantage over banks and other financial institutions because they are better able to meet the needs of poor households. MFIs 'internalize' fewer transaction costs, which is a direct result of access to better information and more effective use of community social capital to assess the integrity of potential clients and externalize information dissemination and deposit collection transactions costs. Similarly, the risk management strategies of MFIs enable them to keep default costs down and on-time repayments high, despite the lack of any widespread alternative to the use of collateral substitutes to screen and monitor borrowers. Taken together, borrower screening and monitoring constitutes the largest share of the operating costs of MFIs.[23]

In the area of savings mobilization, too, the MFI has a comparative advantage based on familiarity with the client, cemented by the fact that staff work closely with poor households. Regular contact makes access for withdrawals less of a problem than it is for banks, which are typically located some distance from the village. Moreover, there is general understanding among village residents that their voluntary savings with the MFI will be recycled back into their own communities. Banks, on the other hand, do not recycle savings back into the village to serve the needs of poor people. Rather, as Bartolome Peirano put it at the 1989 Feldafing conference on self-help and credit: 'Banks do not lend money to the poor, but they lend money to the rich ...' (Bedard, 1989, p. 31.). Unlike the traditional approach to poverty alleviation of development planners, civil servants and aid officials, MFIs have tended to eschew paternalism and tokenism in favour of active participation by the poor in the microfinance implementation process. As Bedard has put it: 'Past theories and concepts did not leave any active role for the poor. They have always been assigned a passive role' (ibid. p. 30).[24]

Conditions for Sustainable Success

If one defines 'success' in the MFI arena as 'the ability to deliver appropriate financial services to a significant number of the target population profitably', there are no successful MFIs anywhere in the world. This rather depressing conclusion is supported by all the case studies reported in Hulme and Mosley, 1996; Schmidt and Zeitinger, 1996; Christen, Rhyne and Vogel, 1995; Gurgland, Pederson and Yaron, 1994; and Yaron, 1994. In not one instance did these studies find a single MFI that is covering all costs, including the opportunity cost of funds employed, and making a profit from which it might strengthen its balance sheet. At best, there are MFIs that are covering their operating costs, though several of the better-known MFIs are also able to at least partially cover the 'subsidized' cost of capital employed. While this result is laudable, in the long term it does not make for 'financial viability'.

There is reason to believe that MFIs should be treated as if they belong to an 'infant industry' that warrants subsidies to enable operators to expand to the point where economies of scale and the productivity fillip that comes from 'learning by doing' are realized. Case studies of individual MFIs strongly support this view, though this is no reason to be lax in imposing strict performance requirements for the continuation of existing subsidies for on-lending, human resource development, or infrastructure investment. The aim must be, as Christen (1996) has so aptly remarked, 'to make MFIs as bankable as their clients'.

The argument that MFIs are a special form of infant industry has great appeal. The importance of economies of scale in the finance sector applies as much to microfinance as it does to conventional banking, insurance and money market activities. There are also significant 'external' benefits to the economy and society at large from the operation of MFIs that further justifies some subsidies. In time the clients of MFIs bring to their economic contacts with banks, retailers, government employees and suppliers of production inputs skills dealing with money management, contractual obligations and resource management that have been learnt or honed as a result of their involvement with the MFI. These skills can be expected to reduce the transactions costs of economic activity generally, disseminate information to the benefit of all, and increase the ability of individuals to be discerning in the assessment of the information available to them in their economic decisionmaking. In each of these respects society benefits from what is, in effect, a productive process leading to the creation of 'public goods' as spin-offs from the growth of microfinance. To the extent that these public goods have value they are a legitimate basis on which to provide subsidies to MFIs while the transition to widespread outreach to poor households is ongoing.[25]

If we accept that MFIs are part of an infant industry, it is clear that the criteria for success should reflect the goals towards which an MFI must aspire if it is to become financially independent of subsidies or the regulations that protect it from the predatory behaviour of potential competitors. The literature on what these criteria ought to be is increasing rapidly, but there is already a discernible consensus emerging that has been most comprehensively expressed in Yaron (1994), 'What Makes Rural Finance Institutions Successful?'. This consensus can be summarized as follows:

A successful MFI will:

- charge positive 'real' interest rates on loans; rates that are also above the cost of capital;
- offer positive 'real' interest rates on voluntary savings deposits;
- have high (i.e.: > 80 per cent) on-time loan repayment rates, supported by a default insurance programme of one sort or another;
- have a rising proportion of its loan portfolio financed from voluntary savings;
- adopt management systems and administrative procedures that are transparent and designed to allow operation and overhead expenses to fall as a proportion of a rising loan portfolio;
- focus its 'new' business on significantly increased outreach to the poorest households; and
- adopt collateral substitutes, deposit collection and repayment enforcement procedures that are consistent with the 'social capital' of the community within which it operates.

A few clarifying comments on the above list of seven success 'strategies' are appropriate. First, 'real' interest rates are defined relative to the local rate of inflation. Hence, if inflation is running at 10 per cent per annum, lending and deposit rates should be above this level, unless there are special circumstances to justify a lower rate. Typically the premium above the inflation rate should reflect an opportunity cost of capital that is consistent with the long-term social rate of return to capital and not necessarily the current private rate. The long-term social rate of return to capital is likely to be lower than the current private rate if there are externalities that are not reflected in current private-sector investment rates of interest, which will be affected by evolving short-term economic conditions.

Second, it is important to distinguish voluntary from compulsory savings. Most MFIs have compulsory savings programmes as a form of loan guarantee or repayment default insurance. Typically no interest is paid on these deposits and clients are given little or no access to their accumulated deposits. In effect compulsory savings form an addition to the asset base of the MFI in the balance sheet, though in strict accounting terms they remain a liability. As the amount of compulsory savings has increased in size there has been a parallel growth in disquiet among MFI members to gain easier access to 'their' savings. As the pressure mounts, one can expect that MFIs will not want to avoid loosening their hold on these members' savings. However, as a proportion of the total value of the outstanding loan portfolio of MFIs, compulsory savings are a minor proportion.

Third, for successful transition to financial viability and more aggressive outreach to the poorest of the poor it is not compulsory savings that are crucial but voluntary savings. In this respect it is a concern that only a minority of MFIs have made savings mobilization the key to their future strategies for growth and outreach to the poorest households. Grameen Bank has not been one of these few, nor have most Grameen Bank replications, but this is changing. Why MFIs have eschewed savings as a source of finance for on-lending is not clear, but the situation is changing rapidly. There is now growing recognition, strongly reflected in the response of practitioners at the Asia-Pacific regional conference on microfinance outreach, Bank Poor '96, held in December 1996 in Kuala Lumpur, that the emphasis placed on the importance of savings by researchers and academic commentators on microfinance is justified and should be adopted by them as a key platform for future growth strategies.[26]

Fourth, the emphasis given to transparency and cost containment in this list should not be divorced from the respect accorded to potential and existing clients from the poorest households by staff and volunteer representatives of the MFI. Nothing can destroy the good work of an MFI more quickly than the perception among the target population that the programme is patronizing, operating to the personal gain of operatives, or subject to losses due to moral hazard and outright corruption. The inclusive 'participatory' approach of both group-based and other MFIs is intended to assist in overcoming these problems, but more is needed. The discipline of peer review and active exploitation of the web of social responsibilities and obligations, that are termed here as the 'social capital' of the community, need to be harnessed. Transparency of procedures, open access to records and staff and regular reporting to the community on microfinance transactions facilitated or completed are some of the tools by which this aspect of the community's social capital can be harnessed.

In order for an MFI to meet all of the seven strategies for success, there are a number of subsidiary requirements that are implied in the conventional wisdom, but which are not always in the control of the MFI. For example, if an MFI is to charge rates of interest on its loans that more than cover the cost of capital, including the opportunity cost of members' funds and subsidized funds received from donors, governments or other sources, the MFI must be free to charge whatever interest rate is needed. Regulated interest rate ceilings may prevent MFIs from doing this. Where such regulations exist, it is necessary for the government to deregulate the financial sector dealing with MFIs. Another example arises in the case of savings mobilization. As already noted, very few MFIs can boast a voluntary savings programme that raises enough in deposits to fund a significant proportion of their lending to members. This is partly due to the use of compulsory savings as pseudo-loan and catastrophe insurance, but the more important reason is that most MFIs operate in a legal limbo and so find it difficult if not impossible to present themselves as deposit managers legally able to guarantee the security of deposits. In some countries, notably China, it is illegal for MFIs to gather voluntary savings without specific government approval. In this situation it is difficult for the MFI to present itself to a potential depositor as free and able to pursue restitution of members' deposits in the case of fraud, a run on the MFI or financial losses covered from members' savings. There is an important role here for close collaboration between government (i.e. the central bank) and MFIs. In addition to the determination of appropriate prudential guidelines, there are procedural arrangements and documentation standards that must be agreed to. It is possible to set these as a result of 'self-regulation', as in the case of credit union leagues overseen by a peak body self-regulation can work well. However, there are benefits that flow from the existence of due-process procedures that are reflected in the confidence that MFI members can have because legally binding requirements have been negotiated and put in place. This is especially important for savings mobilization, the history of which is littered with the disillusionment that follows the collapse of a chit fund or the disappearance of the village banking representative with the records of deposits and members' funds.[27]

Is a Group Approach Essential?

There are few issues of greater interest to MFI staff than the importance that should be attached to the role of groups in the work of MFIs. Supporters of the Grameen Bank model tend to believe that groups are essential as a means of risk management, cost containment, the empowerment of clients, delegation of economically useful functions to promote 'participation', and avoidance of occasions of moral hazard. Those of a contrary view are equally keen in their belief that the integrity of the individual does not need the peer pressure of group membership to ensure repayment and manage the transaction costs of deposit and repayments collection. This contrary view points to the self-interest of borrowers and the power of transparent processes as effective substitutes for group activity. Moreover, the advocates of group-based MFIs must also demonstrate that the added costs associated with group formation and group operations are at least compensated by the gains in cost containment, improved repayment rates, empowerment, etc.,

etc. before those who have a bias favouring individualistic, free-enterprise-based systems will concur.

Researchers have sought to test the value of group work to risk management and cost containment, but the results reported in the literature have not been unequivocal. There are MFIs that appear to have gained significantly from 'solidarity' groups, while other MFIs have done no less well lending to individuals without the benefit of groups. While peer monitoring can be effective, so can the incentive of access to repeat loans to a client who has nowhere else to go for working capital. Researchers point to the heavy cost of group work in terms of time commitment; a cost that may be external to the budget of the MFI but can be a significant burden on one or more members of the group. Also, there is always the risk of the group having to bear the cost of free riders if loan default threatens from within the group.

While the literature on group versus individual loan activity is contrary, the fact remains that Grameen Bank and the many Grameen bank replicators that have sprung up in Asia and the Pacific use their group structure for more than the delivery of microfinance services and products. Microfinance is not a panacea for poverty. Poverty reduction also requires that individuals and communities address the root causes of the non-economic dimensions of poverty. Group-based MFIs have tended to use their group structures as vehicles through which the benefit of solidarity and co-operation can be brought to bear to complement the economic activities supported. Thus far researchers have not succeeded in allowing for these complementary social products in their assessments, though it is clear that the incentive of ongoing access to working capital loans is a powerful force for on-time repayments, whether there is peer group pressure or none at all.[28]

Does Microfinance Help the Poor?

There is no doubt that MFIs do benefit the poor. The weight of evidence from the very few but increasing number of surveys and case studies confirms this. In a major study of MFIs in Asia, Africa and Latin America, Hulme and Mosley (1996) were drawn to conclude: '... our study confirms the emerging consensus that well designed credit schemes can raise the incomes of significant numbers of poor people ...' (p.114). Table 2.2 summarizes their findings on the impact of loans on household income compared to control groups of non-borrowers. Across a sample of almost 4000 borrowers, the increase in family income of borrowers was three times what it was for the control group.

Not all clients of MFIs are poor. Growth in repeat business should be associated with flows of benefits to borrowers who are no longer poor. There is no need to traverse this path again, but it serves to draw us to consider whether there is significant 'unintended and inappropriate' leakage of MFI

Table 2.2 Increase in Family Income of Borrowers and Control Groups of Non-borrowers

Country	Annual Average Change in Family Income % 1988–92 Borrowers	Annual Average Change in Family Income % 1988–92 Control Group	Borrowers as a Ratio of the Control Group Control	Sample Size No. of Borrowers ('000)
Indonesia	12.9	3.1	3.80	2,500
Bangladesh	29.3	22.2	1.34	608
Sri Lanka	15.6	9.9	1.57	700
India	46.0	24.0	1.91	25

Source: Hulme and Mosley, 1996, p. 88.

resources to persons who are not poor. This is an important question, but not one that the literature addresses adequately. Instead the literature notes what one should expect: i.e. that the poorest clients benefit least from MFI loans. Why there is this bias in the literature is unclear, but it is a question that is complicated by the subjective judgement involved in determining if the balance of resources devoted to outreach is 'appropriate' to firms that aim to retain existing clients, especially if they have graduated above the poverty line. Little wonder, therefore, that researchers have discovered among the beneficiaries of microfinance an increasing number of clients who are not among the poorest of the poor, or not even poor. If researchers did not find MFIs dealing with clients who are now above the poverty line, it would be a sign that MFIs are not succeeding in reducing poverty. The opposite is the case. Nonetheless, it remains true that the poorest of the poor benefit less from involvement with an MFI programme than the not-so-poor, the near-poor, or the not-poor.

The distribution of the benefits of microfinance can be interpreted in many ways. For example, just because the poorest households benefit less from access to microfinance than households further up the income scale in the poverty pyramid does not mean that MFIs should concentrate on poor households at the upper rungs of the income range below the poverty line. The vulnerable poor should not be denied access just because they have fewer investment opportunities than their poor but not-so-poor neighbours. Nonetheless, it should also be expected that if the allocation of loan funds is left to open competition, it is likely that the bulk of funds disbursed will flow to poor clients who are not from the least poor households. Does this matter? Isn't the critical thing that the activities of MFIs loosen the liquidity constraint that oppresses and chokes economic growth in poor communities to the benefit of all? Is it enough that MFIs reach out to poor households, even if most beneficiaries are not among the poorest of the poor? These questions are not adequately addressed in the published literature on microfinance and poverty alleviation.

It is impossible to answer these questions without more information than is currently available on the trickle-down and multiplier effects of microfinance across all households in poor communities. Nonetheless, many MFI practitioners are satisfied that they are serving the poor if new beneficiaries are recruited exclusively from the ranks of households that are clearly below the poverty line, even if many of these are not among the most vulnerable. One might also speculate that because outreach to the poorest of the poor is especially difficult and costly, MFIs may not achieve financially viable growth unless they concentrate on the higher strata of the poverty pyramid, leaving the poorest of the poor to benefit from what 'trickle-down' effect is generated by the spread of microfinance to a rising proportion of poor households in poor communities. It may also be, however, that if MFIs discriminate in favour of the poorest of the poor at the expense of the need that the less poor have for ongoing access to working capital, savings services and the like, these less poor households will slowly but surely slide back into the mire of chronic poverty. In the absence of evidence on the multiplier effect of microcredit or other microfinance services, it is impossible to decide this issue objectively. But, it would be surprising if the trickle down of benefits from increased levels of economic activity by and for poor households was not greater than the trickle down of benefits from investments by households with incomes above the poverty line. Hence, although the overall judgement of researchers is that the direct benefits of MFIs 'rarely' reaches the poorest households, it does not follow that MFIs do not play a vital role in sustained poverty reduction.[29]

Gender and Microfinance

An aspect of the distribution of the benefits of microfinance disbursements that has occupied an increasing number of writers is whether the borrower is also the primary beneficiary. Researchers have explored this question in part because MFIs have claimed a special ability to reach out to women, who dominate the ranks of the most vulnerable at the lowest ranks of the poverty pyramid. As a result, MFIs have targeted women as part of their poverty-targeting commitment and claimed a benefit from so doing because women are more diligent at observing on-time repayment schedules than are men. However, several researchers have questioned the effectiveness of the female gender bias in microfinance programmes, noting that in the course of their fieldwork they discovered instances where loans were predominantly made to female borrowers but control over spending passed to the male members of the household even though repayment obligations remained with the borrower. This observation caused some researchers to dig deeper and to question whether the distribution of loans by gender is a reliable indicator to the distribution of the benefits.[30]

Other researchers, Helen Todd (1996b) in particular, questions whether these are important issues. She suggests that writers who have disparaged

Grameen Bank and other microfinance programmes because they have found examples where the primary beneficiary appears to be someone other than the borrower, may be interpreting their results in socio-culturally insensitive ways. Todd's in-depth study of the impact of Grameen Bank loans after an interval of ten years is a powerful, moving and sobering piece of anthropological research. Her findings confirm that in poor households, and especially the poorest households, resources are highly fungible and it is rarely possible to determine whose money is used by whom and for whose benefit. Moreover, Todd shows that the motivation of female borrowers is often drawn from her ability to help her husband, sons or other relatives attain higher status and economic prospects. It is wrong to assume that all women in poor households are oppressed and exploited by the men in their lives. Even if this is the case for too many women, for those who find life in the family environment rewarding, the act of accessing a new source of loans or other financial services is rarely taken independently. Hence, while research into the gender dimension of the distribution of the benefits of MFI activity should heighten awareness to gender issues, it has not weakened the claim that women are major beneficiaries of microfinance programmes.

Microfinance is intimately linked to household economic activities. In the case of female-headed households the data is unequivocal that female borrowers are the major beneficiaries. In the case of other households, however, it can be that the involvement of another member of the household in the application of the borrowed funds means loss of benefits to the borrower or loss of a meaningful input into how the money will be used, but this is not normally the case. In the final analysis one is drawn to conclude that most poor households are able to assess what is in their own best interests and can be trusted not to squander borrowed funds, irrespective of who in the household has borrowed the money or for what purpose the funds appear to have been expended. At the practical level, therefore, there is little to justify the allocation of significant resources to attempt to monitor or second-guess how poor households use the very small amounts of money that they borrow from MFIs. The broader implication is that not only may it be 'uneconomic' to devote scarce resources to monitoring whether or not female borrowers retain control over the use of very small loans, but it may equally be unproductive to monitor whether borrowers spend these small loans on investment or consumption expenditures. This observation becomes less true the larger is the amount borrowed.

Can MFIs Have a Sustainable Impact on Poverty Reduction?

Microfinance may not be a panacea for poverty, but as a component of the fight against poverty the services that MFIs bring to poor households clearly can make a significant difference to economic welfare and the capacity for self-reliance. There are those, however, who question whether attention to improving the functioning of finance markets serving the poor is enough. In 1995 Michael Lipton and Martin Ravallion wrote: '... it is hard to maintain hope that chronic poverty can be reduced appreciably by credit-based interventions. Chronic poverty is not typically due to 'market failures' in credit or other markets, but to low factor productivity, and/or low endowments-per-person of non-labour factors' (p. 2630). The Lipton-Ravallion view is not uncommon among development economists, but it is not a consensus view. The Lipton-Ravallion thesis can be interpreted as saying that microfinance is but a component of the fight to achieve sustained poverty reduction; necessary but not sufficient. Moreover, the effectiveness of the microfinance component is influenced by the economic and institutional environment in which they are provided to clients. If the supply of finance is increased in an environment of civil unrest and insecurity or in circumstances of general economic decline, it is not obvious that the results for borrowers will be a permanent improvement in their circumstances. There is, therefore, an important prior question that cannot be ignored: i.e.: What needs to be done to make microfinance-based interventions more effective as a tool for sustained poverty reduction? The answer to this question has several parts:

1. The impact of investment loans on the income of poor households and the productivity of savings is positively related to the macroeconomic environment. Microfinance interventions are more effective in reducing poverty when the economy is improving than when it is in decline. Responsibility for macroeconomic settings are beyond the ken of MFIs, but if these are wrong or inappropriate, the MFI will be fighting an uphill battle to nurture sustained poverty reduction.

2. MFIs will always remain marginal to the big picture so long as MFIs remain small and insignificant in their outreach to poor households. Currently microfinance providers are reaching out to less than 5 per cent of poor households in most poor economies. The exceptions are Bangladesh, Indonesia and Malaysia, where outreach has either approached or exceeded one-third of poor households since 1980. It is also in these three countries where the situation of the poor has improved the most over this period, and is therefore at most risk because of the Asian financial crisis of the late 1990s. If the outreach of MFIs can be sustained in these economies and similarly increased to poor households in all developing countries, the likely impact of a loosened finance constraint is greater robustness, quicker recovery and a far higher multiplier effect on sustained growth in the income of poor households than has been the case so far.

3. Microfinance is more than simply credit. It is as important to ensure that savings, insurance and money management services are offered to poor households, as it is to bring them access to credit.

4. There is a mounting stock of micro-level data on the benefit that poor households are receiving from access to microfinance that gives us reason to question the Lipton-Ravallion view. The difference that access to microfinance has made to poor households is significant. In recent years there have been at least eight major studies of the impact of micro credit on the incomes of poor households. Without exception these studies confirm that household income of families with access to credit is significantly higher than for comparable households without access to credit. Poor households that have had access to microfinance services also show significant increases in asset accumulation, providing them with both a safety net against misadventure and resources for self-help investments.[31]

5. Jones (1994 and 1995) reports that the multiplier effects of greater credit outreach and reduced hoarding in favour of interest-earning deposits with MFIs are not trivial. There is a 'competition' dividend from greater MFI outreach that is observed as a fall in informal-sector interest rates and an increase in the range of finance 'products' offered to poor households by traditional informal-sector financial services providers. This dividend is in addition to any increase in productivity associated with more investment and less hoarding.

Taken together with all of the foregoing, these five observations indicate that there is an increasing weight of evidence that not only can microfinance make a difference to the economic welfare of poor people, but also that access by the poor to the services of MFIs are a necessary if not sufficient requirement for sustained levels and rates of poverty reduction in poor economies. This realization underlies the mounting pressure for increased investments in microfinance by the international aid community, bilateral donors, private-sector NGOs and commercial banks.

Management Issues

Reliable data on management issues are notoriously difficult to assemble about MFIs. Nonetheless, there are some statistical relationships that have been identified as characteristic of MFI growth and about which there is broad-based agreement. The case studies presented in this book add to the stock of evidence that support the following observations:

1. Successful Microfinance Institutions are Replicable Across Cultural Borders

The remarkable success of microfinance institutions in Bangladesh has prompted the observation that this success is either the result of the remarkable performance of charismatic leaders in that country or the unique appropriateness of the MFI strategy to the socio-cultural milieu in Bangladesh. However, with the successful replication of MFIs in many countries across Asia and the Pacific, this concern has lost what little credibility it may have had.

2. High Real Interest Rates Are Not an Insurmountable Obstacle

It is a myth that poor householders cannot or will not pay high positive rates of interest on borrowed money. In fact, data gathered from most of the major MFIs reported here and in Hulme and Mosley, 1996, shows that there is no apparent statistical relationship between the arrears rate, measured as the percentage of the loan portfolio that is delinquent by six months or more, and the rate of interest charged on loans. In other words, at any given rate of interest there are a number of MFIs, each with a unique arrears record. Similarly, among MFIs with given arrears rate, the pricing policies each employs is not consistent, resulting in a range of interest rates. Hence, although the data clearly shows that all MFIs that have on-time repayments rates of 90 per cent or more all charge positive real interest rates on loans made, the level of real interest rates charged appears to have no consistent relationship to the arrears record. Given the high cost of making small loans it is essential that MFIs reject the notion that poor households cannot or will not pay high real rates.

3. Small and Regular is Beautiful

The most important management indicator for the business health of an MFI is the on-time repayment rate. An overwhelming number of MFIs have discovered that poor markets respond well to repayment collection procedures and deposit collections that accept small amounts frequently (sometimes daily, often weekly, but certainly not less than monthly). It has been the received wisdom in rural development that farmers need loan repayment procedures that called for a single balloon payment after the harvest had been brought in and sold. MFIs have found, however, that even farmers prefer regular repayments in small amounts, so that money that does come to hand can be immediately applied to reduce the debt, so avoiding the danger that competing demands will slowly eat into funds at hand until there is nothing left.

4. Save for the Future

The most successful MFIs have an active voluntary savings programme and fund an increasing share of an expanding loan programme from savings deposits collected. The importance of this management strategy for financial viability has only recently been realized by even some of the biggest MFIs, but its importance has yet to be accepted across all existing MFIs. Savings remain one of the most important but grossly under-utilized sources of new resources for accelerated outreach by MFIs.

5. The Level of Poverty is an Obstacle to Benefiting from Microfinance

The impact of loans disbursed on the income of a borrower is not independent of the level of income from which the borrower begins. This is not unexpected, for as one moves up the poverty pyramid towards the poverty line and then above it, the number of economic opportunities that present increases. In addition, the marketable skills and asset base of the most vulnerable of the poor at the bottom of the poverty pyramid are well below those of households further up in the poverty pyramid. Consequently, MFIs find that new borrowers benefit least from loans taken up, but this return increases as the cycle of repeat loans unfolds.

Concluding Observation

Thinking on microfinance by development practitioners and researchers is evolving as more and more information comes to hand. Even so, there is a remarkable consistency in views among those who have written on the topic. Few are so bold as to see microfinance as a panacea for the entrenched poverty in the developing world. However, few would deny the importance of including access to financial intermediation services as essential to the sustainability of a place in the economic spectrum above the poverty line. Equally, few would deny the critical role that access to these services plays in assisting poor households to escape from the poverty pyramid and achieve a quality of life denied to those trapped in the mire of low income and low productivity below the poverty line.

Acknowledgement

The author would like to thank all those who have commented on various drafts of this chapter. He is especially indebted to Dale Adams, H. Dieter Seibel, Helen O'Neill and Michael Thorp. Any shortcomings or errors that remain are wholly his responsibility.

Notes

1 The books that have come to my attention are: ADB, 1997; Albe and Gamage, 1996; Count, 1996; Garson, 1996; Goodwin-Groen, 1998; Hulme and Mosley, 1996; Ledgerwood, 1999; Morduck, 1997; Rutherford, 1996; Seibel, 1996a; Todd, 1996a and b; Versluysen, 1999. The two-volume work by Hulme and Mosley is especially valuable for its statistical case studies of Asian and Latin American MFIs, while the two volumes by Todd and that by Seibel are valuable 'practitioners' accounts that contain a great deal of detail and documentation for microfinance experiments in Asia.
2 To take some examples from the mainstream journal literature that appeared in 1996 only, the topic of sustainability was addressed in Bennett and Cuevas, 1996; Cuevas, 1996; and Schmidt and Zeitinger, 1996; the impact of microfinance on microenterprise development and the distribution of benefits in Ghate, Ballon and Manalo, 1996; Groetz and Sen Gupta, 1996; Groh and Somolekoe, 1996; Hashemi, Schuler and Riley, 1996; and Pitt and Khandker, 1996; the way in which the operations of MFIs represent responses to market failures in Herath, 1996; Hunte, 1996; Mosley, 1996; Srinivas and Higuchi, 1996; and Rajasekhar, 1996; and lessons from the operation of specific MFIs by Jain, 1996; Khandker and Khalily, 1996; and Tendler and Alves Amorim, 1996.

3 There is a wealth of literature dealing with rural credit in the decades before 1990, but some very influential examples are: Ardener, 1964; Firth and Yamey, 1964; Geertz, 1962; Schultz, 1964; Anderson, 1966; Mosher, 1966; Mellor, 1970; Hayami and Ruttan, 1971; Lipton, 1976; Drake, 1980; Howell, 1980; and Desai and Mellor, 1993. The goals, processes and structures involved in these early rural credit programmes are well described in the classic volume by Adams, Graham and Von Pischke, 1984, entitled *Undermining Rural Development with Cheap Credit*. Other significant contributions to this literature are by Padmanabhan, 1988; Adams, Gonzales-Vega and Von Pischke, 1986; and Adams and Vogel, 1986. A useful retrospective and outline of the intellectual heritage on the topic that is easy to read and informative is given in Hulme and Mosley, 1996 and Adams and Von Pischke, 1992.

4 See for example, Holdcroft, 1982 and Robertson, 1984.

5 These 'failures' are well documented in Von Pischke, Heffernan and Adams, 1981; Von Pischke, Adams and Donald, 1983; World Bank, 1984, 1993b; Adams, Graham and Von Pischke, 1984; Adams and Vogel, 1986; Besley, 1995; and Hulme and Mosley, 1996.

6 Other useful and recent accounts are presented in Adams and Fitchett, 1992; and Bouman and Hospes, 1994. Accounts from the perspective of key donors is presented in Ashe and Cosslett, 1989, for the UNDP; Bechtel and Zender, 1994, for the IFAD; Seibel, 1996, 1985; Binhadi, 1995; and Patten and Rosengard, 1991, for various bilateral supporters of financial innovation and reform in rural Indonesia; and Pulley, 1989, and World Bank, 1993b, 1990b, 1989a for the World Bank.

7 It is too early to assess the impact of the MicroCredit Summit, held in Washington, DC, in February 1997, but the contrast in enthusiasm is evident in comparing Getubig *et al.*, 1997 with Schneider, 1997 and Hulme and Mosley, 1996.

8 See, for example: IFAD, 1985; Fuglesang and Chandler, 1986; deSoto, 1986; Bedard, 1989; Osner, 1991; Remenyi, 1991; Yunus, 1991; Drake and Otero, 1992; Lovell, 1992; Wahid, 1993; Rutherford, 1995; Albe and Gamage, 1996; Count, 1996. Many of these works are in the genre of an institutional 'biography'. As individual examples they accumulate to form a mass of evidence that is more persuasive than that which an individual contribution can sustain. The remarkable consistency of findings across them adds further to their usefulness as reliable insights into the world of microfinance for poverty reduction.

9 See, for example Hulme and Mosley, 1996, Gurgland *et al.*, 1994; Khandker, *et al.*, 1995, 1996; Schmidt and Zeitinger, 1996; Todd, 1996a; and Yaron, 1991, 1994. In addition, there is the major study in preparation by the SBP programme, based at the World Bank, which can be accessed in 'progress report' or 'working paper' format through the SBP, CGAP and World Bank home-pages on the internet. There is a parallel set of literature dealing with microenterprise development and the informal sector that is a source of data on the impact of microcredit to the poor on entrepreneurial activity and income generation by the poor for the poor. See especially Harper, 1998 and Remenyi, 1991.

10 This view has not been so forcefully put elsewhere, but it is consistent with the views expressed in Seibel, 1996a; Todd, 1996a; UNIFEM, 1996; Marx, 1994; Morrison, Solignac and Oudin, 1994; Otero and Rhyne, 1994; Poudyal, 1994; Reidinger, 1994; Remenyi, 1994, 1991; Getubig, 1993; Colter and Suharto, 1993; Yaron, 1991; Amenomori, 1990; and Hulme, 1990. A useful discussion of the role of social capital in the adaptation process can be found in Moser, 1996. A related set of literature concerns the need to protect and strengthen the capacity of poor communities to offer members 'safety nets' in times of emergency or temporary setbacks in personal fortunes. See especially Jayarajah, Branson and Sen, 1996.

11 Readers who have a mind to follow up literature on poverty lines and the

dimensions of poverty would do well to consult Jayarajah, Branson and Sen, 1996; UNDP, 1996, 1990; World Bank, 1996a, 1993b, 1990a; Chambers, 1995; Lipton and Ravallion, 1995; Greeley, 1994; Ravallion, 1994, 1992; Lipton and van der Gaag, 1993; Townsend, 1993; and Lewis, 1988.

12 The MFI best practice literature is also directed at best practice in microenterprise development. Both fields overlap and place the twin goals of 'flexible adaptation' to market requirements and 'financial viability' at the core of sustainable poverty reduction through microfinance. See in particular: Getubig, Quiñones and Remenyi, 1997; Schneider, 1997; Christen, 1996; Hulme and Mosley, 1996; Remenyi, 1996, 1991; Schmidt and Zeitinger, 1996; Seibel, 1996; Tendler and Amorim, 1996; CGAP, 1995; Conroy, Taylor and Thapa, 1995; Malhotra, 1992; Yaron, 1991; World Bank, 1989b, 1990a; Hossain, 1988; and Mosley and Dahal, 1986.

13 The dilemma of whether to focus on economic poverty or broaden the base of intervention to embrace social and political action is nicely dealt with in the histories of the ASA, the BRAC and Grameen Bank in Bangladesh by Rutherford, 1995; Lovell, 1992; and Count, 1996, respectively. Chambers, 1995 is especially apposite in relation to the 'systemic' nature of the root causes of poverty.

14 These issues are not new, as is evident if one returns to classics such as Darling, 1924 and Bailey, 1958. More recent accounts focus significantly on gender as a key issue, such as in Groetz and Sen Gupta, 1996; Hashemi, Schuler Sidney and Riley, 1996; Todd, 1996b; Jones, 1995, 1994; Geddes *et al.*, 1994; Afshar, 1991; Holt and Ribe, 1991; Redclift and Sinclair, 1991; Berger, 1989; and McKee, 1989. The importance of specialization and the effectiveness of minimalist approaches to microfinance for microenterprise development from the 'economist's perspective' can be found in World Bank, 1996c, 1989b; Getubig, 1993; FDC, 1992; Jacklen and Rhyne, 1992; Biggs, Snodgrass and Srivastava, 1991; Everett and Savara, 1991; Schreurs and Richmond, 1991; BKI, 1990; Ashe, 1989; and Bouman, 1989.

15 For further details on linkage MFIs and linkage programmes see: Garson, 1996; Bouman and Hospes, 1994; Quiñones, 1992; Bell, 1990; Kropp *et al.*, 1989; and Seibel, 1988.

16 Though there are many MFIs that do not target the poorest of the poor and deserve to be identified as neglecting the difficult work of reaching out to the poorest of the poor, there is reason to believe that criticisms of this nature levelled at Grameen Bank, MFI programmes in Indonesia and those in other places is misplaced because inadequate attention has been given to this dilemma. See for example: Bennett and Cuevas, 1996; Groetz and Sen Gupta, 1996; Hulme and Mosley, 1996; Jain, 1996; Schmidt and Zeitinger, 1996; Copestake, 1995; Hulme, 1995; Rashid and Townsend, 1994; Lipton and van der Gaag, 1993; and Holt and Ribe, 1991.

17 There is an increasing stock of training-related literature that addresses such matters. Readers who wish to explore such operational issues in greater detail should consult: CGAP, 1996, 1995; Hunte, 1996; Jain, 1996; Pitt and Khandker, 1996; Remenyi, 1996, 1995, 1993; Rutherford, 1996, 1995; Seibel, 1996, 1988; Todd, 1996b; Gibbons, 1994; Rashid and Townsend, 1994; Reidinger, 1994; Tomlinson, 1994; Getubig, 1993; Quiñones, 1992; Lovell, 1992; Von Pischke, 1991; Yaron, 1991; Gibbons and Kasim, 1990; Kropp *et al.*, 1989; Levitsky, 1989; and Devereux and Pares, 1987.

18 There is a long history of economic theories that characterize the mechanisms of poverty and the poverty trap, including Galbraith, 1979; Schultz, 1979; Lewis, 1988; Feder *et al.*, 1990; UNDP, 1990; Bencevinga and Smith, 1991; Wahid, 1993; Wigg, 1993; Lipton and van der Gaag, 1993; Remenyi, 1994a; Jayarajah, Branson and Sen, 1996; Pitt and Khandker, 1996; Moser, 1996; and World Bank, 1996a, 1993a, 1990a.

19 Economists like to present these supply and demand relationships in algebraic or diagrammatic form. Readers who are interested in how this might be done and find diagrams a heuristically more informative way to examine the relationship between economic variables can find a simple set of diagrams presented in the appendix to Remenyi, 1991. More rigorous mathematical formulations can be found in Besley, 1997; Hulme and Mosley, 1996; deAghion, 1995; Coate and Ravallion, 1993; Hoff, Braveman and Stiglitz, 1993; and Llanto, 1990.

20 See especially Darling, 1924; Bailey, 1958; Geertz, 1962; Anderson, 1966; Lipton, 1976; McKinnon, 1973; and U Tan, 1977.

21 Grameen Bank replications are dealt with at length in Count, 1996; Jain, 1996; Todd, 1996a,b; Rutherford, 1995; Bouman and Hospes, 1994; Marx, 1994; Poudyal, 1994; Adams and Von Pischke, 1992; Colter and Suharto, 1993; Getubig, 1993; Yunus, 1991, 1983; Gibbons and Kasim, 1990; Hulme, 1990; and Von Pischke, 1980.

22 See Adams, Graham and Von Pischke, 1984; Ahmed, 1989; deAghion, 1995; Lipton and Ravallion, 1995.

23 There is probably more written in the economics of microfinance on collateral substitutes and their uses by MFIs in risk management, market failures and containment of transactions costs than any other topic. The literature appears to be at pains to show why collateral substitutes work and the conditions under which alternative collateral substitutes work best. Modelling of the economic mechanisms at work has also been given considerable attention; much of it based on the classic works by Varian, 1990 on peer monitoring and Llanto, 1990 on markets with asymmetric information. See also, Besley, 1997, 1995, 1994; Herath, 1996, 1994; Hulme and Mosley, 1996; Besley and Coate, 1995; Balkenhol, 1995; deAghion, 1995; Banerjee, Besley and Guinnane, 1994; Coate and Ravallion, 1993; Aleem, 1990; Hoff and Stiglitz, 1990; Stiglitz, 1990; Anderson and Khambata, 1985; and Bester, 1985.

24 This comment is indicative of the importance that must be attached to 'style and process' in the successful implementation of microfinance delivery to clients from poor households. This lesson has not come easily, but it is one that many writers have attempted to highlight. See, for example, deSoto, 1986; Egger, 1986; Fuglesang and Chandler, 1986; Aleem, 1990; Gibbons and Kasim, 1990; Remenyi, 1991; Quiñones, 1992; Coate and Ravallion, 1993; Getubig, 1993; Ahmed and Kennedy, 1994; Albe and Gamage, 1994; Banerjee, Besley and Guinnane, 1994; Bester, 1994; Balkenhol, 1995; Rutherford, 1995; Herath, 1996, 1994; Hunte, 1996; Todd, 1996b; and Basu, 1997.

25 I am not aware of any estimates of the benefit to society of these public goods' 'complementary outputs' of MFI expansion. However, the issue is not new and has been addressed or alluded to by a large number of writers over the years. See, for example: Hulme and Mosley, 1996; Mosley, 1996; Besley, 1994; Hulme and Montgomery, 1994; Deaton, 1991, 1990; Devas, 1991; Everett and Savara, 1991; Huppi and Feder, 1990; Udry, 1990; Cuevas, 1988; Fischer, 1988; Egger, 1986; Gadgil, 1986; Vogel, 1986; Seibel, 1985; and Bouman, 1982.

26 Proceedings of Bank Poor '96 are available from the APDC, Kuala Lumpur. However, the main themes of that conference on savings and strategies for growth of MFIs are also reflected in Getubig, *et al.*, 1997 and Remenyi, 1996.

27 There is an extensive literature on the control of moral hazard in circumstances where enforcement options are limited. However, it would be stretching the evidence to claim that this literature is unanimous on the optimal role of government or the effectiveness of any one strategy for avoiding the worst aspects of moral hazard. It is difficult to avoid a return to the importance of having staff that are honest and deal with MFI members openly and with genuine mutual respect.

Useful comments on these matters can be found in: Darling, 1924; Bailey, 1958; Geertz, 1962; Ardener, 1964; Firth and Yamey, 1964; Anderson, 1966; Howell, 1980; Jones and Rolls, 1982; Bouman, 1984; 1989, 1995; Collier and Lal, 1984; ILO, 1984; Anderson and Khambata, 1985; Adams, Gonzales-Vega and Von Pischke, 1986; Gadgil, 1986; Gersovitz, 1988; Pulley, 1989; Bell, 1990; BKI, 1990; Hoff and Stiglitz, 1990; Huppi and Feder, 1990; ADB, 1991; Braveman and Huppi, 1991; Patten and Rosengard, 1991; Remenyi, 1991; Ghate, 1988, 1992a,b; Besley, 1994; Bouman and Hospes, 1994; Gurgland, Pederson and Yaron, 1994; Binhadi, 1995; Khandker, Khalily and Khan, 1995; Rutherford, 1995; Cuevas, 1996; Herath, 1996, 1994; Hulme and Mosley, 1996; Hunte, 1996; Groetz and Sen Gupta, 1996; Khandker and Khalily, 1996; Rajasekhar, 1996; and Todd, 1996b.

28 These matters are well reviewed in Hulme and Mosley, 1996, especially Chapters 1, 2 and 7, but readers may also wish to consult Srinivas and Higutchi, 1996; Besley, 1995; deAghion, 1995; Mosley, 1995; Otero and Rhyne, 1994; Coate and Ravallion, 1993; Huppi and Feder, 1990; Llanto, 1990; Siamwalla *et al.*, 1990; Stiglitz, 1990; Varian, 1990; Hossain, 1988; and Adams, Graham and Von Pischke, 1984.

29 Hulme and Mosley, 1996 have been especially critical of MFIs as failing to deliver benefits to the poorest of the poor, but this is a common judgement shared by Rajasekhar, 1996; Hulme, 1995; Jones, 1995; Biggs *et al.*, 1991; and Holt and Ribe, 1991.

30 Much of the seminal literature on this topic has appeared in the journal *World Development*. In particular see: Berger, 1989; McKee, 1989; Groetz and Sen Gupta, 1996; and Hashemi, Schuler Sidney and Riley, 1996. Other recent contributions of note are by Moser, 1996; Pitt and Khandker, 1996; Todd, 1996b; UNIFEM, 1996; Ardener and Bouman, 1995; Jones, 1995; Holt and Ribe, 1991; Lyon, 1991; Hoff and Stiglitz, 1990; and World Bank, 1989b.

31 The eight studies are reported in Hossain, 1988; Wahid, 1993; Gurgland, Pederson and Yaron, 1994; Khandker, Khalily and Khan, 1995; Hulme and Mosley, 1996; Moser, 1996; Pitt and Khandker, 1996; and Todd, 1996b.

II
Microfinance in South Asia

3
Bangladesh:
The Pioneering Country

Iftekhar Hossain, Javed Sakhawat,
Ben Quiñones and Stuart Rutherford

Introduction

Bangladesh is the cradle of microfinance. If necessity is indeed the mother of invention, then this may not be surprising. The need was great in Bangladesh when the new nation arose three decades ago, from the ashes of political and civil unrest between West and East Pakistan, as one of the world's poorest countries with the least developed finance sectors. The microfinance providers of Bangladesh can be rightfully proud of leading the world in reaching the poor. The success of Grameen Bank, the availability of large number of NGOs formed after liberation of the country in 1971, and pressure on the NGOs to be less dependent on donors have all contributed to this success.

Despite chronic political instability, Bangladesh has not fostered a grossly hostile environment for the MFIs. The Bangladesh economy has steadily grown during the last 25 years at a rate considered to be 'moderate' by Asian standards, with the average annual growth rate of GDP hovering around 4.2 per cent during the period 1970–94. There has been no hyperinflation to contend with in the 25 years since Independence. Rather, a steady decline in the international value of the Taka has allowed MFIs to get ever more value, in local terms, out of the hard currency grants given them by donors. The relatively low inflation rate has also contributed to the lowering of interest rates from 9.75 per cent in 1990–1 to 5.50 per cent in 1994–5 (Table 3.1).

Although population growth has been falling through the years, and currently stands at 2.2 per cent p.a., in absolute terms the population of Bangladesh has almost doubled since Independence to 120 million in 1996,

Table 3.1:   Selected Macroeconomic Indicators for Bangladesh, 1990-5

Item	1990–1	1991–2	1992–3	1993–4	1994–5
GDP per capita (at market price), Taka	7613	8137	8374	8913	9443
GDP per capita (at market price), US$	213.37	213.29	213.95	222.83	234.90
GDP per capita growth	–	3.4%	4.2%	4.5%	4.2%
Inflation rate	8.8%	5.1%	1.3%	1.8%	5.2%
Currency (Taka) exchange rate to US$	35.68	38.15	39.14	40.00	40.20
Bank rate	9.75%	8.50%	6.50%	5.50%	5.50%

Source: Iftekhar Hossain and Javed Sakhawat, 1996.

and it is forecasted to again double in the next twenty years to reach 250 million by the year 2015. Some 50 million Bangladeshis remain in absolute poverty, half of them 'hard-core' poor. Poverty is defined in terms of the required per capita daily caloric intake of less than 2122 for absolute poverty and less than 1805 for hard-core poverty. Although this definition is the most commonly used, there is increasing recognition of the need to measure the index of human development which includes other factors affecting the quality of life of the people such as nutrition, health and sanitation, housing, personal security, access to state distribution system, participation and institutional capability, and crisis-coping capacity.

The majority of Bangladesh's population (80 per cent) continues to live in rural areas where the rice harvest has grown to keep pace with population growth. But rice yields per hectare have stagnated and despite a shift away from agriculture in the composition of rural incomes there is little evidence yet of the development of rural industry on any scale. Decreasing availability of farming land and the lack of rural employment opportunities have fuelled urban migration. The fairly high incidence of urban poverty indicates the likelihood of a transfer of rural poverty to the towns resulting from the migration of the rural destitute in search of work in the urban areas. In the towns, the ready-made garments industry sprang into life in the 1980s and is now the country's biggest source of hard currency earnings. This has been accompanied by a quickening of the growth rate of the urban population, and attention is turning increasingly to the problems of urban poverty.

Poverty Alleviation Policies and Programmes

The Fourth Five Year Plan (1990–5) of the government of Bangladesh explicitly emphasized the importance of poverty reduction and employment generation. It has vigorously supported social safety net programmes such as Food For Work (FFW), Vulnerable Group Development (VGD) and the Rural Maintenance Programme (RMP) to deal with the problem of poverty, sometimes in close collaboration with NGOs. However, these programmes have had limited coverage and the foodstuff distributed under the FFW and VGD actually declined in recent years.

The government has attempted to use the co-operative model developed at the Bangladesh Academy of Rural Development at Comilla as the basis for a nationwide credit programme for small and landless farmers. This programme fell into difficulties but is now being revived with group-based lending technology borrowed from Grameen Bank. (A successful example is the BRDB's Rural Development Project 12 (RDP-12), one of the case studies.) Starting with a series of experiments in the 1970s facilitated by the USAID and known as the Rural Finance Experimental Project (RFEP), government-owned banks have also been encouraged to test many innovative approaches to rural credit. None of these efforts proved as successful as that of Grameen Bank, which started in 1976 as a private experiment by Professor Muhammad Yunus, then linked up with a government-owned bank and finally, with Central Bank support, obtained its own unique ordinance as a 'bank for the poor' in 1983.

More recently, the government has set up the PKSF, with Professor Yunus on its board, which provides low-cost funds to more than a hundred NGO partners with poverty-targeted credit programmes. It will soon receive about $120 million from the World Bank on International Development Association loan terms. The NGO Bureau, the body that exerts government control over NGOs, has for some years asked NGOs to become involved in credit for the poor. Most use Grameen-type delivery systems. Several of the larger NGOs have also been developing their own models, and the largest of these, the BRAC and the ASA, now use credit delivery methods not dissimilar to Grameen's, though they began differently. Proshika, another big NGO (not included in our case studies), continues to promote and then lend to small neighbourhood-based savings-and-loan co-operatives, and several other NGOs follow this older model.

Financial institutions and their outreach to the poor

Public-sector institutions providing credit to priority sectors include two agricultural banks (the Bangladesh Krishi Bank and the Rashaji Krishi Unnayan Bank), the Bangladesh Rural Development Board (BRDB) with its various Rural Development Projects (RDP-12, RDP-9, RDP-5, etc.), and government line agencies operating their respective credit programmes for specific target groups. Government-owned banks still have by far the largest share of formal bank branches in the country. In addition to these public-sector institutions, three nationalized commercial banks (Agrani, Janata and Sonali) have also traditionally been directed by the government to lend to priority sectors, including poor households and women. Having been used extensively by the government as delivery channels for its subsidized credit programmes, these banks have fallen into disarray: they are technically bankrupt, deliver less rural credit than Grameen and the NGOs, and have not managed to raise the country's domestic savings rate above a measly 8 per cent of GDP. Despite continuous prodding by donors, the government is still undecided about what to do with them.

Complementing the efforts of the government are member-based MFIs, including Grameen Bank, the ASA, Proshika, the BRAC, co-operatives, and NGOs estimated to be around 200. A recent World Bank report on rural finance estimates that a little over 5 per cent of rural households are being serviced annually by public-sector institutions and 25 per cent by member-based institutions.

At the other end of the scale, and especially in the towns, there are an infinite number of informal user-owned savings intermediation clubs such as RoSCAs and annual savings clubs. They are reliable, innovative and growing fast, but have yet been little noticed.

Financial Policy Environment

The 'invisibility' of the NGO-MFI sector to the formal regulators has, so far, largely worked to the advantage of MFIs in Bangladesh. It has allowed them to charge high rates of interest on loans – a factor that has been crucial to the growth of the bigger MFIs. It has also allowed them to set their own rules. The ASA, for example, does not have to worry about formal liquidity ratios when it lends out its customers' savings. It has allowed them almost unrestricted access to donors, and has allowed them the freedom to develop their own special market and to learn as they grow. It is not surprising therefore, that until very recently the general mood among MFI practitioners, as far as regulation was concerned, was to 'let sleeping dogs lie'. Things may now be changing.

It is probably merely a matter of time before MFIs come under the scrutiny of a more formal supervisory body of some sort – the Central Bank, Ministry of Finance, or some special new second-tier regulatory body. Several trends will ensure this : (1) The very growth of the MFIs brings them every day more to the attention of the authorities and of the big donors. (2) The continuing decline of the government-owned rural banks makes MFIs look ever more like the nation's main banking instrument in the countryside – one donor has contemplated the total demise of the formal banking sector and the spread of MFIs to every sub-district. (3) International attitudes – expressed not least at the Bank Poor '96 Regional Workshop in Kuala Lumpur – are turning in favour of a formal status for MFIs, and Bangladesh's MFIs are now much more aware of international trends than they were three or four years ago. Finally, (4), as MFIs think about mobilizing more savings from the general public the need for formal protection of savings grows stronger.

Indeed, there have already been several instances of rogue or simply incompetent MFIs going out of business at the expense of poor rural savers, but because this is a new discussion in Bangladesh it is not at all clear what form the regulation might take. There are, however, still many ways of delivering financial services to the poor that have simply not yet been thought about or tried. For instance, there are no rural shareholder banks, or district-level private banks, nor has there been much innovation in thrift co-operative (or credit union) management. In addition, no one has seriously tried to link the growing number of spontaneous user-owned savings clubs together.

Microfinance Capacity Assessment

To assess the breadth and depth of microfinance outreach in Bangladesh, eight MFIs were selected for in-depth case study. Table 3.2 gives a brief description of the eight sample MFIs: Grameen Bank, the BRAC, Rural Development Project 12 (RDP-12), the ASA, the Bangladesh Unemployed Rehabilitation Organization (BURO)-Tangail, the Shakti Foundation, the Rangpur Dinajpur Rural Service (RDRS), and the Marginal and Small Farm Systems Crop Intensification Project (MSFSCIP).

Excluding the government projects – the BRAC and RDP-12 – only two (i.e. the ASA and the Shakti Foundation) of the other six MFIs have experienced board members playing a significant role in policy-setting. Though the BRAC, the BURO and Grameen have a governing body, the members of this body do not play a very active role in the affairs of those organizations. Nine of Grameen's thirteen board members (the highest policy

Table 3.2 Description and Number of Clients of Eight Sample MFIs in Bangladesh, 1995

MFI	Number of Clients	Description
Grameen Bank	2,065,661	A formal bank which lends to the rural poor, with a board including elected borrower-members.
BRAC	1,510,802	An NGO with a wide range of activities including credit.
RDP-12	461,452	One of a number of rural credit and income-generation projects run by the government; formally a co-operative, but uses credit delivery methods similar to Grameen's.
ASA	404,218	An NGO which since 1991 has specialized in low-cost lending to poor.
BURO-Tangail	20,924	A local NGO based on Grameen principles but pioneering new savings and loan products.
Shakti Foundation	10,710	An urban NGO using Grameen delivery methods.
RDRS	N.A.	A local NGO with a wide range of activities including credit. Works with 18,308 groups.
MSFSCIP	N.A.	A partnership between government, an NGO and some formal banking institutions under which groups of poor farmers are linked to formal bank services. Works with 1713 groups.

body) are elected from its members. BURO-Tangail has consultative groups at the branch level and plans to have elected representatives to advise its executive committee. The Shakti Foundation and RDP-12 have no plans to increase participation of members/clients in programme decision-making. The BRAC has a seven-member governing body made up of eminent social workers. In the field, all decisions which affect the group members are taken by the members themselves. At the time of the study in 1996, the RDRS has been operating as a project of the international NGO – the Lutheran World Service with headquarters in Geneva, Switzerland – and as such it had no governing body but only an advisory body, which is not very active.

In most of the programmes, the clients are organized into groups with membership ranging from a minimum of ten (MSFSCIP) to a maximum of 50 or 60 individuals (RDP-12). Group members are usually selected taking into account the following factors: economic homogeneity, physical fitness (in order to take up manual labour), having a fixed address and not being shelterless, and being within a certain age range (not too old, not too young). All the groups have elected officials who represent the interests of the members in the higher bodies.

Outreach

As of the end of 1995, the total number of members of these eight MFIs had reached over 4 million (Table 3.2). Of the eight MFIs included in the study Grameen Bank, the BRAC and RDP-12 do not plan to open new branches. The ASA, the BURO-Tangail and the Shakti Foundation are still expanding. Some of the MFIs face various constraints to expansion: funding for the ASA and the BURO-Tangail; management capacity for the Shakti Foundation; and for the RDRS, a shift of vision from relief/rehabilitation work to credit, and which means it requires an overhaul not only of its operating system but most importantly of the attitude towards development work of all its staff, including senior management.

All the MFIs select members on the basis of defined criteria and all have a client base which is more than 90 per cent women. No records are maintained by any of the eight MFIs on the number of non-poor clients, but all of them claim that their borrowers and savers are all poor (Table 3.3). The targeting test conducted by Hossain and Sakhawat, 1996 (applied to all MFIs except Grameen Bank and the BRAC) shows the percentage of non-poor below 10 per cent. While it is generally acknowledged that the very poor are not reached (and there is a lively debate over exactly what percentage is thus excluded), no serious research has ever suggested that more than 10 per cent are non-poor. Most rural MFIs use means tests, usually based on land and asset holdings, to exclude the better-off households in the villages, and urban operators such as Shakti use household income tests. Moreover, many take only or mostly women account holders. Shakti, for example, serves only

Table 3.3 Number of Savers and Borrowers of Eight Sample MFIs, 1995

MFI	Number of Borrowers[a]	Poor Borrowers as % of All Borrowers[b]	Number of Savers[c]	Poor Savers as % of All Savers
ASA	326,255	100	404,218	100
BRAC	1,059,199	100	1,510,802	100
BURO-Tangail	11,694	100	20,924	100
Grameen Bank	1,870,371	100	2,065,661	100
MSFSCIP	1,468	100	1,713	100
RDP-12	328,102	100	461,452	100
RDRS	7,877	100	18,308	100
Shakti Foundation	9,425	100	10,710	100

Notes:
a Strictly, these figures represent a count of loan accounts, but in the Bangladesh situation this is very close to the number of borrowers. The same is true of savers, who are often borrowers-in-waiting.
b As assessed by the MFIs.
c Most Bangladesh MFIs attract clients by offering loans and then require all clients to make regular forced savings.
Source: Hossain and Sakhawat, 1996.

women, and the percentage of men among the customers of the BRAC (8 per cent), Grameen (6 per cent), the ASA (4 per cent), and the BURO-Tangail (2.5 per cent) is minimal. Conventional thinking has it that women in Bangladesh are poorer, or more disadvantaged, than men. They are also better at repaying loans, and many of their loans enter the household cash flow and are not used exclusively by the women borrowers.

The targeting of poor clients is considered an important factor for the high repayment rates achieved by the MFIs, but it has also been blamed for the exclusion of the extreme poor. It is now widely accepted by microfinance practitioners in Bangladesh that not all poor households have benefited from microcredit programmes. There is growing recognition that 'the poor' is not a homogeneous group with broadly similar needs. The extreme poor constituted 22 per cent of the rural poor in 1994, while the moderate poor comprised 52 per cent and non-poor households constituted 26 per cent. The emphasis of the last fifteen years on the poverty-alleviation model of financing enterprise expansion has been found to be valid for 'middle' and 'upper' entrepreneurial poor households, but inappropriate for the poorest households, those with a high degree of income insecurity, and the disabled.

Range of Financial Services

Until recently, the major financial service the MFIs were providing was pure and straightforward loans, with Grameen Bank being the leader in credit delivery. Their experience indicates that loan demand continues to exceed their fund capacity. Nonetheless, the MFIs are responding, albeit slowly, to the needs of the rural clients for a more flexible financial service. The slow response of the MFIs is attributed to the widespread belief that the poor cannot save, or can save very little, and that the only appropriate financial service for them is credit. Where this assumption has been tested, both in the countryside and in the urban slums, it has proved to be incorrect, but these experiments are little known. Moreover, it is still popularly believed that the only 'proper' use for credit is in production-based or trading enterprises that produce a stream of income.

It is now becoming clear that for many borrowers of Grameen-style loans, the role of MFIs in intermediating household savings is as much valued as their role in providing working capital for businesses. That is, many clients are happy to make a series of tiny weekly payments out of their normal income in exchange for a usefully large annual lump sum, and to go on doing this year after year. In fact, some, but by no means all, of these lump sums do get invested in businesses or in land purchases, although much is still used for other vital needs such as house repairs, coping with illnesses, dealing with ceremonies and other major life-cycle expenditures, or paying off older more expensive debts.

As the behaviour of poor customers becomes better understood, and as customers are understood not to constitute an undifferentiated mass, MFIs have begun to respond with new products. Grameen has been offering housing loans for many years, and further experimenting through the Grameen Trust with health insurance. The BRAC has an established programme with special terms for extremely poor rural women. Among our case studies, the BRAC, the ASA and the BURO-Tangail are all trying to introduce voluntary savings into their Grameen-style operations, while the BURO has gone furthest and is the most committed to this approach so far. Several smaller NGOs and private operators (not represented in the case studies) have gone further, for example by selling accumulating fixed-term deposits in the villages, or by setting up low-cost ultra-simple life insurance schemes in which the premiums collected are immediately re-invested in the neighbourhood through Grameen-style lending, or by setting up door-step daily collection savings schemes for the urban poor.

Several MFIs are now ready to add variety to their portfolios of small annual weekly-repaid loans by tailoring bigger loans with other repayment schedules for those having larger-scale entrepreneurial potential among the poor. The BRAC, which has tried this before, started a further set of trials in 1996; the Shakti Foundation is already doing it through a partnership with a specialized microenterprise bank; and the BURO is offering 'lines of credit' to selected rural businesswomen.

This fresh wave of innovation is extremely welcome, and the APDC can help to accelerate this deepening of outreach by bringing the soundest practices from other parts of Asia to the notice of Bangladeshi MFIs, perhaps through the fledgling microfinance network known as the Credit and Development Forum (CDF). Moreover, basic training to build up a cadre of competent and informed microfinance workers with appropriate business-like attitudes was identified by several of the sample MFIs as a current need.

In sum, the outreach to the poor of MFIs in Bangladesh is spectacularly wide but still shallow. One particular product − a small loan delivered in a group setting in the village and paid back in weekly instalments over a year − has reached millions. It is this high-volume low-cost standardized (and rather inflexible) product that has made Grameen Bank the world's biggest, and the ASA the world's fastest growing, MFI. Grameen has grown to close on two million loan accounts in twenty years, the ASA to half a million in five. The BRAC, which started lending to the poor in the mid-1970s, has around one million. Many other programmes using a similar product (including the BURO-Tangail and the Shakti) push the total number of accounts of this type to at least six million. A recent World Bank report estimated that not less than one in every four rural households is reached by such services, and others have suggested an even higher figure. The number will rise − Grameen has stopped opening new branches but most other established MFIs are still growing rapidly. Moreover, there is a constant stream of new entrants, sometimes encouraged by donors who themselves want to be associated with what the world has come to see as a great success story. Excellent repayment rates testify to the popularity of these annual micro-loans.

Viability and Sustainability

Availability of free or very low cost money from international donors has been the essential engine driving the growth of MFIs in Bangladesh. However, their progress towards viability and sustainability has come about because the MFIs have built on this advantage in three ways. First has been the policy of standardization, second of exploiting the liberal interest rate environment, and third of taking forced savings for which there seems enormous potential.

We have already noted their standard product: a single loan type with a fixed repayment schedule and a narrow range of face values, which can be delivered en masse by cheap labour with only a few days of training. The ASA, for example, trains recruits for only six days before deploying them in branches, which handle 1600 accounts each but have only five staff and no accountant. Interest rates charged on these loans have not been restrained by law and are only now starting to be contained by competition (and that, only in some congested areas). Those MFIs that charge lower interest rates usually demand very high rates of forced savings: Grameen, for example, deducts 5 per cent of the face value of each loan at disbursement and holds it for at least ten years. In this way Grameen has, over the years, mobilized more forced savings than its total receipts of donor grant money. Nor is it barred from on-lending these deposits. A standardized product, high interest rates and

Table 3.4 Selected Viability Data, of Eight Sample MFIs in Bangladesh, 1995 (All percentages on annual basis)

MFI	AIRD[a]	AIRB[b]	OTRR[c]	ETFS[d]	OTFS[e]	COFB[f]
ASA	5.0%	24%	[99.7%]	14%	20%	6%
BRAC	6.0%	25%	[97.5%]	12%	10%	N.A.
BURO-Tangail	10.0%	25%	[98.0%]	16%	26%	N.A.
Grameen Bank	8.5%	20%	N.A.	14%	6%	6%
MSFSCIP	N.A.	7%	N.A.	N.A.	N.A.	N.A.
RDP-12	a	16%	90.0%	15%	18%	N.A.
RDRS	N.A.	16%	N.A.	9%	145%	9%[d]
Shakti	4.5%	16%	99.5%	10%	23%	N.A.

Notes:
a AIRD = average interest rate on client deposits. See the text and note that many Bangladesh MFIs collect more forced than voluntary savings. In RDP-12 members of individual co-operatives decide the rate to be paid.
b AIRB = average interest rate charged to borrowers. Most Bangladesh MFIs take a 'flat' interest payment along with the weekly loan repayment. The figures shown here convert such systems into annual percentage rates.
c OTRR = on-time repayment rate. Not fully available from the assessment studies. Note that MFIs use differing systems of measurement: most of these indicate rates above 90 per cent. Figures in square brackets are claims made by MFIs in data provided to the CDF and refer to June 1996.
d ETFS = Earnings (interest + fees) as a proportion of total financial services.
e OTFS = Operating costs as a proportion of total financial services.
f COFB = Cost of fund, where borrowed. Not common in Bangladesh where most loan funds have come from donors. The ASA and the RDRS borrow from commercial sources and from the PKSF (see text) though the RDRS' PKSF borrowings are not included in the 9 per cent figure given (if they were, the figure would be lower).
Source of basic data: Hossain and Sakhawat, 1996.

copious forced savings lead, in a well-managed MFI, to good rates of retained earnings (see Table 3.4). This is well demonstrated by the ASA, with its loan fund comprising roughly equal shares of donor capital, savings and retained earnings.

Even within Bangladesh, the ASA's rise to an exceptional position has been a recent phenomenon so, how has it been achieved? The ASA came late to microfinance, and was able to offer a simplified version of the Grameen loan product. It did away with five-person solidarity cells within larger 'centres' and went for twenty-person groups of women, all of whom save, borrow and repay similar or identical sums on the same day. Customers may have only one loan at a time, cannot make pre-payments, cannot (until recently) withdraw their savings and cannot save more than a fixed amount. Bookkeeping is extremely simple. This allows the ASA to employ a powerful combination of delegation and standardization where modestly-paid briefly-trained staff are given full authority to approve loans but do it within such an inflexible set of norms that they rarely have to exercise much judgement. The loan sizes are also small, even by Bangladesh standards (the ASA gives no loan greater than US$175), and the weekly repayments are well within the capacity of most borrowers to pay from their regular or normal income.

The result, helped by the ASA's highly disciplined weekly meetings, is very high repayment rates. Cash taken in through savings and repayments is turned around very quickly and re-lent, so the ASA keeps very little money idle at the bank. Organizationally the ASA has only two layers – the branches and the Dhaka headquarters. There are staff with supervisory duties at area or regional level but they are not given an office of their own so they sit at a table in a branch. The organizational life-style at headquarters is exemplary in its modesty and there are only three vehicles to serve the staff, which totals 3300. All this is enforced by a leader with a clear vision who takes care to hammer home the message of sustainability at every opportunity, and insists on highly transparent accounts, which are regularly published.

Financial Self-sufficiency

Grameen Bank leads all other MFIs with full financial self-sufficiency reaching 81.2 per cent in 1994 and 85.7 per cent in 1995 based on the formula commonly used for the Bank Poor '96 study (Table 3.5). The ASA already reached full financial self-sufficiency of 97.5 per cent in 1994. The ASA's microfinance technology is reportedly capable of recovering fully the operating costs of a newly established unit office within eleven months. But the ASA's financial self-sufficiency dropped to 58.9 per cent in 1995 as 625 new field staff joined the organization, increasing its work force by 30 per cent and its operating costs by 110 per cent.

The design of RDP-12 and the MSFSCIP, being government projects, does not take into consideration the concept of viability/sustainability. The BURO-Tangail and the Shakti Foundation have projections for attaining financial self-sufficiency within a specific number of years. The BRAC and the RDRS, while striving for self-sufficiency in financial services, still provide various social development services, which are subsidized and cannot be looked at in a cost-effective way. The BRAC has a number of profit-making enterprises whose profits are ploughed back into its development activities. The RDRS is primarily a social and human development organization and therefore does not account for all its inputs and outputs in quantifiable money terms. The RDRS and the BRAC measure their performance and effectiveness through other pre-determined performance criteria.

The strategies used by the MFIs to achieve viability/sustainability are as follows:

– recruiting and retaining committed staff
– scaling up outreach and taking advantage of economies of scale
– increasing the size of loans and savings
– enlarging the range of financial products and services and
– obtaining grant funds.

It is widely known among NGO-MFIs that setting up a revolving loan fund

Table 3.5 Operating and Full Financial Self-Sufficiency of Eight Sample MFIs in Bangladesh, 1993–5 (Amounts in US$'000, exchange rate averaged at US$1 = Taka 40 for all the years)

Year/Item	ASA	BRAC	BURO-Tangail	Grameen Bank	MSFSCIP	RDP-12	RDRS	Shakti Foundation
1993								
Interest and Fees from clients	273.7	4,334.4	32.8	26,298.8	8.3	N.A.	46.6	9.8
Total Costs	2,207.8	8,325.7	81.5	32,891.6	N.A.	N.A.	31.1	34.7
Adjusted Total Costs	2,214.3	N.A.	88.0	33,325.9	N.A.	N.A.	31.5	47.0
Operating Self-sufficiency (%)	12.40%	56.56%	40.25%	79.96%	N.A.	N.A.	146.59%	28.36%
Full Financial Self-sufficiency (%)	12.36	N.A.	37.28%	78.91%	N.A.	N.A.	145.05%	20.96%
1994								
Interest and Fees from Clients	2,507.4	6,213.6	78.1	41,103.8	54.7	1,485.0	158.8	26.3
Total Costs	2,546.1	10,481.7	109.6	49,919.8	N.A.	3,573.1	37.5	73.0
Adjusted Total Costs	2,571.5	N.A.	134.9	50,642.6	N.A.	4,870.2	56.6	102.0
Operating Self-sufficiency	98.48	61.75%	71.26%	82.34%	N.A.	41.56%	423.98%	35.96%
Full financial self-sufficiency	97.51	N.A.	57.86%	81.16%	N.A.	30.49%	280.70%	25.76%
1995								
Interest and Fees from clients	2,857.5	9,613.1	105.8	49,073.6	97.5	2,991.3	441.4	57.8
Total Costs	4,847.3	15,549.5	183.7	56,721.2	N.A.	3,841.3	176.7	144.6
Adjusted Total Costs	4,854.6	N.A.	198.5	57,289.9	N.A.	4,870.2	171.5	176.1
Operating Self-sufficiency	59.04%	67.12%	57.63%	86.52%	N.A.	77.87%	249.77%	39.97%
Full Financial Self-sufficiency	58.86%	N.A.	53.33%	85.66%	N.A.	58.66%	257.38%	32.83%

Source: Hossain and Sakhawat, 1996.

is the surest way out of economic dependence on donors. When funds from donors have been lent out to the poor as loans and repaid with interest, these funds become the assets of the NGO-MFIs.

Only a handful of MFIs in Bangladesh pursue the single-minded strategy of low cost, high interest rate and standardization to the point where economies of scale become important. The ASA, Grameen Bank and RDP-12 are committed to a similar approach. The BURO-Tangail has plans to reach self-sufficiency as a regional MFI with a hundred thousand customers early in the twenty-first century. The Shakti, an urban lender, has also set a target date for self-sufficiency, though at end 1995 it had only 11,000 customers. The BRAC and the RDRS see financial services as one component in a holistic development approach, much of which does not attempt to recover costs, but the BRAC is gradually separating its banking work from its wide range of subsidized social programmes. RDP-12 and the MSFSCIP do not keep accounts that allow viability to be analysed.

Many NGOs continue to run credit programmes as subsidized social services, though those taking loans from the PKSF are tightening up their procedure to meet the stipulated loan servicing schedules. MFIs with social development agenda undertake motivation work more intensively than MFIs dealing only with credit. The former approach, sometimes referred to as 'maximalist' (also called 'credit-plus' or 'microfinance-plus), is more costly than the latter, which is sometimes called 'minimalist'. The 'minimalist' MFIs (Grameen Bank, the ASA, the BURO-Tangail and the Shakti Foundation) do not provide technical assistance for clients. RDP-12 provides training on skill development funded by the project. 'Maximalist' MFIs place social and human resource development in the forefront or concurrently with economic development (e.g., the RDRS, the BRAC, Proshika, etc.) They provide relatively more technical assistance directly or facilitate the access of such technical assistance from government agencies or other sources.

A large replication of Grameen, run by the government, receives massive support from the Asian Development Bank (ADB) but does not seriously aim at independent viable status by covering costs from the margin. The government-owned banks themselves, some of which have services aimed at the poor, are technically bankrupt.

As competition heats up between MFIs, interest rates may fall and a wider range of products – less standardized and more expensive to deliver – may be increasingly demanded by their customers. In particular, better savings bank services will be required. These trends will challenge the fragile viability of Bangladesh's MFIs, making them progressively more like MFIs in other countries and less and less a special case. As a result, they will have to focus ever more sharply on new forms of resource mobilization and on a business-like approach to the task of delivering microfinance to the poor.

Resource Mobilization

Owing to the large number of people living below the poverty line, both government and NGO sectors of Bangladesh have received considerable donor grants. During the last few years, however, donors have become more concerned about institutional viability. Donors particularly of poverty alleviation and microcredit schemes are increasingly making their support dependent on two major factors – outreach, as measured in terms of the number of poor clients, and sustainability, as measured in terms of the degree of financial self-sufficiency. Consequently, NGOs that show possibilities of self-reliance are given preference for donor funding. Compared to the late 1980s and early 1990s donor funding has become tighter in Bangladesh and the smaller NGOs have been more affected than the big ones. Bilateral donors almost exclusively fund only public-sector projects. However, the World Bank has recently decided to provide funds to the NGOs through the PKSF. The ADB is formulating a project with the government, a component of which will provide funds to NGOs through a nationalized commercial bank.

Some MFIs simply consume the donor grants while others have built on them by combining them with forced savings and substantial interest earnings. This leaves other forms of savings broadly untouched as mobilizable resources which include voluntary savings from customers, voluntary savings from the general public, and stores of both voluntary and forced savings represented by the funds held by banks and other financial institutions. More exotic sources such as socially motivated investors (trusts, service organizations or sympathetic business leaders) are not yet visible in any strength. There are some recent exceptions, however. Grameen, for example, has used its status as a formal bank to take funds from the market by issuing bonds, while the ASA has taken a loan from a commercial bank (a very small one because it had to provide its headquarters building as collateral); and a pharmaceutical company puts part of its profits into a small urban programme which lends to poor women. Despite these, it remains the popular view in Bangladesh that donor cash is essential to fund the continued growth of the microfinance sector in Bangladesh.

However, it is clear that donor attitudes are changing, and those of the government with them. The clearest signals come from the PKSF, the government-owned fund which lends to NGOs rather than making grants to them, and from the World Bank, which is about to make an advance of $120 million to the PKSF. Though it is a late-comer to financing MFIs, the World Bank still managed to lecture the donors in Dhaka for their old-fashioned addiction to handing out grants, while advertising their loan policy as more likely to encourage MFIs to become viable and therefore long-lived institutions. There were rueful smiles around the table, especially from those donors with a long history of sympathetic support to MFIs, but the message

Table 3.6 Savings and Loans of Eight Sample MFIs in Bangladesh, as at end 1995 (Amounts in Bangladesh Taka '000 and in US$'000 at $1 = Taka 42)

| MFI | I Savings Held | | II Loans Outstanding | | Ratio of Column I |
	Taka	US$	Taka	US$	to Column II
ASA	246,034.1	5,857.9	559,680.9	13,325.7	0.44
BRAC	801,813.9	19,091.0	2,335,344.1	55,603.0	0.34
BURO-Tangail	6,509.4	155.0	20,424.8	487.0	0.32
Grameen Bank	3,591,203.7	85,505.0	10,811,755.1	257,423.0	0.33
MSFSCIP	5,430.2	129.3	53,602.5	1,276.0	0.10
RDP-12	270,557.9	6,442.0	538,424.9	12,820.0	0.50
RDRS	65,952.0	1,570.0	134,329.0	3,198.0	0.49
Shakti	4,758.0	113.0	17,606.4	419.0	0.27

Note: Much of the savings shown in this table are forced savings.
Source: Hossain and Sakhawat, 1996.

was well taken by them, and several (but by no means all) had already scaled down their grant plans and begun to re-engineer their role as providers of technical assistance rather than loan funds.

Faced with this, and led by very public examples such as the ASA, the MFIs are beginning to explore ways to reduce their dependence on donor favours.

Savings Deposits

Table 3.6 shows, for some of the case study MFIs, the balance held of savings mobilized by them, the value of loans outstanding, and the ratio between the two. The table is included partly for comparison with other country summaries: for example, the highest savings-to-loan ratio in this table is 0.5 compared to 1.57 for BPD, a successful MFI in Indonesia. This illustrates the historic difference in the development of MFIs in the two countries.

Despite the significant record of savings mobilization recorded in Table 3.6, the dominant strategy remains the one already pioneered by Grameen and the ASA – increased earnings on an expanded loan portfolio, in addition to forced savings. Getting capital from the formal banks is still dogged by mistrust and a genuine belief on the part of bankers that financing MFIs is simply not their job. In fact, the ASA's loan from the Agrani Bank needed strenuous midwifery from the donors before this rather under-sized financial infant saw the light. And again, despite the new interest in the mobilization of voluntary savings which is increasingly seen (quite properly) as an important service for poor people in its own right, its role in resource mobilization is still down-played. For example the BURO-Tangail, an MFI which of all the Grameen-style programmes is moving fastest to introduce various savings products, still intends to rely on $4 million of donor money and a high rate of interest on loans made from it to secure self-sufficiency in the early years of the twenty-first century, as indicated in its financial projections.

Finally, some small-scale experiments, and the rapid proliferation of user-owned spontaneous savings clubs, tend to confirm that Bangladesh's poor are not exceptional. Indeed, like the poor in other Asian countries, they both can and want to save. This suggests room for a more radical move by MFIs towards the direct mobilization of savings, though the regulatory environment needs to be clarified before that can be done on any scale.

Commercial Sources of Funds

There is an increased encouragement, particularly by the donors, for the MFIs to look for commercial sources of funds. As this is a new area for the MFIs, the donors are thinking of agents to help institutions in the commercial financial system. Some donors have already set up or are in the process of setting up second-tier institutions whose function it is to raise funds from commercial sources and on-lend to MFIs, make full or partial guarantees of loans made by commercial banks to NGOs, help leverage private investment, etc.

Many public-sector banks and some private-sector banks are currently experimenting with group lending along the lines of the Grameen Bank model. Most of these initiatives fall under their poverty-alleviation programmes. There are some instances of banks lending to NGOs for on-lending to their members, Agrani Bank to the ASA being the most notable. The NGO is responsible for the loan, bearing all credit risk, in exchange for the difference between the loan terms and the on-lending rate.

In some other cases the NGO acts as facilitator (Bank of Small Industries and Commerce with the Shakti Foundation). The bank bears the credit risk by lending directly to the borrowers and shares a part of its spread with the NGO as commission for identifying borrowers and ensuring repayment. A variant of this model (i.e. the MSFSCIP) is observed for government projects where the bank lends to the borrowers at the behest of the MFI, but the MFI services are paid for by a donor.

In sum, availability of donor funds has for so long restrained MFIs in Bangladesh from tapping the commercial market for funds, but with the scaling down of donor funding and growing confidence on the part of the MFI management, the search for alternative funding is becoming a significant factor for financial sustainability. The BURO-Tangail now gives greater emphasis on savings as a source of on-lending funds; the ASA and the Shakti Foundation have established linkages with commercial banks; and Grameen Bank has floated debentures. The government is also doing its part to protect the microfinance sector. It is actively promoting closer co-operation between commercial banks and NGOs and also arranging for World Bank funding of the PKSF for re-lending to NGOs, big and small.

Policy and Regulatory Environment

Given the country's extremely low rates of literacy, especially among women, and a very high incidence of malnutrition and chronic ill health (again affecting women disproportionately), successive governments have understood the need for massive investments in human resource develop- ment if poverty is to be overcome. However, progress has been slow. Governments, finding themselves unable to mobilize enough resources at home, have been unhealthily dependent on international donors. A second policy approach of accelerating the growth of industrialization through macroeconomic reform, deregulation and privatization, and to make the country attractive to foreign investors, has been hampered by political instability and an unresponsive bureaucracy.

Arguably, therefore, Bangladesh has had more success with a third approach to poverty alleviation – income and employment generation programmes targeted at the poor by both government and NGOs. This has been the arena in which the big MFIs such as the BRDB in the public sector and Grameen Bank, the BRAC and the ASA in the private sector – all featured as case studies – have been active.

The fact that no definite policy has been purposively set for regulating MFIs in Bangladesh is a boon rather than a bane to the microfinance sector. While Bangladesh Bank, the central bank, supervises the activities of all registered banking institutions in the country, it has not placed member- based NGOs under its regulatory control. NGOs are being monitored by government ministries like Social Services or, more recently, the NGO Bureau (part of the Prime Minister's Office), rather than by the country's formal financial regulators in the Ministry of Finance or the Central Bank. In 1994, officials reviewed a number of applications for a banking licence, and a handful of small operators who presented themselves as banks got their licences, but the giant among them – the BRAC, with its million clients – was the only NGO and the only one denied a banking licence.

NGOs are currently deemed to be operating outside the supervisory control of the central bank since they are not classified as banking institutions. NGOs also claim that they do not provide financial services to the 'public', only to their members. This has allowed them the independence to develop their own credit and savings programmes with no interference from the Central Bank or any other regulatory body. They set their own interest rates, and devise their own credit delivery mechanisms and accounting practices. However, the lack of regulatory control has also resulted in depositors having no legal recourse against the management of some MFIs which collapsed due to mismanagement and fraud.

While exercising no regulatory controls, the government on the other hand has been providing support to the microfinance sector. In 1983 the government helped Grameen to its banking ordinance, and, later, the NGO Bureau went out of its way to request NGOs to extend loans to the rural poor, thereby giving them quasi-legal status. The government has in fact recommended NGO microfinance technology – above all the annual loan paid back in weekly instalments – to its own banks for emulation, and run its own replication of Grameen (within the Ministry of Youth and Sports).

Although politicians could not resist promising loan forgiveness in the run-up to elections, the major MFIs have been able to present their programmes to the public as a special sector to which such loan forgiveness does not apply. Finally, when it was clear that Grameen Bank had become an international success story, the government became happy to bask in its reflected glory. There have of course been enemies within; for example some fundamentalist groups have targeted MFI groups and placed anti-MFI stories in the local language press, but the leaders of big NGOs are not without their own power and influence, and little lasting damage has been done. In a country where formal employment opportunities are scarce, organizations with thousands of jobs at their disposal are important. Grameen Bank had almost 12,000 staff at the end of 1995, the ASA almost 3000.

Concluding Observations

The world will not forget that it was in Bangladesh where it was first proved that an institution lending exclusively to the poor could become a large, successful and self-sufficient financial institution. Bangladesh's case shows how one good idea in the right place at the right time can spark off a whole new industry. A small loan that can be paid back in tiny instalments over the following year suits millions of poor people, almost irrespective of what they use it for. Professor Yunus had the idea and the ruthlessness to set aside a host of other complicating issues – skills training, collateral, illiteracy – and to focus on how such a loan could be delivered quickly and cheaply to thousands and finally millions of poor villagers. The high point of the industry was the ASA's rise from nothing to half a million clients – and to self-sufficiency – in the first half of the 1990s.

Although the idea has still a long way to run, things will never be quite the same again. Grameen has stopped growing, and many of its existing branches are suffering lower repayment rates than they have been used to, as clients find that loan sizes that grow year by year finally turn out to be more expensive than they can handle out of weekly income. Furthermore, competition in areas densely populated by MFIs is beginning to force interest rates down. Donors are also having second thoughts. Meanwhile, the MFIs themselves are looking at new ideas – savings, regulation, or bigger loans with special terms for genuine entrepreneurs. As this happens, so Bangladesh will become less and less of a special case, and will look more like other Asian countries in the development of a full range of intermediation services for the poor and not-so-poor.

Some substantive reforms will have to take place if the microfinance sector of Bangladesh is to strive towards a more fully developed financial intermediation system for the poor. Most NGO-MFIs will have to segregate their credit programmes from social development programmes. They should put more emphasis on developing 'bare-foot-bankers' instead of social workers. They should develop cost-effective training programmes to address the lack of competent and skilled staff. They need to design viable credit programmes that reach significant number of poor households. Of the big and middle-size MFIs, only a very few have seriously tried savings mobilization, although there is a growing realization that savings are plentiful in the villages. Donor agencies should encourage their partner-MFIs to mobilize savings more earnestly. They could also provide technical assistance to networks of MFIs for the development of deposit insurance.

With its strategic role in providing support for microfinance initiatives, the PKSF can actively promote the replication of viable and sustainable microfinance technologies. The CDF can also play a leading role by initially providing the motivation to the MFIs, educating the society to the need for viable/sustainable MFIs which require reasonable rates of return, and then assisting the MFIs in developing long-term plans for viability/sustainability.

4

Microfinance in India: Adjusting to Economic Liberalization

Sanjay Sinha, John Samuel and Ben Quiñones

Introduction

Until the financial policy reforms in the 1990s, credit to the poor in India has largely been viewed as a government programme that requires huge doses of subsidy. Although this view continues to hold sway among politicians, government bureaucrats and bankers, deregulation of the financial system is gradually changing the financial landscape. As a result of interest rate deregulation, a growing number of commercial banks, with support from the national apex institution, the NABARD (National Bank for Agricultural and Rural Development), are now establishing linkages with informal self-help groups (SHGs) of the poor in order to mobilize deposits among the poor and provide credit to them at affordable rates.

The financial reforms were part of a structural adjustment policy package introduced by the government of India in 1990–1 with the aim of accelerating the country's economic growth and alleviating the worsening living conditions of the greater part of its population. With a GDP in excess of US$293 billion in 1994, India ranked sixteenth in the world in terms of size and as high as fifth in terms of purchasing power parity. But with a per capita income estimated at US$320, the country ranks among the poorest in the world.[1] India's manufacturing economy is the world's largest in absolute terms, but the country remains a rural economy with two-thirds of employment (of main workers) still engaged in the primary sector. These two-thirds of the total employed labour force account for only one-third of the net national product.[2]

Historically the Indian economy has registered GDP growth rates of 2 to 5 per cent per annum.[3] During the period 1985–6 to 1989–90,[4] economic growth accelerated to an annual average of 5.8 per cent, but this rate was not sustained following the introduction of major structural adjustment policy reforms in 1990–1. The economy almost ground to a halt in 1991–2 and then expanded at a relatively slower pace of 4.9 per cent average annual growth during the next five years to 1995–6. Although the import dependency of the Indian economy is relatively low,[5] particularly for basic consumer goods, the drastic depreciation of the Rupee (around 23 per cent p.a.) during the early years of structural adjustment brought inflation that further worsened the lot of the poor.

Evidently, the Indian economy has to grow much faster than it has ever achieved in the past if the characteristics of under-development with a persistent and widespread poverty are to be eliminated. Poverty in India has come to be known as endemic because it has persisted for as long as people can remember. It is also extensive: one of every three persons in India live below the poverty line. Using the calculations made by the Expert Group On Estimation of Proportion and Number of Poor over the fifteen-year period from 1973–4 to 1987–8, it is estimated the number of households living below the officially defined 'poverty line' is around 300 million, or 34 per cent of the total population in 1993–4.

The government of India measures the incidence of poverty in terms of the proportion of population with incomes less than the poverty threshold, also referred to as the 'poverty line' and defined officially as annual household income of Rs 11,000 (US$317). Estimating the number of poor in India has evoked a lot of controversy. Estimates of poverty incidence have been made by a government Expert Group as well as by the Planning Commission.[6] The Expert Group's calculations suggest that rural poverty is now proportionately less prevalent than urban poverty, but the Planning Commission's estimates place rural poverty at substantially higher levels than those in urban areas (Table 4.1). Notwithstanding these differences, both estimates portray a common historical trend: (1) the poverty ratio displayed a declining trend in both urban and rural areas over the past twenty years, and

Table 4.1 Proportion of Population in India with Income Less Than the Poverty Threshold

Areas	% of total population				
	1973–4	*1977–8*	*1983–4*	*1987–8*	*1993–4*
Rural – Expert Group[7]	56.4	53.1	45.6	39.1	33.6
– Planning Commission[8]		51.2	40.4	33.3	26.3
Urban – Expert Group	49.2	47.4	42.2	40.1	35.7
– Planning Commission		38.2	28.1	20.7	15.2
Combined – Expert Group	54.9	51.8	44.8	39.3	34.0
– Planning Commission		48.3	37.4	29.9	23.2
– Economic Survey[9]				25.5	19.0

Source: Sinha and Samuel, 1996.

(2) the decline in poverty incidence accelerated in more recent years. Poverty tends to be more prevalent in some states of eastern/central India such as Bihar, Orissa, West Bengal, Uttar Pradesh and Madhya Pradesh. The household incomes in these states are much lower than in other parts of the country.

Poverty Alleviation Policies and Programmes

Over the past fifteen years, the government placed subsidized credit as the centrepiece of its policy on poverty alleviation. It has established and continues to implement the Integrated Rural Development Programme (IRDP), which was designed to be 'a direct instrument for attacking India's rural poverty'.[10] The IRDP is reputed to be one of the largest poverty-alleviation programmes in the world with the number of loans advanced since its introduction in 1978 having reached some 45 million individuals and financial assistance worth US$6.17 billion (Rs214 billion) disbursed as of March 1995. It was meant to provide the rural poor with access to assets, skills, services and institutional support in order to enhance their employment and income sufficiently so as to enable them to cross the poverty line.[11] This was to be achieved through the acquisition of productive assets by the rural poor (including at least 30 per cent women) by means of credit advanced by the commercial banks and subsidy provided by the government of India, varying from 25 per cent for small farmers, 33.3 per cent for agricultural labourers, marginal farmers and rural artisans, and 50 per cent for scheduled castes, tribes-people and the physically handicapped.

Three support programmes were linked with the implementation of the IRDP for the purpose of enhancing the earning capacities of borrowers: (1) TRYSEM (Training of Rural Youth for Self Employment) – to provide technical skills to young people in rural areas for self-employment; (2) DWCRA (Development of Women and Children in Rural Areas) – to provide women with skills and support (e.g. child care and nutrition for children) for economic activities so as to enable them to generate income through group entrepreneurship; and (3) infrastructure – 10 per cent of government funds were allocated to provide support facilities at the district level such as shop buildings, feeder roads or electric lines, common deep borewells and milk collection vans which help the borrowers realize the potential of their income-generating activities. There was a requirement that more than 40,000 rural bank branches should participate in providing loans to IRDP clients. This extensive organizational infrastructure was meant to ensure that the programme was implemented at the district and sub-district levels in every corner of the country.

Despite the massive support, a government evaluation in 1989 revealed that the IRDP has not achieved the expected results: only 28 per cent of those assisted under the IRDP had, in fact, been able to cross the poverty line. In contrast, private-sector-led services and business microenterprises performed somewhat better with 33 per cent of those involved in this sector crossing the poverty line. The government study identified the following factors that contributed to the IRDP's poor performance:

- *Loose Targeting*: The subsidy orientation of the scheme created tremendous temptation for the non-poor to participate in the programme, inescapably by dishonest means. There was no effective mechanism for enforcing the selection of poor clientele based on the official definition of the 'poverty line'.
- *Bureaucratic Delivery System, High Transactions Costs*: As they rationed out low-cost credit to a great number of people, the handling banks increased the paperwork required for obtaining a loan, thus also increasing the processing fees. According to some estimates, the transactions costs entailed in obtaining an IRDP loan were as high as 20 per cent of the total investment cost. The net effect was to limit access to subsidized credit by the poor, particularly the usually less literate and assetless female poor.
- *Unsuitable Financial Products*: In an attempt to regulate the cost of implementation and limit malpractices, the government and the handling banks prescribed the activities and purposes to be financed and the size of loans for each activity or purpose. In effect, the IRDP created financial products and services that were ill suited to the needs of the poor.
- *Poor Co-ordination of Programme Support*: There was no effective co-ordination between the handling banks and the other support programmes of TRYSEM, DWCRA and infrastructure. Being implemented by different agencies, these support programmes were run independently of each other, thus failing to create a concerted impact on poverty.
- *Political Tolerance of Loan Defaults*: From the start, people regarded the IRDP as a political programme. The mendicant attitude of the borrowers towards a government-subsidized programme explains a great deal of the extremely poor loan recovery performance[12] of the IRDP, which has never exceeded 45 per cent. Instead of combating this negative attitude and encouraging prompt repayment of loans, the government in 1990 took the politically motivated act of condoning defaults on small loans made up largely of agricultural credit and IRDP loans. As a result, IRDP recoveries dropped to even lower levels (30 to 35 per cent) in recent years, prompting the Expert Committee on the IRDP to conclude that the deficient functioning of the programme has affected its credibility. Low recovery further discouraged the banks from lending to poor borrowers in rural areas[13] and slowed down the recycling of programme funds.

Financial Institutions and their Outreach to the Poor

As of March 1995, there were more than 30,000 rural and sub-urban branches of the public-sector banks and around 15,000 branches of the 196 regional rural banks (RRBs) in the country, all of them mandated by the government to provide financial services to the poor. The latter were established in the late 1970s as subsidiaries of the scheduled public-sector banks for the purpose of meeting the credit requirements of the poor – classified into small and marginal farmers, landless workers, artisans and small entrepreneurs. Altogether, these institutions comprise an impressive part of the country's banking system which consists of over 40,000 branches of 28 public-sector 'scheduled' commercial banks and another 4400 branches of 55 smaller private-sector banks.[14] Foreign banks are growing in number but their reach, through some 160 branches, is limited to the main cities.

Involvement of banking institutions in microfinance for the poor is directed by the RBI, the country's central bank. With its vast supervisory and regulatory control of the banking system, the RBI applies pressure on commercial banks to participate in government-subsidized credit programmes. In 1982, the RBI established the NABARD to act as the apex bank for rural credit and oversee the functioning of the co-operative sector including the State Co-operative Banks (SCBs). The NABARD provides short- and medium-term credit to the SCBs and the RRBs for approved agricultural purposes as well as medium- and long-term credit to all banks for investments in agriculture. The RBI encouraged the establishment of RRBs to streamline commercial bank lending to priority areas and synchronize the delivery of loans to designated areas under the Service Area Approach. But the response of banking institutions has been lukewarm in the face of prudential banking regulation (high reserve requirements and liquidity ratios) and interest rate ceilings which limited the credit resources that could be made available for on-lending to small borrowers.

The tens of thousands of primary agricultural co-operative societies (PACS) are an ideal grassroots alternative for purveying microfinance for the poor because they are present in every village. But many of them no longer have the capacity to provide financial services. Co-opted by the government to implement subsidized credit programmes, the PACS have incurred huge losses from enormous loan arrears. A survey in 1984–5 revealed that some 43.5 per cent of PACS were operating at a loss. Another report disclosed that the proportion of overdue loans among PACS stood at 40 per cent in 1989–90, more than half of which were loan arrears older than three years.[15] Most of the PACS failed to mobilize savings, having been dependent on government for the bulk of their loanable funds. Furthermore, the village elite has taken over PACS management and they allocate loan funds based on patronage, which really means that those who borrow larger sums more frequently are given priority to borrow much larger amounts. The lion's share of PACS advances went to farm-owners with larger landholdings. In 1991–2, for instance, farm-owners with holdings of less than two hectares received 35 per cent of all loans advanced by the PACS while the poorer members such as tenant farmers, sharecroppers, landless workers received only 5.1 per cent.

Another alternative delivery mechanism of microfinance for the poor are the non-banking finance companies (NBFCs). Their fairly extensive network of agents providing financial services to enterprises in the village could well play an important role in poverty-oriented lending. In practice, however, NBFCs function mainly as mobilizers of savings from the rural and sub-urban middle class and make these funds available to borrowers in more urbanized areas.

The failure of banks, co-operatives and NBCFs to provide financial services to poorer sections of society contributes to the predominance of traders, moneylenders, friends/relatives and neighbourhood SHGs as the primary sources of credit for the poor. Poor women in particular tend to borrow small sums from informal sources primarily for domestic consumption. Most of them, being illiterate, are less able to cope with formal mechanisms outside their local environments. Apart from their accessibility both in physical and procedural terms as they are located within the village or neighbourhood and require virtually no paperwork, informal credit sources also operate with a high degree of flexibility. Their loan terms and loan sizes are negotiable and they do not restrict the uses of credit.

A revamp of the formal financial system was initiated in recent years to make it more sensitive to the needs of small businesses and microentrepreneurs. The NABARD introduced a financial innovation to promote banking with the poor by establishing linkages between banks and SHGs. Launched in 1991–2, the NABARD microfinance initiative otherwise known as the 'Linkage Banking Programme' involved 28 commercial banks, 60 RRBs, 7 co-operative banks and 129 NGOs as of March 1996. (See Table 4.2.) The project covered some 4757 SHGs in sixteen states, and around 85 per cent of SHGs were women's groups. Loans totalling US$1,745,820 had been sanctioned by the banks to the SHGs against which the NABARD had provided refinance amounting to US$1,631,124. Among the NGOs participating in the programme are the sample MFIs reported in the next section of this chapter.

Compared to the 45 million loans worth US$6.17 billion disbursed under the IRDP, the exposure of the NABARD in the Linkage Banking Programme

Table 4.2 Progress of the NABARD's Linkage Banking Programme (Cumulative)

Year	Number of SHGs	Total Loan (US$ '000)
1992–3	255	86.46*
1993–4	620	223.63
1994–5	2122	704.61
1995–6	4757	1745.82

* Estimated.
Exchange rate: US$ = Rs.34.70.
Source: Sinha and Samuel, 1996.

is obviously miniscule. But the NABARD and the RBI are increasingly convinced of the suitability of the Linkage Banking Programme for increasing access of the poor to formal financial services. Having seen the initial success of the programme, commercial banks responded positively to the initiative of the NABARD. An outstanding example is the Small Industries Development Bank of India (SIDBI) which launched its microcredit scheme (MCS) in March 1994 using the Linkage Banking approach. Established in April 1990 as a wholly owned subsidiary of the Industrial Development Bank of India, the SIDBI aims to serve as the principal financial institution for promotion, financing and development of industry in the small-scale sector, and to co-ordinate the functions of the institutions engaged in promoting, financing and development of industry in the small-scale sector.[16] The bank recognizes SHGs 'as a promising tool for job creation and income generation' among the poor. Through the MCS, the bank provides funds to well-managed NGOs for on-lending to individuals as well as groups of rural borrowers, particularly women. The SIDBI also provides capacity-building grants to more than 50 NGOs for meeting managerial salaries, for strengthening accounting and managerial capabilities and for training SHGs in credit utilization and delivery to the target group.

Encouraged by the success of the Linkage Banking Programme, NGO intermediary organizations such as the Friends of Women's World Banking (FWWB), the Rashtriya Gramin Vikas Nidhi (RGVN – National Rural Development Fund) and the government-sponsored Rashtriya Mahila Kosh (RMK – National Women's Fund) have also adopted the strategy of sponsoring SHGs to be financed by banks. If the outreach of these intermediary NGOs were combined with those of the NABARD and SIDBI, the overall size of the domestically sponsored microfinance initiatives is estimated to reach 211,175 clients as at end-March 1996 (Table 4.3).

Although foreign funding agencies (e.g. the United States Agency for Internal Development (USAID), the Netherlands Organization for International Development Cooperation (NOVIB), the Swiss Development Co-operation and Deutsche Gessellschaft fur Technische Zusammenarbeit (the

Table 4.3 Outreach of Institutions Involved in the Linkage Banking Programme

Funding Source	No. of NGOs/SHGs*	No. of Members	Amount Sanctioned*
NABARD	4,757*	50,000	1,745.82
SIDBI	53	19,000	1,373.78
RMK	97	98,000	5,475.50
FWWB	74	42,000	1,057.35
RGVN	109	2,175	115.85
Total	5,090	211,175	9,768.30

* Cumulative as at end of March 1996, US$ '000. Exchange rate: US$1 = Rs34.70.
Source of basic data: Sinha and Samuel, 1996.

GTZ)) run a variety of assistance programmes for SHGs, on-lending funds from these agencies are not significantly large and can only support small pilot projects. However, foreign funding agencies may have the comparative advantage in providing support for staff training and institutional capacity building of NGOs and SHGs. The bulk of on-lending funds for credit to the poor will have to be generated locally. Backed by large volumes of funds at their disposal, both the NABARD and the SIDBI have the capacity to provide refinance for credit to the poor.[17]

Financial Policy Environment

The financial policy reforms initiated by the RBI in the 1990s created an environment that encouraged financial innovations. Interest rate controls for credit to the poor and other types of credit were scrapped. The interest rate ceiling on small loans of less than US$720 (Rs25,000)[18] was first increased from around 10 per cent to 12.5 per cent in early 1996, but at the end of August 1996 the ceiling was scrapped altogether. Interest rates payable on time deposits of over twelve months duration have also been deregulated. The RBI has encouraged banks to avoid requiring physical collateral on such small loans, and to rely instead on group and peer pressure to ensure full repayment of the loan.

These financial liberalization measures made it possible for the NABARD to transform its small research project into a full-blown microfinance programme for the whole country. The NABARD project incubated for several years and failed to take off owing to lack of policy support. The project started in 1986 when the NABARD provided support to the Mysore Resettlement and Development Agency (MYRADA) in Bangalore to assess the adequacy SHGs of poor persons as channels for credit to the poor. The project was based on the idea that SHGs can provide the vulnerable poor in general, and poor women in particular, 'with the space and support necessary to take effective steps towards greater control of their lives in private and in society'.[19] It fosters a participatory approach to development and is based on the principle of mutual co-operation and trust.

In 1988–9, the APRACA supported a wider survey[20] of SHG experiences in India. The results of these studies contributed significantly to the design of the NABARD's pilot programme for linking SHGs with banks. The NABARD's Linkage Banking Programme also made extensive use of the operating manuals produced by a similar programme in Indonesia implemented by Bank Indonesia with technical assistance from the German technical agency, the GTZ. The programme seeks to augment, through bank financing, the internal resources of the SHGs for lending to their members 'while maintaining a strong correlation between savings and credit'.[21] The programme recognizes both production and consumption needs as being inclusive of the total credit requirements of the poor and eligible for bank financing.

The Linkage Banking Programme envisions developing the SHGs as informal financial intermediaries. During the 'initiation period', the SHGs are encouraged to mobilize savings and on-lend the funds to their members prior to the injection of bank funds into their system. The savings of members are deposited in the SHG's group account with the participating bank. In a radical departure from conventional banking, the RBI instructed banks to accept deposits in the name of the unregistered SHG. At the end of the 'initiation' period, which could last up to twelve months, the bank extends a group loan to the SHG without collateral, either directly or through an NGO associated with the latter.[22]

Loans from the bank to the SHGs are normally repayable over a three-year period, whereas loans from the SHGs to their members have flexible and varying loan terms determined collectively by the members. Banks lend directly to SHGs at 12 per cent per annum. When NGOs are involved as intermediaries, banks lend to them at 10.5 per cent p.a. and NGOs in turn on-lend to SHGs at 12 per cent p.a. Banks receive re-financing from the NABARD at 6.5 per cent p.a. interest. The SHG is free to determine the interest rate it may charge its member-borrowers. The collective wisdom of the members is accepted as the most appropriate basis for determining the cost of capital at the village level. SHGs normally fix interest rates in the range 24 to 60 per cent per annum – usually just below the cost of capital from local informal sources but well above the interest rates in the formal banking sector.

So popular has the 'SHG route' to microfinance become that most NGOs in India have adopted it for the financial empowerment of the poor. A Working Group constituted by the RBI to study the functioning of the programme reported that the SHG linkage programme 'is a cost effective, transparent and flexible approach to improve the accessibility of credit for the formal banking system to the rural poor. It is expected to offer the much-needed solution to the twin problems being faced by banks: viz. recovery of loans in the rural areas and the high transaction cost in dealing with small borrowers at frequent intervals.'[23]

Microfinance Capacity Assessment

Most of the institutions working with the poor in India are NGOs providing microfinance services as an alternative to informal sources. These MFIs can be classified into three types: (a) *Grameen Bank Approach replicators* – these are organizations replicating the model developed by Grameen Bank of Bangladesh in providing credit to the hard-core poor; (b) *Co-operatives* – these are mainly the primary and secondary co-operative societies; and (c) *NGOs with SHG linkage programmes* – these are organizations working with formal financial institutions to provide financial services to informal, self-organized groups of poor households.

The eight sample MFIs covered by the study in India include two Grameen Bank Approach replicators (the SHARE and Nari Nidhi), two co-operative networks (the WWF and the SEWA Bank), and four NGOs with SHG linkage programmes (the Rural Development Trust (RDT), Shanthidan, the MYRADA and the Sri Padmavathy Mahila Abyudaya Sangam (the SPMS)).

- **SHARE**: Initially registered under the Societies Act to provide educational services, the SHARE commenced its credit operations in 1993 after four years of research on various savings and credit models. Its primary aim is to provide poor women access to small amounts of capital and support services for self-employment and income-generating activities. With two branches at the Guntur and Gurnool districts in Andhra Pradesh state, the SHARE is the largest replication of Grameen Bank in India so far.
- **Nari Nidhi**: Nari Nidhi is a credit fund for poor women promoted by Adithi, a Patna-based NGO working for the socio-economic empowerment of poor women. Its long-term objective is to facilitate direct linkages between groups of poor women and the formal banking institutions.
- **WWF**: Established in 1978, the WWF is a renowned grassroots union of poor women workers extending credit to its members. Its members are spread over three states of south India, namely Tamil Nadu, Karnataka and Andhra Pradesh. At first, the WWF acted as a mediator between the banks and its members, assuring the banks of the credit discipline of its members. It soon abandoned this strategy because banks doubted the creditworthiness of its members while the poor women themselves faced psychological barriers in approaching banks. In 1981, the WWF established the Working Women's Co-operative Society, renamed in 1994 as the Indian Co-operative Network for Women.
- **SEWA Bank**: The Sri Mahila SEWA Sahakari Bank has its roots as a trade union established in 1972 in Ahmedabad City in Gujarat state. The SEWA, literally meaning 'service', organizes women who work in their homes and are employed in the informal sector. Initially, the SEWA tried to link its members with the scheduled commercial banks, but the latter were both untrained and unwilling to deal with illiterate women who were not familiar with banking procedures. This prompted the SEWA to establish a co-operative bank with support from 4000 women members, each of whom contributed Rs10 as share capital.
- **RDT**: The RDT is a registered voluntary organization promoting integrated development activities in the Ananthapur district of Andhra Pradesh since 1969. Its target population consists of the 'scheduled' caste and 'scheduled' tribal people who are traditionally the most exploited and marginalized communities in India. Starting initially with health education and community-organizing activities, the RDT initiated a women's programme in 1982 through which it introduced a savings scheme in 1983.

- **Shanthidhan**: Founded in 1983, Shanthidhan is an NGO based in Nagarcoil, Tamil Nadu and working among the fishing communities. Its main aim is the social and economic empowerment of self-employed rural women. Having identified the lack of savings as the root cause of women fish vendors falling into the moneylender's debt trap, Shanthidhan established the Women Fish Vendors Social and Credit Programme which organizes fish vendors into village-level *sangams* (community groups).
- **MYRADA**: Founded in 1968, the MYRADA until 1978 was involved in the resettlement of Tibetan refugees in the state of Karnataka. Since 1978, it has been involved in rural development with the rural poor. The MYRADA identifies potential borrowers, forms them into credit management groups, and helps them access loans from banks by using their influence and by providing collateral. Currently, the MYRADA operates in the states of Karnataka, Tamil Nadu and Andhra Pradesh.
- **SPMS**: The SPMS is a federation of SHGs in the urban slums of Tirupati region of Andhra Pradesh. Originally, the SHG members were borrowers of local banks participating in the differential interest rate scheme of the government, which provides loans to the poor at a subsidized interest rate of 4 per cent p.a. To help improve the loan recovery rates under this government programme, two NGOs – the Rayalseema Seva Samithi (RASS) and the Professional Assistance for Development Action (PRADAN) – formed women's groups called *Podupu Sangams*, a Telugu phrase meaning women's savings groups. As the *sangams* spread in the slums of Tirupati region, they formed the SPMS as a federation.

These eight sample MFIs reflect the historical evolution of MFIs in India. The two co-operative networks (the WWF and the SEWA Bank) are the oldest with some 15 and 22 years' experience respectively. Following them are four NGOs with SHG programmes (the RDT, Shanthidhan, the MYRADA and the SPMS) that have been operating for some 13–14 years. The most recent entrants in the microfinance sector are the Grameen replicators (the SHARE and Nari Nidhi), having three and five years' experience respectively.

All the MFIs focus their microfinance programmes on women only, except the MYRADA, which has 63 per cent women members in its management credit groups (see Table 4.4). Though all the organizations claim that 100 per cent of their clients are poor, not all of them undertake assessments to verify this. An attempt by Sinha and Samuel (1996) to determine the proportion of poor clients among the clients of MFIs using the Housing Index method failed to obtain useful results. Many SPMS and SEWA members lived in urban slums mostly, with more stable construction materials than those used in rural areas. On the other hand, some MYRADA members had benefited from housing loans with which they have improved their houses in the recent past.

Table 4.4   Outreach of the Eight Sample MFIs in India (As at end of March 1996, except as indicated)

MFI	No. of Groups	No. of Members	% of Women	Poverty Ratio	Staff in Programme	Client to Staff Ratio
SHARE	299	1,495	100	100	33	45 : 1
Nari Nidhi	297	2,350	100	100	24	98 : 1
WWF[1]	No groups	59,870	100	100	232	258 : 1
SEWA Bank[1]	[2]	56,541	100	100	60	942 : 1
RDT	867	13,201	100	100	68	194 : 1
Shanthidhan[1]	69	4,221	100	100	64	66 : 1
MYRADA, Kamasamudram[3]	172	3,075	63	100	43	72 : 1
SPMS	233	2,621	100	100	17	154 : 1
Total	1,937	143,374	99	100	541	265 : 1

1 Figures for 1994–5 (April–Mar.).
2 The rural clientele – 6403 members, 11.3 per cent of the total – is organized into 171 groups.
3 Figures for 1995.
Source: Sinha and Samuel, 1996.

Four MFIs – Nari Nidhi, the WWF, the SEWA, and the RDT – have predominantly women staff, with only a few men, usually engaged in the accounts department. The other MFIs have relatively fewer women on their staff, but they have not found this to be a deterrent to their outreach to women.

Outreach

The total combined outreach of the eight MFIs was 143,374 'clients' as of March 1996 (Table 4.4). This level of outreach[24] is not very impressive considering that six of the sample MFIs have been in operation for more than ten years, and that the poor in the country number in hundreds of millions. As a point of reference, Grameen Bank and the ASA of Bangladesh expanded their outreach at the rate of over 100,000 new clients annually. Compared to this record, the rate of outreach expansion (at 2500 to 4000 new clients annually) of the two largest MFIs in India, the SEWA Bank and the WWF, appears to be quite slow. On the other hand, the pace of outreach expansion of the two Grameen replicators in India among our sample, i.e. the SHARE and Nari Nidhi, is even slower at around 500 new clients annually.

One obvious reason for the slow growth of the MFIs' outreach is the relatively small number of clients supervised by each MFI staff. Five MFIs had a client-to-staff ratio lower than 100:1, which means a staff member was handling less than 100 clients. This is rather low compared with a standard client-to-staff ratio of around 300:1 adopted by the fast-growing MFIs of Bangladesh. Standardizing the client-to-staff ratio sets a target load for each staff member and helps the MFI control operating costs. The case of the SEWA Bank which has a high client-to-staff ratio of 942:1 is unique. This ratio does not take into account the volunteer workers of the SEWA who do most of the developmental and motivational work among its members.

Resource Mobilization

Availability of lump-sum funds that warrant significant outreach expansion within a short period of time is a crucial factor for outreach expansion. The previous chapter tells us how generous donor support to MFIs of Bangladesh has been instrumental in their unprecedented outreach expansion. Contrary to this experience, the MFIs of India relied heavily on local sources of funds, except for the two Grameen-type MFIs whose compulsory savings constitute an insignificant proportion of their total resources. In five of the sample MFIs, internally generated funds comprising member savings and retained earnings accounted for 70 to 90 per cent of their total resources. It has taken these MFIs considerable time to build up their own resources, thus slowing down their outreach growth.

With total resources of US$2.5 million, the SEWA Bank is by far the

Table 4.5 Financial Services and Resources of Eight Sample MFIs in India (As at end of March 1996, except as indicated) (Amounts in US dollars)

MFI	Financial Service		Resource Mobilization				
	Loan Outstanding (1)	Savings[1] (2)	Soft Loans and Grants[2] (3)	Internal Resources[3] (4)	Commercial Loans (5)	Total (6)	% of (1) to (6) (7)
SHARE	66,237	12,684 (16.1%)	117,031 (73.8%)	12,684 (8.0%)	28,818 (18.9%)	158,533 (100.0%)	41.8 %
Nari Nidhi	50,039	12,233 (19.6%)	128,156 (91.3%)	12,233 (8.7%)	Nil	140,389 (100.0%)	35.6%
WWF[4]	465,743	113,743 (19.6%)	44,967 (28.3%)	113,743 (71.7%)	Nil	158,710 (100.0%)	293.5%
SEWA Bank[4]	1,363,041	2,488,028 (64.6%)	N.A.[5]	2,488,028 (100.0%)	Nil	2,488,028 (100.0%)	54.8%
RDT	138,386	92,771 (40.1%)	12,236 (8.8%)	124,334 (89.8%)	1,816 (1.4%)	138,386 (100.0%)	100.0%
Shanthidhan[4]	177,704	112,875 (38.8%)	35,303 (22.2%)	123,955 (77.8%)	Nil	159,258 (100.0%)	112.3%
MYRADA[4]	122,748	37,776 (23.5%)	105,878 (70.4%)	37,776 (25.1%)	6,790 (4.5%)	147,444 (100.0%)	83.3%
SPMS	177,564	116,051 (39.5%)	61,769 (11.6%)	167,638 (88.4%)	Nil	229,407 (100.0%)	77.4%

Exchange rate: US$1 = Rs34.70.
1 Figures in parentheses are the percentage share of Savings to Total Financial Services.
2 Figures in parentheses are the percentage share of Soft Loans and Grants to Total Resources.
3 Savings plus internal accruals.
4 Figures as of end of March 1995.
5 N.A. – not available. The SEWA Bank receives significant grants for fixed assets, staff training and other expenditures. However, information on this was not available on the date of study.
Source: Sinha and Samuel, 1996.

largest of the sample MFIs in India in terms of business volume. The other MFIs had smaller total resources amounting to US$100,000 to US$200,000 (Table 4.5). The extent to which the MFI utilizes its total resources for on-lending certainly affects its credit outreach. The two Grameen replicators, the SHARE and Nari Nidhi, held less than 50 per cent of their total resources in loans outstanding. The other MFIs had much higher proportions of their total resources in their loan portfolios. The SEWA Bank's case is special because its total resources are comprised solely of internally generated funds, the bulk of which are savings deposits of SEWA members.

In terms of savings outreach, the SEWA Bank's performance is outstanding. The Bank's average deposits per member was highest among the sample MFIs. The Bank has several savings products including interest-paying recurring deposits and long-term fixed deposits. It also offers incentives to savers such as small gifts of silver or kitchen utensils at the end of the savings period. The Bank benefits from the services of the highly committed, often voluntary, staff of its mother organization, the SEWA, which helps market the Bank's financial products. It is not clear, however, why the Bank held only 55 per cent of its total resources in its loan portfolio and invested the balance elsewhere when it could have been used more productively to provide credit resources to new poor clients. But if the Bank were behaving rationally, it would not be surprising if it invested its scarce resources in higher yielding assets — after meeting the credit needs of its member-clients. The lesson of essence here is that success in savings mobilization does not guarantee that the resources generated will be ploughed back and made available as credit resources for the poor.

The RDT, Shanthidhan and the SPMS also had significant proportions (between 80 to 90 per cent) of their total resources generated internally. They achieved this by making good use of their extensive community network and by offering savings products with attractive rates of interest and linked to future access to housing and marriage loans. SPMS *sangams* pay 12 per cent p.a. interest on regular savings. Shanthidhan pays 9 per cent interest p.a. on member savings and encourages its staff to mobilize savings by paying them a salary that is determined on the basis of the volume of savings generated.

But these efforts at mobilizing savings are mainly confined among the member-clients of MFIs. Unlike the SEWA Bank, the NGO-MFIs do not have a banking licence, hence they could not offer savings facilities to other potential savers and exploit the full potential of their presence in the community. The SEWA Bank has taken full advantage of its banking licence and demonstrated that mobilization of savings in depressed communities can be a highly rewarding activity.

A practical approach of mobilizing savings that has in recent years become highly attractive to NGO-MFIs is to encourage poor households to form their own SHGs. This approach has gained more prominence among NGO-

Table 4.6   Loans Outstanding, Savings, and Total Resources Generated Per Member by Eight Sample MFIs in India, 1995 (All amounts in US dollars)

MFI	Loan Outstanding Member (1)	Savings/ Member (2)	Total Resources per Member (3)	Percentage of Column (1) to Column (3) (4)
SHARE	44.30	8.47	97.55	45.4
Nari Nidhi	21.30	5.22	54.52	39.1
WWF	7.78[a]	5.19	7.26	107.2
SEWA Bank	65.42	44.01[b]	44.01[c]	148.6
RDT	10.49	7.03	10.49	100.0
Shanthidhan	42.10	26.74	37.72	111.6
MYRADA	37.41	11.50	45.85	81.6
SPMS	67.75	44.27	82.85	81.8

Notes:
a The number of savers is reported at 22,000 compared to nearly 60,000 members. If the borrowers were over counted on account of multiple loan accounts, loan outstanding per member would amount to Rs739.
b No. of borrowers = 20,840 compared to 56,541 savers. If the number of savers were considered and not the number of savings accounts, savings per member would amount to Rs4,142.
c Excluding grants received for training, asset acquisition and other activities on which information was not available.
Exchange rate: US$1 = Rp34.70.
Source: Sinha and Samuel, 1996.

MFIs in recent years owing to advances made by the NABARD Linkage Banking Programme, which encourages SHGs to mobilize savings. As shown in Table 4.6, internal resources of MFIs working closely with SHGs comprise a relatively high proportion of the loan outstanding per member, with the SEWA Bank leading (182.5 per cent) followed by the RDT (89.8 per cent) and the SPMS (65.5 per cent).

The two Grameen replicators, the SHARE and Nari Nidhi, devote a small proportion of their total resources for on-lending because they need funds for capacity building as well as for other 'non-financial services'. Both the SHARE and Nari Nidhi train their staff for up to six months before the new recruits are given responsibility to handle loans. In addition to its capacity-building requirements, Nari Nidhi also incurs additional costs in providing design and marketing services to handicraft producers.

Provision of 'non-financial services' to the member-clients is prevalent among other NGO-MFIs. For example, the RDT promotes group enterprises such as groundnut marketing for its marginal farmers, while the MYRADA assists marginal farmer-members to have access to irrigation through watershed development programmes. These non-financial services are funded by donor grants but separately so from microfinance activities. NGO-MFIs view non-financial services as a means for increasing the credit absorptive capacity of client-members in the belief that the client's ability to use productive loans is limited by his/her lack of assets such as agricultural land or shop space, or skills to undertake appropriate productive activities, or marketing facilities for their products. However, the ability of such NGO-MFIs to expand service outreach is generally limited owing to the lack of staff and management personnel with adequate skills, knowledge and commitment to undertake both financial and other support services.

In spite of their lack of profitability, the NGO-MFIs continue to implement their social services and/or very costly financing programmes because there are donors willing to give them grants. Nari Nidhi received some funds from the government of India for meeting part of its operating costs. Soft loans at very low or zero interest rate were also obtained by the SHARE and Nari Nidhi from such organizations as the APDC and the Grameen Trust for Grameen Bank replication projects. International donor agencies actively engaged in funding local development initiatives include the Friedrich Ebert Stiftung (FES) of Germany, the Dutch Embassy, German NGOs and Community Aid Abroad of Australia. On-lending funds from these donor agencies, however, are available for specific projects only and cannot be depended upon on a sustained basis.

In the light of these realities, the question arises: What strategy should be adopted to increase significantly the outreach to the poor of MFIs in a financially viable and sustainable way? This issue is addressed in the discussion following.

Financial Viability and Sustainability

Conventional wisdom tells us that MFIs with significantly large outreach will gain economies of scale. This appears to be supported by the experience of MFIs in India. As Table 4.7 shows, MFIs with larger outreach (i.e., the WWF,

Table 4.7 Cost Structure of Eight Sample MFIs in India, 1995

MFI	Operating Costs as % of Total FS*	Total Costs as % of Total FS	Ratio of Salaries to Average Assets	Ratio of Operating Costs to Average Assets	Ratio of Financial Costs** to Average Assets
SHARE	53.5	57.2	0.215	0.526	0.020
Nari Nidhi	32.8	39.3	0.124	0.218	0.034
WWF	18.5	29.2	0.094	0.153	0.076
SEWA Bank	3.8	8.5	0.019	0.049	0.052
RDT	7.2	12.7	0.080	0.121	0.091
Shanthidhan	2.0	6.5	0.011	0.035	0.080
MYRADA	49.2	51.2	0.128	0.514	0.006
SPMS	5.3	10.9	0.039	0.092	0.075

* Financial Services = savings + loans outstanding.
** Total financial costs.
Source: Sinha and Samuel, 1996.

the SEWA Bank and the RDT) had lower operating costs per unit of asset compared to MFIs with much smaller outreach (i.e., the SHARE, Nari Nidhi and the MYRADA). It thus appears that increasing outreach is a promising route towards financial viability in working with the poor.

It takes time to build up a significant outreach programme, during which it is essential for MFIs to adopt a cost-efficient method of mobilizing, motivating and training its clientele. Although working with the poor can be costly, this should not pre-empt efforts to provide microfinance services in a more cost-efficient way. A promising approach is to work with SHGs. Shanthidhan and the SPMS have demonstrated that operating costs can be minimized by involving the community in the microfinance programme. Community involvement is expressed not only through people's participation in membership expansion and training of new members, but also in mobilization of savings and equity contributions.

Some evidence can be found in India that 'minimalist' MFIs (i.e those who provide microfinance services only) are more cost-effective than the 'maximalist' or 'microfinance-plus' MFIs (i.e. those who provide other support services in addition to microfinance). In 1995, for example, the unit operating cost of the SPMS, a 'minimalist' MFI, were lower than that of Shanthidhan, a 'microfinance-plus' MFI. Both of these MFIs are working with SHGs. The MYRADA also works with SHGs but as a 'microfinance-plus' MFI, the cost burden of non-financial support services has not only weighed down its outreach capacity but also raised its operating costs relative to its total financial services. The two young Grameen Bank replicators, the SHARE and Nari Nidhi, are 'minimalist' MFIs and do not work with SHGs, but they invest much time and resources in clientele training, motivation and mobilization, all of which contribute substantially to operating costs.

While the staff are important assets of the MFIs, staff salaries generally comprise 40 to 60 per cent of their operating costs (see Table 4.7). This being so, MFIs must train their staff to handle a minimum volume of business that could support the field unit's operating costs, lest the viability of the MFI's microfinance programme is undermined. MFIs of Bangladesh usually adopt a standardized staff-to-client ratio in observance of efficiency principles. With highly simplified lending procedures, the MFIs of Bangladesh aim to establish within the shortest possible time a financially viable field unit catering to a minimum number of active clients. Some of the sample MFIs in India have not yet fully developed a cost-efficient service delivery mechanism, but the others (e.g. the SEWA Bank, WWF and SPMS) managed to minimize administrative costs by tapping volunteer workers from among the clientele groups and relying on them for member mobilization, motivation and supervision. As a result, the number of clients and volume of business their regular staff actually handle are much higher than they can normally manage. The sample Grameen Bank replicators in India have not achieved such economies of scale so far.

The strategy of minimizing costs, however, is not sufficient to ensure the MFI's viability. This strategy should be accompanied by a vigilant collection system and a market-oriented pricing policy for the MFI's financial products. In similar vein, an excellent on-time repayment rate is crucial, but it alone cannot ensure the MFI's viability. MFIs with excellent repayment performance are those that have first decided to become viable, and they are more predisposed towards inculcating and practising credit discipline and minimizing costs. The on-time repayment rates of four MFIs are outstanding (e.g. the SHARE, 100 per cent; the MYRADA, 96.8 per cent; the SEWA Bank, 96 per cent; and the SPMS, 90 per cent) – which indicates the tight credit discipline they practise with their clients. But two of these MFIs (the SHARE and the MYRADA) have very low levels of financial self-sufficiency, which only confirms the argument that high repayment rates do not guarantee viability.

The SEWA Bank is the most sustainable of the sample MFIs of India, with partial financial self-sufficiency recorded at 132.1 per cent (Table 4.8). Partial financial self-sufficiency is the ratio between 'Returns' (i.e. interest and fees from clients) and the 'Unadjusted Total Cost' (i.e. total cost unadjusted for inflation and opportunity cost of capital). Shanthidhan and the SPMS have also attained high levels of partial financial self-sufficiency (109.7 per cent and 89.2 per cent, respectively). For the rest of the sample MFIs, the level of financial self-sufficiency is quite low. The RDT is a good example of an MFI that has taken the right step towards self-reliance by sourcing a substantial part of its loanable funds from savings, but it failed to manage its resources very well. Its practice of paying 24 per cent p.a. on long-term deposits (which comprise a sizeable chunk of RDT deposits) and of charging interest of 24 per cent p.a. flat rate on loans of 3–12 months does not leave RDT any margin adequate enough to cover its

Table 4.8 Return on Assets and Financial Self-Sufficiency of Eight Sample MFIs in India, 1995

MFI	Interest Charged % +	Interest and Fees from Clients/Total FS* %	Return on Average Assets, %	On-time Repayment Rate, %	Degree of Partial Financial Self-sufficiency %	Degree of Full Financial Self-sufficiency %
SHARE	15 (flat)	11.2	11.0	100	19.6	15.0
Nari Nidhi	12(flat)	9.4	6.5	67.7	23.8	15.6
WWF	18 (reducing)	14.0	11.6	N.A.	49.5	47.9
SEWA Bank	12-16.5 (reducing)	11.2	14.6	96	132.1	N.A.
RDT	24 (flat)	6.4	10.6	N.A.	50.2	47.7
Shanthidan	13 (flat)	7.1	12.6	60	109.7	89.0
MYRADA	12–24 (flat)	3.5	3.6	96.8	6.8	5.8
SPMS	24-60 (flat)	9.7	16.8	90	89.2	73.6

+ ... on the main loan products. * Financial Services
Source: Sinha and Samuel, 1996.

costs. This has resulted in a very low level of financial self-sufficiency (50.2 per cent). The WWF also has a very low level of self-sufficiency and this again can be traced to the practice of charging an interest rate (18 per cent p.a.) which does not adequately cover the cost of funds (11 per cent for 72 per cent of all resources mobilized) and the operating costs. For the Grameen replicators, partial financial self-sufficiency is extremely low (the SHARE, 19.6 per cent and Nari Nidhi, 23.8 per cent). This has been brought about by high operating costs at low volumes of business as well as relatively low spread even on funds obtained from development banks.

MFIs with very low levels of financial self-sufficiency tend to look up to donors for low-cost funds. Indeed, donor-dependent MFIs have much lower financial costs relative to assets (e.g. the MYRADA, 0.6 per cent; the SHARE, 2.0 per cent; and Nari Nidhi, 3.4 per cent), but ironically, they are also the very ones that have very high operating costs.

To stress an important lesson, near perfect on-time repayment rates must combine with sufficient spreads to ensure financial viability and sustainability of the MFI. The interplay of outreach, loan collection and interest rate results are eventually reflected in the profit performance of MFIs, as shown in Table 4.8. The SPMS registers the highest returns (16.8 per cent), and the MYRADA the lowest (3.6 per cent). The SEWA Bank has a fairly large outreach by Indian standards, maintains a healthy on-time repayment rate, and charges rates of interest that are competitive in the formal banking sector. Unlike the SEWA Bank, the SPMS has a small outreach but it charges a higher interest and operates at a repayment rate of 90 per cent. The MYRADA has a modestly large outreach and a high on-time repayment rate, but it charges a very low interest rate. Nari Nidhi charges an interest rate comparatively higher than that of the MYRADA but it suffers from a low repayment rate and a very small outreach.

As is borne out by the experience of MFIs from India, setting appropriate interest rates is a vital step towards financial viability. The spread between the cost of funds (i.e. the interest paid on savings and/or on external borrowings) and the interest charged on loan products must be sufficient enough to cover the MFI's operating cost, plus some profit. Among the sample MFIs of India, those working with SHGs tend to charge much higher flat rates of interest and to be more flexible in repayment terms compared with the Grameen MFIs. Five MFIs charge their borrowers a flat rate ranging from 12 per cent p.a. to 24 per cent p.a. with loan maturities ranging from 12 to 36 months (Table 4.9). Under a weekly repayment schedule, SHARE's interest rate of 15 per cent p.a. works out to over 29 per cent p.a. while Nari Nidhi's interest rate of 12 per cent p.a. translates into nearly 21.5 per cent p.a. given its monthly repayment schedule.

The effective interest rates charged by SHGs can run up to 5 per cent per month. This relatively high rate of interest is acceptable to the SHG members as it is still comparatively lower than those charged by the informal credit

Table 4.9 Interest Rate Charged and Repayment Terms of Eight Sample MFIs in India

MFI	Interest Charged (in %)	Repayment Schedule	
		Term in Months	Instalments
SHARE	15 (flat)	12	Weekly
Nari Nidhi	12 (flat)	12	Monthly
WWF	18 (reducing)	10–36 negotiable	Monthly
SEWA Bank	12–16.5 (reducing)	36	Monthly
RDT	24 (flat)	3–12 negotiable	Monthly
Shanthidan	13 (flat)	20 negotiable	Negotiable
MYRADA	24–36 (flat)	Negotiable	Negotiable
SPMS	24* (flat)	Up to 24 negotiable	Negotiable

* Funds lent by the Federation to the *sangams* at 18 per cent on reducing balance. The *sangams* on-lend the funds to their members at an interest rate of 5 per cent per month.
Source: Sinha and Samuel, 1996.

sources, and after all, the surplus will revert back to the members in the form of dividends. The co-operative MFIs, by contrast, charge much lower rates of interest – the WWF at 18 per cent and the SEWA Bank at 12 to 16.5 per cent – on reducing balance. The SEWA Bank provides mainly three-year term loans whereas the WWF repayment terms range from 10 months for loans up to US$86 (Rs3,000) to 36 months for loans greater than US$432 (Rs15,000).

The SHARE, MYRADA and SPMS also provide housing loans with longer repayment periods of three to four years, but they charge lower interest rates on these loans which are calculated on reducing balance. The MYRADA's housing loan programmes are re-financed by national-level housing development finance companies such as the public sector Housing & Urban Development Corporation (HUDCO) and the private sector Housing Development Finance Corporation (HDFC). While these housing loan programmes may be beneficial to some members of the MFI, the MFI should ascertain whether it is profitable for it to carry these loans and be sure that principles of viability are the guide in determining the credit terms of the programme.

Policy Environment

Partly on account of the poor experience of the IRDP, the commercial banking system in India has consciously avoided the market for microfinance. But this is slowly changing. Policy reforms abolishing interest rate ceilings have allowed institutions like the NABARD and SIDBI to introduce financial innovations that aim to provide poor households easier access to financial services of formal financial institutions. The Linkage Banking Programme of the NABARD is attracting commercial banks to channel the NABARD funds to NGO-MFIs for on-lending to poor clients.

For as long as NGOs and SHGs are linked with the banks, the legality of their savings and credit activities will not arise as a substantive issue inasmuch as the RBI and the NABARD consider these activities as an integral part of the bank's normal functions in the context of the Linkage Banking Programme. Scaling up outreach to poor households will therefore hinge on the willingness of banks to channel more resources to their partner NGOs and SHGs and the availability of refinance facilities from the NABARD on which banks almost entirely depend for funding support. It is unlikely that banks will continue lending to NGOs and SHGs in the near future without refinance facilities from the NABARD.

The government should take vigilant steps to put a stop to this 'dependency syndrome' of banking institutions and to induce them to engage more vigorously in banking with the poor. But a thorough change in their practices may require an overhaul of the restrictive liquidity requirements which tend to discourage banks from using their own resources for on-lending to NGOs and SHGs. Under the Banking Regulation Act of 1949, banks are required to maintain a Cash Reserve Ratio (CRR, currently 12 per cent of net demand and time liabilities of banks) and a Statutory Liquidity Ratio (SLR, around 30 per cent of net demand and time liabilities over and above the CRR). The RBI uses the CRR and SLR as instruments of monetary policy to control the availability of credit in the system and keep a lid on inflation. The RBI recognizes that these ratios are regressive and it is inclined to reduce the CRR and the SLR to 10 per cent and 25 per cent, respectively. In line with this policy direction, the RBI should also consider providing special incentives to encourage lending to NGOs and SHGs working with the poor by allowing bigger reductions on the liquidity requirements for: (a) savings mobilized by these grassroots organizations; and (b) savings generated by the bank that are on-lent to NGOs and SHGs.

Concluding Observations

Most of the microfinance programmes in India have not reached a significant number of the poor nor have they achieved financial viability and sustainability. But their initiatives are slowly gathering momentum. To sustain the momentum and scale-up outreach to a significant number of poor in a financially viable way, MFIs of India should take the fundamental step of setting appropriate interest rates as this is vital for their viability.

The experience from India provides some evidence that working with SHGs allows the MFIs to increase outreach and to approach viability and sustainability. 'Minimalist' MFIs working with SHGs that manage their own group funds have been more successful in keeping their operating costs low and in approaching financial self-sufficiency. As SHGs increasingly take over the motivational work and service delivery functions of the MFI, the latter's capability to cover more clients increases. Federating village level savings and credit groups has the effect of reducing the MFI's unit cost of servicing clients and also strengthening the capacity of SHGs to handle service delivery functions at the grassroots level.

Another advantage of working with SHGs is that it facilitates the generation of internal resources through mobilization of savings. By encouraging SHGs to attract savings into their revolving funds, the MFI helps the poor develop their own financial intermediation system. Whether such grassroots financial system should be established into a bank or maintained as an informal system but linked with the formal financial system is an issue that should be left to the MFI to decide. Most of the non-bank MFIs in India, however, prefer not having a banking licence because of fear of abandoning their other socio-cultural objectives as NGOs, but perhaps also because the equity requirements for establishing a bank is some huge amount that they cannot put up. With the support of the NABARD's Linkage Banking Programme, the NGO-MFIs of India find it more attractive to take the 'SHG route' rather than to establish a bank that exclusively caters to the poor.

But the dramatic influx of NGOs to poverty-oriented lending during the early 1990s could not have transpired without a fundamental change in financial policy. The financial liberalization measures of the RBI and the deliberate effort of the NABARD to promote SHGs as a channel for microfinance services to the poor were instrumental in bringing NGOs to their new role of microfinance providers to the poor. Similarly, the policy reforms abolishing interest rate ceilings have renewed the interest of banking institutions in microfinance for the poor either as funding partners of NGO-MFIs or as direct providers of financial services.

Perhaps owing to their limited outreach and volume of business, SHGs and NGOs have not yet been subjected to RBI regulations and restrictions on deposit mobilization, liquidity ratios, and prudential norms that are routinely applied to formal financial institutions and non-banking finance companies. To the extent that SHGs and NGOs are linked with the bank in the context of the NABARD's Linkage Banking Programme, the lack of legal personality of NGOs and SHGs will remain a non-substantive issue. But as they scale-up outreach significantly and aspire to greater independence from formal banking institutions, the NGO-MFIs' impact on the financial market will be felt and their lack of legal personality will increasingly become a bone of contention. As the number of NGO-MFIs and their constituent SHGs are likely to increase into tens of thousands in the ensuing years, it appears imperative for the RBI to address now the issue of appropriate supervision and regulation of the microfinance sector.

Notes

1 Estimated by the World Bank for 1996d.
2 Summarized in Misra and Puri, 1995.
3 The average of 3.5 per cent growth per annum is referred to tongue-in-cheek as the 'Hindu rate of growth'.

4 Virtually all organizations in India, including the government, adopt the April-March fiscal year.
5 According to official figures, the value of imports was 10.3 per cent of GDP in 1993–4.
6 At one stage, in the late 1980s, accusations were rife that the government was trying to 'define away' poverty for political reasons.
7 Government of India, 1993. The propositions for 1993–4 were estimated by Sinha and Samuel (1996) based on trends indicated by the Expert Group's estimates.
8 Poverty ratio estimated by the Planning Commission based on the quinquennial Consumer Expenditure Surveys conducted by the National Sample Survey Organization (Misra and Puri, 1995).
9 Government of India, 1996.
10 Reserve Bank of India (RBI), 1995, p. 3.
11 For this purpose, the poverty line is 'drawn' by the government at a family income of Rs11,000 p.a.
12 Defined as amount repaid as a proportion of the amount due to be repaid.
13 It has led to the coining by bank staff of a new expansion of the acronym for the IRDP, *'Itna Rupya Dubona Padega'*, translated from Hindi as 'so much money down the drain'.
14 Much of the discussion in this section is adapted from BASIX, 1996.
15 Misra and Puri, 1995.
16 Small Industries Development Bank of India (SIDBI): Micro Credit Scheme (SIDBI leaflet).
17 Outstanding portfolios of around US$17.3 billion and US$3.2 billion, respectively, or a total equivalent to some US$20.5 billion.
18 Including larger loans to groups of borrowers such as SHGs who cumulatively borrow more than US$720 (Rs25,000) but individually require much less.
19 IFAD, 1995a, Annex 6: Self-Help Groups.
20 NABARD, 1989.
21 NABARD, 1995.
22 In an overwhelming majority of cases so far the SHGs have actually been initiated and promoted by the NGOs.
23 RCPD No. PL BC 120/04.09.33/95-96 dated 2 April 1996. Issued by the Rural Planning and Credit Department and signed by the Executive Director of the RBI.
24 This outreach figure does not include the clients served by some of the MFIs through other projects. In the case of the MYRADA, for instance, its overall programme includes thirteen projects with over 3000 credit management groups – the MYRADA's version of SHGs – and 67,000 members. The information required by the study was not available on a consolidated basis for all credit management groups. For this reason, only one of the MYRADA project areas – Kamasamudram – was included in the study on a sample basis. Similarly, the *sangams* of SPMS of Andhra Pradesh were once directly supervised by the Madurai-based PRADAN and the local RASS under a joint project called 'Rural Women's Banking Project'. This project has a total coverage of over 600 *sangams* and 9000 members. Having recently emerged as an autonomous federation of the *sangams* in urban slums of Tirupati region, the SPMS was chosen for the Bank Poor '96 study instead of either the PRADAN or RASS.

5

Microfinance in Nepal: Coping with Dispersed Markets

Harihar Dev-Pant, Dipak Dhungel
and H. Dieter Seibel

Introduction

Nepal is among the poorest countries in the world. With a Human Development Index (HDI) of 0.332, Nepal ranks number 151 among 174 countries (average HDI for South Asia: 0.444). Some of the HDI indicators for Nepal's low level of social development are: a life expectancy of 53.8 years; an infant mortality rate of 98 per thousand; an adult female literacy rate of 13 per cent; and a daily calorie intake of 1957 per capita. While average holdings of arable land are about one hectare, the poor possess little more than the land on which their home is built: 0.14 ha in the plains and 0.05 ha in the hills (Nepal Rural Credit Review Survey, 1994). In 1991 the World Bank estimated that 70 per cent of the Nepalese population were below the poverty line (set at a per capita annual income of $150).

The country's 20 million population grows at the rate of 2.1 per cent per annum and comprises some 3.2 million households of an average size of 6.2 persons. They live in dispersed villages which are clustered into some 4000 administrative units referred to as Village Development Committees (VDCs). Per capita income was Rs12,092 ($212) in the fiscal year (ending mid-July) of 1995–6 of which agriculture generated 41 per cent. During the last five years, the economy grew at a rate of 5.0 per cent p.a.; per capita income went up by 2.9 per cent; and the rate of inflation averaged 10.5 per cent. The economy is projected to grow over the next five years at annual rates around 5–6 per cent while inflation is expected to drop to rates between 5 per cent and 8 per cent.

At 12.4 per cent (fiscal year June–July, 1994–5) the domestic savings ratio is low, amounting to only about half the investment ratio of 23.5 per cent. This large gap poses a major constraint on the country's economic stability and growth. In failing to mobilize the potential savings of the population, financial institutions lack the resources to satisfy the demand for credit; while households lack access to deposit facilities to accumulate the funds for the self-financing of their enterprises. The failure of formal financial institutions to penetrate dispersed villages has given the informal financial institutions much space to grow and flourish. Non-rotating local savings and credit groups are active in the rural areas, where over 90 per cent of the population of Nepal live, more than half of them in hills and mountains under precarious environmental conditions. The outreach particularly of non-rotating local savings and credit groups, on which there are no statistics, appears to be far greater than that of the formal system. Unlike urban rotating savings groups (*dhikuti*), which have evolved into *the small businessman's self-help bank*[1], non-rotating groups mainly recruit their members from among the poorer section of the rural population. As these institutions mobilize their resources internally, there is invariably a strong emphasis on savings. Recently, finance companies have started to mobilize savings throughout the informal sector. The financial services are mostly concentrated in urban areas. One of them, the Himalaya Savings and Finance Company, employs some 600 daily deposit collectors.

Poverty-Alleviation Programmes Using Microfinance

Poverty-oriented programmes in Nepal have largely ignored the role played by non-rotating local savings and credit groups in financial intermediation in the rural areas. Five programmes targeted on the poor with some outreach of significance have been focused on providing credit to their target clientele:

1. the Small Farmer Development Programme (SFDP) with 189,000 borrowers, accounting for about half the total outreach of poverty lending programmes;
2. the IBP with 85,000 borrowers;
3. Production Credit for Rural Women (PCRW) with 27,000 borrowers;
4. Grameen replicators comprising five Grameen Bikas Banks and two NGOs (Nirdhan and the Centre for Self-Help Development) with 32,000 borrowers in July 1995 and 48,000 borrowers as of July 1996; plus
5. an estimated 12,000 registered and unregistered savings and credit organizations and co-operatives with an overall membership of 792,000 members.

In addition, there are some small programmes like BP, the RSF and the Micro Credit Project for Women (MCPW) with a total outreach of less than 10,000 borrowers. Women's participation in the PCRW, Grameen and the MCPW is

Table 5.1 Outreach of Poverty Lending Programmes in Nepal, 1995 and 1996

Programme	Borrowers		Loans outstanding (in US$ '000)**
	Number	*Percentage female*	
SFDP, 1/1996	188,757	22*	23,266
IBP, 7/1995	84,811	n.a.	22,774
PCRW, 7/1995	26,974	100	1,661
Grameen replicators:			
7/1995	32,119	100	1,916
7/1996	48,392	100	3,431
Savings and credit organizations and co-operatives, 7/95	n.a.	n.a.	98,266
BP, 7/1995	3,585	80	328
RSF, 7/1995	2,931	n.a.	
	201		
MCPW, 7/1995	1,750	100	365

* This official statistic is based on the percentage of all-female groups; the Project has in the past lumped together all-male and mixed groups. Hence, the actual percentage of female members is presumably higher than 22 per cent.
** Exchange rate: US$1 = Rp54.8.
Source: Dev-Pant and Dhungel, 1996.

Table 5.2 Deposits and Loans of Banks in Nepal, July 1995

	US$million	*Percentage*
Total deposits	1230.4	100.0%
Commercial banks	1114.0	90.5%
ADBN	116.5	9.5%
Total loans	975.8	100.0%
Commercial banks	856.1	87.7%
ADBN	119.7	12.3%
Poverty-focused credit	73.7	100.0%
Priority sector	51.0	69.3%
ADBN-SFDP	22.6	30.7%

Source: Dev-Pant and Dhungel, 1996.

notably high since these programmes exclusively target women (Table 5.1). The majority of borrowers of the SFDP, the IBP and co-operatives are male heads of households acting on behalf of the family. The Agricultural Development Bank, Nepal (ADBN) plans to increase the share of female borrowers in the SFDP to at least 40 per cent. Average loan sizes of the various programmes are between US$60 and US$120, except in the IBP which has an average of $260.

The contribution of poverty-oriented programmes to resource mobilization in the country is very small. As of July 1995, the financial sector of Nepal mobilized US$1.24 billion (Rp68 billion) in deposits (Table 5.2). Commercial banks accounted for about 90 per cent of that amount, the

Table 5.3   Financial Viability Indicators of Poverty-lending Programmes in Nepal

Programme	Repayment rate*	Arrears ratio*	On-lending Interest Rate		Subsidy Dependency Index***
			Actual**	Required**	
SFDP	43.6	20.1	18.1	42.5	1.35
IBP	41.4	23.6	15.55	43.5	1.80
PCRW	82.0	n.a.	15.55	72.4	3.66

*   1994–5
**   1991–2
***(Required rate − average rate)/average rate.
Source: Dev-Pant and Dhungel, 1996.

ADBN about 9 per cent, and the recently formalized finance companies about 1 per cent. Together, Grameen-type development banks, co-operatives and NGOs accounted for only 0.1 per cent of total deposits. Commercial bank loans outstanding amounted to US$856.1 million (88 per cent), and ADBN loans to US$119.7 million (12%). Poverty-focused credit amounted to US$73.7 million, 31 per cent of which were handled through the ADBN's SFDP, the biggest single provider of poverty loans. The ADBN's main business is not poverty lending, as was indicated by the fact that in mid-1995 SFDP loans accounted for 18.9 per cent of the ADBN's total loan portfolio.

Data concerning outreach to the poor are mostly on credit rather than savings. The savings of the poor go largely uncollected. While the poor make up the majority of the population, their share of credit has remained minuscule, with poverty-focused credit amounting to 7.5 per cent of total bank loans outstanding. As of mid-1992, 17 per cent of rural households reported loans outstanding from the formal sector and 49 per cent from the informal sector. These proportions were 6 per cent and 42 per cent, respectively, among the landless. The savings ratio of rural households was estimated at 7 per cent. With an outreach of credit to about 20 per cent of the poor in January 1996, progress since the mid-1970s when the central bank first embarked on poverty lending has been moderate.

Most government-supported poverty lending programmes in Nepal have been a big financial failure. Two factors have rendered them financially non-viable: a historically low repayment rate and grossly insufficient interest rate spreads. There were times when borrowers considered loan defaulting as an act of political defiance in the pursuit of democracy while the winning party felt subsequently obligated to reward its followers by waiving the repayment of their loans.

As of July 1995, the repayment rate was 44 per cent in the SFDP and 41 per cent in the IBP, while arrears (amount overdue in percentage of amount due) were 20 per cent and 24 per cent, respectively.[2] (See Table 5.3.) With a repayment rate of 82 per cent, the performance of PCRW, which is targeted on women, has been much better, but is still far from satisfactory. Only the

Grameen replicators, established between March 1993 and July 1995, report a repayment rate of 100 per cent as of July 1996. The SFDP and the IBP similarly reported a repayment rate of 100 per cent during the year of their inception (1976/7 and 1981/2 respectively) but this dropped rather sharply to 86 per cent and 63 per cent, respectively, in the following year. In subsequent years, their repayment peaks were 63 per cent (1983/4) and 80 per cent (1985/6) respectively while their lows were 39 per cent (1990/1) and 40 per cent (1992/3) respectively.

For the three major programmes, the SFDP, the IBP and PCRW, the World Bank calculated their subsidy dependency during the three fiscal years from 1989 to 1992. It found wide discrepancies between actual and required cost-covering interest rates: 18.1 per cent vs. 42.5 per cent in the SFDP; 15.6 per cent vs. 43.5 per cent in the IBP; and 15.6 per cent vs. 72.4 per cent in PCRW.

Policy and Regulatory Framework

In recent years, the institutional development of rural financial institutions has gained much attention in Nepal's two chief monetary and financial policymaking institutions: the Ministry of Finance and the central bank, Nepal Rastra Bank (NRB), which is in charge of bank supervision. New legal forms have been created that are of relevance for microfinance services, among them development banks for Grameen replicators, savings and finance companies and the Small Farmer Co-operatives Ltd (SFCL). A Co-operative Banking Act was under preparation at the time of the study. To promote the establishment of banks with a local outreach, the NRB has recently differentiated equity capital requirements for rural development banks: Rs2.5 million − US$45,620 − for banks working in a single district, Rs5 million − US$91,240 − for banks working in two or three districts and Rs10 million − US$182,482 − for those working in four to ten districts.

The deregulation measures of the NRB readily drew a robust response from the co-operative and NGO sectors. Subsequently, two types of financial institutions with a considerable outreach potential to the poor have emerged in recent years: the SFCL and the Grameen replicators.

SFCL: One of the more interesting microfinance innovations in the Asian-Pacific region is the transformation of the sub-project offices (SPOs) of the SFDP into autonomous local financial institutions owned and managed by their members in the form of the SFCL − apparently with a remarkable impact on institutional viability and sustainability, as is indicated in Table 5.4.

The SFCL has its roots in the SFDP, which the ADB, Nepal has built up since 1975 with major support from the IFAD (US$27.5 million) and the ADB, Manila (US$30 million). By mid-1996 the SFDP had reached 189,000 heads of households organized in some 23,000 small farmer

Table 5.4 Performance of Four SFCLs in Dhading after Two Years of Autonomy, July 1995 (Handover date: 16 July 1993)

Loans from own resources in % of all loans outstanding:	20%
Excluding handover loans:	28%
Repayment rate of:	
ADBN handover loan:	28%
New ADBN channelling loans:	79%
Loans from internal resources: July 1995:	98%
January 1996:	100%
Arrears ratio:	
ADBN handover loan:	62%
New ADBN channelling loans:	5%
Loans from internal resources: July 1995:	0%
Transaction costs in % of loans outstanding:	1.5%
Increase of loans outstanding from internal resources during preceding six months:	19.5%

Source: Dev-Pant and Dhungel, 1996.

groups. Credit disbursement and technical support of the SFDP were administered through 422 SPOs. The programme incurred substantial losses, with repayment rates barely above 40 per cent and loss ratios fluctuating mostly in the 20s and 30s. Its savings mobilization component was largely symbolic as it depended totally on donor resources throughout its existence. In July 1993, with technical assistance from the GTZ, the ADBN embarked on a new course of institutional transformation and turned the SFDP operations in four SPOs in Dhading over to the small farmers themselves, establishing the first four SFCLs owned and managed by their members.

Each of the four SFCLs comprises on average 709 small farmers in 100 small farmer groups (73 per cent of them male or mixed and 27 per cent female), organized in turn into eleven inter-groups. It appears that this transformation achieved a miracle. The SFCLs started mobilizing their own resources, which reached 20 per cent of all loans outstanding within the first two years of their existence; the repayment rate of ADBN channelling loans (which continued unabatedly) virtually doubled; and the repayment rate of loans from internal resources jumped to 98 per cent as of July 1995 (Table 5.4). While the SFCLs still have quite some way to go to full autonomy, there is at least incipient evidence that there is a route of transforming the unsustainable operations of a state-owned agricultural development bank into viable MFIs that cover their costs from the margin and might eventually mobilize their own internal resources.

By mid-1996 the operations of 30 SPOs had been converted into autonomous SFLCs, with a total outreach of over 20,000 families (representing a population of about 130,000). While the ADBN continues to establish new small farmer groups through its existing network of SPOs that are to be converted into SFCLs in due course, it is expected that within six to eight years about 400–500 SFCLs will have been established with an outreach of more than 200,000 predominantly poor families (i.e. a population of 1.2 million). Given their low level of transaction costs and the excellent repayment performance, their viability does not appear to be threatened. However, full institutional autonomy and self-reliance (including the cessation of loan channelling on the ADBN's terms), appropriate supervision and the establishment of an apex structure are among the many issues that need to be resolved if savings and credit co-operatives of the SFCL type are to evolve into a self-sustained movement with an ever-increasing deepening of financial services to the poor.

Grameen Bank replicators: In 1992 the government of Nepal embarked on a Grameen Bank replication programme, announcing its plans for the establishment of five Grameen-type rural development banks, one in each of the five geographical regions of the country. In 1996 the Development Banking Act was passed under which the five Grameen Bikas Banks have been registered. In addition there are two NGO replicators existing side by side, testing the appropriateness of a bank vs. NGO approach.

The main resource base of the Grameen Bikas Banks has been their share capital amounting to Rp60 million (US$1.1 million), of which the central bank, the NRB, has provided two-thirds. The two NGOs were supported by international donors. In addition, commercial banks lent Rp148.7 million (US$2.71 million) to the Grameen Bikas Banks and Rp31.6 million (US$576,642) to the two NGOs under the compulsory deprived-sector credit programme, totalling Rp180.3 million (US$3.29 million), which is barely less than the total volume of Grameen loans outstanding. Like the commercial banks in Nepal, the Grameen replicators are excessively liquid. Government vs. private ownership of the Grameen-type development banks has been an issue of critical debate, reflecting the fear that government intervention might interfere with sound banking practices and keep the banks from attaining resource self-reliance and financial viability. The Grameen replicators target exclusively poor women. Starting in 1993, outreach has grown rapidly from about 12,500 in mid-1994 to over 50,000 in mid-1996 (Table 5.5).

With a repayment rate of 100 per cent loan recovery so far has been perfect. Members' savings constitute 20 per cent of loans outstanding. Compulsory savings in the group fund are the chief instruments of internal resource mobilization, with personal voluntary savings amounting to a mere 12 per cent of total savings. Transaction costs of the Grameen-type group approach have been substantial and are a big threat to the viability of the institutions. If this issue could be resolved and if self-reliance were to replace their donor-dependency, they could continue to widen their outreach and greatly enrich the financial infrastructure that is accessible to the poor.

Table 5.5 Performance of Seven Grameen Replicators within their First Three Years (amounts in US dollars)

	July 1994	July 1995	July 1996
1. No. of group members	12,561	34,910	51,437
2. No. of borrowers	10,839	32,119	48,392
3. Loans disbursed, cumulative	897,810	4,056,569	9,901,460
4. Loans repaid, cumulative	375,912	2,136,861	6,463,504
5. Loans outstanding	521,898	1,919,708	3,436,131
6. Overdue loan	Nil	Nil	Nil
7. Group fund savings	252,920	235,401	593,066
8. Personal voluntary savings	131,022	54,744	87,591
9. Members' total savings	85,766	291,971	682,482
10. Loan from group fund savings	7,482	62,044	260,949

Source: Dev-Pant and Dhungel, 1996.

Microfinance Capacity Assessment

Six MFIs were selected as case study illustrations to analyse the performance of MFIs in Nepal in terms of their outreach, resource mobilization, and viability/sustainability. These MFIs are:

(a) Two pioneering Grameen replicators: Purbanchal Grameen Bikas Bank (PUGBB), one of five government-sponsored Grameen-type banks with legal status under the Development Bank Act, and Nirdhan, one of two NGO replicators and the first of all replicators in the field. Both are located in the plains of Nepal

(b) Two out of 49 NGOs sponsored through the governmental RSF: Adarsha Krishak Samanbaya Samiti (Adarsha) and Vyccu Bachat Tatha Rin Sahakari Samstha (Vyccu).

(c) Two out of 233 co-operatives engaged in microfinance and registered under the Co-operative Act of 1992: the SFCL in Bhumisthan, Dhading, which is one of by now 30 pioneers of the ADBN's new GTZ-supported strategy of transforming some 400+ SFDP SPOs into autonomous local financial intermediaries owned and managed by their members; and the privately organized Navajiban Co-operative Limited in Dhangadi (Navajiban), as one out of ten commercially oriented co-operatives authorized to undertake banking functions.

Of the six cases, PUGBB, a government-owned regional development bank, has been singled out for a more elaborate presentation (see below). Originally registered in 1992 under the Commercial Bank Act of 1974, it started its financial operations on 8 August 1993; as of March 1996, it fell under the newly enacted Development Bank Act. Two years after its start, its equity capital of Rp30 million (US$547,445) was doubled to Rp60 million US$1,094,891) of which the NRB held 66.75 per cent, the government 8.25 per cent and each of the five state-owned commercial banks 5 per cent. The bank has been selected here as an example of the Grameen approach geared to a disadvantaged segment of the Nepali population, namely women below the poverty line. After little over two years of operation, it attained about the same outreach as the third-largest poverty lending programme of the government, PCRW; it accounted for 75 per cent of the poor women covered by the seven Grameen replicators in 1995; and it is projected to reach about half the number of households in its region of operation within the next three years that the SFDP has covered nationally after twenty years of existence. Both its capital and governance structure indicates that PUGBB is a government bank. Its board of directors is exclusively recruited from government institutions: the NRB, the Ministry of Finance and the state-owned commercial banks; the chairman (so far from the NRB) and the executive director (from one of the commercial banks) are elected from among the board members – with prior government approval. PUGBB also illustrates the severe struggle for viability of a government-owned poverty lending institution.

Outreach

The outreach figures for the six sample institutions (Table 5.6) reflect different policies. The Grameen replicators, foremost among them the Bikas Bank with over 26,000 clients, cover a wide geographical area. The other institutions tend to be limited to a small number of villages, usually under one VDC. Only informal institutions, which are excluded from the sample, tend to recruit their members from single villages. The Grameen replicators and the SFCL recruit their members from among the poor only; in addition, the former restricts participation to women. In all three programme approaches, the number of savers exceeds that of the borrowers, which mostly reflects the fact that saving is a compulsory programme requirement.[3] In non-discriminating institutions, men, who are usually the heads of

Table 5.6 Outreach of Six Sample MFIs in Nepal, December 1995

MFI	Borrowers			Savers[4]		
	No.	% poor	% female	No.	% poor	% female
(a) Grameen:						
Bank: PUGBB	25,028	100	100	26,297	100	100
NGO: Nirdhan	1,936	100	100	2,131	100	100
(b) RSF:						
Vyccu	49	35	37	313	24	24
Adarsha	87	0	38	160	0	37
(c) Co-operatives:						
SFCL, Bhumisthan	741	100	20	793	100	25
Navajiban	212	46	27	1,661	18	22

Source: Dev-Pant and Dhungel, 1996.

households, outnumber women by a wide margin. This is usually due to a policy of limiting memberships or loans to only one family member at a time, resulting in a restriction of access to credit for women's own income-generating activities. To widen outreach, programme managers may be encouraged to lift that restriction; and to promote the establishment of women's own units or sub-units, e.g. at the village or village-group level.

Whether MFIs should broaden their outreach or put more emphasis on deepening their services and impact is a challenging issue to be left to their member-customers and management rather than policymakers and donors. There does not seem to be an inherent advantage of one strategy over the other.

PUGBB[5] is located in the eastern plains. Its objective is the provision of financial services, particularly access to credit, to all women in the eastern region that fall under the poverty line.[6] The bank has a dual delivery structure, comprising a bank structure and a member structure. As of 1995/6, the bank consisted of a head office, six area offices and 29 branches. On average there are five branches per area office. Each branch has a staff of 6–10. The total number of staff is 256. Of these, 35 (14 per cent) are in the head office. There are 127 field assistants (comprising about half the total), who work directly with the women's groups in the field. Incentive schemes have not been introduced.

During its first fiscal year, 1993/4, the bank enrolled 8294 women; in 1994/5 14,992; and in 1995/6 another 5667, bringing the total to 28,953 (Table 5.7). The members are organized in about 5800 groups of five women who in turn form 827 centres of seven groups each. The bank's growth projection until the year 1998/9 is about 81,500 members (this would equal half of the SFDP's present national outreach) in some 16,300 groups and 2000 centres.

Prospective members are attracted through public meetings and house-to-house visits. Groups of five women each are formed, and the members of three groups jointly receive one or two weeks of training, one hour per day,

Table 5.7   Outreach of PUGBB: 1993/4–1995/6 (July)

	1993/94	1994/95	1995/96
Number of members	8,294	23,286	28,953
Number of borrowers	6,890	21,538	28,271
Percentage of borrowers	83.1%	92.5%	97.6%
Av. loan disbursed (US$)	80.30	102.10	129.56
Av. loan outstanding (US$)	49.91	60.55	78.17
Average savings (US$)	6.90	8.43	14.36
Loans outstanding (US$)	343,066	1,304,744	2,177,007
Savings deposits (US$)	56,569	197,080	416,058
Savings as % of loans outstanding	16.5%	15.1%	19.1%

Source: Dev-Pant and Dhungel, 1996.

in the Grameen technology – reportedly with only little adjustment to the Nepali context. Five of the fifteen participants usually drop out, and the remaining ten form two solidarity groups. Reasons given for dropping out include fear of losing property, ignorance, husband's interference and discouragement from landlords, moneylenders or politicians. As in Bangladesh, Grameen banking seems to be perceived by local authorities and leaders not just as a financial business but as a type of social revolution centring on the role of women in society.

The bank is very much credit-oriented, with virtually every group member becoming a borrower. There are three loan products: general loans with a one-year maturity and weekly instalments accounting for 98 per cent of all loans outstanding (1995/6), six-months seasonal loans due upon maturity, and irrigation loans. In addition, 50 per cent of the compulsory group savings, which are not withdrawable, can be lent by the groups to their members at interest rates fixed by the group for emergency and consumption purposes. The percentage of borrowers during the three years was 83 per cent, 92.5 per cent and 98 per cent respectively. During the same time average loan size (disbursed) grew from Rp4,400 to Rp7,100 (US$80 to $130) and average savings from a meagre Rp378 to Rp787 (US$7 to $14).

The demand for loans of larger sizes outstrips the supply by far. The bank practises a system of incremental repeat loans, with a ceiling of Rp15,000 (US$274) for third-term borrowers. The total volume of loans outstanding grew from US$343,066 1993/4 to US$2,177,007 in 1995/6, and total savings from US$56,569 (16.5 per cent of loans outstanding) to US$416,058 (19.1 per cent of loans outstanding) in the same years. With 92.5 per cent of the savings accumulated through regular compulsory group savings in 1995/6, the mobilization of irregular voluntary savings of varying sizes is of negligible importance.

Financial Viability and Sustainability

Of the six MFIs studied in Nepal, only the two Grameen replicators are low in both operational and financial self-sufficiency, which may be partially attributed to their recent origin. However, this does not explain the difference between the bank and the NGO, as both became operational in 1993. In terms of self-sufficiency, the bank performs much more poorly than the NGO: surprisingly as it is a bank, perhaps unsurprisingly as it is government-owned. However, in 1995/6, the bank's self-reliance indicators jumped from 18 per cent to 47 per cent and from 15 per cent to 34 per cent, respectively, bringing it somewhat closer to the level of the NGO. The organizations under the RSF and the co-operatives are operationally fully self-sufficient; the conventional co-operative is also financially fully self-sufficient. Vyccu, Adarsha and the SFCL have rates of full financial self-sufficiency from 71 per cent to 84 per cent (Table 5.8). The on-time

Table 5.8   Operational and Financial Self-sufficiency of Six MFIs in Nepal, 1995

	Grameen Replicators		Rural Self-reliance		Co-operatives	
	Bank	NGO	Vyccu	Adarsha	SFCL	Navajiban
Lending rate of interest	20	20	18	18	15–18	12–21
On-time repayment rate	100	100	97	100	64	92
Mean loan size (US$)	57.48	61.86	167.88	250.36	121.53	1,535.22
Degree of partial financial self-sufficiency (in %)	18	64*	103	96	136	127
Degree of full financial self-sufficiency (in %)	15	59*	71	84	82	113

* These data pertain to July 1996.
Source: Dev-Pant and Dhungel.

repayment rate is perfect, or near-perfect, among the Grameen replicators and the RSF organizations. The on-time repayment performance of Navajiban is near satisfactory. The SFCL is a special case, as the figure of 64 per cent conceals wide variations depending on the source of funds: the repayment rate of loans from internally mobilized resources is 100 per cent; of loans channelled on behalf of the ADBN since their institutional autonomy around 80 per cent; and of loans handed over at the time of its establishment as an SFCL (shrunk by now to a portfolio of bad debts) around 20 per cent.

On the whole, co-operatives appear to be the most outstanding performers while the Grameen replicators still have a long way to go to become self-reliant. Despite the recent deregulation of interest rates, the MFIs continue to charge rates of interest around and below 20 per cent, which is usually not sufficient to cover the costs and risks of micro-loans. Navajiban is an exception as its average loan size (approximately US$1,500) is more than 25 times the loan size of the Grameen replicators and 6–13 times the size of loans of the other organizations.

After three years of operation, PUGBB is still far from breaking even. In absolute terms its net loss was Rp4.86 million (78 per cent of total expenditure) in 1993/4, Rp12.98 million (78 per cent of total expenditure) in 1994/5 and Rp 10.96 million (46 per cent of total expenditure) in 1995/6.[7] In terms of the volume of loans outstanding, the losses amount to 25.8 per cent, 18.2 per cent and 9.2 per cent, respectively. In terms of total assets, the losses are 6.8 per cent, 11.0 per cent and 5.9 per cent, respectively. The bank's degree of partial financial self-sufficiency has jumped from 0 per cent in 1993/4 to 47 per cent in 1995/6 and it hopes to achieve a 100 per cent-rate in 1996/7. Its degree of full financial self-sufficiency has increased from 0 per cent in 1993/4 to 15 per cent in 1994/5 and 34 per cent in 1995/6.

The bank projects to become financially fully self-sufficient within three years, i.e. until 1998/9. However, the bank ignores the fact that the value of the subsidy element has been increasing rapidly in terms of actual costs, namely from 17 per cent in 1993/4 to 39 per cent in 1995/6, making the bank donor-dependent and vulnerable. If the opportunity costs of the bank's equity capital contributed by the government are taken into consideration, the dependency (and, concomitantly, lack of autonomy in decision-making) is even more pronounced. While some consider these projections as overly optimistic, others derive hope from the fact that 8 of the 29 branches have reported operational profits within three years (disregarding the value of grants and soft loans). Additional indicators of performance are given in Table 5.9 below.

There is a host of factors militating against viability in PUGBB. But as important as they are, there is at least one factor that so far has not undermined the bank's viability, and that is the repayment behaviour of its customers. The women repay their loans; to date no loan losses have been reported.

The first factor, which militates against viability, lies in the bank's governance structure. Being owned by government institutions, there is no

Table 5.9 Performance Indicators for PUGBB: July 1993–4, 1994–5 and 1995–6 (all amounts in US dollars)

	1993/4	1994/5	1995/6
Operating expenditure	110894	272,628	353,996
Interest paid on deposits	2,044	7,372	19,288
Interest paid on soft loans:			
Amount actually paid	639	18,814	63,066
Value of payments at market rate	12,774	69,416	194,215
Loan loss provision:			
Actual amount	0	3,193	2,135
Value of 2% of loans outstanding	6,879	26,077	43,522
Total cost:			
Actual cost	113,577	302,007	438,467
Subsidy element*	19,014	73,485	172,536
Adjusted cost	132,591	375,493	611,004
Subsidy element/actual cost (in per cent)	16.7%	24.3%	39.3%
Groups per branch	638	803	998
Groups per FA (field assistant)	82	185	233
Loan amount per FA	3,412	10,347	17,555
Savings per FA	567	1,551	3,431
Average salary of FA in % of GDP	256%	363%	440%
Loanable savings deposits	54,963	186,460	395,036
Soft loans and grants	182,482	658,960	1,560,547
Loans outstanding	343,905	1,303,996	2,176,314
Loss/Total expenditure	78%	78%	46%
Loss/Loans outstanding	25.8%	18.2%	9.2%
Loss/Total assets	6.8%	11.0%	5.9%
Degree of financial self-sufficiency:			
Partial	0%	18%	47%
Full	0%	15%	34%

* The subsidy element is calculated as the total of the value of payments on borrowings at the market rate minus actual soft loan interest payments (lines 5 and 4) plus loan loss provisions of 2% of loans outstanding minus the actual loan loss provision (lines 8 and 7).
Source of basic data: Dev-Pant and Dhungel, 1996.

vested interest in profitability. To the contrary, the bank finds itself under political pressure to lend to the poor at low interest rates at which it cannot cover its costs. This lack of interest in the bank's viability relates not only to its owners but also to its management and staff. The branches are not run as profit centres; nor are there any employee incentive schemes. While access to cheap central and commercial bank funds may be considered an asset as it lowers the costs of loanable funds, its actual impact is the opposite, leading to a distortion of the cost structure and, presumably, a general lack of cost awareness among the bank's management and staff.

The bank's delivery system is expensive — a second factor impeding viability. Salaries alone accounted for 57 per cent to 58 per cent of total expenditures in each of the last three years of operation; while salaries and office expenses together accounted for 98 per cent in 1993/4, 90 per cent in 1994/5 and 81 per cent in 1995/6. During the three years interest expenses on savings deposits were 1.8 per cent, 2.4 per cent and 4.4 per cent respectively of total costs; while interest expenses on borrowings grew from 0.6 per cent to 6.2 per cent and 14.4 per cent, respectively. In terms of loans outstanding as recorded in the balance sheet, expenditures for salaries and office expenses were 32 per cent, 21 per cent and 16 per cent during the three respective years — a declining trend. There are already signs of a decline in the dynamics of expansion indicated by the number of groups formed on average by field staff: 82 groups during the first year, 119 during the second year and only 45 during the third year, while the number of field staff grew only slightly, namely from 101 in 1993/4 to 126 in 1994/5 and 127 in 1995/6. Political interference is cited as one of the background factors, which includes changes in bank leadership parallel to changes in the political system of the country. Another factor is of course that the field staff have reached the limits of their capacity, as they are obligated to participate in group and centre meetings.

A third factor lies in the interest rate of loans which is below a genuine rural market rate. The bank pays 7.5 per cent on savings deposits (close to the commercial bank savings deposit rate of 8 per cent), 6 per cent on old soft loans (US$1.16 million) and 8 per cent on its most recent soft loan (US$372,263). Under political pressure to approximate poverty lending standards, the bank charges 20 per cent on its loans to the groups, which is only slightly higher than the commercial bank rate and a fraction of informal lending rates. Interest rates are not differentiated according to loan product, which makes it unattractive for the bank to offer products with customer-friendly services, such as doorstep collection of instalments. This would lower borrower transaction costs substantially while of course increasing the lender's transaction costs — however, with the result of a net decrease in overall transaction costs! Under political pressure, the bank finds itself unable to raise interest rates sufficiently to cover its costs. As elsewhere, this invariably leads to loan rationing, curtailing loan sizes as well as the overall lending volume. This limits the women's access to credit and thus restricts their ability to invest a sufficient amount of resources into income-generating activities with the highest rate of return. The low interest rates may be beneficial to politicians; but they certainly do not benefit the poor women. In this case, small is not beautiful. To the contrary, inadequate loan sizes tend to keep the women in poverty.

The groups are not considered as financial intermediaries – a fourth factor. Serving only as credit channels with joint liability functions, they cannot set their own interest rates on loans received from the bank; nor can they add a margin. Given the standardization of loan sizes and compulsory savings deductions, individual transactions are all reduced to the lowest level affordable by each group member. However, there is a 5 per cent compulsory savings deduction from every loan disbursed, 50 per cent of which the groups can lend on their own terms. This might open the door to the proper pricing of loan products provided the fields' assistants do not advise against it.

Another factor lies in the bank's exclusive targeting of poor women who accept the solidarity group approach. This leaves out some wealthier community members and their potential savings deposits and others with a potential request for larger loan sizes, which would contribute to the bank's economies of scale.

Closely related to this is a sixth factor: the bank's sole reliance on the group approach. This is likely to save transaction costs when banking with the poor. But it excludes bigger customers with widely diverging savings potentials and credit needs that might be better served with an individual technology.

The bank faces a great challenge. According to the NRB/ADB Rural Credit Survey of 1991/2, only 6 per cent of the landless and 12 per cent of marginal farmers have access to institutional credit. The percentage of the poor with access to savings deposit facilities (not to mention collection services) is close to zero. Moreover, the fact that vast numbers of the poor need savings deposit services much more than access to credit is widely ignored. Yet it is the accumulation of savings which would strengthen the much-needed self-financing capacity of the poor. To overcome its shortcomings, the bank would have to undergo a major transformation in order to effectively meet the challenge of serving a substantial portion of its potential market.

Resource Mobilization

Of the six samples MFIs studied in Nepal, the two Grameen replicators are among the weakest in terms of internal resource mobilization (Table 5.10). With savings constituting only 16 per cent and 18 per cent, respectively, of loans outstanding, they largely depend on donor funding. In case of withdrawal of external funds, they would not be sustainable. The two

Table 5.10   Resource Mobilization by Six MFIs in Nepal, December 1995

	Grameen replicators		Rural Self-reliance		Co-operatives	
	Bank	NGO	Vyccu	Adarsha	SFCL	Navajiban
Savings (US$'000)	254.0	18.8	4.2	21.9	10.2	325.9
Loans outstanding (US$'000)	1,436.8	119.7	8.2	21.7	90.1	325.5
Savings/loans outstanding(in %)	18	16	51	100	11	100

Exchange rate: 1US$ = Rp54.8.
Source: Dev-Pant and Dhungel, 1996.

organizations under the RSF present a discrepant picture: Vyccu has savings equivalent to half the amount of loans outstanding, while Adarsha's loans outstanding are fully matched by its internal resources. Similarly, Navajiban fully mobilizes its own resources while the other co-operative, SFCL, Bhumistan, still continues to serve as a channel for ADBN funds. Within the first three years of its operation, the SFCL has mobilized from its 788 members Rp0.58 million (a mere US$13 per member). Interestingly, the raising of compulsory share capital contributions has been of minor importance, accounting for only 7.1 per cent of its own resources as of January 1996. Voluntary savings, 72.5 per cent of resources, make up the bulk. In addition, livestock insurance, accounting for 20.4 per cent, has contributed in an innovative way to the group's internal resources. In all MFIs, voluntary withdrawable savings have the greatest growth potential, particularly when collected through doorstep services, as recently demonstrated by the Himalaya Finance and Savings Company Ltd.

On the whole it is concluded that resource mobilization and the range of financial services offered by the MFIs, comprising nominal fees, share subscriptions, regular compulsory savings and, to a restricted extent, voluntary savings, are quite limited. A wider range of savings products and collection services is generally lacking. There are virtually no reciprocal products of combined savings and instalment collection. Donor and government funding and the policy of interest rate subsidization of bank micro-loans have greatly undermined the motivation of the MFIs to mobilize their own resources. In addition, an inverse interest structure which resulted from the channelling of government funding through MFIs at preferential terms has in the past greatly impeded the mobilization of voluntary savings.

PUGBB has been remarkably successful in mobilizing external resources. For its start it obtained Rp24 million (US$437,956) in equity capital from government sources which were augmented to Rp60 million (US$1.09 million) after two years. The central bank, the NRB, with two-thirds of the paid-in capital, is the major equity holder. The state-owned commercial banks and the government contributed the rest. In addition, the bank has borrowed

Table 5.11 Resource Mobilization by PUGBB: July 1993–4, 1994–5 and 1995–6 (Amounts in US$'000)

	1993/4	1994/5	1995/6
Paid-up capital	438.0	10,344.8	10,344.8
New commercial borrowing	182.5	658.8	901.5
New borrowings/Loans outstanding in per cent	53.1%	50.5%	41.4%
Borrowings outstanding	182.5	658.7	1,560.2*
Borrowings outstanding/Loans outstanding in per cent	53.1%	50.5%	71.7%
Compulsory savings/Total savings in per cent	.	85.0%	94.0%
Savings deposits/Loans outstanding	16.5%	15.1%	18.8%

* This includes US$1.52 million from commercial banks and US$41,423 from Grameen Trust.
Source: Dev-Pant and Dhungel, 1996.

Rp10 million (US$182,481) in 1993/4, Rp36.1 million (US$658,759) in 1994/5 and Rp49.4 million (US$901,460) in 1995/6. The amount of borrowings outstanding as of July 1996 was Rp85.5 million (US$1.56 million) (Table 5.11). In the framework of the compulsory lending programme for the deprived sector, government-owned banks supplied 46.5 per cent of the borrowings and private banks another 50.8 per cent. The remaining 2.6 per cent came from the Grameen Trust in Bangladesh for the scaling-up for one of the branches.

Despite the fact that development banks are authorized by the banking law to mobilize savings from the general public, the bank has restricted its internal resource mobilization to the group members. It offers two types of savings products: compulsory group savings amounting to a 5 per cent deduction from every loan and voluntary savings. Little effort is being made by the bank to tap the savings potential of its members. In 1994/5 compulsory group savings accounted for 85 per cent and individual voluntary savings for 15 per cent. In the following year, 1995/6, the share of compulsory savings increased to 94 per cent while voluntary savings fell to 6 per cent. The future of voluntary savings in PUGBB appears bleak, with projections of the share of voluntary savings of 1.7 per cent for 1996/7, 1.4 per cent for 1997/8 and 1.3 per cent for 1998/9.

During the preceding three years there was no clear trend concerning the proportion of savings deposits in terms of loans outstanding. Their share was 16.5 per cent in 1993/4, 15.1 per cent in 1994/5 and 19.1 per cent in 1995/6 (cf. Table 5.9). There does not seem to be a policy within the Bank to step up its internal resource mobilization. To the contrary, the bank's projections until 1999 show proportions of 10.4 per cent for each one of the next three fiscal years. The Bank's resource mobilization policy seems to be geared to external resources rather than internal savings. During the three preceding years, new borrowings from commercial sources amounted to 53.1 per cent,

50.5 per cent and 41.4 per cent, respectively, of loans outstanding; while borrowings outstanding amounted to 53.1 per cent, 50.5 per cent and 71.7 per cent of loans outstanding. For each one of the next three years the Bank has projected the share of borrowings at 93 per cent of loans outstanding.

Some observers have concluded that there is only one way of reversing the bank's trend towards increased external resource dependency: privatization. While this may appear as an ideological issue to some, others have pointed out that time and again governments have been generous in supporting new poverty-lending initiatives, but sooner or later, under budgetary constraints and concerns for macroeconomic stability, they have retracted their support. This has usually led to the collapse of those institutions that did not possess the foresight of preparing for the day of enforced self-reliance. This is a thorny issue for the bank. For its government owners would have to foresee, and prepare for, their own withdrawal.

Regulatory Framework

During the 1990s the government has created a new policy environment focusing on democratization, decentralization and local participation, economic and financial liberalization including interest rate deregulation, poverty alleviation, and a legal framework for MFPs. While opening up to the outside world including external markets, the government also showed a new positive attitude to NGOs and their role as facilitators in the process of development at the grassroots level. The government renewed its emphasis on alleviating the plight of the rural poor, including women. While poverty alleviation was considered a matter of charity in the past, it is now being increasingly realized that rural financial systems development along the lines of a market economy, with an emphasis on the viability of institutions and programmes, opens up new avenues for sustainable poverty alleviation on an ever-increasing scale of outreach.

The government first responded to the problems of extreme rural under-development at the time of absolute monarchy. In 1968, it set up the ABDN and subsequently, in 1975, established the SFDP to stimulate agricultural production by providing credit and related training and consultancy services through the ADBN. Other interventions followed, among them the Intensive Banking Programme in 1981, with preferential credit being the principal tool to alleviate poverty. As usual at that time among governments and donors, the approach was supply-driven and top-down, resulting in the rapid deterioration of the financial health of the programme and its handling institutions. Groups were established as a grassroots channelling mechanism, without a notion of institutional autonomy as local financial intermediaries. Pre-existing self-organized savings and credit groups, many of them of indigenous origin, were ignored. To some extent, there might have been a positive impact on agricultural production, but that impact remained restricted by the failure of credit services to grow dynamically and by the neglect of savings deposit facilities.

Indeed, the partial liberalization of the financial system of Nepal in recent years has brought some conspicuous changes in the banking system of the country. Average bank lending rates have increased to around 18 per cent in commercial lending and 11 per cent in preferential lending. This is still low compared to the interest rates in the informal financial sector, which hover at around 35 per cent in the mountains and 43 per cent in the plains. The average inter-bank rate was below 10 per cent in July 1996; the Treasury bill rate was 12.8 per cent (up from 3.8 per cent in January 1994).

Despite the liberalization measures, a number of restrictions continue to constrain the performance of the financial system. The banks' freedom, for instance, is restricted by two major factors: an NRB directive limiting the spread between deposit and lending rates to 6 per cent (except for the Grameen-type development banks and NGOs); and the prevalence of subsidized credit, which includes a provision for commercial banks to allocate 12 per cent of their loan portfolio to priority sectors in agriculture, cottage industry and services. Financial institutions are obligated to lend against collateral. An exception is made up to a certain level for loans to low-income families and solidarity groups. As average transaction costs from institutional sources in rural Nepal have been estimated at 6 per cent (at presently given terms and conditions), ranging from 1 per cent on large loans (above Rp50,000, or about US$912) to 11 per cent on small loans (below Rp5,000, or about US$91), restrictions on the margin militate against lending to small and marginal borrowers, lead to risk-aversive lending and shift transaction costs to borrowers (i.e. eliminating customer-friendly services). They are also likely to undermine the financial viability of the banks.

The remedies to the disease of non-viability seem clear: elimination of interest rate subsidies in favour of cost-covering rates of interest; insistence on, and incentives for, timely repayment; and lowering of transaction costs. How this can be achieved has recently been demonstrated by the ADBN in its SFDP. By transforming its SPOs into autonomous co-operative local financial institutions (SFCLs), owned and managed by their members, the repayment rate of funds has improved from around 40 per cent to 79 per cent. These funds were channelled by the ADBN through the SFCL against a commission that has subsequently been increased since its adoption in the first four SFCLs established in Dhading, one of the poorest areas in Nepal. The repayment rate of funds mobilized by the SFCLs from its own members was 100 per cent as at January 1996; and their administrative expenses according to project statistics were a mere 1.5 per cent of the amount of loans outstanding.

Much as the MFIs would want to mobilize savings from communities they are serving, they cannot do so because of some legal impediments. Deposit taking from the general public continues to be restricted to commercial and development banks as well as finance companies. NGOs and savings and credit organizations including co-operatives with NRB permission for limited banking operations are only authorized to accept deposits from their members. Deposits collected by finance companies, co-operative credit societies and savings and credit organizations are limited to the ten-fold of their equity capital. They also have to maintain a minimum of 10 per cent liquidity of their deposit liabilities. Banks and finance companies have to adhere to capital requirements as a percentage of total assets and risk assets as prescribed by the NRB.

On top of these restrictions, a number of other issues have to be resolved at the policy and regulatory level if microfinance outreach for the poor in Nepal is to grow significantly and in a financially viable way:

- the adoption of an overall microfinance systems development approach, which includes the systematic co-ordination of the various measures and donor contributions;
- the establishment of self-organized second-tier regulatory authorities for the various networks of MFIs, providing guidance, business representation, institution-building, supervisory and refinancing services that exceed the capacities of the NRB and the Department of Co-operatives respectively;
- the actual implementation of differentiated, market-oriented interest rates, which would generally have to be far above the commercial bank prime rate in order to cover the costs of intermediation;
- the curtailment and, eventually, the abolishment of preferential lending programmes, which distort rural financial markets and set up an unfair competition to market-oriented MFIs;
- the abolishment of micro-loan interest rate subsidies, which undermine savings mobilization;
- a stop to all practices of using MFIs as channels for programmes with terms and conditions set by governments and donors, to be replaced by an emphasis on internal resource mobilization which may be complemented by a system of liquidity exchange among related institutions and access to sources of portfolio refinancing at market terms;
- the promotion of innovative linkages between institutions belonging to the various financial sub-sectors;
- the selection and testing of successful microcredit, microsavings and microinsurance products and strategies and their dissemination throughout the formal, semi-formal and informal financial sectors;
- the strengthening of the autonomy of all financial institutions including the central bank, the NRB;
- the promotion of governance structures and incentive schemes which are conducive to the viability and growth of microfinance institutions; and
- the privatization of government-owned MFIs.

These issues will only be resolved in the best interest of the poor if there is adequate co-ordination and close co-operation between MFIs, their customers or members, government agencies and donors.

Notes

1 Seibel and Shrestha, (1988). Acharya, Shrestha and Seibel (1988). Seibel and Dhakhwa (1997).
2 In the past there was usually no write-off policy in these programmes.
3 However, half of these institutions and programmes are credit-driven and borrower-oriented, namely the two Grameen replicators and, at least to date, the SFCL. Unlike some of the institutions from Indonesia where poor savers outnumber poor borrowers by a wide margin, these three institutions in Nepal fail to appeal to savers. Indeed, access to cheap donor and government funds makes it in the short run economically rational behaviour to rely on external resources rather than own savings with their high mobilization costs.
4 Borrowers and savers cannot be simply added up to arrive at the total number of members or customers; the larger one of the two figures is usually equivalent to the total.
5 Reported figures usually pertain to one of two reporting dates, the end of the fiscal year, 16 July and the end of the calendar year, 31 December. Due to differences in reporting time, there may thus be wide divergences between figures for the same year.
6 A household of five with land holdings not exceeding 0.68 ha (1.0 big ha) is officially defined as poor. Participants are mainly identified on the basis of land ownership and the quality of their housing. According to a housing indexation test in one of the poorest areas of the bank, Jhumka, 84 per cent in a sample of 50 households were poor, 12 per cent not so poor and 4 per cent non-poor. Outreach to the non-poor is usually defined as *leakage* (supposedly of scarce government or donor funds earmarked for poverty lending) by Grameen replicators and not welcomed.
7 Data for 1993/4 and 1994/5 are audited, data for 1995/6 are provisional.

6
Microfinance in Sri Lanka: The Importance of Adapting to Local Conditions

Sunimal Fernando and Joe Remenyi

Introduction

Sri Lanka is a country of more than 18 million people, at least three-quarters of whom find their livelihood in the rural districts. By the start of the 1980s, in comparison to developing countries as a whole and South Asian economies in particular, Sri Lanka had achieved the most impressive records for improved health, educational attainment, life expectancy and many other quality of life indicators. However, these gains were made at the expense of substantial taxes on the export sector, massive growth in government expenditures and the number of government-owned enterprises, spreading dependence on welfare hand-outs among urban and rural residents alike, increasing food aid receipts, declining food self-sufficiency, a stagnant plantation sector, and growing disquiet over the inability of government to maintain roads, bridges and other social overhead capital and deteriorating equity trends that contributed to political and civil unrest.

Economic growth trends, adjusted for inflation, for Sri Lanka in recent years are contrasted with those for earlier decades in Table 6.1. These data show that the trend to a more diversified economy did gather pace as economic growth rates accelerated in manufacturing, construction and service trades ahead of those in agriculture in the years since 1990. Despite this recent spurt in the nature and absolute level of economic growth, Sri Lanka in the late 1990s is still a predominantly agricultural country and official unemployment levels appear stuck at well above 10 per cent of the workforce, with demand from females to enter the waged employment rising.

Table 6.1   Real Growth Trends in Sri Lanka, 1970–95

	Real Average Annual Growth Rates		
	1970–80	*1980–90*	*1991–95*
Real GDP	4.0	4.3	5.4
Agriculture output	2.7	2.2	2.3
Manufacturing	2.0	4.6*	8.9
Construction	5.1	N.A.	5.7
Services	4.8	4.8	5.6
Gross Domestic Investment	N.A.	1.7	10.8
Inflation	N.A.	10.9	9.5
Population	1.9	1.6	1.3
Real GDP/person – Sri Lanka	2.6	2.7	4.0
Real GDP/person – South Asia	1.2	3.2	3.2

* Includes construction
Sources: Ministry of Plan Implementation (Sri Lanka), various statistical sources from 1980 to 1994; Central Bank of Sri Lanka, *Review of the Economy*, various, reports from 1980 to 1994; World Bank, various issues of *World Development Report*, 1980 to 1996; and Economist's Intelligence Unit (EIU), 1996.

The macroeconomic performance of the Sri Lankan economy is distorted by the influence of civil unrest and the resource demands of military action across significant areas of this small and beautiful island state. In the fifteen years to 1995, the share of government expenditure devoted to defence[1] increased from a low 1.6 per cent in 1980 to a burdensome 21 per cent, including significant expenditures on imported military equipment and supplies that helped keep the balance of trade in deficit and worsen national indebtedness. Nevertheless, government budget deficit as a share of national expenditure declined significantly. This result is directly tied to the successful privatization of large sections of public-sector enterprises, especially in the plantations industries that had moved into the government domain as part of the post-independence reorganization of the Sri Lankan economy. The manufacturing sector increased its share of GDP by almost ten percentage points in only fifteen years (Table 6.2). Gradually, Sri Lanka has shed the burden of a bloated public-sector-dependent economy that had evolved in the decades to 1990. That Sri Lanka has done so without sacrificing gains made in overcoming widespread illiteracy, high levels of gross fertility and infant mortality rates, is an achievement that deserves to be recognized and heralded.

However, the economic welfare and structural adjustment gains made in the ten years to 1995 have been significantly limited, and in some areas reversed, by a number of factors:

1. The recurrence of political and civil strife in 1995–6 caused military activity to quicken and essentially halted government attempts to remain strictly true to the hard medicine of policy reform that it had engaged in since 1989.
2. The government made several failed attempts to reform the civil service

Table 6.2   Structural Macroeconomic Performance Indicators, Sri Lanka, 1980–95

	1980	1991	1994	1995
Per cent of government expenditure devoted to:				
– defence	1.6	12.3	11.6	21.0
– social services	23.6	37.7	33.0	39.4
– health	5.6	4.9	6.0	6.0
– education	10.8	9.5	11.7	10.8
– budget deficit	N.A.	51.7	45.4	37.9
Per cent of GDP represented by: Output in:				
– agriculture, forestry and fishing	28.0	22.6	20.5	20.0*
– manufacturing & construction	18.0	24.4	26.6	27.3
– services	54.0	53.0	52.9	52.7
Debt service ratio (%)	12.4	N.A.	8.7	N.A.
Exchange rate (Rupees per US$)	N.A.	41.4	49.4	52.8
Inflation rate (%)	N.A.	12.2	8.4	7.7
Unemployment rate (%)	N.A.	13.8	12.1	12.7
GDP per person (US$)		470		

* In 1995 an estimated 36.9 per cent of the workforce was engaged in agriculture.
Sources: World Bank, 1997, 1996a and 1990a; EIU, 1996.

during the period 1985–95, the result of which was that the gains made in increasing national productivity were significantly limited, and leakage from the public purse to privileged groups continued largely unabated (reflected in part by the fact that the share of national income received by the richest 20 per cent of households remained at more than ten times that by the poorest 20 per cent).

3. There was a break in the trend towards increased international competitiveness (which can be measured in various ways, but is reflected in long-term strengthening of the terms of trade and growth in foreign trade, both of which faltered as Sri Lanka entered the mid 1990s).

4. There was a failure of financial sector reform to stimulate the level of domestic savings sufficiently, so that national savings achieved, the rate of which almost doubled between 1980 and 1995, still fell short of the finance needed to fund domestic investment demand plus debt servicing. As a result, Sri Lanka depended on foreign aid, remittances by nationals resident overseas, foreign private investment inflows and increased levels of overseas borrowing to cover the resource gap.

The slowing of economic progress in Sri Lanka since 1994 prompted the World Bank to conclude in its 1997 Operations Evaluation Department report, that sustainable escape from the economic doldrums that have beset Sri Lanka in the late 1990s, will be contingent on more broadly based financial sector reform, renewed improvements in public-sector management to ensure better targeting of social services and welfare, reform of the civil service to place it on a more professional basis, and cessation of political unrest and armed conflict (World Bank, 1997). Success in each of these areas will be crucial to future significant reduction of both urban and rural poverty in Sri Lanka.

Incidence of Poverty

Despite relatively high levels of growth in measured GDP per head in recent decades, productivity in rural Sri Lanka remains so low that an estimated two-fifths of the rural population, where three-quarters of households engaged in economic activity in Sri Lanka reside, were officially declared to be in absolute poverty at the beginning of the 1990s. For the country as a whole, the share of the population living below the poverty line was around one-third, with the most recent estimates showing some success in poverty reduction through the 1980s and the first half of the 1990s, but also a deterioration in the proportion of households in poverty in 1994–6. There are competing estimates of the head count index for Sri Lanka in recent years (see Table 6.3), but to agree that it was not less than 25 per cent in 1995 would be a conservative estimate that puts the fight against poverty in Sri Lanka in the best light.

Poverty for the hard-core rural poor in Sri Lanka is reflected not only in low incomes in return for low levels of productivity, but also in vulnerability to changing economic conditions, limited access to a broad range of economic institutions, isolation and a deteriorating environment. The rural poor struggle with the persistence of food insecurity and low levels of agricultural and non-agricultural asset accumulation. Sri Lanka's rural poor have extremely limited access to productive resources from which to forge an improved income stream, including both land and credit, despite reforms implemented in the past decade to liberalize factor markets and impose the discipline of the market place on the resource-allocation process.

Poverty-Alleviation Policies and Programmes

The poverty-alleviation strategies implemented by successive governments in Sri Lanka included a nationwide Food Stamp Programme (FSP) that has operated continuously since 1979; a midday meal programme for school children initiated in 1989; a household-level cash grant programme called the Janasaviya Programme (JSP), launched in 1990; and a complementary poverty-alleviation programme originally called the Janasaviya Trust Fund (JTF), introduced in 1992, which was reformed in 1994 and again in 1995 as the renamed National Development Trust Fund (NDTF), to provide assistance with community projects, village and household-level human development projects, including nutrition intervention and credit. Details of each of these programmes are given below.

The poor relief FSP is an income-augmentation and consumption-support

Table 6.3   Competing Recent Estimates of Poverty in Sri Lanka

Estimated by	Year	Head Count Index (% of population below poverty line)
DOCS (1)	1980/1	50.5
World Bank (2)	1982	27.0
DOCS (3)	1985/6	40.0
HLCO (4)	1988	44.5
MPI (5)	1986/7	27.8
Korale (6)	1985/6	39.5
Average	1980s	35.5
GoSL (7)	1991	37.0
IFAD (8)	1992	46.0
GoSL (7)	1994	39.0

Poverty line (Rupees per family per month):		Rupees
– Official government rate	1977	700.0
– Official government rate	1989	700.0
– Janasaviya Programme (JSP) rate	1989	1500.0
– World Bank/UNDP (Janasaviya Trust Fund – JTF) rate	1991	1500.0 (= approx.US$30)
– Official government rate	1995	1500.0
– National Development Trust Fund (NDTF) rate	1995	3000.0
– National Bank rate	1996	3000.0 (= approx. US$55)

Sources:
DOCS (1) and (3): Department of Census and Statistics, Sri Lanka, 1981 and 1986, cited in Chandrasiri, 1993, p. 45.
World Bank (2): *World Development Report 1990*, Washington, DC, and Oxford University Press for the World Bank.
HLCO(4): The High Level Committee of Officials on Poverty Alleviation 1988, 'Poverty Alleviation Through People-Based Development', Government of Sri Lanka Press, Colombo. HLCO estimates are based on the population receiving food stamp relief, which is known to overstate the number of persons below the poverty line.
MPI (5): Sri Lanka Ministry of Plan Implementation (MPI), 1990, 'Strategies for Poverty Alleviation: The Sri Lanka Experience', Working Paper Presented at the Fifth SAARC Meeting of Planners, March, 1990.
Korale (6): R.B.M. Korale, 1987, 'Income Distribution on Poverty in Sri Lanka', quoted in ISACPA/SAARC, 1992, p. 5.
GoSL (7): Government of Sri Lanka statistics on numbers in receipt of poverty relief payments.
IFAD, 1992.

programme that was started in 1979. The FSP sought to improve the nutrition status of poor households by increasing their disposable income using food coupons instead of subsidized rations of rice. At the time of launch, the FSP covered households with incomes less than Rp300 (US$5.68) per month and catered for more than 60 per cent of all households in the country.[2] In 1986 the value of the food stamps was doubled and coverage of the FSP was extended to assist households with a monthly income up to

Rp700 (US$13.26) but on a sliding scale. The FSP had no microfinance component.

The second of the above programmes was launched in 1989 because of the government's concern that widespread child malnutrition was limiting the social and private benefit of subsidized education expenditures due to irregular or low school attendance and restricted student alertness. The programme provided on-sight feeding as an incentive to ensure school attendance. Initially targeting all children attending primary and secondary school, the programme was changed in May 1990 to involve parents and reduce costs by substituting a subsidy of Rp3 (US$0.057) per day to every child bringing a nutritious meal to school. In 1993 the programme was again restructured to target FSP recipient households with school-age children. Under this scheme, which is still in force, a monthly allowance of Rp50 (US$0.95) is given to every school-age child in the household.

The JSP was also introduced in 1989 as the government's official poverty-alleviation programme aimed at enabling poor households to engage in income-generating enterprises or acquire skills to get better-paying jobs. Target beneficiaries of JSP were households with a monthly income less than Rp700 (US$13.26), but the selection criteria was subsequently changed to include a special set of qualitative measures. JSP provided eligible beneficiaries with a consumption support grant of Rp1,458 (US$27.61) a month for two years, of which Rp438 (US$8.30) per month was compulsorily saved in the name of the receiving household in the National Savings Bank. These savings deposits earned an interest rate of 12 per cent p.a., but access to these deposits was strictly regulated. Other village-level savings schemes in the form of a Common Fund and a Group Fund paid up to 6 per cent interest on savings and against which very short term loans could be accessed at an interest rate of between 24 and 60 per cent p.a. In the period 1989–93, the JSP mobilized a total of Rp2,163.79 million (US$40,980,871) in savings, or about US$5 per household p.a.

The JSP also provided credit to beneficiaries for self-employment projects with a median loan size of Rp1500 (i.e. < US$50), for a period of two years at an annual interest rate of 16 per cent. Loans were made on the basis of a referral from the village level Janasaviya Support teams and from the relevant extension officers responsible for the working of the programme. In the period 1990–5, a total of Rp1,314.02 million (US$24,886,367) was distributed to 238,889 beneficiaries through state banks, the CRB and the RRDBs.

The JTF, launched in 1992 with World Bank funding, is complementary to but independent of the JSP, working in the four project areas of community development, human development, credit dispersal, and nutrition intervention projects. Under its credit component the JTF provided credit funds at 7 per cent p.a. to partner organization (NGOs, banks and government agencies) for on-lending at 21 per cent p.a. to the poor for self-employment and small-enterprise establishment or expansion. Between 1992 and 1996, by which time the JTF had been renamed the NDTF, Rp2,400 million (US$45.45 million) had been spent in the four project areas, with Rp733 million (US$13.88 million) (30.5 per cent) being devoted to credit disbursement to a total of 372,604 families at a rate of interest of 21 per cent p.a. This represents an average loan size of Rp1967 (= approximately US$37). Little detail is available on the uses to which the margin of 14 per cent on NDTF funds disbursed is put or on the performance of the on-lending programmes of collaborating agencies.

In addition to the above-mentioned programmes, a different type of programme was initiated in 1994. At this time a change of government brought a change in the official poverty-alleviation programme, to what became known as the Samurdhi Programme (SP). Households that qualify for SP aid are categorized into two types. The first is the poorest of the poor which comprises households that have a monthly income of only Rp500 (US$9.47) or less, and so require a subsidy of Rp1,000 (US$18.94) a month as government assistance to bring them up to or near the new poverty line. At the time the SP was introduced there were an estimated 100,000 households in Sri Lanka (3.3 per cent of the total households in Sri Lanka) eligible for this level of assistance. The second type of poor household were those with monthly income in excess of Rp500 (US$9.47), which were eligible for a subsidy of Rp500 (US$9.47) a month as government assistance. An estimated 1.1 million households in Sri Lanka (36 per cent of the total) were believed to be of this 'less-poor' type. Adopted as official government policy from the beginning of 1995 and intended to eventually replace the JSP, the FSP and the midday meal scheme, the SP does little to remove cash handouts as the primary thrust of the government approach to poverty alleviation in Sri Lanka. Nevertheless, the government envisions that in addition to direct income transfers, the SP should facilitate income-generating activities of poor households. Credit eligibility will be tied to savings mobilization, where beneficiary households are encouraged to save 10 per cent of the income supplement they receive as the foundation of future credit entitlements of up to Rp10,000 (US$189.40) each at concessionary rates of interest (as low as 10 per cent p.a.) for self-employment and small-industries projects.

Another poverty-alleviation measure currently in the very early stages of design is the Self-Employment Promotion through Micro Enterprise Credit (SEPMEC) scheme. Under SEPMEC, the poverty line is established at an income of Rp3,000 (US$56.82) per family per month, which is twice the official poverty line of Rp1,500 (US$28.41). Its objective is to deliver to poor households credit facilities and support services for self-employment through microenterprises. Project plans reveal a special focus on educated youth, among which unemployment is rife, in an attempt to break away from the tradition that new graduates will find employment in the public sector. Present planning calls for commercial banks with an adequate branch network throughout the country to participate in this programme, which will be monitored and supervised by the Central Bank of Sri Lanka.

Regulatory Framework for Microfinance

Despite the growing importance of microfinance as a major strategy for poverty alleviation, the official financial sector regulatory framework in Sri Lanka, as expressed in the Banking Act, the Monetary Law Act and the Finance Companies Act, continues to present some serious constraints on the range of financial services in which MFIs can engage.

Licence to mobilize savings: There is a widespread consensus among microfinance specialists that a cornerstone of success for an MFI must be the ability to offer savings services and, over time, to see an increasing share of the loan portfolio funded from savings mobilized from borrowers and other customers. However, under current laws only banks can legally mobilize savings from any client. The Co-operatives Ordinance also only permits co-operatives or thrift and credit societies to mobilize savings from their members but not from non-members or the public at large. In practice, however, there are many NGOs that do offer savings services to their clients, and in most instances the government has been turning a blind eye to their activities. However, this is not always the case, as was exemplified by the celebrated case of Sarvodaya, which the government of President R. Premadasa prosecuted in 1992, in part as an example to all others that the government's compliance is not to be presumed upon. Since then, pressure has been brought on the government to reconsider its position, but with little success. This has prompted large NGOs such as Sarvodaya to consider the possibility of setting up their own savings banks within the framework of the existing laws.

Interest Rates: Under current arrangements, the norms of Central Bank regulation (including centralized controls over the setting of interest rates, the spread between loan and deposit rates, acceptable collateral requirements, permissible debt-equity ratios and liquidity requirements) apply solely to commercial banks and formal financial institutions, which add to their transactions costs and limit their ability to be flexible enough to offer financial intermediation services to very poor households profitably. These same restrictions do not apply to NGOs, RoSCAs or other informal-sector MFIs, nor to co-operatives and credit unions that are regulated under their own ordinance, with the result that NGOs and MFIs are free to adapt to the markets they serve without having to observe rules and regulations tailored to the needs and economics of formal-sector banking. In contrast to the close supervision of savings mobilization, interest rates on savings and the margin between deposit and lending rates are largely left for market forces to determine. However, interest-rate movements are influenced significantly by the state of the Central Government budget deficit, setting the Treasury bill rate as the lead rate in Sri Lanka. The higher the deficit the greater the 'crowding out' effect as government Treasury Bills and other financial paper soaks up liquidity in the economy.

Taxation: The prevailing tax system in relation to MFIs favours co-operatives and NGOs, both of which are exempt from income tax. Banks, on the other hand, including specialist niche banks established to provide microcredit services for the poor, are subject to tax according to the prevailing income tax laws of the country. The RRDBs are exempt from income tax for the first ten years of their operation, but from the eleventh year they are subject to the payment of income tax on their profits. In a perverse way, therefore, existing taxation arrangements in Sri Lanka provide a disincentive to the formation of village banks or any other sort of MFI that is not a co-operative or an NGO.

Women's Participation

Poor women have access to credit made available through government-facilitated microcredit programmes and similar programmes run by NGOs. Nevertheless, there is little evidence to suggest that increasing awareness of the viability of female participation in microfinance has had anything more than a marginal impact on the female participation rate in the credit programmes of either formal-sector financial institutions or NGOs in Sri Lanka. So much is this so that the programmes that maintain gender-desegregated data are the exception, and are typically restricted to programmes tailored to 'women in development' initiatives, such as the credit programmes associated with the IFAD, the CIDA, the JTF and Sarvodaya.

Among the MFIs consulted for this study, all report that, in their experience, women are much more reliable than men in the matter of loan repayment. Also, very poor women are much keener to repay their loans than the not-so-poor because they have a special self-interest in ensuring access to another loan. However, the paucity of gender-desegregated information on borrower records prevents an assessment of the extent to which Sri Lankan women have been able to overcome poverty through the productive activities that access to microfinance services has facilitated. In many parts of both rural and urban Sri Lanka, women pursue their private savings and borrowing activities by joining SHGs of up to twenty members, often formed for the primary purpose of establishing a traditional *seetu* or revolving savings and loan 'club'. Many NGOs promote the work of these *seetu* by providing assistance with their formalization and resource mobilization.

Financial Institutions and their Outreach to the Poor

In 1993, the Central Bank of Sri Lanka estimated total rural credit needs of Sri Lankans at Rp16 billion (US$303 million) per annum, of which only Rp900 million (US$17 million), or 5.6 per cent, was met by the formal financial sector, composed of state banks, commercial banks, RRDBs, CRBs and Thrift and Credit Co-operative Societies (TCCSs). The balance of more than Rp15 billion (US$284 million) was left to be met by informal-sector finance providers, which a decade earlier the Central Bank reported in its annual report for 1981–2 consisted of private money lenders (60 per cent), family and friends (35 per cent) and NGOs including grassroots-level self-help groups (5 per cent). (See Zander, 1992.) In almost any village in Sri Lanka, two or three people, usually elderly women, engage in short term lending of small amounts to the very poor for meeting short term cash needs at interest rates ranging from 5 to 30 per cent per month. The persons engaged in this 'highly valued' activity are very different from the stereotype village moneylender, who is supposed to be rapacious, dishonest and willing to enforce repayments by violence if necessary.

Only a proportion of the estimated demand for rural credit can be attributed to demand from poor households. The Rural Credit Division of the Central Bank has suggested in the course of consultations and research for this chapter, that the credit demand of the rural poor might represent around one-third of the total credit needs of the rural sector. The same source offered the opinion that, 'the credit needs of the very poor are not even marginally met by the formal sector'. One result of this is that 'pawning' has become a crucial way in which poor households meet their need for cash resources. In response to this demand, both state banks in Sri Lanka – the Bank of Ceylon and the People's Bank – plus the fourteen RRDBs in Sri Lanka and the Hatton National Bank, which is a commercial bank, have been authorized by government to engage in pawning services, which appears to be the main source of working capital for many rural households.

In 1995, the Sri Lanka National Savings Bank (SLNSB) reported to the World Bank that it held deposits from rural customers exceeding Rp10 billion (US$189.4 million), from 10 million separate accounts in a country that had less than 4 million households. This is a considerable achievement in savings mobilization, but it is one that has also contributed to the persistence of poverty in Sri Lanka. Very little of these rural savings is recycled back into the communities from whence it was raised. As a result, the very success of the banking system in mobilizing savings also robs rural economies of the liquidity that they could otherwise use to support informal-sector microenterprises and household-level investments that increase the range of sources from which poor households derive income. In this sense, the banks in Sri Lanka are not performing the financial intermediation role that MFIs must play if they are to contribute effectively to poverty reduction.

According to the inventory of MFIs in Sri Lanka undertaken by the World Bank's SBP programme, by the end of 1992 thirteen MFIs in Sri Lanka had been operating for at least three years and had at least 1000 current borrowers, including the SLNSB and the countrywide network of credit unions. In alphabetical order these thirteen are:

Christian Children's Fund
Federation of Thrift and Credit Co-operative Societies (FTCCS)
Jeeva Sanwardhanaya Ayathanaya
Lanka Evangelical Alliance Development Services
People's Rural Development Association (PRDA)
Postal Savings
Praja Naya Niyamaks
Research and Applications for Alternative Financing and Development
SANASA (this is the Sri Lankan acronym for the 'reformed' or 'reawakened' credit co-operative/union movement, of which FTCCS and most TCCS members are a part)
Sarvodaya
Savcred
SLNSB
TCCS

These thirteen MFIs do not include NGO-based microfinance providers, such as those that are operated by CARE (Cooperative for American Relief Everywhere), the Opportunity Foundation or World Vision International. Nor does the list include the very many small programmes that have less than 1000 clients or have come into being since 1992, from which date the SBP programme collected its data. In addition, the list does not include rural credit programmes operating through official development assistance channels with funding from agencies such as the IFAD, the UNDP or bilateral donors such as the USAID, though many of the MFIs in the list are collaborators with and beneficiaries of grants and loans sourced from these and other development assistance agencies. A comprehensive list of MFIs that includes all these would be likely to run to a large number of separate microfinance programmes, each serving a niche market or a specifically targeted group of Sri Lankans.

Microfinance Capacity Assessment

In what follows the microfinance activities of a small sample of four MFIs is examined in some detail in order to explore the constraints facing MFIs in reaching out to a larger proportion of poor households in Sri Lanka in a financially viable manner.[3] The sample consists of:

1. **The RRDB of the Kalutara District** – a bank that was established under the Regional Development Banking Act of 1985 by the Central Bank of Sri Lanka with a government grant of Rp33.5 million (US$634,470). Its major funding was intended to come from the mobilization of rural savings. The

RRDB is governed by a board of five directors that meets monthly. Each board member is, in practice, an appointee of the Central Bank and drawn from a list of persons 'recommended' from the Kalutara District. In this way the political patronage system that prevails in Sri Lanka is made an intimate part of the governance and policymaking structures of the MFI, strengthening the influence of the Central Bank in the resolution of moot or contentious issues. The CEO of the RRDB also serves as chairperson of the board. By 1996 the RRDB had established sixteen branches to serve the 175,500 households resident in the Kalutara District. The RRDB has a yearly internal audit and an annual external audit conducted by the Government Auditor General's Department. Costs are analysed once in three months, but an institutional financial analysis has never been done.

2. **The GPU of the Hatton National Bank (HNB)**, also known as the Village Reawakening Programme of the HNB, was established in 1989 with the objective of mobilizing rural savings and supporting micro-enterprise development with a special focus on poverty alleviation. The GPU comes under the general administration and management of the HNB and is the special responsibility of the Deputy General Manager. At the start of 1996 the GPU had 71 branches established across the country, but accounting of these is subsumed within the broader accounting processes and records of the HNB, so that no separate data on operational costs and other management information is directly accessible. Data on operation costs of the GPU were estimated on the assumption that these are in proportion to the volume of financial services delivered through the GPU. In 1996 this was found to be 1.8 per cent of the total financial services of the bank, though the GPU management sees its potential client base consisting of all 4 million households on the island, especially the million or so that are below the poverty line. The GPU is subject to an internal audit, which is the responsibility of the audit department of the HNB. A monthly analysis is made of Savings, Loans Disbursed, Loan Recoveries and Interest Payments, but an institutional financial analysis of GPU has never been made.

3. **The PRDA** has a credit programme in the Puttalam District in the west of Sri Lanka which is part of a larger programme of a national-level NGO with 22 member entities making up the association. The PRDA is governed by an elected board of thirteen directors, drawn from the national business community, the national professional community, development NGOs and grassroots organizations in the districts in which the Association works. The chairperson of the board is a leading banker while the two alternate chairpersons are leading members of the national business community. The PRDA's strategy is to assist the poor by entering into alliances with community-based organizations that can assist it in its effort to promote microenterprise development among the poor in the villages in which it works. At the end of 1996 the PRDA had activated

this programme only in the districts of Puttalam and Gampaha. The Puttalam district has around 11,000 households, the majority of which are believed to be below the poverty line. The PRDA has an annual audit conducted by a firm of recognized auditors appointed by the board. There is no internal audit and no cost analysis on a regular basis, and an institutional financial analysis has never been done.

4. **TCCS** in the Colombo District. This MFI is one of 27 district level co-operative credit unions representing more than 700,000 members through some 7500 community level 'societies' that make up the national peak body, the FTCCS. The TCCS seeks to serve the estimated 310,000 households resident in the district of Colombo. The TCCS programme has a history of 75 years of operation, but its reincarnation as a revitalized and reformed MFI dates only from the early 1980s, based on three fundamental concepts – savings mobilization through the practice of thrift, provision of loans to members out of savings, and the promotion of mutual assistance among members. At the start of 1996 the Colombo District Union consisted of nine branches representing 256 registered community-based 'primary thrift and credit co-operative societies' (PTCCS) functioning at village level with a membership of 27,712 persons, of whom 18,193 were women. Membership is not limited to the poor but is open to all villagers without exception, and loans are given for both investment and consumption purposes, including emergencies, house repairs and the financial cost of weddings, funerals or other social obligations. The Colombo District Union is governed by an active but honorary board of directors, elected by the members at an annual general meeting. The chief executive is the General Manager who works in close co-operation with the chairperson. The district level TCCS, such as the Colombo District TCCS, draw strength from membership of the national federation, the FTCCS, which by the mid-1990s could boast a membership with outreach to all corners of the island representing one-fifth of rural households, in excess of Rp700 million (US$13.26 million) disbursed in outstanding loans and Rp600 million (US$11.36 million) held in savings deposits and share capital. FTCCS members represent around 80 per cent of the SANASA movement in Sri Lanka, but by the start of 1995 only an estimated two-thirds of local level credit co-operatives had reformed their operating procedures and core goals sufficiently to conform to the requirements for SANASA and FTTCS membership. The TCCS is audited annually by the audit division of the Department of Co-operatives. The MFI is also closely monitored on a three-monthly basis by the internal audit branch of the Department of Co-operatives, but an institutional financial analysis of the Colombo TCCS District Union has never been conducted. (An excellent overview of the all district TCCS, the umbrella federation and the SANASA movement can be found in Huppi and Feder, 1990; and Hulme and Mosely, 1996 (at Vol. 2, Chapter 13)).

The areas served by the sample of four MFIs examined are representative of the diversity of environment, level of economic activity and availability of social overhead capital across most of Sri Lanka. The Colombo district includes the national capital, Colombo, but the rural foundations of the district are still clearly evident from the distribution of land area by agricultural activity. Moreover, the degree to which the district of Colombo may be perceived as privileged or otherwise grossly unrepresentative of the microfinancial services and opportunities available to poor households in the rest of Sri Lanka is dispelled by almost all the indicators of socio-economic status and infrastructure, especially the sparse distribution of banks. The figures in Table 6.4 confirm that, taken together, the four MFI programmes examined (GPU, TCCS, RRDB and PRDA), provide a microcosm of the main markets for microfinance activity in Sri Lanka.

Table 6.4 Infrastructure and Socio-economic Characteristics of the MFI Sample Areas, 1994

MFI studied	Sri Lanka GPU	Colombo District TCCS	Kalutara District RRDB	Puttalam District PRDA
Year MFI programme established	1989	1985	1985	1989
Population: (As % of total island population)	100.0	11.4	5.6	3.3
Population Density: (Persons/sq. km)	235	2659	527	171
Per cent of total land area devoted to:				
– major cash crops – tea, rubber, coconut	6.4	13.7	19.4	7.9
– double-cropped paddy	4.2	4.2	5.6	2.1
– highland crops	0.7	0.2	0.1	1.2
Per cent of paddy land that is:				
– single cropped	53	36	80	29
– irrigated	69	8	15	89
Per cent of roads motorable all year	63	81	82	83
Per cent of households with:				
– electricity	31	49	50	51
– access to safe water	69.9	89.9	64.7	74.2
– flush or water sealed toilets	26.9	59.7	41.2	26.5
Literacy rates: (% of adult population)	87.2	94.1	90.3	90.0
Education: (No. of pupils per school)	426	906	488	459
Education: (No. of pupils per teacher)	22.5	23.6	24	26.7
Education: (Drop out rates up to year 9)	3.9	2.3	3.3	6.1
Health: (Hospital Beds per 1000 population)	2.8	5.1	2.1	2.2
Health: (Medical Officers – per 100,000 people)	19.6	61.3	30.7	21.7
Health: (Midwives per 100,000 people)	24.6	12.1	30.7	21.7
Banking Density: No. of bank branches per 10,000 of population	1.2	1.5	1.4	1.1

Sources: Sri Lanka Central Bank, Annual Reports, 1995 and 1996. Government of Sri Lanka, Department of Census and Statistics, Annual Reports, 1995, 1996.

A Note on Management Capacity and the Reliability of Data

Accounting standards are not the place where the founders of MFIs begin. A consequence of this is a lack of consistent accounting standards and the need for great care before accepting data given as a true and fair representation of the health of the MFI or the effectiveness with which it is delivering its services. There are no sources against which to check the veracity of the performance data summarized in Tables 6.5, 6.6 and 6.7 for the four MFIs surveyed. The co-operation of officials of the four sample MFIs was exemplary and greatly appreciated; nonetheless, the figures reveal a lack of consistency in the performance records reported, which are a surprise only in so far as the variations are far greater than expected. The variations are greater than can be explained because of differences in date of establishment or diversity of approach to the delivery of microfinance services. It is difficult to avoid the conclusion that some of the differences may be the outcome of incomplete or 'creative' data that deserve to be treated with some scepticism.

Outreach

The poverty focus ratios presented in Table 6.5 for four sample MFIs describe flows of savings by the poor into loans to the not-poor. If this record is in any way indicative of the poverty focus of all MFIs in Sri Lanka, then MFIs tend to do more business with households that are not poor than with those that fall below the poverty line. In addition, although it is laudable

Table 6.5 Poverty Status of Clients of Sample MFIs, 1995

	GPU		TCCS		RRDB		PRDA	
	Poor	*Not-poor*	*Poor*	*Not-poor*	*Poor*	*Not-poor*	*Poor*	*Not-poor*
A. Borrowers								
– male	1,054	2,460	690	1,035	4,978	7,466	487	325
– female	263	615	2,070	3,105	2,489	5,807	1,463	975
– total	1,317	3,075	2,760	4,140	7,467	13,273	1,950	1,300
B. Savers								
– male	11,509	26,854	2,460	3,690	17,174	5,725	562	375
– female	2,877	6,714	13,837	4,613	25,761	8,587	1,687	1,126
– total	14,386	33,568	16,297	8,303	42,935	14,312	2,249	1,501
Ratio of Poor to Not-poor:								
– borrowers		1:2:3		1:1:5		1:1:8		1:0:7
– savers		1:2:3		1:0:5		1:0:3		1:0:6
Borrowers: Savers	1:11	1:11	1:6	1:2	1:6	1:1	1:1	1:1

Source: Sunimal Fernando, 1996.

that MFIs have so successfully mobilized the savings of rural households, they have been less successful at recycling these as loans to support the investment and consumption needs of poor households. Only in the case of the GPU are there more savers from not-poor households than from poor households, and only in the case of the PRDA programme are there more borrowers from poor households than not-poor households. Most surprising is the programme of the TCCS, which has a reputation for being poverty focused, but which the data clearly shows favours the not-poor in loan activity at the expense of savings mobilized from poor households. Because most MFIs require aspiring borrowers to fulfil a preliminary savings programme, it is normally true that all borrowers from MFIs are also savers, but not all savers with MFIs are also borrowers. In the main, borrowers from MFIs in Sri Lanka are not the poorest of the poor or even households below the poverty line. Most borrowers are from households that are recognized by microfinance providers as not-poor or 'near-poor' at best.

The overall bias revealed in the sample MFI profile of borrowers and savers favouring clients who are not poor is further highlighted by the financial balances dealing with loans and deposits held. These are summarized in Table 6.6. Though there is some variation across the four programmes, the general trend favouring the better-off clients is unequivocal. Savings deposits are not normally recycled to meet the needs of the poor, but the opposite is true. While some of the savings of the poor are recycled as loans to poor clients, in the main the bulk of savings deposits finds its way into loans to the not-poor clients of these four MFIs, a situation that is consistent with what common opinion holds about the activities of MFIs in general in Sri Lanka.

On the basis of the foregoing, it is difficult to avoid the conclusion that poverty targeting is a constraint to greater outreach by MFIs in Sri Lanka to poor households. Moreover, the failure to target is also a constraint on the success with which MFIs can contribute to poverty reduction. This constraint will remain so long as MFIs in Sri Lanka continue to eschew poverty targeting as a strategic policy guiding future growth in MFI intermediation in the delivery of loan and savings services.

Efficiency and Financial Viability

Efficiency can be measured in many ways, but ultimately the viability of an MFI depends on the extent to which it has access to reliable long-term cash flows sufficient to meet its expenses. In the case of the four MFIs examined here, each has been established with the express intention of remaining in business for the long term. For this to happen each MFI must achieve financial viability and independence from a continuous flow of subsidies, which not only demands that the MFI establish a firm basis on which to earn an income flow from the microfinance services it delivers, but develops a cost

Table 6.6 Loan and Deposit Activity of Sample MFIs, 1995

	GPU		TCCS		RRDB		PRDA*	
	Poor	Not-poor	Poor	Not-poor	Poor	Not-poor	Poor	Not-poor
Loans Outstanding (US$, 1995):								
– male	356,818	832,576	110,606	166,098	570,833	826,250	62,500	298,295
– female	89,205	208,143	313,818	497,727	335,038	616,288	14,205	41,667
– total	446,023	1,040,719	424,424	663,825	905,871	1,442,538	76,705	339,962
Poor as % not-poor		42.98		66.6		61.5		22.6
Average Loan (Rp'000)	17.89	17.87	8.46	8.47	6.58	5.83	3.64	25.36
Average Loan (US$, 1995)	339	338	160	160	125	110	69	480
Savings Deposits (US$, 1995):								
– male	1,619,318	3,776,515	29,545	44,318	224,053	896,402	27,083	53,030
– female	405,503	943,182	88,447	132,578	273,864	1,095,644	79,545	17,992
– total	2,024,821	4,719,697	117,992	176,896	497,917	1,992,046	106,628	71,022
Poor as % not poor		42.9		66.6		25.0		150.1
Average Savings (Rp.'000)	7.43	7.42	0.49	1.08	0.63	7.52	2.52	4.16
Average Savings (US$, 1995)	141	141	9.30	20	12	142	48	79
Average Savings as % of Average Loan	41.5	41.5	5.8	12.8	9.8	129.0	69.2	16.4

* PRDA obtains the bulk of its on-lending funds via a line of credit from the HNB amounting to Rp20,375,000 or US$385,890. The credit provided by the bank is guaranteed by a combination of the USAID, ILO and the RAFAD Foundation through a letter of credit issued by a Swiss bank. These guarantees are not shown as an asset in the PRDA balance sheet and hence the PRDA appears to be lending far more than its on-lending asset base. Exchange rate: 1US$ = Rp52.8.
Source: Sunimal Fernando, 1996.

structure that is affordable beyond the time when start-up grants or soft loans are no longer available.

In Table 6.7 data on costs and revenues of MFIs in Sri Lanka and South Asia generally are explored. These show that it is not unusual for MFIs to offer staff salaries that are considerably in excess of the average income per

Table 6.7 Indicators of Efficiency and Viability of Sample MFIs, Average 1993–5

Performance Indicators	GPU	TCCS	RRDB	PRDA	SBP[1]
Average Salary as % GDP per capita	381	81	256	352	410
Average Loan as % GDP per capita	42.9	28.0	15.2	33.9	18.0
On-time repayment rate (%)	97.2	99.9	81.3	96.7	96.0[2]
Default rate (%)	6.1	1.3	5.4	1.2	N.A.
Ratio field : Headquarters staff	7.2	1.5:1	4.7:1	3.8:1	N.A.
Per cent of field staff that are female	0.0	83.0	40.0	10.0	N.A.
Clients per field assistant	794	641	709	342	N.A.
No. Loans Outstanding per field assistant[4]	66	104	236	211	141
Savings per field assistant	5,261	360	1,360	936	N.A.
Savings as % Loan Portfolio (1995)	4.54	0.27	1.05	0.43	N.A.
Effective Interest rate to borrowers (% p.a.)	21	21	21	22	N.A.
Effective Interest rate on deposits (% p.a.)	11	16	13	10	N.A.

Financial Performance Indicators	GPU	TCCS	RRDB	PRDA	SBP
Degree of Full Financial Self-Sufficiency (%)[3]	24	83	77	64	N.A.
Interest and Fees received as % assets (%)[4]	32	13	13	33	N.A.
Financial costs as % of assets (%)	32	7	5	55	N.A.
Operating costs as % of assets (%)	16	4	5	44	N.A.
Active Grants as % Loan Portfolio (1995)	0.0	16.3	0.01	0.03	54.0[5]
Years to full financial viability[6]	5	2	1	3	N.A.
Forward estimates[6] of additional funds (US$) needed during 1997–9, for:					
– on lending	3.0	4.9	6.5	7.0	N.A.
– capacity building	7.7	1.3	1.9	4.4	N.A.

1. The SBP figures refer to 1992 data from a sample of 98 MFIs in South Asia, as reported by the World Bank's SBP programme.
2. Based on a reported arrears rate of 4 per cent. Though there are important differences between arrears and on-time repayment rates, they are sufficiently similar to allow for some comparisons when also considered in relation to the default rate.
3. As defined by the CGAP, using the prime lending rate as the opportunity cost of grants for on lending.
4. Effectively gross income as a proportion of assets used.
5. The SBP programme found that for the 98 MFIs in South Asia that responded to their survey, in 1992 approximately 54 per cent of all funds came from donors, 29 per cent from deposits and 13 per cent from commercial sources. The balance of only 4 per cent was equity, government and earned income.
6. As assessed by senior executives of the MFI.
Sources: Sunimal Fernando, 1996: *Sustainable Banking for the Poor (SBP)*, World Bank, 1997.

person. This finding is in line with expectations and the received wisdom about the shortages that characterize the market for staff skilled in finance and grass roots community development. However, the experience of the TCCS, which has been able to operate at least as successfully as most other MFIs with staff that require salary levels well below the national average income per head, suggests that the personnel costs accepted by MFIs in South Asia and Sri Lanka in particular, may be significantly above what is achievable.

The importance of transaction costs is directly related to loan size. The larger the loan the easier it is to cover a given level of transactions costs at a given interest rate. However, by definition microfinance is about adopting operating procedures that enable the MFI to cover transaction costs on very small loans. As average loan size rises, so too does the leakage of loan activity to those clients who are not poor. Typically MFIs in Sri Lanka have a mean loan size that is more than twice the average of US$78 for South Asia as a whole. This higher average is consistent with the absence of strict targeting of poor households in Sri Lanka, even by poverty-focused MFIs such as the TCCS and NGOs such as the PRDA. Nonetheless, taken together with other performance indicators, such as above average on-time repayment rates, higher average number of loans per fieldstaff than is typical in South Asia, and exceptional success in savings mobilization, MFIs in Sri Lanka appear to be on a firm base from which to achieve financial viability.

There is reason to believe that the figures shown in Table 6.7 on financial viability may overstate the true situation. For example, GPU programme costs have been 'estimated' on the assumption that GPU operating costs are in proportion to GPU loan and savings mobilization activity as a share of all loan and savings activity for the HNB as a whole. In effect this is equivalent to assuming that there are no economies of scale in banking, which is clearly untrue. Second, it is impossible to completely factor-out the impact of programme cross-subsidization, which can be substantial in the case of MFIs that are in receipt of significant donor resources, even though the benefit received may be indirect and delayed, as may well be the case with the TCCS. Third, it is possible that the redirection of savings deposits to servicing the needs of the poorest households will drive up the operating costs of MFIs in Sri Lanka as the client base shifts to reflect a greater number of more difficult-to-reach poorer customers. These reservations notwithstanding, the overall picture on financial viability of MFIs in Sri Lanka is encouraging if the four programmes studied are in any way representative, which we believe they are.

The financial viability of the RRDB is estimated at close to 80 per cent over the three years 1993–5, which is more than three times better than the HNB had achieved. Also, the performance of the PRDA and TCCS provide support for the view that grassroots-based community organizations can successfully deliver microfinance services to significant numbers of poor households while also achieving significant levels of financial independence from donor grants and cheap loans. The fact that these four MFIs in Sri Lanka have reached financial viability levels in excess of 50 per cent on the basis of exceptionally limited use of flexible pricing policies and niche marketing suggests that there is considerable scope for doing even better.

The degree of financial viability achieved by the MFIs studied has been built largely on the success with which they have attracted rural savings. The exception is the PRDA, which has, nonetheless, shown remarkable innovation and break with tradition by sourcing most of its on-lending funds from the commercial banking system. However, the strategy that the PRDA has adopted is not one that is consistent with increasing financial sustainability. Although the PRDA has paid market interest rates on the funds it has borrowed, it has on-lent these at the very same interest rate to its clients, keeping no spread for itself. The PRDA then sought grant funds to cover the costs of intermediation. As an NGO with a good network of international contacts and access to information about the international aid system, the PRDA has been able to access grants from donors, but its success in this respect is not a strategy that one can commend to MFIs that seek to achieve financial independence as commercially viable 'businesses' in the microfinance arena. The PRDA could significantly reduce its costs if it replaced funds for on-lending that are borrowed at commercial bank rates by savings of the people associated with the community-based organizations through which it operates its programme. Even so, one ought to add that despite the appearance of donor 'dependence' associated with the PRDA strategy, at the national level the NGO also operates a parallel programme to build up a trust fund devoted to investments in income-generating enterprises that are intended to make PRDA largely independent of donor funds for its operating expenses by the year 2005. At the end of 1995, the PRDA Trust Fund reported a financial corpus in excess of Rp6 million, which was earning net income of around Rp1 million per year; clearly not enough to maintain a significant flow of subsidies to support an expanding microfinance programme. These funds are not reflected in the estimates of PRDA subsidies received, as the extent of the flow from this source to the microfinance programme is not known.

From the figures in Table 6.7 one gets the impression that the TCCS is the most donor-dependent of all four MFIs studied. Yet, it is the TCCS that has consciously chosen to follow a strategy of outreach and growth based on the principle that it did not want to develop donor dependency by accessing grants as the source for its on lending funds or for its operational expenses. RRDB executives, on the other hand, reported that they have relied on savings deposits as the main basis of growth in their activities and did not seek donor funds because they did not have the contacts or the information needed to do so. The relatively poor financial viability status of the GPU stands in sharp relief to that of the other three MFIs, yet this result could easily be transformed if the GPU recycled a higher proportion of its savings on hand rather than continuing to allow some other programme within the HNB to benefit from the use of these funds. In the case of the GPU there is in fact a negative subsidy equal to the flow of benefits realized by these other programmes. This negative subsidy has not been calculated in assessing the GPU's financial viability status, but GPU executives were confident that they would be able to more than double their client base and achieve financial viability in only three more years of operation. All four MFIs confidently expressed the view that doubling the number of their borrowers within four years was a realizable objective, and the figures indicate that if growth is associated with increased use of female fieldstaff, growth will be associated with increasing financial viability.

Constraints to Greater Microfinance Outreach

Sri Lanka is at once a shining example of what can be achieved to lift the socio-economic indicators of development to levels that are the envy of most developing countries and an enigma. Despite the great strides made in bringing mortality rates down, raising literacy levels and bringing the benefits of a safe water source and electricity within the reach of most citizens, the proportion of the population in Sri Lanka that remains below the poverty line is still unacceptably high and the number of people living below the poverty line is increasing. The reasons for these trends in poverty are many and greater access to microfinance is not a panacea for them. However, greater commitment to an expanded microfinance programme in Sri Lanka is part of the solution.

The government of Sri Lanka has sought to provide an enabling environment for the growth of MFIs through the stimulus of macroeconomic growth. This is important but it is not enough. The advance of economic welfare also requires peace and the certainty that comes with assured national security. In this respect there is much yet to be achieved in Sri Lanka. The persistence of civil unrest and military action remains the single most important constraint to effective growth and reduced poverty through the expansion of microfinance services to poor households in Sri Lanka.

The skills needed to manage and guide the growth of an MFI from a small community-based initiative to a significant, financially viable institution requires skills that are scarce in all countries with higher than acceptable head-count indices. Sri Lanka is no exception, as shown by the lack of consistency between MFIs in accounting standards, management practices and documentation. At lower levels of staffing, the experience of the TCCS suggests that there is a rich load of qualified workers available to be tapped, without the need for salary levels that are many multiples of the national average income per person. The savings that can be made in salaries can then usefully be used in providing new recruits with the sort of hands-on practical training that is needed to convince even high school graduates that the poor are trustworthy and bankable.

As a South Asian country with many socio-cultural features that appear common to Bangladesh, India, Pakistan and Nepal, it is a mistake to assume that successful models of MFIs operating in those neighbouring economies will transfer easily into Sri Lanka. In fact there is likely to be a strong bias against attempts to replicate, for example, the Grameen Bank model, because it is from Bangladesh. This opposition is an expression of cultural pride and a deeply felt sense of competition between the nationals of the region. MFI programmes must be so acknowledged as to encourage local people to develop their own MFIs, without pressure to credit Grameen, the BRAC, AIM or BKK or any other successful MFI in Asia for particular design and management features of the local model.

A great strength of existing MFIs in Sri Lanka is the productivity of their savings mobilization efforts. However, the contribution that this success has made to the alleviation of poverty in Sri Lanka is limited by the failure of these same MFIs to recycle these funds into poor households as loans. This is a poverty-targeting issue, that present bias among microfinance operators in Sri Lanka does little to overcome. Reasonably widely held negative attitudes towards the bankability of the poor and especially the poorest of the poor (which was encountered in all the MFIs visited in the course of fieldwork for the research reported here), is a constraint to enthusiastic outreach and poverty targeting in Sri Lanka. If savings mobilization is to make the contribution that it ought to the alleviation of poverty through the intermediation activities of MFIs in Sri Lanka, these attitudes must change.

At an institutional level, there is a need for further financial sector deregulation in Sri Lanka to enable all MFIs to mobilize savings and adopt strategies of growth that lead to financial viability. Without the legal right to offer savings services to their members, NGOs can never expect to see their fledgling microfinance activities develop the range of intermediation roles that an effective MFI must have to facilitate poverty reduction and increasing capacity for self-help. In Sri Lanka this will entail the lifting of current legal restrictions on savings activity and the rationalization of current taxation regimes. While financial sector deregulation along these lines is to be welcomed, some additional guidance from the agencies of government is also warranted to ensure the healthy development of the MFI sector. Guidelines are required on acceptable fiduciary standards, the transparency of accounts and accountability of MFI staff to members for deposits held and income disbursed. Action by officials in these areas would go a long way to ensuring that new or expanded MFIs receive from potential clients the same sort of confidence in their integrity and reliability as is given to formal-modern-sector banks in Sri Lanka.

Notes

1 The numbers in the Sri Lankan armed services increased from only 20,000 in 1983 to more than 175,000 in 1996.

2 Though the figures on the number of poor in Sri Lanka vary widely, statistics show that more than 44 per cent (7.5 million) of the population qualified for food stamps in 1988. Since food stamp beneficiaries are supposed to be only those considered as low-income receivers living below the official poverty line, one is forced to conclude either that poverty is rife in Sri Lanka or the FSP is being seriously abused, as suggested in Peiris and Nilaweera, 1985. The Sri Lankan High Level Committee of Officials which was charged with examining poverty in Sri Lanka in 1988 concluded that: 'On the basis of calorie intake, nearly 25 per cent of the people (4.25 million) are below the poverty line ... 7.5 million people (44.2 per cent) live on food stamps. 37 per cent of children 0 to 5 years suffer from chronic malnutrition. Over 50 per cent of the pre-school children are affected by nutritional anaemia' (pp. ii–iii).

3 The fieldwork on which the data reported in this chapter is based was gathered by Sunimal Fernando on behalf of the APDC Microfinance Assessment Programme in preparation for Bank Poor '96 held at the APDC in December 1996. The survey results were originally reported in Sunimal Fernando, 1996.

III

East Asia and the Pacific Islands

7

Microfinance in Indonesia: Experiments in Linkages and Policy Reform

Uben Parhusip and H. Dieter Seibel

Introduction

Since research for this chapter was begun, Indonesia has experienced what can only be described as a radical financial meltdown such as has never before been recorded in the modern history of economic development. The value of the Indonesian Rupiah has collapsed by 800 per cent in less than a year. Despite greatly increased international assistance, the flight of capital and the disintegration of import-dependent economic activity continues. The incidence of poverty is estimated by the World Bank to have increased at least three-fold and the rush to the bottom of the economic downswing showed no sign of abating, even six months after the change of leadership from Suharto to Habibie.

In this chapter we have not found it necessary to 'revise' what we have written about microfinance in Indonesia in the light of Indonesia's economic crisis. Instead, we judge that the crisis has made it all the more urgent that MFIs should be given top priority as institutions that are able to help poor households weather the storm. Unlike the import-dependent manufacturing enterprises of Java, for example, poor people operate in an economic world that is largely insulated from the grossest effects of the collapse in the value of the exchange rate. Poor households need the assistance of institutions that can help them establish or rebuild the income streams they need to survive and recover. While it is likely that MFIs are not well suited to the dispersal of relief, rescue payments or emergency assistance, microfinance providers can accelerate the rate at which people recover and establish 'sustainable' investments in their own economic future.

Table 7.1   Inflation, Exchange and Interest Rates in Indonesia, 1990–5

Year	Inflation Rate	Exchange Rate	Changes	Average Lending Rate		Average Fixed Deposit Rate
				Working Capital	Investment	
1990	7.8%	1905	–	21.0%	20.2%	17.75%
1991	9.5%	1997	4.8%	25.1%	19.3%	21.18%
1992	6.9%	2074	3.8%	22.1%	18.4%	21.13%
1993	9.7%	2118	2.2%	18.0%	16.0%	16.25%
1994	8.5%	2205	4.1%	17.0%	15.0%	12.96%
1995	9.4%	2305	4.5%	19.3%	16.0%	16.22%

Sources: Central Bureau of Statistics: *Indonesia Economic Report 1994*; Bank Indonesia: *Indonesian Financial Statistics*, March 1996.

The economic crisis has not destroyed the impressive capacity for outreach MFIs in Indonesia. On the contrary, it is the capacity of these institutions to support, nurture and encourage local-level investment in income and employment generation that is critical to helping the poor of Indonesia to cope with the collapse of economic activity. In order to ensure that this capacity is utilized, the government of Indonesia would do well not to ignore microfinance in its effort to overhaul and strengthen institutions delivering services to the poor. It is to a study of that capacity to which we now turn.

Incidence of Poverty

Since 1983 Indonesia has pursued, with considerable success, a policy of growth and stability based on the gradual deregulation of the finance sector, privatization and budgetary reform. During the period of 1990–5 the per capita gross domestic product grew at an annual average rate of 5.0 per cent. The rate of population increase is declining and is forecast to fall to 1.9 per cent by the end of the twentieth century. The inflation rate during 1990–5 was maintained at one digit, the lowest 4.6 per cent in 1992 and the highest 9.7 per cent in 1993, and the Rupiah lost only 4 per cent of its US$ value during that period. These data are summarized in Table 7.1.

Economic historians will record that the almost two decades of sustained economic growth brought about a sharp reduction in the incidence of poverty in Indonesia from more than 60 per cent of the population in the period prior to 1970 to less than 20 per cent at the start of the 1990s, and with urban poverty almost abolished. The financial meltdown of 1997 has largely reversed this achievement, with the locus of poverty in the urban centres of Java. Three major factors have been cited for the economic gains made before 1997: clear and explicit government policies that encouraged agricultural growth and private investment, sustained economic growth

Table 7.2 Provinces with High Incidence of Poverty in Indonesia, 1990 and 1993

Province	1990	1993
East Timor	43.0%	36.20%
Maluku	29.0%	23.93%
West Kalimantan	24.0%	21.84%
East Nusa Tenggara (NTT)	28.0%	25.05%
Central Kalimantan	24.0%	20.81%
West Nusa Tenggara	23.1%	19.52%
South Kalimantan	21.0%	18.61%

driven by massive public sector infrastructure expenditures, and, since 1983, financial and economic deregulation. Statistics show that the annual rates of poverty reduction increased after the financial deregulation of 1983. Microfinance has played a role in this process, but it has done little to alter the remarkable inequality in the distribution of income and wealth that persists in Indonesia. The poorest 40 per cent of households receive less than 15 per cent of total national income.

Officially the poor are categorized as those people who live below the poverty line defined by the Bureau of Statistics as the capability to afford expenditures for 2100 calories of food per capita per day plus expenses for essentials like housing, fuel, clothing, education, health and transport. In 1993 this was equivalent to an annual per capita income of Rp258,000 (US$112) or Rp334,000 (US$145) in urban and Rp219,000 (US$95) in rural areas.

Poverty distribution varies from province to province (Table 7.2), but the largest number of poor people is found on Java, by far the most populous island of Indonesia. In 1993 the poor on Java comprised 58 per cent of the total number of poor people in Indonesia. The highest incidence of poverty was found in East Timor, Maluku, East and West Nusa Tenggara, West, Central and South Kalimantan. On the whole, the incidence of poverty and the degree of poverty is greater, although more variable, in eastern Indonesia due to isolation, difficult agroclimatic conditions, poor infrastructure, and the low level of commercial activities and economic growth. The economic reversal that started in 1996–7 is changing this pattern, and is expected to result in a concentration of poor households in Java and in the urban centres where unemployment arising from the shut-down of factory production is also concentrated.

In their microcredit design study of 1993, Development Alternatives Inc. and P.T. Indoconsult identified the following prominent characteristics of the poor in Indonesia: female-headed households (generally divorcees and widows); elderly – over 65 years of age the majority of whom are women; the unemployed, under-employed and the intermittently employed; fishermen who do not own boats; agricultural labourers; plantation and factory workers paid below the minimum wage; petty traders; low-paid artisans;

unskilled construction workers and miners; tenants and sharecroppers; owners of less than a quarter hectare of agricultural land; shifting cultivators; tribal people; people living in isolated villages; hunters; sea nomads; transmigrants and resettled families; urban village residents in congested areas with inadequate facilities; recent migrants to city living and working in the informal sector; and scavengers.

Poverty-Alleviation Policies and Programmes

Several prominent programmes had been developed prior to the 1990s to alleviate poverty, the most relevant to microfinance being:

P4K (Income Generating Project for Marginal Farmers under the Ministry of Agriculture in co-operation with BRI);
BRI-Udes (rural credit and savings by a state-owned commercial bank, BRI);
PHBK (linking banks and SHGs under Bank Indonesia, the central bank);
UPPKA (Income Generating Project for Family Planning Participants); and
IDT (*Presidential Instruction on Backward Villages*).

The most recent and largest poverty-alleviation programme is *Inpres Desa Tertinggal (IDT)* No. 2/1993 or *Presidential Instruction on Backward Villages* issued in August 1993. It is based on the positive experience of the PHBK, P4K, UPPKA and other projects working through financial SHGs. It is a national programme centring on poor villages rather than poor households or individuals. The villages are identified through economic and social infrastructure indicators. The IDT programme covers approximately 34 per cent of rural villages or 20,633 in absolute terms.

The IDT funds are provided to SHGs (Kelompok Masyarakat, POKMAS) consisting of poor families and on-lent by the SHGs to their members on the basis of an approved plan for their utilization, mainly as working capital. Loans have to be repaid with interest. The IDT allocations are expected to be seed money for viable and ultimately self-reliant local financial institutions modelled after semi-formal institutions such as BKK (Central Java), LPD (Bali) or LPN (West Sumatra) to be eventually transformed into formal village banks (BPR). An additional component of IDT is rural infrastructure development for improved access to markets, health services, training and employment opportunities, and for rural institution building.

Like any large-scale government programme IDT is fraught with hazard. An evaluation mission concluded in April 1995 that there is no guarantee that the project results are sustainable, the most immediate result of this project, improved understanding of the IDT programme on the part of the villagers, being constantly undermined. Furthermore, the structures designed to provide community assistance have been largely ineffective and failed to be committed to the principles of participatory development. Facilitators have no skill in the preparation and implementation of business plans; they have little production or commercial experience; and they tend to recommend activities with limited scope for profit. One may surmise that IDT will only be successful to the extent that concerns for institutional viability and sustainability will outweigh the concern for short-term political gains from liberal disbursement of funds.

Financial Institutions and Their Outreach to the Poor

Access to credit has been considered by the government as a major instrument in the promotion of equitable growth and the reduction of poverty. Since the early 1970s, the government has used two major instruments of promoting access to credit: the provision of subsidized credit mainly through government banks; and the establishment of semi-formal financial institutions at the provincial level which largely mobilized their own resources and were exempt from the interest rate regulations that prevailed until mid-1983. The subsidized credit approach was largely given up as ineffectual and wasteful in 1990 when 30 of the 34 major programmes were scrapped.

Microfinance constitutes a growing business for government-owned BRI which counts under its mandate 3500 sub-branches, 9000 registered local financial institutions (unit desa or village institutions), numerous subsidiary private and public banks, plus literally hundreds of thousands of informal institutions scattered across virtually every village in Indonesia. They provide financial services to a segmented market of the poor, the not-so-poor and the non-poor, the market shares of which are not exactly known. Data on microfinance services by MFIs and BRI are presented in Table 7.3.

Rural MFIs are quite heterogeneous. They are classified into: BPR-Non-BKD, BPR-BKD and LDKPs/SFIs (Lembaga Dana dan Kredit Pedesaan/SFIs). The banking law of 1992 provides rules for the establishment of a fully licensed rural credit bank (BPR) under central bank supervision and the transformation of LDKPs into BPR (BPR-Non-BKD). The minimum paid-up capital for a new BPR is Rp50 million (US$21,692). A new BPR cannot operate within the provincial and district capital cities. It is only allowed to operate within the sub-district where it is located (though it appears that this rule is not rigidly enforced). The second type of BPR is BPR-BKD. The BKD (Badan Kredit Desa) is a village-based hitherto semi-formal financial institution established and owned by local villages and supervised by BRI. The third type of BPR is called the LDKP (Lembaga Dana dan Kredit Pedesaan) or *rural fund and credit institution*. Included in this third type are the BKPD (Bank Karya Produksi Desa), LPK (Lembaga Perkreditan Kecamatan), BKK (Badan Kredit Kecamatan), KURK (Kredit Usaha Rakyat Kecil), LPD (Lembaga Perkreditan Desa), LKP (Lembaga Kredit Pedesaan) and LPN (Lumbung Pitih Nagari). Sponsored by provincial and local governments in the early 1970s as

Table 7.3 Formal and Semi-formal Financial Institutions in Indonesia (December 1995) (All amounts in US$ million)

Type of Financial Institution	Number	Credit		Funds Mobilized		Total Financial Services	
		Accounts ('000)	Amount ($ Million)	Accounts ('000)	Amount ($ million)	Accounts ('000)	Amount ($ million)
1. BPR (Rural Credit Bank) and secondary banks	1,948	1,232	679.4	2,969	531.9	4,252	1,211.3
2. LDKPs (small financial institutions (SFIs))	1,978	261	97.2	456	51.2	716	148.4
3. BKDs (village credit body, include BPR ex BKD)	5,435	955	40.3	1,176	27.3	2,130	67.7
Sub-total MFIs	9,361	2,448	816.9	4,601	610.4	7,098	1,427.4
4. BRI-Udes	3,482	2,264	1,385.7	14,483	2,610.0	16,747	3,995.7
Total, 1 to 4	12,843	4,712	2,202.6	19,084	3220.4	23,845	5423.1
5. Commercial banks	240	91,168	101,783.5	49,904	93,173.1	141,072	194,956.6

Sources: 1. Bank Indonesia: *Annual Report 1995/6*, May 1996; 2. *Indonesian Statistical Report*, March 1996; 3. *Statistik Kredit Koperasi dan Kredit Kecil* (KUK), January 1996; 4. BRI.
Exchange rate: US$1 = Rp2,305.

non-licensed rural credit institutions, LDKPs are now required to receive a BPR licence within five years or close down.

Until 1983 BRI was a major provider of subsidized targeted credit in rural areas, with a repayment performance around 40 per cent. After the deregulation of June 1983, it carefully crafted two commercial products: a rural savings scheme with a lottery component (SIMPEDES) to mobilize its own resources at village level; and a rural credit scheme (KUPEDES) which operate on market terms. All its sub-district operations were commercialized, i.e. the banking units were turned into profit centres; and they were to mobilize their own resources, cover their costs from the margin, and recover their loans (which they did at a rate of 97.5 per cent) − lest sub-branch managers lose their credit authority (and opportunities for promotion). All other operations, particularly programmes carried out on behalf of the government and of donors, were kept from sub-district branches and confined to the branch level. With this model, BRI became one of the most successful banks with a rural mandate in Asia-Pacific, serving by the end of 1996 some 18 million clients, with its rural banking network completely self-reliant (fully mobilizing its own resources) and viable (covering its costs from the margin and making a profit from which the expansion of the system is being financed).

As of 31 December 1995, 9271 semi-formal and formal MFIs provided small loans to 2.45 million borrowers amounting to US$816.9 million loan outstanding − compared to 2.26 million borrowers of BRI sub-branches with a total volume of US$1,385.7 million loan outstanding. At the same time MFIs served 4.60 million savers and mobilized savings amounting to US$627.7 million − compared to 14.48 million savers at BRI sub-branches and US$2,610 million in savings. The BRI thus outperforms the totality of MFIs by a considerable margin: 16.75 million microfinance accounts in BRI vs. 7.10 million accounts in over 9000 MFIs. However, while they are competitors, their competition serves a healthy purpose: to increase the supply of financial services to the lower segments of the rural population. Together, they provide for 4.51 million loan accounts and 19.08 million savings deposit accounts, totalling 23.6 million accounts.

The lending volume of MFIs is only 2.2 per cent of that of the commercial banking sector; while MFI savings deposits are equivalent to only 0.7 per cent of commercial bank deposits. In terms of outreach, which is somewhat difficult to determine as figures relate to accounts rather than clients, MFI loan and savings accounts amount to 7.8 per cent and 9.5 per cent respectively, of those of commercial banks. However, a number of national and provincial commercial banks do provide a considerable volume of microfinance services in rural and urban areas. No data are available to determine the exact proportions. The overall volume of microfinance services in Indonesia may thus be somewhat higher than indicated by the figures on MFIs and BRI.

Perhaps one of the most remarkable features of microfinance in Indonesia is the sector's self-financing capacity. Together, BRI and MFIs fully finance their lending operations from internal resources, but BRI more so than local MFIs. This is all the more remarkable as BRI as a government-owned agricultural development bank was accustomed, until 1983, to obtain most of its resources from the government at preferential terms.

BRI's rural financial operations have been very profitable. The consolidated totality of MFIs, however, has been taking losses in recent years: US$11.7 million in 1993, US$11.3 million in 1994, and US$9.5 million in 1995, amounting to 1.6 per cent, 1.3 per cent and 0.9 per cent respectively, of financial operations. In the three preceding years, the sector as a whole showed substantial profits, amounting to 1.5 per cent of its financial operations in 1990, 2.2 per cent in 1991 and 1.5 per cent in 1992.

Regulatory Framework

Starting in June 1983 Indonesia has gradually and consistently deregulated its financial system. This has been paralleled by the deregulation of its foreign trade regime. There are many that would argue that the process has been too slow and lacking in transparency, but the steps taken since 1983 can be summarized as follows:

- *1983*: Interest rate autonomy is given to all banks, state-owned and private. Bank Indonesia as the central bank drops direct interest rate controls and adopts market-oriented monetary policies. Between 1983 and 1990 savings mobilization increased 6.7-fold, bank loans outstanding 6.4-fold. From 1990 to 1995 savings mobilization increased 2.5-fold, bank loans outstanding 2.4-fold.
- *1988*: Bank Indonesia deregulates the institutional framework by easing the establishment of new banks and the opening of branches. A new rural banking law was passed, permitting the establishment of rural banks (BPR) with an equity capital of Rp50 million, requiring the existing semi-formal financial institutions to be eventually transformed into formal banks (BPR). Up to 1995 1643 formal rural banks (BPR) were established. The total number of registered SFIs grew from 8003 in 1990 to 9271 in 1995. During the same period the number of commercial banks increased from 171 to 240 and the number of their branches from 3563 to 5191.
- *1990*: Bank Indonesia withdraws most of the interest rate subsidies. Commercial banks are required to allocate at least 20 per cent of their portfolio to small, either directly or through BPR (with little if any direct benefit to the poor).
- *1991*: In response to some spectacular bank failures, Bank Indonesia steps up bank supervision and imposes a capital adequacy ratio.
- *1992*: A new banking act deregulates bank ownership. Only two types of

banks are recognized: commercial banks with a paid-in capital of Rp10 billion (US$4.34 million) and rural banks (BPR) with a paid-in capital of Rp50 million (US$21,692).

With the deregulation of interest rates in 1983, financial services in terms of savings deposit facilities and credit for the lower sections of the population have greatly increased, particularly through government-owned BRI, provincial government-owned BPDs, and a number of private banks and smaller institutions. None of them has exclusively targeted the poor, but has included the poor among their clientele.

With the bank deregulation of 1988, the number of village banks and rural branches grew rapidly, increasing the outreach of this banking segment to both the non-poor and the poor. This deregulation has also increased competition, forcing small institutions like BSD, our second case study from Indonesia, first to register as a BPR and then to increase its outreach. This bank did so, among other things, through the addition of the group approach as a cost-effective approach of banking with poor, almost doubling the number of its borrowers and increasing the number of its savers by about one-third. The new banking law of 1992 also requires all registered MFIs in Indonesia to be transformed within five years into formal village banks. Some NGOs, among them Yayasan Bina Swadaya as one of the leading institutions, have been inspired by the law on village banks to establish their own banks. Very few MFIs target exclusively the poor, but many do include the poor among their clientele. These are the financial institutions that have helped to reduce poverty in Indonesia by giving the poor access to savings and credit services.

There are also hundreds of thousands of informal SHGs with savings and credit activities, either of indigenous origin or founded by government organizations or NGOs. There are numerous programmes, most under NGO guidance, that have demonstrated the ability of either upgrading the capacity of existing SHGs or establishing new SHGs. Most importantly, under the umbrella of central bank permission, an increasing number of them have gained access to banks, particularly through Bank Indonesia's own linkage banking programme (PHBK). In the process substantial training capacities have been built up in NGOs geared at the upgrading of SHGs; and the promotion of linkages with national, regional and local banks.

Microfinance Capacity Assessment

Out of a vast number of institutions and programmes with microfinance services in Indonesia, four case studies focusing fully or partially on the poor have been selected, each with a special story to tell:

- Mitra Karya of East Java (MKEJ) established in 1993, a Grameen Bank replicator with funding from the Grameen Trust Fund and Bank Negara

Indonesia (BNI) and implemented by the Research Centre of Brawijaya University in East Java.

- BPR BSD, a self-financed private village bank established in 1970 in D.I. Yogjakarta on Java which in the past dealt mainly with individual clients but, inspired by Bank Indonesia's linkage banking programme, also adopted the group lending approach.

- P4K (Proyek Pembinaan Peningkatan Pendapatan Petani Kecil – Income-generating Project for Small Farmers) first established in 1980/1 and restarted in 1989/90, a large national poverty-lending project of the Ministry of Agriculture and BRI with substantial financial assistance from the IFAD and technical assistance from the UNDP.

- the BPD in Semarang, Central Java, established in 1990 as a commercial bank with financial assistance from Misereor, Germany, by an Indonesian NGO that was established in 1963. This NGO had a longstanding experience in the promotion of microenterprise activities among the poor including microsavings and microcredit programmes since 1973. By setting up a bank of its own the NGO was able to formalize its savings and credit operations on a commercial basis.

Of the four cases, BPR BSD has been singled out for a more elaborate presentation. To readers familiar with donor-supported approaches to banking with the poor, BSD presents an outstanding example of a private institution that is self-reliant in terms of resource mobilization, financially viable, has financed its expansion from profits, and has substantially increased its outreach to the poor as a market segment on commercial terms. As it employs both the individual and the group methodology of financial services, it also permits an assessment of the effectiveness of the two strategies. Its five private founders established the then *PT Bank Madya Shinta Daya* as a limited liability company with an equity capital of Rp1.0 million (US$40,000 at the 1970 exchange rate) in the sub-district of Kalasan-Prambanan. As Prambanan was the site of a famous Hindu temple dating back to the eighth century, the bank derived its name and philosophy of lending to the rural people including the poor from Dewi Shinta who stand for honesty and self-reliance. Operations started on 20 August 1970, with a staff of eight in a small building of 80 square metres floor space. The bank, which is far from unique in its outlook and operations, has grown considerably since then but has retained its modest appearance.

Outreach

Specialized programmes with a sole or major focus on the poor have had a limited outreach. Using end-1995 data, the outreach of the institutions and programmes covered by these four case studies in terms of borrowers was only 9.7 per cent of that of BRI and 4.7 per cent of BRI and MFIs combined.

Their outreach in terms of savers was 2.6 per cent of that of BRI and 1.9 per cent of BRI and MFIs combined. While the role of these special programmes on a national scale is small with regard to access to credit, it is almost negligible with regard to access to savings deposit facilities. However, some of them have made illuminating inroads into the market segment of the poor and demonstrated how the poor can be reached by institutional finance in cost-effective ways.

An example of very restricted outreach is a Grameen replication project, MKEJ in East Java, our first case study. In 1993 it started with 105 participants organized in 21 small groups. In 1994 it expanded to 178 groups with 889 members and in 1995 to 225 groups with 1125 members, all of them women. Following the Grameen Bank system, it strictly adheres to a group size of five, a cultural novelty on Java where almost every woman and man belongs to a multitude of groups, including financial SHGs of a much larger size. The project is now under consolidation, with limited expansion capacities. MKEJ strives for what it considers its optimum size of 2000 members in 400 groups as of 1998. There is certainly a place for small institutions with a purely local outreach. However, MKEJ is unlikely to achieve the size required for registration as a formal rural bank (BPR).

BSD, our second case study, is a rural bank that was established with private money and funded its expansion from profits, not subsidies. With 43,000 accounts and a clientele of over 30,000, comprising 30,340 savers and 12,656 borrowers as of December 1995, it has shown that privately owned village banks can have a considerable outreach at the local level that does not need to be subsidized. Moreover, as it records 69 per cent of its borrowers and 85 per cent of its savers as poor, it has also demonstrated that financial services to the poor by private banks can be profitable and self-sustained.

For the first twenty years of existence the bank made no conscious effort of financial deepening among the poor. This began to change in 1989 when the bank started to participate in a project *Linking Banks and Self-Help Groups* under the umbrella of Bank Indonesia. After an expensive and ultimately abortive attempt of working through a local NGO as a financial intermediary, the bank decided to seek out its own savings and credit groups, set up a special group lending department, and hired its own fieldworkers, some of them former NGO staff. As of December 1995, the bank effectively worked with 310 groups comprising 7750 members. This has allowed the bank to virtually double its outreach to borrowers from 6456 to 12,656 and to increase its outreach to savers by about one-third from 22,940 to 30,340. The impact of the newly introduced group approach, discussed in great detail in the last section of this chapter, is most dramatic with regard to access to credit to the poor.

The following conclusions can be drawn from the experience of BSD:

● Private rural banks can and do provide financial services to the poor;

- the non-poor are somewhat more likely than the poor to be borrowers while the poor are far more likely to utilize the bank's deposit facilities than the non-poor;
- the group approach extends the outreach of the bank to the poor;
- in terms of additionality and financial deepening, the group approach is most successful in providing access to credit for the poor; and
- there may be an additional impact of bank access on the volume of internal savings and credit operations within the groups, which was beyond the scope of this study.

The biggest outreach example is probably P4K, our third case study, which is a national poverty-alleviation programme with a rapid expansion rate. Using the most recent data for March 1996, P4K now reaches 486,000 carefully screened poor and very poor families (with a per capita income equivalent to less than 320 kg, or 240 kg respectively, of rice per annum) in 45,400 groups and 2762 self-organized associations with their own autonomous savings and credit activities. A total of 37,300 of the groups are active borrowers; the remaining 18 per cent are either under preparation, have died or have opted for self-reliance. However, despite its spectacular growth, P4K still has reached less than 10 per cent of the population officially recorded as poor. During the six-year period, March 1990 to March 1996, bank and internal group savings have surged from US$28.6 million to US$2,759.2 million; credit disbursed from US$384.4 million to US$32,518.9 million. Its impact has been remarkable, though data gathered from the informal sector need to be interpreted with great caution. According to an evaluation by the IFAD, income has increased by 33 per cent after the first loan and 46 per cent after the third loan, to which indirect multiplier effects from multiple reinvestments have to be added. Eighty-two per cent of the beneficiaries report an increase in the volume of production, and 65 per cent in the quality of production. Employment in each beneficiary household has gone up by 27 hours per week. There are also psychological and social effects on the self-confidence of the poor and their standing within the community. In addition, there are institutional effects with regard to the emergence of self-sustained savings and credit associations at the grassroots level and the building of a group formation and guidance capacity within the ministry with its unique delivery structure of 33,000 field extension workers.

A particularly interesting case is the BPD in Semarang, our fourth case study. As an NGO with a social mandate, the BPD has focused on financial services to the poor, particularly the financing of their income-generating activities. To put its activities on a legal basis, it made use of the deregulation of 1988 and with substantial donor assistance it established a commercial bank in 1991 with an equity capital of Rp10 billion (US$5 million at the 1991 exchange rate), only to find out that it takes substantial capacity-inputs until a bank of that size has trained the staff to serve vast numbers of the poor.

Through a unique system of ambulant bankers who are the bank's substitute for branching out, its clientele by the end of 1995 comprised 13,315 accounts (the number of physical clients being smaller, presumably less than 12,000), 89 per cent of them savings accounts and 11 per cent debit accounts. Of its savers, 91 per cent are poor, but only 37 per cent of its borrowers are poor. Under pressures of viability, the bank is forced to concentrate its business, in terms of volume, on the non-poor. At the same time, it is swamped by savings. It finds itself unable to expand its lending business at the same rate and is left with a huge liquidity surplus. With less than 500 poor borrowers, the poor can hardly be said to be benefiting from the heavily donor-subsidized services of the bank.

The inadequacy of the various approaches to fully eradicate poverty has caused great concern in the office of the President, which has, in 1992, declared war on poverty with a focus on poor villages through IDT. Discussions were held on whether this objective was best achieved through a massive supply of subsidized credit or through a strengthening of institutions supplying microcredit at market rates. The final decision was in favour of a combined group lending and local financial institution-building approach modelled after the P4K and the PHBK experience. Up to US$200 million are lent annually to 20,633 poor villages, each of which may receive Rp20 million ($8,677) per village for three years. Funds are on-lent by the groups to their members at locally determined terms. With the help of facilitators of widely varying competence, the groups are required to either evolve into an autonomous local financial institution, or merge with an existing one.

There is a notable absence of financial institutions or programmes of any significance specialized on women in Indonesia. To varying degrees, women are part of the market of any financial institution; but most of them have no financial products differentiated by sex, nor do they report sex-specific data. Few formal institutions, including formal and semi-formal MFIs, have focused on women only. On the other hand, informal financial institutions of the RoSCA type are almost considered a female monopoly in Indonesia; upgrading them would greatly contribute to financial deepening for the women participants and indirectly contribute to their outreach a deepened outreach in this case. Special programmes focusing solely on the poor like P4K made the case that a strong though not necessarily exclusive focus on women will greatly contribute to the viability of the programme and also be more effective in poverty alleviation in terms of donor investment. If this course is pursued further, it might pave the way for transforming project operations into large numbers of autonomous local MFIs owned and run by women.

In Table 7.4 below, summary data as of December 1995 are given on outreach of the four institutions covered by the case studies: Grameen-replication-project MKEJ for some 1125 women; BSD, a rural bank with about 30,000 customers; the BPD, a new NGO universal bank with close to

Table 7.4   Outreach of Four MFIs in Indonesia, 1995*

MFI	Number of Borrowers	% of Poor Borrowers	Number of Savers	% of Poor Savers
MKEJ	1,078	100%	1,125	100%
BSD	12,656	69%	30,340	62%
BPD	1,322	37%	11,893	91%
P4K	203,790	100%	328,670	100%

* Some of the data given in the text are more recent than December 1995. The original data on P4K were on groups of an average size of ten members. Borrowers and savers normally overlap and cannot be added up. In programmes with a forced saving component the number of savers usually equals the total number of participants; in banks the total number of customers is likely to be somewhat larger than the number of savers. BSD and the BPD, like any other bank, give no breakdown by sex of customer.

11,000 customers; and P4K with some 330,000 participants (1995) below the poverty line, about half of them women.

In sum, Indonesia has made great progress in extending financial services to almost all segments of the population. Instead of replicating successes of other countries, Indonesia, during a period of over a hundred years, has found its own unique way of coping with poverty and rural finance. In rural and microfinance, BRI with its almost three million small borrowers and now almost eighteen million small savers, is perhaps the biggest single provider of financial services. Numerous other banks, including provincial government-owned banks (BPD) and private banks like Bank Dagang Bali have extended their services to the poorer sections of the population, including SHGs of the poor. The 9000 registered MFIs, 1650 of them banks while the others are semi-formal financial institutions not falling under the banking law, represent a financial infrastructure which can potentially serve a large proportion of the population spread over 60,000 villages and cities. However, there are still poor areas and pockets of poor people that have been left out. How can they be reached?

If there is one major conclusion to be drawn from the Indonesian experience it might read: It is viable financial institutions that reach the poor; but programmes can pave the way! The main emphasis of any further attempt at poverty alleviation must concentrate on institution building: the establishment and upgrading of institutions owned by the poor, and of institutions providing services for a clientele that includes the poor. It is clear that no single approach or single type of institution will achieve this end. A systems approach to microfinance may be needed which promotes the access of all segments of the population to the services of financial institutions through a variety of strategies and gives special emphasis to the poor as a market segment and, at the same time, as potential owners of member-based financial institutions:

● Assist informal financial institutions to upgrade their financial operations and acquire an appropriate legal status, thus evolving into semi-financial institutions with deepened services and increased outreach.

- Assist semi-formal financial institutions to upgrade their financial operations and evolve, where feasible, into village banks (BPR).
- Assist informal, semi-formal and formal MFIs to link up with banks as refinancing institutions, thus strengthening their financial service capacity and deepened outreach.
- Assist the poor in poor villages, in the informal sector and in pockets of poverty to organize themselves in SHGs by using the P4K experience; assist them in upgrading their activities and in gaining access to the financial services of banks.
- Assist MFIs to open a window for targeting the poor through the group approach, linking the MFI to existing SHGs.
- Assist poverty-alleviation projects in increasing women's participation and in transforming their local financial operations into autonomous local MFIs owned and run by women.
- Assist rural and commercial banks in establishing business relations with MFIs to refinance their activities, thus strengthening their financial deepening and outreach.

Financial Viability and Sustainability

In the long term, only viable financial institutions with sustainable financial services can increase their outreach. The issue of viability is thus not only of relevance to the health and survival of the institutions but also to the poor themselves as clients and owners of such institutions.

Before the onset of deregulation in 1983, financial viability was not a concern in the government's subsidized credit programmes. Repayment rates averaged about 40 per cent, and billions of dollars were lost over the years, with BRI as one of the major lenders involved. After 1983, government banks were increasingly forced to rely on their own resources. With technical assistance from the HIID, BRI responded by converting its 3400 village sub-branches into profit centres and introducing KUPEDES, a credit scheme with market rates of interest and powerful incentives for timely repayment. On the whole the BRI village units became fully self-reliant and profitable within six years since 1984, proof that government-owned agricultural banks can be successfully restructured into viable institutions with sustainable financial services to the poorer (though not the poorest) sections of the population. (The costs of foreign technical assistance are usually not included in the calculations of viability.)

The semi-formal financial institutions established through government initiative at village (like LPN, LPD, BKD) and sub-district levels (like BKK), after an initial equity booster by the government, were meant to turn into viable institutions. As they did not fall under the banking law, they were permitted, even before the deregulation of 1983, to charge rates of interest covering their costs and producing a profit. Many of the small village-based BKDs, which fell under BRI supervision, became dormant. Of the programmes under provincial bank supervision, approximately half the institutions were active. Those that fell under the USAID Financial Institutions Project (FIP) turned into viable institutions with a range of credit products. High interest rates ranging from about 30 per cent to 60 per cent p.a. not only covered their costs but also served as a major instrument of resource mobilization, financing the rapid expansion of the programme. They are proof that MFIs that are registered but do not fall under the banking law can be viable by charging market rates of interest even in the adverse policy environment before 1983.

The newly established formal sector village banks, BPR, and the older MFIs converted into BPR like BSD, have usually been successful in attaining viability, covering their costs through a variety of credit products adapted to the needs of their clients including some of the poor. This seems also to apply to the BPR set up by NGOs, which mostly cater for the poor. However, if such institutions are set up as universal banks requiring an equity capital of Rp10 billion (US$4.34 million), as in the BDP, our fourth case study, the attainment of full viability may be a long way off.

Indigenous informal financial institutions, among them hundreds of thousands of rotating and non-rotating savings and credit associations and other financial SHGs, but also moneylenders, are self-reliant from the onset, mobilizing their own resources, and they are viable, covering their costs and risks from the margin. Savings, credit and insurance services are sometimes combined in ingenious ways. Through the PHBK and other programmes, increasing numbers are given access to capacity building by NGOs and to bank sources of refinance.

Government organizations and NGOs have set up considerable numbers of solidarity groups with financial functions in Indonesia. Supplied with government or donor funds, such groups have rarely attained self-reliance and viability. With some success, the linkage-banking project, the PHBK, of Bank Indonesia and GTZ, has attempted to introduce a commercial approach to them, providing training to NGOs and SHGs to turn them into viable financial intermediaries. In response, some NGOs have established their own banks while some banks have established their own groups; and most of the groups under the programme are now viable, repaying their loans and covering their costs from the margin. However, access to bank refinancing has drastically increased their external resource base, simultaneously decreasing the degree of their self-reliance.

Donor-supported programmes and institutions like MKEJ, P4K and the BPD have generally not been self-reliant as they depend to a large degree on outside resources. However, viability is feasible, though at present not in reach for the two programmes.

Grameen-replicator MKEJ reports liabilities in the form of soft loans received (outstanding as of December 1995) to the amount of US$46,507 (about half from government-owned BNI and half from Grameen Trust Fund) compared to assets in the form of loans outstanding amounting to a mere US$32,104. With an interest rate of 10 per cent on savings deposits and 3.5 per cent on soft loans, a lending interest rate of 30 per cent and an on-time repayment rate of 98 per cent, its spread should be more than sufficient to cover its costs. This is indeed the case, as indicated by the degree of partial financial self-sufficiency of 110 per cent. However, given its dependency on donor funds, its degree of full financial self-sufficiency is only 39 per cent. MKEJ is a young institution with a relatively costly delivery system using the Grameen Bank's small group approach. It employs a field staff of four, one on average for 56 groups with a total of 280 members. During its third year, 1995, MKEJ showed its first profits (amounting to Rp11.7 million, or US$5,076), excluding, however, the honoraria paid to the university advisory team of three and ignoring the market value of the soft loan (on which MKEJ pays only 3.5 per cent interest), which contains a subsidy element of Rp7.0 million (US$3,037) if we use the rate of interest paid by MKEJ to its depositors (10 per cent), or Rp11.8 million (US$5,119) if we use the average savings deposit rate paid by BPR-type rural banks (14.5 per cent) as a calculatory basis. Moreover, all these calculations ignore the value of the time spent by the group members on their weekly meetings, which substantially add to borrower transaction costs. With total assets amounting to Rp127 million (US$55,098), loans outstanding of Rp74 million (US$32,104) and a deposit base of Rp12.3 million (US$5,336) and virtually no equity base, MKEJ would have to come a long way to grow into a formal village bank, a BPR, which would require a minimum paid-in equity capital of Rp50 million (US$21,692). So far MKEJ has not been able to demonstrate convincingly that the replication of the Grameen Bank approach in Indonesia may substantially improve the poor's access to financial services.

BSD is a private rural bank that was established with private capital (US$40,000 in 1970, equivalent to Rp92.2 million in 1995) and financed its expansion from its profits. Its net worth as of December 1995 stood at Rp495.8 million (US$215,098), comprising Rp179.5 million (US$77,874) in capital and Rp316.3 million (US$137,223) in retained earnings. Access to subsidized funds was not of any vital importance in the history of BSD. When Bank Indonesia scrapped most of its subsidized programmes and instead required commercial banks to allocate at least 20 per cent of their loan portfolio to small enterprises either directly or through rural banks, BSD took advantage of this offer. In 1993 and 1994, the bank obtained these funds amounting to Rp439.4 million (US$190,629) and Rp178.5 million (US$77,440) outstanding respectively, at interest rates below the market rate, namely at 8.0 per cent and 9.8 per cent respectively. Meanwhile these rates have been adjusted. In 1995 the bank's outside funds amounted to Rp163.0 million (US$70,716) on which it paid 16.6 per cent interest, which is

Table 7.5 Indicators of Efficiency, BSD, as of December 1995

Ratio of salaries to average assets:	*6.3%*
Ratio of operating costs to average assets:	10.0%
Ratio of financial costs to average assets:	12.9%
Return on average assets:	27.4%
Operating costs/total financial services:	16.5%
Total costs/total financial services:	22.7%
Average salary as % of GDP/capita:	325.5%
Degree of partial financial self-sufficiency:	111.0%
Degree of full financial self-sufficiency:	96.0%

above the average three-months fixed deposit rate as well as above the average rate paid by the bank to its depositors.

The average interest rate paid to its depositors was 15.2 per cent; the average interest rate charged to borrowers was 27.4 per cent; the default rate was 2.0 per cent. In 1995 the bank had access to outside funds but, unlike during the preceding years, not at a subsidized rate. Its total income as of June 1995 amounted to Rp822.5 million (US$356,833) comprising of interest income (95.4 per cent), operational income (3.4 per cent), and non-operational income (1.2 per cent). Net profit of the year according to the balance sheet was Rp63.3 million (US$27,462), which is equivalent to 7.7 per cent of its total income and 12.8 per cent of its net worth. Other efficiency measures provided on the basis of the case study are shown in Table 7.5.

BSD has a field staff of 17, each of which serves an average of 1767 customers. The bank employs two technologies: retail financial services to individuals and wholesale services through groups. By adding the wholesale technology the bank has substantially increased its outreach in terms of number of customers. However, in terms of viability, the crucial issue to the bank is: How much does the group technology add to the bank's business volume? And how profitable are the two technologies to the bank? The group technology is found by BSD to be viable as such, but adds little to the bank's overall viability. Why then does the bank engage in business with small groups? The bank's management explains this with future expectations. By providing financial services to group members with microenterprise activities, it contributes to their growth. As the members' microenterprises grow, so will their business with the bank. Besides providing a service to the community which covers its costs and even yields a profit, the bank hopes to grasp a larger market share which might pay off substantially in the future.

Can programmes that are government-implemented and donor-funded be viable? When BRI as a wholesale bank for P4K insisted on market rates of interest and timely repayment, not only was viability approximated, but outreach, which is affected by viability, substantially widened. P4K works through a fieldstaff of 2384 (December 1995) provided by the Ministry of Agriculture; each staff members serves an average of 14 groups with about 140 members.

P4K has taken several steps in the direction of viability and sustainability. It strengthens group associations which have spontaneously emerged in large numbers; they function as autonomous institutions, mobilizing their own resources and providing short-term credit at their own terms. The arrears ratio is still a mere 2.5 per cent, reflecting the seriousness of the borrowers, the effectiveness of incentives set up by BRI (groups, villages and districts with arrears over 10% are automatically cut off from repeat loans) and the quality of supervision by project staff. And finally, BRI has agreed to provide refinancing from its own resources beyond the availability of IFAD funds. In Table 7.6, some selected indicators of viability are presented. While the project is profitable to BRI as executing bank, the indicators show that P4K as a project is still a long way off financial self-sufficiency.

The BPD in Central Java is a commercial bank for the poor, which uses fieldworkers as itinerant banks, rather than branches. The expansion of the bank depends on its success in training fieldstaff in which the bank invests considerable time and resources. As a large part of the bank's equity has been provided by a donor at no cost to the bank, the assessment of the bank's viability hinges on whether or not a market rate of interest is included in the calculation as a hidden subsidy. In Table 7.6 the hidden subsidy element is excluded from the sustainability calculations. The degree of partial financial self-sufficiency is 90 per cent, and the degree of full financial self-sufficiency 58 per cent (157 per cent if income from interbank deposits is included).

The provision of equity capital has also contributed to the BPD's over-liquidity, which it has deposited in other banks. The loan to deposit ratio is still very low, but has increased substantially from 9.9 per cent in 1993 and 24.25 per cent in 1994 to 38.62 per cent in 1995. With an average interest rate on deposit of 14 per cent, a lending interest rate of 24 per cent and a default rate of 1 per cent, the BPD may eventually become viable, provided it

Table 7.6 Selected Indicators of Viability in Four MFIs in Indonesia, 1995

Indicator	MKEJ	P4K	BSD	BPD
Average interest rate on deposits	10.0%	10.0%	14.7%	14.0%
Interest rate to borrowers	30.0%	21.15%	27.4%	24.0%
On-time repayment rate	98.0%	94.0%	96.5%	96.5%
Default rate	1.0%	3.2%	2.0%	1.0%
Operational cost/Total financial services	20.0%	32.0%	16.5%	10.0%
Average cost of outside funds	3.5%	7.4%	16.5%	0.0%*
Savings available for lending	50.0%	20.0%	99.0%	168.0%
Partial financial self-sufficiency	110.0%	37.0%	111.0%	90.0%
Full financial self-sufficiency	39.0%	35.0%	96.0%	58.0%** (157.0%)

* The BPD has received a major proportion of its equity capital of Rp10 billion in the form of a grant which is thus not a (soft) loan and on which no interest is due.

** The BPD has placed a substantial amount of excess liquidity in other banks (Rp11.4 billion; + Rp0.54 billion as required reserves in Bank Indonesia). If income from interbank deposits is included, the rate of full financial self-sufficiency jumps to 157 per cent in 1995.

continues to expand its lending business. However, to cover the costs of an expanding microcredit business with the poor, it would have to substantially increase its interest rate.

In sum, the Indonesian experience shows that viability and sustainability can be attained in banking with the poor and the near-poor. Technical assistance has usually played a key role in the transformation of subsidized programmes into savings-driven viable institutions. Indonesia also shows that institutional viability can be achieved even under repressive policy conditions (before 1983), provided the institutions remain non-formal and apply their own sound practices. Capacity building through training that may be provided by specialized bank-training institutions and by qualified NGOs are a key input in the transformation process.

Resource Mobilization

The sustainability of microfinancial services hinges on two main factors: the mobilization of internal resources and the soundness of financial practices in dealing with these resources. Internal resource mobilization makes MFIs independent of government and donor funding. It is the heart of self-help. Major resources include share capital, savings deposits and profits. For some MFIs operating in the microeconomy, high interest rates on loans may be a very effective instrument of internal resource mobilization in addition to the collection of voluntary savings; this is a form of self-imposed compulsory savings mobilization frequently chosen by small institutions in the informal financial sector.

Resources can be mobilized under any policy regime; but it is under an environment of deregulated interest rates that resource mobilization flourishes, providing a source of self-financing to small farmers and entrepreneurs and a basis of self-reliance to financial institutions. The effect of deregulation in Indonesia has been more pronounced on savings proper, an instrument of the poorer sections of the population, than on time deposits, an instrument of the non-poor.

Convenient and safe savings deposit facilities are of particular importance to the poor, who have demonstrated, time and again, a high propensity to save. In the case of BSD, savings deposits amount to 105 per cent of loans outstanding. But while the poor account for the majority of the bank's depositors, their share of the total amount of deposits is small. This has also been the experience of the BPD, our fourth case study. After it turned from an NGO intermediary into a formal bank, it was swamped with savings which, according to data from its balance sheet (end-1995), amounted to US$6.03 million by 1995. Only US$4.64 million of a total of about US$9.54 million in loanable funds were loaned out, and only 1 per cent of this amount to poor borrowers. At the same time, its poor clients contributed 5 per cent of the savings while 95 per cent came from non-poor clients as of December

Table 7.7 Savings and Loans of Four MFIs in Indonesia, 1995 (amounts in US dollars)

MFI	Savings Mobilized	Loans Outstanding	Savings Ratio
MKEJ	5,336	31,931	0.17
P4K	1,803,557	8,875,490	0.2
BSD	2,191,800	2,093,275	1.05
BPD	6,033,839	4,645,553	1.30

Table 7.8 Number of Depositors and Average Deposits of Poor and Non-poor Clients of Four MFIs in Indonesia, 1995

Depositors/deposits	MKEJ	P4K	BSD	BPD
Depositors (in thousands)	1.1	328,67	30	12
Poor (in thousands)	1.1	328,67	26	11
Non-poor (in thousands)	0	0	5	1
Average deposits (US$)	4.8	5.6	72.5	620.4
Poor (US$)	4.8	5.6	26.9	30.4
Non-poor (US$)	–	–	284.6	6,633.4

1995. The bank now realizes it will take years to train the staff required to reach the vast numbers of savers and borrowers it ultimately wants to serve.

P4K has another story to tell with regard to the poor's interest in savings. The project has a compulsory savings component adjusted to the average regular savings capacity of a group. As this is far from exhausting the savings capacity of the members and as the small groups of ten members each were found to be too small to serve as financial intermediaries, some groups started to join together in associations with weekly meetings at which savings are collected, loans disbursed and loans repaid. The number of associations grew from 181 in July 1992, comprising 910 groups with 9100 members, to 2051 comprising 9287 groups with nearly 100,000 members, i.e. about 28 per cent of all project participants. They continue to spread like wildfire: during the half-year period from December 1995 to June 1996 their number grew by 36 per cent. These associations form the nucleus of self-reliant and self-managed local financial intermediaries that might eventually grow into rural banks (BPR). As they are by-products of the project, no statistics are available of their financial transactions.

Some data are given in Table 7.7 on the volume of savings and loans in the four MFIs studied, yielding a very low savings ratio of not more than 0.2 for the two projects which heavily depend on donor funds, and a high savings ratio above 1.0 for the two banks which mobilize their own resources.

Average deposits in the two projects, amounting to Rp11,000 and Rp13,000 (Table 7.8) respectively are substantially lower than in the two banks with average deposits of Rp167,000 (US$72) and Rp1,430,000, (US$620) respectively. To some extent this is due to the fact that the two projects exclusively cater for the poor while the banks work with both the poor and the non-poor.

However, this does not fully explain the difference as average deposits of the poor in the two banks, Rp62,000 (US$27) and Rp70,000 (US$30), respectively, are more than five-fold the deposits in the project-supported institutions. The decisive factor here is the savings mobilization technology: the two projects rely on regular compulsory savings which are invariably fixed at a minimum affordable by all group members while the two banks have more innovative savings products such as doorstep collection of savings and voluntary savings. The projects do not exhaust the savings capacity of their customers; or in other words: their savings deposit facilities for the poor are inadequate. The vast difference between the two banks in terms of average deposits from the non-poor, namely Rp656,000 (US$285) and Rp15,290,000 (US$6,633), is probably due to type of bank and their location, BSD being a rural bank located in a rural area and the BPD, a commercial bank located in the capital of the Region of Central Java.

In sum, given the need of the poor for savings deposit facilities, it is all the more surprising that projects focusing exclusively on the poor as in the various Grameen Bank replications (including MKEJ) and SFDPs (including P4K) continue to be credit-driven. They offer little in terms of innovative savings products with attractive returns and convenient collection services, with regular compulsory savings as promoted by these projects tending to restrict savings to the required minimum. Unless this is reversed, credit-driven poverty-alleviation projects might miss the chance of assisting the poor in using their financial resources and the technical and financial assistance offered for establishing or strengthening their own MFIs.

Regulatory Framework

The Indonesian experience shows that the establishment of MFIs and the outreach of existing financial institutions to the poor has been greatly influenced by two events: the deregulation of interest rates in 1983 which led to a surge in national resource mobilization and a multitude of financial innovations; and bank deregulation in 1988, which led to the establishment of a rapidly increasing number of village banks and the transformation of small institutions into rural formal-sector banks. Both have greatly eased access of the poor to banking services and contributed to the reduction of poverty in Indonesia. However, there is still a felt need for another nationally recognized legal status for MFIs below the level of rural banks, including very small institutions such as SHGs and self-help associations of the poor, or at least a recognized form of registration, particularly for the associations of groups formed under P4K. The need is also felt in Indonesia to create second-tier regulatory authorities, other than the Co-operative Department, which render appropriate guidance and supervision services to MFIs.

Indonesia has a deep experience in the promotion of MFIs, the expansion of microfinancial services and the alleviation of poverty. This experience indicates that changes in the policy and regulatory environment have been of crucial importance in that field. The Indonesian experience allows us to draw some general conclusions in that respect. For the further development of MFIs and microfinancial services for the poorer segments of the population, four policy measures are of particular importance:

- Deregulation of interest rates to permit institutions to pay interest rates with positive real returns to savers and to charge interest rates on loans that cover their costs and permit profits from which their expansion is financed and owners are rewarded (*under conditions of nationally regulated interest rates:* granting of exemptions from interest rate regulation for a specific area, institution and time period). Deregulation also allowed institutions to differentiate their interest rates according to loan product, depending on loan size, maturity and collection service. The four MFIs studied have used opportunities offered by deregulation in varying ways, offering deposit rates ranging from 10 per cent to 14.7 per cent and charging average lending rates from 21 per cent to 30 per cent.
- Bank deregulation to ease the establishment of new banks, branching out, *taking the bank to the people,* and to allow for the establishment of local MFIs with equity capital requirements that substantially differ from those for national banks. The transformation of the financial activities of the NGO BPD into a commercial bank has been the direct result of this deregulation.
- Provision of adequate forms of governance and legal status for MFIs that may be owned by members, communities and stockholders (as in the case of BSD) including NGOs (as in the case of the BPD). There is still a need for adequate forms of non-bank status for small and very small MFIs such as financial SHGs (i.e. member-based *micro*-institutions).
- Establishment of second-tier regulatory authorities, which guide and supervise large numbers of small financial institutions that cannot be effectively controlled by the central bank: still largely a task of the future.

Individual vs. Group Microfinance Technologies

The effectiveness of the individual vs. the group microfinance technology is at present (at the time of writing) being hotly debated, sometimes to the point of holy warfare as evidenced during the Bank Poor '96 workshop in Kuala Lumpur in December 1996 and the MicroCredit Summit in Washington, DC in February 1997. Examples for the success of each basically attest to the feasibility of each approach but leave open the question as to the conditions under which each is most appropriate and to their relative effectiveness. What makes a comparative evaluation difficult is the fact that most institutions or programmes are specialized on one of the two technologies. The individual technology is usually employed by banks and

Table 7.9   Savings Mobilization through Individual and Group Technologies in BSD

	Individual	Group	Total
Depositors:			
Number	22,940	7,400	30,340
Per cent	75.6%	24.4%	100.0%
Poor depositors only:			
Number	18,352	7,400	25,752
Per cent	71.3%	28.7%	100.0%
Amount of deposits in %:			
All	96.9%	3.1%	100.0%
Poor only	89.9%	10.1%	100.0%

the group technology in NGO and government organization projects (for instance, MKEJ and P4K which exclusively cater for the poor are specialized on the group technology; the BPD which caters for the poor and the non-poor on the individual technology), which means that any result is simultaneously determined by type of technology and type of institution. Further limitations derive from the fact that the two technologies are frequently not applied to both savings deposit collection and credit. How are we then to compare the effectiveness of NGOs lending to the poor indirectly through groups with banks collecting savings from and lending directly to the non-poor as individuals?

Among the four sample MFIs there is one which employs both technologies; applies them to deposit collection as well as credit delivery; and caters for the poor and the non-poor: this is BSD in Kalasan. The existing data for December 1995 (Table 7.9) allow us to analyse the effectiveness of the two technologies with regard to savings deposits, credit and profitability to the bank.

BSD started its individual savings and credit business in 1970. In 1989 the bank started experimenting with the group approach through a local NGO as a credit channel that had been previously involved in the disbursement of donor-provided funds to a large number of widely dispersed groups. The experience ended in disaster. Losses amounting to about $50,000 were equally shared between the bank and Bank Indonesia, which had supported the experiment. Instead of giving up on group lending, BSD, like any good banker, learnt from the experience. It abandoned its co-operation with the NGO and its pampered groups and started to select and train local SHGs with well-established internal savings and credit activities through its own SHG department. The bank's experience with the group technology is thus relatively young. Its business with SHGs has been rapidly expanding and is expected to expand further.

As of December 1995, the bank worked with 310 groups selected from within the vicinity of the bank, with a total of 7750 members among whom

7400 were active savers and 6200 active borrowers through their respective SHGs. At the same time the bank had 22,940 individual depositors and 6456 individual borrowers. Savers and borrowers cannot be added up to arrive at the total number of customers. Small banks in Indonesia require their clients to open a savings account before they can borrow, with the result that the number of savers equals more or less the total number of customers.

The group technology has enabled the bank to expand its outreach to poor depositors by 40 per cent, namely from 18,352 individual poor savers by 7400 group members, who are all poor, to a total of 25,752. Of the bank's poor depositors 71 per cent are individual customers and 29 per cent group members. Among the poor customers of the bank, 90 per cent of the volume of deposits has been collected from individuals and 10 per cent through groups. However, there is a wide differential between individual and group savers in terms of the amount deposited: of the total amount of savings deposits, 96.9 per cent have been mobilized from individuals and only 3.1 per cent through groups. The difference is due to savings techniques: savings from individuals are voluntary whereas savings through groups are compulsory, regular and standardized at a minimal level that is affordable by each member of a group.

With regard to borrowers, the group technology has enabled the bank to double its outreach: from 6456 to 12,656 borrowers, but has added relatively little to the volume of loans outstanding. Group members represent 49 per cent of borrowers but only 11 per cent of the volume of loans outstanding. Through the group technology the bank has increased its outreach to poor borrowers substantially, namely from 2582 by a margin of 240 per cent to a total number of 8782. Of its poor borrowers, 29 per cent are individual customers and 71 per cent are group members (Table 7.10). Average loan sizes of individual borrowers are more than two times bigger than those of group members, with the result that the volume of loans outstanding from the poor are in the hands of the much smaller number of individual borrowers.

Both technologies are profitable to the bank (Table 7.11). However, the

Table 7.10   Credit Delivery Through Individual and Group Technologies in BSD

	Individual	Group	Total
Borrowers:			
Number	6,456	6,200	12,656
Per cent	51.0%	49.0%	100.0%
Poor borrowers only:			
Number	2,582	6,200	8,782
Per cent	29.4%	70.6%	100.0%
Loans outstanding in %:			
All	89.3%	10.7%	100.0%
Poor only	48.4%	51.6%	100.0%

Table 7.11   Profitability of Individual and Group Lending Technologies in BSD

	Individual	Group	Total
Net profit of the bank	94.0%	6.0%	100.0%
Profit in % of loans outstanding	2.6%	1.4%	2.5%
Profit in % of total financial services	1.2%	1.1%	1.2%

contribution of the group business to the bank's profits is only 6 per cent. On average group lending is less profitable than individual lending, with profits from individual lending amounting to 2.6 per cent of individual loans outstanding and profits from group lending amounting to only 1.4 per cent of group loans outstanding. Yet the bank finds the group technology promising. It allows the bank to capture a new market segment which the bank hopes will benefit from the access to its financial services. As the microenterprises of the group members grow, so will their business with the bank: either mediated by the group or, if their financial needs exceed the capacity of what the group wants to handle, in a direct business relationship, i.e. after *graduation*.

There are two key observations relevant to the replicability of the experience of BSD: (1) Group technology can increase outreach to depositors, including those from poor households, by a notable margin. However, targeting the poorest of the poor households means that the exercise is likely to add very little to the overall volume of resources mobilized for recycling as loans to members. (2) The individual approach proved to be best suited to savings mobilization, so that 'individual banking' was shown to be 'savings-driven'. In contrast, credit activities are 'group-driven'. Both observations have logical appeal but imply very different strategies for delivering deposit and lending services. It is also worth noting that the individual approach appears to allow for larger average loan sizes to the poor than the group approach. However, this finding may well require further research before its importance is understood. It is not clear to what extent individual lending allows for more differentiated loan screening while the group approach suffers from an inherent regression to the mean.

Concluding Observation

Indonesia is going through a remarkably traumatic economic crisis. One of the key victims of the financial turmoil is the Indonesian banking system, which has proven to be under-capitalized and over-extended with foreign currency debts that technically renders them all bankrupt. It is impossible, therefore, to imagine that the MFIs and microfinance programmes that have flourished in Indonesia because of the success with which they have been able to link to the mainstreams of banking, will not be put at risk. However, there is cause for some optimism. In the main the deposits and loan portfolios of Indonesia's many MFIs are separate from the asset and liability holdings of the country's 440 commercial banks. There is no evidence to show that MFIs have been forced to close their doors or stop working with the poor. On the contrary, new microfinance projects are being launched in Indonesia, supported by Bank Indonesia, BRI, the ADB, the IFAD and the World Bank. Let us hope that these initiatives will not only bring desperately needed sustainable assistance to the poor, but also demonstrate to the development community the efficacy of greatly expanded investment in microfinance for sustainable poverty reduction.

Notes

1 Financial deepening refers to an increase in financial services to a given area or market segment. In discussing outreach, it is proposed to take a wider view and include both quantitative and qualitative outreach, i.e. numbers and impact.
2 Indirectly this also indicates that an equity capital of Rp50 million as required for the establishment of a rural bank of the BPR type (or several times Rp50 million for several small autonomous rural banks) would have been adequate for meeting the credit demands of the market segment envisaged by the bank. This would also have avoided overliquidity and donor dependency.

8
Microfinance in Malaysia: Aiming at Success

Siwar Chamhuri and Ben Quiñones

Introduction

Malaysia is one of the 'exemplar' countries in South-east Asia of what came to be called the 'Asian Miracle'. Within six years, from 1990 to 1995, GDP per capita of the country almost doubled, growing at the rate of 10.3 per cent p.a. while inflation was kept at the average of 4.0 per cent p.a. (Table 8.1). The manufacturing sector expanded at the rate of 10 to14 per cent p.a. and contributed about 70 per cent of exports, leading the nation's export-oriented growth and its transformation from a primary commodity producer to a newly industrializing country.

A stable financial environment helped sustain the country's robust economic growth. Between 1991 and 1995, interest rates including interbank, savings and fixed deposits moved upward as Bank Negara Malaysia (BNM) tightened monetary policy. The average base-lending rate increased from 6.83 per cent in 1994 to 8.03 per cent in 1995. The increasing interest rates of saving and fixed deposits attracted household savings into the formal financial system, thus keeping Malaysia's national savings rate at a relatively high level of 32.1 per cent on average from 1991 to 1995. Nonetheless, domestic savings were not sufficient to meet the growing financing requirements of the robustly expanding economy. The savings-investment gap stood at about 7.1 per cent of GNP in 1995, fuelling the country's need for fresh foreign investments.

Until the financial crisis in mid-1997, the Ringgit remained relatively stable in terms of a composite basket of foreign currencies. In fact, the Ringgit appreciated in 1995 against the Japanese Yen, US dollar and Pound sterling, but it depreciated against the Singapore dollar, Deutschemark and

Table 8.1   Selected Macroeconomic Performance Indicators, 1991–5

Indicators	1991	1992	1993	1994	1995	Average (1991–5)
GDP growth (%)	8.7	7.8	8.3	8.5	8.5	8.4
Per capita income growth (%)	1.0	10.9	7.8	10.4	12.2	10.3
Inflation (%)	4.4	4.7	3.6	3.7	3.4	4.0
Agriculture contribution to						
– GDP (%)	17.1	16.5	16.1	14.6	13.6	15.6
– Growth rates (%)	0.0	4.3	4.3	–1.0	2.2	2.0
– Employment (%)	26.0	n.a.	n.a.	n.a.	18.0	n.a.
Manufacturing, contribution to	28.2	28.9	30.1	31.7	33.1	30.4
– GDP (%)	13.9	10.5	12.9	14.7	14.5	13.3
– Growth rates (%)	19.9	n.a.	n.a.	n.a.	25.9	n.a.
– Employment (%)						
Currency exchange rate (%) (change against US$, %, US$1	–0.9	4.5	3.5	5.6	0.7	1.3
Interest rates, annual average						
– 3 month interbank, %	7.57	8.10	7.21	5.14	6.05	6.81
– savings deposit, %	3.25	3.25	3.99	3.54	3.70	3.55
– fixed deposit (12 months)	8.5	8.0	6.29	6.15	6.89	7.17
– base lending rate, %	9.0	9.5	8.22	6.83	8.03	8.32
National savings rate (% of GNP)	28.3	31.5	32.4	34.5	33.9	32.1
Unemployment rate (%)	4.3	3.7	3.0	2.9	2.8	3.3

Source: Bank Negara Malaysia. *Annual Report* (various Years)
Exchange rate at end of 1995: US$1 = RM2.5.

Swiss franc. The Malaysian economy seemed to have reached full employment with the unemployment rate averaging at a relatively low level of 3.3 per cent during the period 1991–5. Sustained economic growth has led to excess employment opportunities for the local population but also attracted workers from abroad.

All these achievements, however, did not spare Malaysia from the 1997 economic downturn brought about by the financial crisis and successive rounds of currency devaluation. So sudden and massive the adverse impact of the crisis had been that even a country with strong fundamentals such as Malaysia could not stem the meltdown's tide. Nonetheless, Malaysia is not as vulnerable as many other South-east Asian economies because its level of external indebtedness is lower and its finance sector has a stronger asset base than is the case in Indonesia, Thailand or the Philippines. Malaysia also entered the crisis period with a far more developed economy and lower incidence of poverty than many neighbouring economies. But Malaysia remains vulnerable to the health of its export markets, which the financial crisis is putting at risk. If export growth cannot be maintained, unemployment will spread and the incidence of poverty will also increase.

The Fight against Poverty

Prior to the Asian meltdown, Malaysia has achieved remarkable success in reducing poverty. Poverty had been more extensive and acute in the rural than in the urban areas. From 1985 poverty incidence in Peninsular Malaysia started to decline, and by 1990, at the end of the NEP (New Economic Policy) period, it has been reduced to 15 per cent, way below the NEP target level of 16.7 per cent. One cannot dispute the fact that the robust economic growth of the country contributed substantially towards improving the general living conditions of the Malaysian people. However, without the specific poverty-alleviation programmes that deliberately targeted the poor, it is doubtful whether the economic gains would have trickled down to the poor to such an extent as to significantly improve their income levels.

Broad poverty-eradication policies and strategies were initially implemented during the Second Malaysia Plan (1971–5), but it was only during the Third Malaysia Plan (1976–80) that explicit targets on poverty reduction and concrete expression of policies into projects at grassroots levels were made. The government's poverty-alleviation programme receives between 24 and 30 per cent of federal development expenditure, indicating the importance placed by the federal government on poverty alleviation in the overall development policy. As absolute poverty declined significantly at the end of the NEP period, the government focused attention on eradicating poverty among the hardcore poor. A special Development Programme for the Hardcore Poor was carried out during the sixth planning period (1991–5) and continued in the seventh planning period (1996–2000) to ensure continuing assistance to the hardcore poor.

Important for the success in the implementation of poverty-alleviation programmes is the involvement of financial institutions as providers of credit and savings services to the poor. Traditionally, the role of microfinance provider was carried out by government agencies, public enterprises or semi-government institutions and credit institutions that were especially created to assist in meeting the NEP objectives of alleviating poverty among the Bumiputras and enhancing their participation in commerce and industry.[1] As poverty incidence was higher in the rural areas, poverty-alleviation programmes laid greater emphasis on the development of the agricultural sector and the provision of subsidized credit to the target beneficiaries. The leading institutions in agricultural and rural finance are the agricultural bank, Bank Pertanian Malaysia (BPM), the Farmers Organisation Authority (FOA),[2] agro-based co-operative societies, some specialized agricultural development agencies like the Federal Land Development Authority (FELDA), and the Credit Guarantee Corporation (CGC).[3] BPM is the largest among the rural credit institutions in terms of resources, branches and loans outstanding. It can accept savings and fixed deposit, including GIRO account. However, all these financing agencies and co-operative societies catered mainly to farmers, fishermen and tobacco growers. They have not been particularly successful in providing financial services to the hardcore poor.

The introduction in 1986 by two social scientists, Dr David Gibbons and Professor Sukor Kasim of the Universiti Sains Malaysia, of a microfinance programme for the poor called Project Ikhtiar marked a high point in the country's fight against hardcore poverty. Patterned after the successful Grameen Bank of Bangladesh, and distinguished as the first replication of Grameen Bank outside Bangladesh, Project Ikhtiar exclusively targeted the poor as clients. The question that intrigued the social scientists from the Universiti Sains Malaysia was: Could Grameen be an effective means of reducing rural poverty in Peninsular Malaysia? The only effective way of getting a reliable answer to the question was by means of a pilot project. Dr Gibbons and Professor Kasim explained: 'Without actually doing Project Ikhtiar, we never could have resolved the academic debate about the feasibility of "transplanting" a successful poverty-reduction programme from one national context to another. We would still be arguing about it today, instead of planning and managing the expansion and institutionalisation of Project Ikhtiar, thereby bringing its benefits to many very poor households in the Peninsular.'

With the success of the pilot project, Project Ikhtiar was later established into an NGO MFI, the Amanah Ikhtiar Malaysia (AIM), which succeeded in attracting funding support from the government. Convinced of the effectiveness of the AIM to provide financial services to poor households, the government allocated generous grants to it to finance the expansion of its programme to other poor states in Peninsular Malaysia as well as in Sabah and Sarawak. With the new interest-free loan from the government amounting to RM200 million appropriated in the Seventh Malaysia Plan (1996–2000), the AIM is geared to expand outreach not only to the poorer Bumiputras in Sabah and Sarawak but also to the poorer households of other ethnic groups in Peninsular Malaysia.

Microfinance Capacity Assessment

Three NGO MFIs were selected for case study to assess the performance of microfinance institutions in terms of their outreach to the poor, viability and sustainability, and resource mobilization, namely:

1. *The AIM.* The AIM started as a pilot project in Northwest Selangor, Peninsular Malaysia to test the effectiveness of the Grameen Bank Approach for the reduction of extreme rural poverty in Malaysia. Yayasan Pembangunan Ekonomi Islam Malaysia (YPEIM) provided the on-lending funds as a grant. The Selangor State Government and the APDC contributed to the operating cost. The success of the pilot project encouraged the founders to expand its coverage and, at a later stage,

institutionalized it by establishing the Amanah Ikhtiar Malaysia as an NGO MFI under the Trustee Incorporation Act 258 (revised 1981) of 20 October 1988. From a modest coverage of about 300 clients during the pilot stage, the AIM's outreach expanded tremendously to about 40,000 clients in 1995. Members participate in the AIM's decision-making process through representation in the board of members. Two representatives are elected from each region, or a total of eight representatives from four regions. The board is chaired by the Managing Director and the Director of Loan Division is designated as the secretary. The board is a forum through which members can air their concerns and raise issues and problems about the AIM's programme. The AIM's management then brings the concerns of members to the board of directors meeting.

2. *Yayasan Usaha Maju (YUM)*. The Grameen Bank Approach replication was extended to Sabah in 1988 through Project Usahamaju. This project was initiated as a one-year pilot project of the Institute for Development Studies (IDS, Sabah) and the Sabah State Government through its development agency, the Rural Development Corporation (RDC), in order to address the problem of high incidence of rural poverty in Sabah. Project Usahamaju was funded through grants from the state government to the RDC. While maintaining the essential elements of the Grameen Bank Approach, the project made some modifications to suit the local conditions and the uniqueness of the type of poverty, economic opportunities, infrastructure and socio-political structure of Sabah (Gunting and Rantau, 1993). After the pilot project phase, the project was expanded by KPD while IDS of Sabah continued its researcher role. On 30 June 1995, the project was registered as a foundation under the Trustees (Incorporation) Ordinance 1951 chapter 148 of Sabah and became known as Yayasan Usaha Maju (YUM). By December 1995, YUM has reached 5697 clients in 659 villages in six zones of Sabah. Members participate in the governance and decision-making of YUM through the council of members, which meets quarterly. The council consists of six members elected from the centre leader and YUM's management. It discusses issues and problems concerning the members, which are then brought to the board of directors by YUM's management.

3. *Kooperasi Kredit Rakyat (KKR)*. Another source of microfinance is the credit unions. One such credit union is the People's Credit Co-operative Society (Koperasi Kredit Rakyat, KKR) which operates in the rural town of Batang Berjuntai in the District of Kuala Selangor. KKR started as a Youth Social Club, which endeavoured from 1970 to 1974 to improve the socio-economic status of estate workers through tuition and tailoring classes and kindergarten for their children. In 1975, the club was registered as a credit co-operative under the Society Act and became a network member of the Credit Union Promotion Centre. KKR sent a number of young officers to the Philippines and India to undergo training on the Co-operative

Movement. Three co-operative projects were initiated from 1975 to 1980 and the idea started to spread to neighbouring villages, estates, mines and rural towns. By the end of 1995, KKR had organized credit unions in 40 communities benefiting 2060 members. Participation of members in the governance and decision-making process of KKR is ensured through the Area Committee, which is further sub-divided into women, youth, children and education sub-committees. These sub-committees meet once a month. There is also the Area Committee General Meeting and the Annual General Meeting where members can voice their concerns and elect members of the various sub-committees.

Outreach

The AIM is the largest poverty-oriented MFI in Malaysia. Of the combined outreach of 47,158 clients of the three MFIs in 1995, the AIM accounted for almost four-fifths (Table 8.2). More important, the depth of the AIM's coverage of hardcore poor in Malaysia is remarkably high: as of end of 1995, almost half of the 88,800 hardcore poor were active clients of the AIM. Women clients comprised over 99 per cent of total clients of the AIM and YUM and 50 per cent of total clients of KKR.

The AIM has the largest portfolio with loan outstanding amounting to US$9.3 million at the end of December 1995 (Table 8.3). AIM's average loan size in 1995 (US$235 per client) is likewise much larger than YUM's (US$139 per client) and KKR's (US$111 per client).

Outreach of both the AIM and YUM grew tremendously during their early stages of expansion, but this declined in more recent years. Two major

Table 8.2 Outreach of Three Sample MFIs in Malaysia, 1995

Item	AIM	YUM	KKR	Total
No. of clients	39,401	5,697	2,060	47,158
Percentage to total hard-core poor in Malaysia*	44.4%	6.4%	2.3%	53.1%
No. of female clients	39,335	5,657	1,030	46,022
Per cent female	99.8%	99.3%	50.0%	97.6%
No. of male clients	66	40	1,030	1,136
Per cent male	0.2%	0.7%	50.0%	2.4%
Classification of clients**				
Poor	37.7%	55.3%	79.2%	59.9%
Not-so-poor	58.4%	36.2%	12.5%	33.1%
Non-poor	3.8%	8.5%	8.3%	7.0%

* Estimated at 88,800 households.
** Results of Housing Index Test, with sample size: AIM = 53 sample clients; YUM = 47 clients; KKR = 72 clients.
Definitions: 'Poor clients' = Housing Index score lower than 4.5 points.
'Not-so-poor clients' = Housing Index score of 4.5 to 5.0 points.
'Non-poor clients' = Housing Index score of over 5.0 points.

Table 8.3 Loans Outstanding* and Savings Mobilized by Three Malaysian MFIs, 1993–5 (In US '000 dollars)

Year/Item	AIM	YUM	KKR
1993			
Loans outstanding	3,478.4	378.4	223.5
Savings deposits	1,310.7	68.5	322.2
Savings as % of loans	37.7%	18.1%	144.2%
1994			
Loans outstanding	6,732.6	426.0	229.1
Savings deposits	2,374.0	58.1	229.1
Savings as % of loans	35.3%	13.6%	100.0%
Growth rate: Loans	93.6%	12.6%	2.5%
Savings	81.1%	−15.2%	−28.9%
1995			
Loans outstanding	9,268.8	790.1	227.7
Savings deposits	3,770.1	64.8	569.1
Savings as % of loans	40.7%	8.2%	250.0%
Growth rate: Loans	37.7%	85.5%	−0.06%
Savings	58.8%	11.5%	148.4%

* Includes current loans and past due accounts.
Exchange rate at end of 1995: US$1 = RM2.5.

factors contributed to the AIM's outreach expansion: generous funding support from the government, and technical guidance from Grameen Bank of Bangladesh. Annual enrolment of new members reached a peak of 9517 in 1992 for the AIM and 1619 in 1990 for YUM. In subsequent years, however, enrolment of new members for the AIM as well as for YUM declined for various reasons. With the increasing coverage of the hardcore poor in the economically depressed states of Kedah, Perlis, Perak, Selangor, Penang, Kelantan, Terengganu and Pahang, the number of poor households who are eligible to participate in the AIM programme naturally dwindled over the years. Moreover, bad borrowers were weeded out of the programme and stricter measures were adopted for selecting new borrowers. In more recent years the AIM geared its expansion towards financial deepening by providing bigger loans to borrowers and generating larger amounts of compulsory savings. The increase in loan sizes fuelled the growth of the AIM's loan portfolio especially during the period 1993–5.

The slowdown of YUM's outreach expansion is a different story. It was largely caused by poor collection performance, and this was exacerbated by the lack of funding support, the geographic distribution of the poor in isolated areas, and the lack of adequate communication and transportation facilities in these areas. Its most critical problem, non-repayment of loans, has beset YUM's operations from the early years. The number of defaulters were only four in January 1989, but this increased to 48 in December of that year and loan arrears accumulated to an amount of RM20,824. Through the years, membership targets were not achieved, and target achievement declined from

74 per cent in 1990 to 52 per cent in May 1991. With its small outreach, YUM's delivery cost remained high, about four times higher than planned for. The IDS of Sabah recommended that the microfinance project should focus on improving staff efficiency and the quality of human resources, implementing cost control measures, and fostering discipline of member-clients as well as staff. Project management adopted these measures and subsequently achieved an almost perfect repayment of 99.6 per cent at the end of 1991. Nonetheless, problems of repayment discipline once again cropped up in subsequent years and continued to plague the project. By the end of 1995, the repayment rate dropped to 72.9 per cent.[4]

KKR draws its membership from the plantation workers. In recent years, many plantations were sold off for real estate development purposes. Plantation workers who lost their jobs migrated to the metropolitan city of Kuala Lumpur and sought whatever odd jobs they could find there. With the closure of the plantations, KKR shut down six of its 40 branches in 1995. In a bid to retain the patronage of its members, including those who migrated to the capital city, KKR entered into an agreement with sister co-operatives based in Kuala Lumpur to recognize its erstwhile members and to extend the usual financial services. Furthermore, KKR is offering its members new financial products and services, among them housing loans and educational loans.

The financial products of the three case studies are mainly loans and savings. Economic loans form the major portion of their loan portfolio, most of which go to trading activities and the rest are shared by agriculture and forestry, livestock and fisheries, processing and manufacturing, and services. Until the early 1990s, the majority of AIM loans went to finance agricultural projects but in subsequent years more loans have been used for non-agricultural activities. In addition to economic loans, the AIM and YUM provide educational loans and housing loans. On the savings side, the products of the Grameen Bank Approach replicators were conspicuously different from those of the co-operative society, KKR. The AIM and YUM mobilize mandatory savings of RM1 to RM3 or 5 per cent of loan amount, which are collected at the weekly centre meetings. In contrast, KKR mobilizes voluntary deposits from its members. It has introduced various savings schemes such as special savings and children's savings. As Table 8.3 shows, KKR relies totally on savings generated from its members, whereas members' savings comprise less than two-thirds and less than one-fifth of the AIM's and YUM's loan portfolios respectively.

Targeting the Poor

A relevant question is whether microfinance providers in Malaysia are reaching the poor. The answer to this question is a resounding 'yes'. To ensure that poor households are selected for their programmes, both the AIM and YUM use an instrument called Means Test for screening potential clients. The AIM uses four indexes for the Means Test: housing index, household profile, income, and land ownership. YUM uses three indexes: per capita income (not exceeding RM106 or around US$42 per month), value of movable assets (not exceeding RM1,000 or US$400 per capita), and value of landholding not exceeding five acres.

As of the end of December 1995, the AIM has completed 134,803 means tests of eligibility and conducted 111,538 re-interviews of which 101,395 or 90.9 per cent were eligible for the Ikhtiar Loan Scheme (ILS). This number is more than the estimated population of the hardcore poor in Peninsular Malaysia and includes the not-so-poor households. About 39 per cent of those who went through the eligibility test have eventually been enrolled by AIM as member-clients while the other 61 per cent remained in the AIM roster as potential clients. Some of the non-enrollees were eligible to participate in the AIM programme but chose not to participate. Those who choose not to join the programme claim that they are afraid of being indebted and/or they are satisfied with current level of living and have no desire to borrow for additional income-generation activities. In the case of YUM, six out of every ten potential clients eventually join the programme. Those who did join were either not interested in the programme or were rejected due to the strict screening process.

KKR does not use any targeting mechanism but it focuses its organizing activities among estate workers, mining workers, contract workers, squatters and industrial manual workers, most of whom belong to the Indian ethnic group. The common characteristics of its target groups are: (a) low income; (b) low level of education; (c) belief in fatalism; (d) belief in caste system; (e) inferiority complex; (f) fear of the landlord/master; (g) superstitious beliefs; (h) alcoholism; and (i) oppression of women (Sinnapan, 1995).

To determine the effectiveness of their poverty targeting, Siwar Chamhuri (1996) conducted a housing index test among 172 clients of the sample MFIs. The results are shown in Table 8.2. An interesting finding is that the incidence of poverty is lowest among AIM clients. Siwar Chamhuri (1996) noted that most AIM and YUM clients live in houses made of sturdy materials. With the housing index as a gauge of poverty incidence, he concluded that a significant proportion of AIM and YUM clients were not-so-poor or non-poor. Does this mean that the AIM has actually been biased for the non-poor at the expense of the non-poor, or has the AIM focused its services on members who have crossed over the poverty line? The fact is that the AIM has retained its good borrowers and gave them access to much larger loans each succeeding loan cycle. Instead of 'graduating' clients who have prospered and handing them over to commercial banks, the AIM has developed its capacity to provide them with better services. This strategy has enabled the member-clients of the AIM to increase investments and generate higher incomes. If incomes of AIM clients have indeed increased, as the series of impact studies reported in the succeeding section of this chapter confirm, and they have crossed over the poverty line after participating in the AIM's programme continuously for a period of time, it should not be surprising to find them living in better quality houses, for when people have money, they are predisposed to invest some of it on the improvement of their houses.

The case of KKR clients is vastly different. Siwar found that 79 per cent of the KKR clients were 'poor'. It must be noted, though, that Siwar arrived at this figure not by using the housing index but by comparing household income obtained from the KKR loan application forms against the official definition of poverty line. Applying the housing index would have classified KKR members as 'non-poor' because they live in estates housing units made of firm materials, asbestos roofing, and of medium size. But plantation workers in Malaysia are largely poor, they earn low wages, and they have low levels of education. By focusing on them, KKR has brought financial services to a section of Malaysian society that other organizations, both governmental or non-governmental, have not reached.

Microfinance providers of Malaysia have learned that the fear of indebtedness is quite strong among the hardcore poor and that motivation work is essential to convince them to borrow. After the client has passed the means test, the MFI's branch manager or field officer conducts a re-interview, and when new clients are selected, he/she commences motivation work. The field officer acquaints the new client about the MFI's activities, rules, regulations and the mechanism on group formation. To avail themselves of a loan, all member-clients must go through a compulsory group training, group recognition test and attend regular centre meetings.

KKR also engages in motivation work in promoting its credit union activities. Mostly done by volunteer social workers, whose number is dwindling due to more attractive jobs elsewhere, motivation work begins with a participatory research in which the social workers survey the community, identify its problems and ascertain its potential in terms of human and financial resources. Members are required to attend an education and training programme which is carried through different media such as theatre, folk arts, cultural presentations and group dynamics. The training programme acquaints the members on: (i) the historical background of co-operative movements; (ii) roles and duties of members; (iii) economic projects and financial products of the co-operative including savings and loan facilities, welfare and insurance scheme, microenterprise, alternative income-generating projects for youth and women; and (iv) opportunities for developing market outlets and small business development. Out of ten people motivated, around eight would eventually join KKR's programme. This high degree of success can be attributed to the effectiveness of KKR's community organizing approach, general acceptance of the co-operative movement, but also to the lack of better alternatives for the poor. Those who reject the programme are mostly illiterate, or who have borrowing needs that the co-operative could not meet.

Credit Delivery System

The credit delivery system of the AIM and YUM is patterned after Grameen's and requires a manpower-intensive organizational set-up. Under the system, clients are formed into small groups with five members in each group. Eight groups comprise a centre. The centre meets once a week to discuss loan proposal, disburse loans, supervise borrowers, and monitor problems and the general welfare of the members. The poorest two members of the group obtain the first loans. The two other members get their loans after eight weeks of perfect weekly repayment by the first two borrowers. The group chairman's turn comes after another eight weeks of perfect repayment by the four members of the group. Group dynamics is deemed crucial in developing group solidarity, cohesiveness and peer pressure. A network of groups binds members into a coherent force through programmes for self-improvement (Gibbons and Kassim, 1990). Loans are provided with no collateral, no guarantors, no interest, no threat of legal action, and simple procedure. If a borrower of good standing dies, their outstanding loans will be written off.

KKR does not form its members into sub-groups or centres. Its staffing is very lean: KKR is run by two permanent staff only. All members of the KKR board are volunteers, including the Internal Auditor and the members of various committees. It has no branch office that is manned by full-time workers similar to those of the AIM and YUM. What constitutes as a branch of KKR is a unit committee consisting of volunteer officers (i.e. President, Secretary, Treasurer and two committee members) of the local chapter. The Treasurer of the unit committee also acts as loan repayment collector and can claim reimbursement for transportation expenses incurred while collecting loan repayments. KKR stresses community participation through co-operative activities. Its programme incorporates people's participatory development methods, continuous education and training of local leaders who administer and co-ordinate the day-to-day activities of the co-operative (Sinnapan, 1995).

As of end of 1995, the AIM, YUM and KKR respectively had 35, 24 and 34 branches. While the total outreach figures of these MFIs may look impressive, the efficiency of their branches is low and can still stand a lot of improvement. The average number of clients per branch was 1124 for the AIM, which falls short of the Grameen Bank Approach standard of 1500 to 2000 clients per branch. Nonetheless, the AIM's record is many times better than YUM's and KKR's, whose branch coverage averaged at only 237 and 60 clients respectively.

Impact of Microfinance Programmes

Malaysia provides solid evidence that microfinance is indeed an effective tool for poverty alleviation. Six separate evaluation studies on the AIM conducted during the period 1990–5 consistently show the positive impact of microfinance programme on the economic well-being of the clients. An evaluation study conducted by Gibbons and Kasim (1990), founding implementers of the Amanah Ikhtiar pilot project, concluded that small loans on reasonable terms to the very poor households for financing additional income-generating activities could be an effective way of reducing extreme rural poverty. The study noted that during the one-year reference period, average monthly income of clients increased by 90 per cent. The clients were able to diversify income sources and their annual return to capital of clients was estimated at 99.7 per cent.

Comparing borrowers and a control group of people who were qualified under the ILS but did not borrow, it can be seen that income of AIM members increased by 124 per cent compared with the control group's 80 per cent. Two-thirds of very poor borrowers have moved out of poverty after only one ILS loan. By the end of the fourth loan, eight out of ten borrowers were able to pull themselves out of poverty. In another study, a survey of 396 borrowers showed that monthly household income increased by 134 per cent with 63 per cent of borrowers having moved out of poverty. Another independent study of 310 borrowers (Chamhuri, 1996) confirmed improvements in the socio-economic status of borrowers in terms of house ownership, food intake, income and the empowerment of women. Average income increased 182 per cent, 61 per cent of which were derived from ILS-supported enterprises, mainly non-agricultural activities. Overall, the incidence of poverty decreased by 53.1 per cent, of which 37.5 per cent was reduction among hardcore poor households. Among the borrowers studied, 58.9 per cent crossed over the poverty threshold.

An internal impact study conducted by the AIM in 1992–3 showed that income of borrowers increased by 139 per cent. The Centre for Policy Research, Universiti Sains Malaysia conducted the latest impact study in 1994–5. The study covered 367 respondents consisting of active members (201), non-active members (40) and a control group consisting of eligible clients but who did not join the AIM (120). The study concluded that average income increased by 272 per cent, more pronounced especially among active members. Using a per capita income of RM50 (US$20) per month to define the poverty line, the study found that 74 per cent of 306 respondents whose income was below the poverty line managed to pull out of poverty. By type of respondent, about 86 per cent of the AIM's active members crossed the poverty line, compared to 67 per cent among non-active members and 56 per cent among the control group. The study also confirmed the increase in the clients' quality of life in terms of value of assets and the quality of housing.

The IDS (1991, 1993 and 1994) conducted at least three impact evaluation studies on Project Usaha Maju. The first study, an assessment of the pilot project, revealed that the credit facilities provided by the project contributed positively towards improving incomes and standard of living of the poor. However, the study expressed serious concerns about the project's low degree of efficiency and viability. Initially, repayment rates were impressive, but later declined and loan arrears increased. The study concluded that with the project's high delivery cost per loan, it is unlikely to attain viability during the expansion plan. The second impact study, conducted in 1993, noted that incomes of members increased 23.2 per cent and the return on each RM1 loan was estimated at RM2.97. However, project efficiency was still not satisfactory. Although repayment rates improved to 98 per cent, organizational efficiency was low as reflected in the low ratios of client per branch and per staff. A high proportion (24.9 per cent) of members discontinued participation in the programme. The third impact study, conducted in 1994, concluded that incomes of members increased between 16 to 57 per cent. In terms of efficiency, however, costs of operation remained high, despite some measures to reduce costs. Recruitment of new members remained low, repayment rates were at 98 per cent, but the amount of loan arrears continued to increase.

The overwhelming evidence supports the conclusion that the poor are bankable: they are creditworthy and can be depended upon to use credit in highly beneficial undertakings. The question, however, is 'Have microfinance providers translated the bankability of their clients into their own financial viability'? We shall focus on this issue in the succeeding discussions.

Viability and Sustainability

Results of the microfinance capacity assessments show that all three MFIs under study are not financially viable: their revenues from interest and fees on loans were much lower than their total costs (unadjusted for inflation and opportunity cost of capital). The lack of viability of the sample MFIs largely owes to their practice of charging low interest rates relative to their costs. In accordance with Muslim faith, the AIM charges no 'interest' on its loans but collects an 'administrative fee' of RM25 (US$10) for the first-cycle loan, RM50 (US$20) for the second-cycle loan, and RM75 (US$30) for subsequent repeater loans. YUM also does not charge any 'interest' but collects an 'administrative fee' of 5 per cent on first-cycle loans, 3 per cent on second-cycle loans, 1 per cent on third-cycle loans, and 0 per cent on fourth-cycle loans. KKR charges an effective rate of 5.5 per cent p.a. on its loans. As a percentage of average performing assets (i.e. assets used for providing financial services to clients), revenues of the AIM and YUM were in the

Table 8.4 Return on Assets and Cost Efficiency of Three Sample MFIs, 1993–5 (Amounts in US dollars)

MFI/Year	Average Performing Assets (APA)	% of Interest and Fees to APA	% of Total Cost to APA	% of Cost of Funds to APA	% of Operating Cost to APA	% of Loan Loss Provision to APA
1. AIM						
1993	4,165,743.2	12.4%	73.7%	10.0%	56.5%	7.2%
1994	7,431,964.0	14.7%	39.3%	6.8%	32.5%	*
1995	N.A.	N.A.	N.A.	N.A.	N.A.	N.A.
2. YUM						
1993	2,172,476.0	9.1%	19.3%	*	14.0%	5.3%
1994	2,139,564.5	10.4%	21.7%	0.1%	15.0%	6.6%
1995	2,166,416.1	13.5%	21.1%	Nil	14.2%	6.9%
3. KKR						
1993	386,271.2	9.2%	11.0%	6.0%	5.0%	Nil
1994	395,641.1	4.7%	9.3%	4.3%	5.0%	Nil
1995	425,595.6	4.7%	6.4%	2.8%	3.6%	Nil

* Less than 0.1 per cent
Symbols used: APA – average performing assets, defined as assets used for providing financial services to clients, averaged between beginning and end of year balances.

vicinity of 13 to 15 per cent while KKR's was less than 10 per cent (Table 8.4).

The practice of charging low interest rates is inappropriate particularly because the operating costs of the sample MFIs are relatively high. In 1993, the (unadjusted) total costs were higher than revenues by 6.3 times for the AIM, around 2.1 times for YUM and 1.2 times for KKR. With comparatively higher costs of operation, the pressure is greater for the AIM as well as YUM to expand outreach and the volume of business in order to reduce costs and become viable and sustainable. The AIM tried to improve its productivity and proved that it can be done. It recruited more fieldstaff and redeployed some of its Head Office staff to the branches. It adopted a salary scale slightly above the public administrative scheme so as to attract and retain experienced staff as well as to curb turnover of staff. Bonuses and additional increments were provided to highly productive staff. As a result, productivity of AIM fieldstaff improved with the average client per fieldstaff increasing from 82 in 1993 to 110 in 1995. The total financial (savings and credit) services provided by AIM fieldstaff more than doubled from 1993 to 1995 (Table 8.5), thus enabling it to reduce its average operating cost per unit of loan.

YUM's attempts to improve staff productivity have been halfhearted and it continues to operate a very costly delivery system. Salary increases in YUM have been marginal, rigidly following the public service salary scheme. Almost all of its staff experienced a horizontal pay increase, indicating no special incentives for excellence in service or higher productivity. In similar

Table 8. 5   Selected Measures of Staff Productivity of Three Sample MFIs, 1993–5 (amounts in US dollars)

MFI/Year	No. of Fieldstaff	No. of Head Office Staff	Ratio of Fieldstaff to Head Office Staff	Clients per Fieldstaff	Loan Outstanding per Fieldstaff ($)	Savings per Fieldstaff	Total Financial Services per Fieldstaff
1. AIM							
1993	312	61	5.1 : 1	82	11,147.7	4,201.0	15,348.7
1994	347	47	7.4 : 1	95	19,399.1	6,841.5	26,240.6
1995	357	55	6.5 : 1	110	25,946.3	10,560.6	36,506.9
2. YUM							
1993	127	28	4.5 : 1	32	2,825.4	539.0	3,364.4
1994	132	28	4.7 : 1	37	2,563.4	440.5	3,003.9
1995	141	36	3.9 : 1	40	4,902.0	459.7	5,361.7
3. KKR							
1993	38	2	19 : 1	53	5,880.3	8,478.8	14,359.1
1994	34	2	17 : 1	58	6,737.4	6,737.4	13,474.8
1995	34	2	17 : 1	61	6,695.8	6,695.8	13,391.6

vein, KKR recently increased the salary of its full-time staff by 33 per cent from RM600 to RM800 per month. But because KKR has only two permanent staff working in a small office and it uses volunteers extensively, it has managed to increase its volume of business without significantly raising its total costs.

Degree of Financial Self-sufficiency

Notwithstanding efforts to improve productivity, all three sample MFIs have not attained financial self-sufficiency. One of two indicators used to gauge this is *partial financial self-sufficiency* which measures the extent to which total costs (operating costs including depreciation plus cost of funds and provision for loan losses) are covered by interest and fees collected from clients. All the three sample MFIs had a less than 70 per cent degree of partial financial self-sufficiency, which simply means total revenues were less than 70 per cent of their total costs, although the degree of financial self-sufficiency for the AIM and YUM improved through the years while that of KKR deteriorated in 1994 and partly recovered in 1995 but was still below the 1993 level (Table 8.6).

The other measure is *full financial self-sufficiency* which adjusts total costs for inflation and the interest subsidy on funds sourced from grants and soft loans and used for on-lending to clients. Inflation rate during the study period was 3.6 per cent, 3.7 per cent, and 3.4 per cent respectively for 1993, 1994, and 1995. Cost of capital was defined as the prime lending rate plus 2 per cent. This worked out to 10.03 per cent, 8.83 per cent, and 10.22 per cent

Table 8.6 Selected Indicators of Financial Viability and Sustainability of Three Malaysian MFIs, 1993–5

MFI/Year	Interest Rate	On-time Repayment Rate	Interest and Fees (US$)	Unadjusted Total Cost (US$)	Adjusted Total Cost (US$)	Degree of Partial Financial Self-sufficiency	Degree of Full Financial Self-sufficiency
1. AIM							
1993	5%	99.99%	518,028	3,071,600	4,230,017	16.86%	12.25%
1994	5%	99.99%	1,094,887	2,919,266	4,545,272	37.51%	24.09%
1995	5%	99.96%	1,774,260	2,653,390	5,154,756	66.87%	34.42%
2. YUM							
1993	3%	98.07%	198,005	420,576	833,210	47.08%	23.76%
1994	3%	97.78%	221,486	463,494	945,068	47.79%	23.44%
1995	3%	98.38%	293,382	457,750	967,291	64.09%	30.33%
3. KKR							
1993	5.5%	95.0%	35,706	42,801	43,757	83.42%	81.60%
1994	5.5%	95.0%	18,680	36,902	37,539	50.62%	49.76%
1995	5.5%	96.5%	19,886	27,206	27,634	73.09%	71.96%

Definitions:
Degree of Partial Financial Self-Sufficiency = [Interest and Fees] / [Unadjusted Total Cost] × 100%.
Degree of Full Financial Self-Sufficiency = [Interest and Fees] / [Adjusted Total Cost] × 100%.

respectively in the same years. The difference between unadjusted and adjusted total costs represents the magnitude of subsidy to the MFIs. The greater the subsidy, the greater is the deviation of one measure of financial self-sufficiency from the other.

A number of measures can be adopted by the sample MFIs to improve their financial viability and self-sufficiency. First, they should improve the productivity of their staff. While the AIM had a relatively high staff-to-client ratio, staff salaries comprised more than two-fifths of its total cost (Table 8.7) as it paid a relatively higher salary. In 1993 and 1994, the average salary per staff as a percentage of GDP per capita was 40 per cent for the AIM, 18 per cent for YUM, and less than 1 per cent for KKR. On the other hand, staff salaries comprised less than 20 per cent of YUM's and KKR's total costs but their staff-to-client ratios were also very low. There is a need for YUM and KKR to increase their volume of business by generating more clients whereas the AIM needs to increase the volume of business from its existing clients.

Second, the sample MFIs should strive to minimize the cost of their funds by mobilizing more savings. This will also enhance their financial self-sufficiency. At present, the AIM's and YUM's capacity to mobilize savings is low due to its compulsory savings limit. They do not offer term deposits or voluntary savings. For KKR, which relies totally on savings as a source of on-lending funds, the cost of fund could not be reduced without adversely affecting the demand for its savings products.

Third, they should also try to reduce their non-performing assets in order

Table 8.7   Percentage Distribution of Total Costs of MFIs By Cost Item, 1993–5

MFI/Year	Salaries	Other Operating Costs	Cost of Funds	Bad Debts Provision	Unadjusted Total Cost	Subsidy*	Adjusted Total Cost
1. AIM							
1993	42.0%	34.7%	13.5%	9.8%	3,071,600	1,158,417	4,230,017
1994	45.8%	36.8%	17.4%	n.a.	2,919,266	1,626,006	4,545,272
1995	n.a.	n.a.	9.1%	0.2%	2,653,390	2,501,366	5,154,756
2. YUM							
1993	17.3%	54.7%	0.4%	27.6%	420,576	412,634	833,210
1994	16.6%	52.5%	0.5%	30.4%	463,494	481,574	945,068
1995	16.9%	50.5%	Nil	32.6%	457,750	509,541	967,291
3. KKR							
1993	10.8%	34.8%	54.4%	Nil	42,801	956	43,757
1994	12.9%	40.7%	46.4%	Nil	36,902	637	37,539
1995	15.6%	40.0%	44.4%	Nil	27,206	428	27,634

* Subsidy = [Grants and soft loans + savings available for on-lending] × [inflation rate + prime lending rate + 2%] – [Actual interest paid on deposits and borrowed funds].

to minimize loan losses and realize full returns from the current portfolio. This is a more urgent measure for YUM to undertake because of its huge and still growing portfolio of non-performing assets. Past due loans of YUM grew from US$19,560 in 1993 to around US$99,000 in 1995. Its provisions for loan losses also grew in terms of percentage share in total costs from 27.6 per cent in 1993 to 32.6 per cent in 1995.

Fourth and finally, apart from the cost-cutting measures, MFIs in Malaysia should increase their administrative charges in order to substantially improve financial self-sufficiency. For instance, YUM's 3 per cent administrative charge covered about 47 per cent of total costs in 1993 and 1994 and a higher 64 per cent in 1995; the rest were financed by government grants. By increasing the administrative charge to a more suitable level, YUM may be able to cover all its costs. YUM has in fact planned to increase its administrative charge but this may take some time to implement.

Resource Mobilization

The AIM and YUM depended largely on donor funds, and this is an abiding reason why their microfinance programmes were not designed at the outset to be financially viable and self-sufficient. The AIM's start-up fund for its pilot project was contributed by YPEIM, the Selangor State Government and the APDC. It continues to receive interest free loans from the federal government for its loan funds (the most recent is a long-term credit amounting to RM200 million, or around US$80 million), various state government line agencies for its operating costs, and grants from YPEIM for its loanable funds. The federal government stipulates that its loan funds should be for the hardcore poor. Funds from the state governments, which have dwindled in recent years, can be used by the AIM to cover the cost of administering its credit programme for the poor in the state. In addition, the AIM obtains soft loans on a very limited scale from some commercial banks like Bank Islam Malaysia Berhad (BIMB), Bank Bumiputra Malaysia Berhad (BBMB), Malayan Banking and the CGC.

The Sabah State Government provided YUM's funds for the primary purpose of on-lending to the poor in the state of Sabah. Previously, the RDC, a state government agency under the Ministry of Agriculture, implemented Project Usaha Maju. Fund sourcing was not a problem then because project funding was included in the state government's budget when YUM was incorporated in mid-1995. No government budget was allocated for YUM during the transition period, and this adversely affected its capacity to expand its programme. YUM has no other sources of funds apart from the government. The government has not acted on YUM's application for tax-exemption privileges, which is quite essential for attracting donations from the private sector. Finally, YUM cannot obtain bank loans at commercial rates because its administrative charge is below the base-lending rate.

The AIM and YUM will not attain full financially self-sufficiency unless they develop the capacity to mobilize savings. Since YUM and the AIM do not pay interest on the savings of their members, they cannot use these funds for on-lending; which is why they are extremely keen to mobilize more savings. The savings of their members are deposited in a commercial bank in interest-bearing accounts (6 per cent p.a. and 3.5 per cent p.a., respectively for YUM and the AIM). While they earn some margin from handling these savings, this is not enough to cover their service costs. On its part, KKR tries to improve its spread by investing surplus funds in fixed deposit with the commercial banks. With a yield of 6 to 7 per cent p.a. on fixed deposit, KKR's spread is higher at 3 to 4 per cent. On a small portfolio (below US$240,000), KKR's spread will not warrant full financial self-sufficiency.

The AIM and YUM could learn from the experience of KKR, which sources funds entirely from savings. KKR has taken several measures to intensify internal resource mobilization, namely: (i) increasing the types and amounts of saving products and intensifying clients education on savings; (ii) increasing the co-operative equity share to at least RM100 per member; (iii) attracting greater patronage of members by introducing various types of loans such as small business loan, equity loans, and emergency loans; and (iv) increasing real interest rates on deposits.

To cap it all, the three sample MFIs need to revise their lending rates upwards. The effective loan charges collected by the AIM and YUM from their clients (5 per cent and 3 per cent respectively for the AIM and YUM) as well as by KKR (1 per cent per month over a period of ten months on a declining basis, or an effective rate of 5.5 per cent p.a.) are not sufficient to cover the cost of funds, the costs of operations and bad debts.[5]

Policy Framework

Malaysia has increasingly liberalized its financial system in recent years to facilitate the free flow of capital that is needed by the rapidly expanding economy. This has helped fuel the growth of the export-oriented manufacturing sector and attracted both long-term foreign investments in the real sector and short-term investments in the capital markets. Liberalization of the financial system, however, has not been accompanied by a deregulation of banks. Establishment of new banks is tightly controlled by BNM and only a few NGO MFIs have been granted a special licence to lend to the poor households. All institutions providing financial services are governed by the Banking and Financial Institutions Act (BAFIA) of 1989 which has tightened regulations on deposit taking to prevent and penalize undue solicitation of deposit. The BAFIA covers three categories of institutions:

(a) scheduled financial institutions – major deposit-taking institutions such as finance companies, commercial banks and discount houses;
(b) scheduled non-financial institutions – major non-bank sources of credit and finance, such as credit card companies, building societies, factoring and licensing companies and development finance institutions; and
(c) non-scheduled institutions – statutory bodies and other persons or corporations not subject to the provisions of BAFIA governing scheduled business and representation offices.

Loosely, the NGO MFIs may be classified under category (c) above. The AIM and YUM, and a few other NGO MIFs, operate under a special licence from the Ministry of Housing and Local Government under the Money-lenders Act to provide credit to the poor. They have been granted special exemptions, which enable them to collect deposits from clients. On the other hand, KKR operates under the Co-operative Act 1993, which allows the co-operative, or credit union, to mobilize savings of members through the purchase of shares and to pay back dividends to members.

In so far as the government is concerned, the AIM is the main implementer of its poverty-alleviation programmes and policies. The government, therefore, continues to provide funding support for the AIM's ILS. The RM200 million long-term soft loan provided by the government under the Seventh Malaysia Plan has boosted the capacity of the AIM to expand outreach to the poor households of Sabah and Sarawak as well as to other ethnic groups. To the extent that the new line of credit results in greater outreach of the poor, the preferential treatment accorded to the AIM may not be a bad thing. The downside of this approach, however, is that other players in the microfinance sector who do not get a similar treatment will continue to be weak and underdeveloped. In the face of the Asian meltdown, the blossoming and capacity build-up of more MFIs catering to poor households might just be the kind of development strategy a country like Malaysia needs to help speed up economic recovery.

Concluding Observations

The biggest challenge for MFIs in Malaysia at present is to translate the bankability of their clients into the bankability of their microfinance programmes. They should develop new savings products (e.g. savings schemes for children, youth, workers and professionals) and offer them at market rates of interest. With a broader mix of fund sources, MFIs can offer loans for purposes other than production, such as education, housing and medical needs or the purchase of shares and equity. They can also broaden their institutional base for resource mobilization by establishing financial linkages with various financial institutions. Malaysia can learn from the experience of other countries such as India on SHGs, Indonesia on how financial linkages have been established and operationalized, and Bangladesh on innovations in the capital market and accessing commercial loan funds.

To effectively meet the challenge, the government should formulate policies that would encourage more institutions to enter the nascent industry of microfinance, and enable them to mobilize voluntary savings and charge market rates of interest. Rather than funding subsidized credit programmes and channelling cheap funds through a favoured few, the government should provide assistance for the capacity building of MFIs, especially in the area of staff training, systems development and institutional networking.

Notes

1 In the 1960s, MARA (Council of Trust for the Bumiputra) was created to assist the Bumiputras in commerce and industry by providing small loans and consulting and advisory services. In support of MARA's thrust, the Urban Development Authority and the State Development Economic Corporations provided business premises for the Bumiputras while the PERNAS (National Corporation) assisted in facilitating marketing links. All these agencies were placed under the umbrella of the Ministry of Public Enterprises, recently renamed the Ministry of Entrepreneurial Development. MARA's role is now confined to providing loans for educational purposes, i.e. for furthering education at local and overseas institutions of higher learning.

2 The FOA initially provided concessionary credit to farmers for various agricultural enterprises, but its lending activities were stopped in 1986 due to heavy arrears and were taken over by BPM. BPM has provided concessionary loans with interest rates ranging from 0 to 4 per cent p.a. under the Special Agricultural Loan Scheme for paddy farmers, fishermen and tobacco growers. BPM also provides commercial loans at market rates of interest to commercial farmers for various agricultural enterprises.

3 The CGC was established in 1972 to provide guarantee cover to commercial banks that extend loans to small-scale enterprises.

4 These figures do not reflect on-time repayment rate but the percentage of loans disbursed and of loan arrears that were repaid.

5 The base-lending rate in the financial system was between 8 to 10 per cent p.a. in 1996.

9

Microfinance in the Philippines: Battling the System

Ruth Callanta, Edgardo Garcia,
Gilberto M. Llanto and H. Dieter Seibel

Introduction

The Philippines was a country of great promise during the 1950s. Since then
it has not lived up to expectations, but has greatly lagged behind a number of
other Asian countries, in terms of both economic growth and poverty
alleviation. It is only within the last few years that this land of 70 million
people (1995) has again dared to hope that the growth and development so
earnestly desired by its peoples will return to the country.

After the crisis years under the Marcos regime, policy and structural
reforms were initiated under the Aquino and Ramos's administration. This
eventually put the economy back in the growth path. Over the five-year
period, 1991–5, overall GNP growth averaged only 3.4 per cent p.a. At the
current rate of population growth, this has meant that per capita income
grew hardly at all. However, there is a marked difference in growth between
the first and the latter part of that time period. During the first three years,
GNP growth rates were 0.1 per cent, 1.4 per cent and 1.3 per cent.
Subsequently, in 1994 and 1995, they jumped to a new level of 5.3 per cent
and 5.7 per cent respectively. At the same time, the government succeeded in
keeping inflation under control, which was brought down from 18.7 per cent
in 1991 to single-digit figures fluctuating between 7.6 per cent and 9.8 per
cent p.a. The value of the national currency, the Peso, stabilized too, with a
slight overall appreciation from P27.5 in 1991 to P25.9 to the US$ in 1995.[1]

With the recovery of the economy from stagnation, a significant increase in real savings was noted after 1993, particularly attributable to a growth in savings of the government and of corporations. At the same time, deposit and lending rates stabilized, starting in 1993. Lending rates of commercial banks averaged at 15 per cent p.a. in 1993–5, down from weighted averages of 23 per cent and 19 per cent in 1991 and 1992 respectively. At the same time nominal interest rates on savings jumped from close to 5 per cent in 1991 to an average around 8 per cent in recent years but mostly failed to exceed the inflation rate, yielding negative or near-zero real returns. Real returns on time deposits were not much higher, averaging only about 1 per cent p.a. during the last two years. This seems to have affected the savings of households and unincorporated enterprises, which not only failed to increase savings but also slowly declined in recent years.

In 1995 the formal financial system was strengthened by the creation of a new and more autonomous central bank, Bangko Sentral ng Pilipinas (BSP). The central bank pursued the financial reforms of the 1980s and increased banking competition by liberalizing bank entry and branching-out. The measures to liberalize the economic and financial policy framework have created a basically favourable environment for microfinance. With interest rate deregulation and a liberal bank entry and branching policy, there is ample room for the creation of more MFIs and the expansion of their activities.

The country was gradually but surely phasing out from IMF support, but less than a year before the phase-out the Asian meltdown hit the Philippine shores. But despite the difficult environment created by the financial crisis besetting the whole of Asia, but especially Indonesia, Thailand and Japan, recent news about the development of the financial sector and the economy as a whole have been positive.

Incidence of Poverty

The persistence of poverty despite recent developmental gains became such a rallying issue in the 1998 presidential elections that the overwhelming majority of the Filipino people elected the erstwhile opposition's candidate who campaigned on an anti-poverty platform. The overall incidence of poverty in the Philippines was 36 per cent in 1994, down by four percentage points from 40 per cent in 1991. According to the Family Income and Expenditure Survey, the total number of poor households has only slightly decreased from 4.78 million to 4.56 million during that period – almost fully matched by a corresponding growth of the population. On inauguration day in June 1998, the newly installed President-elect Estrada announced a strong focus on poverty alleviation in the framework of continued policy reform.

The Philippine poor are largest in number in the agricultural sector, which is attributed by some to a prevalence of large landholdings and a failed land reform. More than half the rural population are poor, with little change in incidence rates: 55 per cent in 1991 and 54 per cent in 1994. The incidence of rural poverty, about two-thirds, was highest among farming and fishing families. The decline in urban poverty, which is somewhat below average, was more marked: from 36 per cent in 1991 to 29 per cent in 1994. In addition to the magnitude of poverty, the government has also to contend with the highly inequitable distribution of income, which is slow in changing. Between 1991 and 1994, the Gini index has negligibly declined from 0.468 to 0.454, indicating a slightly more equitable distribution of income.

Financial Institutions and their Outreach to the Poor

Banks rarely lend to the poor. The poor also have very limited access to credit – from any source. Since 1991, less than 12 per cent of low-income families have borrowed, nearly two-fifths of them from relatives and friends and one-third from private moneylenders and co-operatives. NGOs provided only 2.9 per cent of that credit in urban and 1.9 per cent in rural areas. Co-operatives and rural banks have a much wider outreach, but serve more the non-poor than the poor. To remedy this situation, the government has supported as many as 111 credit programmes of which thirteen are targeted to the very poor (Table 9.1). Among them are the NGO MicroCredit Project of the Department of Trade and Industry with 82,000 borrowers through almost 2000 conduits (March 1996); the Self-employment Assistance Programme of the Social Welfare and Development Department with over 45,000 clients; the Grameen Bank Replication Project of the Agricultural Credit Policy Council, involving 23 NGOs, co-operatives and rural banks as replicators, with 13,500 beneficiaries (December 1994); and the Landbank's agricultural and rural credit channelling programme through rural banks and some 8000 co-operatives.

Experts agree that credit channelling has greatly undermined the viability of these institutions. To divest itself of the task of lending to the poor, Landbank has recently established a finance company, the People's Credit and

Table 9.1   Directed Credit Programmes in the Philippines, 1995

	Agricultural Credit	Ultra-poor	Salaried and Self-employed	Small/ Medium Enterprises	Total
No. of programmes	39	13	21	38	111
No. of implementing agencies	19	4	12	9	
Funds available in million US$	> 472.0	N.A.	> 123.6	> 644.8	> 1,240.4
Interest p.a.	6–14%	0%; 6%; to market rate	3–18%	7–24%	

Source: National Credit Council.
Exchange rate used in this table and in the text: US$1 = P25.90.

Finance Corporation (PCFC). The objective is to use PCFC for poverty lending so that Landbank can concentrate on its original mandate of agricultural reform lending and its new mandate of commercial lending to a growing agricultural sector. Prior to the creation of PCFC, the government used the National Livelihood Support Fund, the NLSF, under the Office of the President to provide microcredit. In 1995, the NLSF provided credit lines to about 60 MFIs valued at P83 million (US$3.2 million). As of March 1996, P46 million has effectively been lent to 28 rural banks and 10 co-operative rural banks. They in turn provided microloans not exceeding P25,000 (US$965) to 4345 end-users. These figures clearly show that such programmes are more symbolic in nature, with only insignificant outreach and impact.

The Philippines is a country in which NGOs abound. According to the National Economic Development Authority (NEDA) Monitoring Study, it is estimated that there are over 30,000 NGOs and community-based People's Organizations listed with the Securities and Exchange Commission. This includes close to 7000 development NGOs and up to 500 credit NGOs with an average of 100–200 borrowers; 50 of them are estimated to provide credit with a commercial orientation. Despite their large number, their outreach remains limited, with the largest NGO serving not much more than 3000 borrowers and savers. It is estimated that only 2 per cent of the credit needs of poor borrowers are actually covered.

On the whole, there is an estimated number of about 2800 MFIs in the Philippines with a total outreach of about 650,000 customers (Table 9.2). Adding more than 1000 rural shareholding banks, with an average of 2000 loan accounts and 6000 savings deposit accounts, and private development banks, total MFI outreach might exceed the one million mark. There are also some 8000 agricultural co-operatives not included in the table which are used by Landbank as credit channels. In addition, there are uncounted informal savings and credit associations, among them the ubiquitous RoSCAs (*paluwagan*), which mobilize and circulate their own resources.

Despite all these efforts, the overall outreach to the poor has remained

Table 9.2 Estimated Institutional Outreach of MFIs in the Philippines

MFI	Number of MFIs	Average Outreach	Total Outreach
Development NGOs	150	150	2,500
Grameen replicators	40	500	20,000
Mature credit NGOs	30	1,000	30,000
Immature credit NGOs	100	250	25,000
Co-operative rural banks	42	2,000	84,000
Credit co-operatives	1,500	300	450,000
People's organizations	500	50	25,000
Total	2,362		636,500

Source: Chua and Llanto, 1995.

small. The credit programmes of the government were found costly and unsustainable, leading to gross inefficiencies, financial market distortion and a weakening of private sector incentives to innovate. Credit NGOs have not fared much better. They may have an almost exclusive focus on the poor. But they are hampered by their weak institutional capacity, which largely appears beyond redemption unless they turn into proper financial institutions. Without a legal personality as a fully-fledged financial institution, the credit NGOs can neither raise sufficient equity nor tap deposits to sustain their operations. Lending funds may be made available from many sources, but the weak absorptive capacity of the NGOs is a binding constraint to a greater outreach. Some claim that only the rural banks have the potential of truly reaching out to the poor, but that they would require thorough familiarization with financial technologies of profitable banking with the poor. Some rural and private development banks in Mindanao have successfully demonstrated that banking with the poor is feasible.

The Philippine experience shows that those institutions that focus on the poor lack the capacity of reaching the poor in large numbers; while those institutions that possess the capacity lack the focus. It is quite clear that the effectiveness of NGOs banking with the poor could be greatly enhanced through the adoption of a legal status providing the authority to act as real financial intermediaries. However, given their small number, this will not solve the outreach problem. At the same time, the capacity of credit NGOs to develop and offer innovative financial products was found to be quite restricted. This is due to two major factors: their lack of competence in product development; and their lack of appropriate legal status, which makes deposit mobilization illegal.

Policy and Regulatory Framework

The eradication of poverty is one of the major concerns of the Philippine government. The Presidential Commission to Fight Poverty, the PCFP, has identified five major strategies to bring the incidence of poverty down to 30 per cent in 1998:

1. Promote and sustain economic growth at 5–7 per cent p.a. to create employment and livelihood opportunities.
2. Sustain growth strategies directly accessible to the poor, including labour-intensive industries, adequate agricultural prices, and credit retailing of co-operatives and NGOs to farmers, marginal borrowers and people's organizations at market rates, and the consolidation of livelihood programmes into a credit facility for the hardcore poor.
3. Expand basic social services.
4. Support income-generating community projects including skill and technology training, credit and livelihood assistance, and extension services.

5. Enhance the capabilities of the poor to help themselves through people's organizations, NGOs and local government.

Starting in the 1980s, a number of financial reforms have improved the policy environment in which MFIs operate. Interest rate ceilings were removed; the interest rates of preferential credit programmes were aligned with market rates; bank entry and branching-out were liberalized; competition in the domestic financial market was strengthened; and a stronger BSP replaced the former Central Bank of the Philippines. As a result, banks compete in deposit taking, offering innovative products directed at different market segments. Similarly, credit unions and co-operatives, which are under the supervision of the Co-operative Development Authority, offer withdrawable and non-withdrawal deposit products, particularly to small savers.

Recognizing the need to provide access to credit to the microeconomy, particularly smallholder agriculture and the small and microenterprise sector, the government has put in place several policies on credit allocation and deposit retention comprising the following interventions:

— requiring 75 per cent of the deposits generated from a region to be invested in that area;
— mandating banks to allocate 25 per cent of their net incremental loanable funds for agriculture, two-fifths (10 per cent) of which are to be lent to agrarian reform beneficiaries while three-fifths (15 per cent) are to be reserved for general agricultural lending;
— mandating all lending institutions to lend at least 10 per cent of their total loan portfolio to small enterprises with total assets up to a ceiling of P10 million;
— liberalizing bank branching regulations to bring banking services to a wider range of the population;
— implementing various directed credit programmes for the basic sectors.

On the whole, policymakers in the Philippines have relied more on government intervention and credit channelling than the self-reliant intermediation of market-oriented MFIs. For example, through credit programmes such as the Department of Trade and Industry's MicroCredit Project, the ACPC's Grameen Replication Project and the NLSF's loan programme, the government has increasingly used NGOs as alternative credit conduits. At the same time, NGOs are regarded as informal institutions, and are hence not permitted to mobilize deposits. This bars them from engaging in financial intermediation and becoming self-reliant, resulting in a loss of resource mobilization. This in turn is to be offset by mandating banks to allocate 25 per cent of their loanable funds to agriculture and 10 per cent to small enterprises: a piece of financial repression which places a heavy burden on the urban banking industry and is unlikely to spur processes of self-sustained growth in banking services to the poor. In fact, it might even prevent the further evolution of grassroots financial institutions owned and managed by the poor. At the same time, the newly liberalized policy environment might eventually pose a serious threat to the survival of non-mature, social-service-oriented credit NGOs, which are already found to operate in a policy vacuum. The government's 111 preferential credit programmes, which have been criticized for being inefficient, over-politicized, unco-ordinated and unsustainable, are presently under review. The Department of Finance, together with the National Credit Council, is in the process of rationalizing these programmes, guided by principles of sustainability and viability. It is not unlikely that a thorough reform of the government's credit programmes will have spillover effects on the NGO credit world.

It is predicted that ultimately there might only be one option: the transformation of mature credit NGOs into formal financial intermediaries. With reference to Grameen Bank in Bangladesh and BancoSol in Bolivia, it is concluded that this strategy seems to be the only realistic approach to the problems of lack of outreach, viability and sustainability. Furthermore, it is argued that placing the NGOs in such a legal structure is the only guarantee that their mission for the poor can be sustained and expanded on an ever-increasing scale. To implement this in the most effective way in the service of the poor, it is recommended that the government provide an appropriate supervisory and regulatory framework for MFIs based on the principle of self-regulation. Donors may be invited to participate in the policy dialogue and eventually provide the required support for the establishment of a self-regulatory authority at the second tier.

All this indicates that the government, inspired by brain trusts such as the ACPC and the Philippine Institute for Development Studies (PIDS) it has helped to support, is getting the message: in the long run only viable institutions will provide sustainable financial services to all segments of the population including the poor. Given the complexity of Filipino society and its formal and non-formal financial sectors, the implementation of this recognition will present a major challenge for some time to come.

Microfinance Capacity Assessment

In the framework of this study, seven MFIs were selected, six of which make explicit use of the Grameen technology in reaching the poor. The remaining one includes poor women as one of several target groups. Six are credit NGOs. One is a co-operative rural bank with regular co-operative as well as Grameen-type operations, which has been singled out here for a more detailed presentation.

> Ahon Sa Hirap, Inc. (ASHI): an MFI established in 1989 and incorporated in 1991; with an equity capital of P2.5 million; serving 2143 poor female beneficiaries organized in Grameen-type small groups; with a volume of

P3.5 million loans outstanding and US$23,166 savings outstanding in 1995.

Alalay Sa Kaulanran Sa Gitnang Luzon, Inc. (ASKI): an MFI established and incorporated in 1987; with an equity capital of US$250,965; serving 1552 poor clients, 85 per cent of them female; offering both group and individual loan services; with US$509,652 loans outstanding and US$61,776 savings outstanding in 1995.

The Centre for Agriculture and Rural Development (CARD): a microfinance and training institution established in 1992; with an equity capital of US$289,575; with 3980 poor beneficiaries, 98 per cent of them women, organized in groups of five; with US$49,806 loans outstanding and US$111,969 savings outstanding.

The Co-operative Rural Bank of Laguna, Inc. (CRBLI): an MFI established as a co-operative bank registered with the Securities and Exchange Commission and the Bureau of Co-operative Development in 1977. Operations started in 1978. Unlike NGOs it was given authority by the central bank to provide financial services to the community and accept savings and time deposits. Its equity capital amounts to US$444,015, comprising US$239,382 million in members' equity and US$204,633 in retained earnings. It serves 2583 savers, 81 per cent of them women and 55 per cent of them poor; and 1792 borrowers, 90 per cent of them women and 74 per cent of them poor; with US$1,088,803 loans outstanding and US$216,216 in savings deposits outstanding.

The Gerry Roxas Foundation Bangko Hublag (GRFHBH): an MFI established in 1987 with an equity capital of US$7,722 and registered with the central bank, providing loans to non-bankable microentrepreneurs and mobilizing internal resources through a capital build-up or savings scheme. Its equity and reserves in 1995 amounted to US$150,579. As of end-1995 it served 1259 savers who are all poor, 84 per cent of which are women; and 1198 borrowers, 73 per cent of them women and 85 per cent of them poor. Loans outstanding amounted to US$270,270 and savings outstanding to US$27,027.

The Negros Women for Tomorrow Foundation, Inc. Project Dungganon (PD): an MFI incorporated in 1986 to serve landless poor women in the depressed communities of Negros. As of 1995 its equity and fund balance was negative at −US$277,992. Its Grameen Bank replication programme started in 1989. It serves 9216 clients who are all women and all poor. As of end-1995 there were 5866 borrowers with active loan portfolios and 6952 active savings accounts. Loans outstanding amounted to US$308,880 in 1995, savings outstanding to US$127,413.

Tulay Sa Pag-Unlad Inc. (TSPI): an MFI established in 1982 targeting the entrepreneurial poor. Starting in 1984, TSPI initiated its Intermediary Lending Programme, lending wholesale to microentrepreneurs through 24 participating NGOs, co-operatives and community-based groups. At the end of 1995 its equity and fund balance stood at US$1,953,667. As of end-1995 TSPI served 3119 individual borrowers who were all poor, 64 per cent of them women, and 12 institutions. Loans outstanding amounted to US$2,158,301, 96 per cent of which were lent directly and 4 per cent wholesale through other institutions. Of the active loan portfolio of direct lending, 90 per cent were lent to men and only 10 per cent to women. TSPI serves a total number of 3024 savers, 64 per cent are women. Total savings outstanding as per December 1995 amounted to US$185,328, but only 18.5 per cent were mobilized from women.

The CRBLI has been singled out for a closer inspection, for two reasons: (1) it is the only institution among the seven which is financially self-reliant and viable, serving both poor and non-poor clients, but among them poor women as the large majority; and (2) since 1991, it is a Grameen Bank replicator, thus combining regular and Grameen-type operations. Does the Grameen approach enable an MFI to reach out to a poorer clientele? And, in doing so, can it cover its costs or perhaps even make a profit? The answer to the latter question is all the more interesting in the face of overwhelming evidence that NGOs microfinance providers in the Philippines are not viable.

The CRBLI was formally established in October 1977 by village-based co-operative farmers' organizations in the province of Laguna led by the president of the Provincial Federation of Samahang Nayon of Laguna. The required equity capital was contributed by the members of 90 participating farmers' organizations who decided to call the institution *Bangko ng Magbubukid*, i.e. *Bank of Farmers*. There are now 11 individuals and 124 farmers' co-operatives that own it. Its board of directors comprises eleven members, nine of them farmers and two representatives of the Landbank and the Department of Agriculture, respectively, which own preferred shares. The board has appointed the son of the founder as a manager. The CRBLI comprises a head office with a staff of 17 and it has no branches. Its operations are confined to the province of Laguna, which consists of 29 municipalities and one city.

Assisted by the ACPC as the pilot-testing agency of the Grameen Bank Replication Programme in the Philippines, the CRBLI adapted the Grameen approach in 1991 to extend its banking services to poor women without collateral. The scheme is called Kaunlarang Pangkabuhayan Project (KPP) Livelihood Development Project. Since 1994 the CRBLI has employed a staff of five, one male and four female, specifically for KPP. The programme was supported by the ACPC with a grant of US$7,722 to subsidize the salaries of the fieldstaff during the first three years and by a grant of US$77,220 from local government in 1995. The CRBLI generates the loan funds internally.

For reasons of cost-effectiveness, it has not provided any technical assistance to the women-microentrepreneurs.

Outreach

The seven MFIs have a total outreach of about 21,000 customers,[2] ranging from about 1260 to 7000 and averaging about 3000 per MFI. The smallest has an outreach of about 1300 customers, the largest about 7000. About 90 per cent of the customers of the MFIs are women. About 94 per cent are poor (Table 9.3). Two of the institutions target exclusively poor women. Five target exclusively the poor. In all seven institutions, women and the poor predominate among the savers and the borrowers. There is no indication that any of these institutions will greatly increase their outreach in the near-future.

Total loans outstanding as of December 1995 amounted to US$4,969,111, savings outstanding being only a fraction thereof, namely US$679,536 or 13.7 per cent (Table 9.4). There is wide variation between the seven sample MFIs, ranging from US$6,563 to US$186,486 in savings balances (a ratio of 1:35) and from US$134,362 to US$2,159,073 in loans outstanding (a ratio of 1:62). Average savings balances per saver ranged from P99 ($3.8) to P1,209 ($47) among the poor and from P2,826 ($109) to P15,400 ($595); average loans outstanding ranged from P744 ($29) to P12,104 ($467) among the poor and from P38,970 ($1505) to P66,545 ($2,569) among the non-poor.

Social preparation and client training in the use of credit are among the services offered by the sample MFIs. Some charge a training and monitoring fee of 2 per cent of the loan amount, while others rely on government and donor funding. Given the narrow scope of products and outreach, the problems associated with the quality and funding of client training as well as supervision and impact evaluation appear as minor issues.

To increase outreach in a cost-effective and sustainable way, it is proposed to confine capacity-building measures to existing viable and sustainable

Table 9.3 Outreach of Seven Sample MFIs in the Philippines, 1995

MFI	Savers			Borrowers		
	Number	% Poor	% Female	Number	% Poor	% Female
A	1,695	100	100	1,695	100	100
B	6,952	100	100	5,866	100	100
C	3,980	100	98	3,980	100	98
D	1,160	99	85	1,307	99	85
E*	1,415	55	81	1,330	74	90
F	1,941	100	64	1,993	100	64
G	1,958	100	84	764	85	73

E* = the CRBLI, singled out for more elaborate presentation in this chapter.

Table 9.4   Savings and Loans Outstanding in Seven MFIs in the Philippines, 1995 (In US dollars)

MFI	Savings	Loans	Ratio of savings to Loans (in %)
A	6,563	134,362	4.8
B	127,799	308,880	41.4
C	110,810	496,525	22.3
D	70,656	511,969	13.8
E*	150,193	1,090,733	13.8
F	186,486	2,159,073	8.6
G	28,185	269,111	10.4
Total	680,692	4,970,693	13.7
Poor only	611,583	4,333,976	14.1
Women only	453,667	2,348,262	19.3

E* = the CRBLI, singled out for more elaborate presentation in this chapter.
Exchange rate: US$1 = P25.9.

Table 9.5   Outreach of the CRBLI, 1995

MFI	Savers			Borrowers		
	No.	% Poor	% Female	No.	% Poor	% Female
1993	3893	40	77	1842	78	92
1994	3763	43	80	1889	77	91
1995	2583	55	81	1792	74	90

financial institutions which exist in the Philippines in large numbers, such as rural banks, co-operative rural banks and credit co-operatives with their nationwide network of unit banks and branches. Through appropriate forms of training in microfinance technologies, these institutions may greatly enhance their services to the poor. In contrast, investing in the creation of new branches of NGOs appears to be more costly and risky. Instead, it is recommended to transform credit NGOs into formal financial institutions such as private banks, finance companies, and non-stock savings and loan associations or credit co-operatives.

In 1995, the CRBLI served 1792 borrowers, down 5 per cent from the previous year, and 2583 savers, down 31 per cent from 1994. Between 1993 and 1995, the percentage of the poor among the savers has increased from 40 per cent to 55 per cent, the percentage of women from 77 per cent to 81 per cent (Table 9.5). The share of women and the poor among borrowers is substantially higher than among savers, but proportions have slightly decreased over the three-year period: from 78 per cent to 74 per cent poor borrowers and from 92 per cent to 90 per cent women borrowers. It appears that the CRBLI has reached the limits of its outreach, with a decline in the number of active borrowers and savers in the period 1993–5.

The CRBLI offers two savings products: passbook savings of a minimum of P500 (US$19) with a yield of 7 per cent p.a. and time deposits ranging from 90-day to 730-day maturities with yields from 9 per cent to 16 per cent p.a. While the number of savers has substantially dropped from 3893 in 1993 to 2583 in 1995, the average amount has gone up during that time period by about 50 per cent, namely from P1,011 to P1,506 (US$39 to $58). There has been no increase in nominal savings during that time period, but a substantial drop in real terms.

Compared to the number of poor savers, the volume of savings mobilized from the poor has been modest; however, its share has increased remarkably over the three-year period: from 4 per cent of all savings to 23 per cent. The total amount of savings mobilized from women has slightly declined over the three-year period: from 76 per cent to 64 per cent. While the volume of the loans grew at an average of 19.5 per cent p.a., it did so at a diminishing rate. The average maturity was 180 days at an interest rate of 18 per cent p.a. The bulk of the loans have been given directly to individual borrowers.

While the vast majority of borrowers are poor, only a small proportion of the volume of the loan portfolio goes to them, increasing from 4 per cent in 1993 to 11 per cent in 1995. The share of the women in the volume of loans is not quite commensurate with their numbers, declining from 61 per cent in 1993 to 57 per cent in 1995 (Table 9.6).

In the field of credit, the Grameen programme KPP has contributed to a very substantial increase in outreach of the CRBLI: 1330 or 74 per cent of the CRBLI's 1792 borrowers fall under the KPP (Table 9.7). Under the influence of the KPP, loans provided through savings groups have been increasing from 1 per cent of total loans granted in 1993 to 15 per cent in 1995. However, in terms of volume, the contribution of KPP borrowers, US$121,621, to the CRBLI's total loan portfolio of US$1,090,733 outstanding is modest, comprising only 11 per cent. Evidently, loans outstanding to poor women averaging P2,367 (US$91) are far below the CRBLI's overall average, which is P15,763 (US$608) per borrower. There are wide discrepancies in terms of average loans outstanding by sex and poverty status in 1995: the average size of loans was P9,987 (US$385) for women and

Table 9.6 Savings and Loans Outstanding in the CRBLI, 1995 (Amounts in US dollars)

Year	Savings			Loans			Ratio of Savings to Loans (in %)
	Amount	% Poor	% Female	Amount	% Poor	% Female	
1993	152,123	4	76	765,637	4	61	19.9
1994	125,096	13	71	959,845	6	59	13.0
1995	150,193	23	64	1,090,733	11	57	13.8

Exchange rate: US$1 = P25.9.

Table 9.7   Savings and Loans in the CRBLI, KPP vs. Entire Bank Operation, 1995

	KPP (Grameen)		Entire Bank Operations	
	Number	Amount in US Dollars	Number	Amount in US Dollars
Savings:				
Total	1,415	35,135	2,583	150,193
Poor	1,415	35,135	1,415	35,135
Non-poor	0	0	1,168	115,057
Women	1,415	35,135	2,087	96,138
Men	0	0	496	54,054
Loans outstanding:				
Total	1,330	121,621	1,792	1,090,733
Poor	1,330	121,621	1,330	121,621
Non-poor	0	0	462	969,111
Women	1,330	121,621	1,609	498,841
Men	0	0	183	470,270

Exchange rate: US$1 = P25.90.

P66,545 (US$2,569) for men; P2,367 (US$91) for the poor and P54,327 (US$2,097) for the non-poor.

In the field of outreach to savings depositors, the Grameen programme KPP has more than doubled the CRBLI's outreach. All of the KPP's 1415 participants have deposited savings in the CRBLI, compared to 1168 non-KPP depositors. Thus, 55 per cent of all depositors are KPP participants. However, in terms of volume, their share is substantially lower, namely 23 per cent of a total of US$150,193, yet much higher than their credit share. This shows once again: the poor can save, and, in particular: women are good savers!

The average size of savings in the bank was P1,506 (US$58). Again, discrepancies exist, but they are by far not as wide as in the field of credit: women saved on average P1,192 (US$46), men saved P2,826 (US$109). The poor saved an average of P642 (US$25), the non-poor P2,553 (US$98).

Resource Mobilization

There are three major sources of loanable funds in the seven sample MFIs: equity and grants, borrowings, and savings mobilized. Among these three sources, savings are least important. They account for only 13.7 per cent of loans outstanding. Savings mobilized from the poor account for 14.1 per cent of loans outstanding to the poor. Among women, savings are slightly more important, accounting for 19.3 per cent of loans outstanding. The amount of savings deposits mobilized by the seven sample MFIs ranges from a minimum of US$6,564 to a maximum US$186,486, a ratio of 1:28 (Table 9.8).

Two-thirds of the savings (67.6%) are mobilized from women and one-third from men. The poor account for nine-tenths (89.8%) of the savings mobilized. The most important source of loanable funds are equity and grants

Table 9.8 Amount of Savings Outstanding, Seven Sample MFIs in the Philippines, 1995 (In US dollars)

MFI	Female		Male		Total
	Poor	Non-poor	Poor	Non-poor	
A	6,564		31		6,595
B	127,799		81		127,880
C	107,722		3,089		110,811
D	54,054	5,792	8,494	2,317	70,657
E*	35,135	61,004	54,054		150,193
F	32,432		154,054		186,486
G	23,166		5,019		28,185
Total	386,872	66,796	224,822	2,317	680,807
Per cent	56.8%	9.8%	33.0%	0.4%	100.0%

E* = the CRBLI, singled out for more elaborate presentation in this chapter.
Exchange rate: US$1 = P25.90.

which account for 58.5% of loans outstanding. The remainder is mobilized through borrowings.

The single most important factor, which undermines the sustainability of the sample MFIs, is their dependency on external resources. Most MFIs in the sample lack resources internally generated in the form of equity capital and savings deposits. The MFIs have all attempted to mobilize resources in various innovative ways but their informal character has hampered the effort. The MFIs have thus failed to evolve into full-service institutions providing the poor with adequate savings deposit facilities.

Under the prevailing practices, the MFIs continue to be subsidy-dependent and donor-driven. As donor funds are invariably short in supply, the institutions lack the potential of dynamic growth. At the same time, the institutions find themselves compelled to devote some of their most creative manpower to the acquisition of donor grants, donor reporting and other forms of donor communication. It is also questionable whether under these circumstances participation in national or international conferences, seminars and workshops is a learning experience or a waste of precious time. It is concluded that grants and subsidies from government and donors have stunted the growth of many credit NGOs into viable and sustainable financial intermediaries.

In order to stay competitive and viable, the MFIs must raise substantial deposits and develop various instruments, especially for the small savers, which will help to build up their financial base. Both financial broadening and deepening are needed, comprising the development of new product lines and services and the implementation of new microfinance technologies and practices that strengthen their financial base.

The CRBLI has an active loan portfolio of US$1,090,733 as of end of December 1995. Its major source of funds are equity capital and retained earnings amounting to US$444,015, i.e. 41 per cent of its loans outstanding. Savings deposits are a minor source of loanable funds, equivalent to only 14 per cent of loans outstanding. In the KPP Grameen scheme internal savings play a larger but still a very restricted role, amounting to 29 per cent of the loans outstanding within the scheme.

Borrowings as of end-1995 amounted to US$514,285, accounting for almost half (47 per cent) of the outstanding loan portfolio. Sources of refinance included the Landbank's Rediscounting Programme ((53 per cent of borrowings); the Co-operative Development Authority's lending facility (19 per cent of borrowings); the MicroCredit II Project of the Department of Trade and Industry for established microentrepreneurs and SHGs (1 per cent of borrowings); the Grains Production Enhancement Programme (GPEP) or Gintong Ani with input subsidies and agricultural support services for rice and maize production (10 per cent of borrowings); the Agricultural Credit Policy Council (15 per cent of borrowings); and local banks (2 per cent of borrowings). With access to such a rich source of external finance, the CRBLI appears to have little motivation to vigorously embark on the cumbersome job of mobilizing savings from its members and the community.

Financial Viability and Sustainability

The overall evidence on the viability of the sample MFIs is conflicting. There are positive indications, such as sound credit practices and response to market signals. Of crucial relevance is the fact that none of the NGOs adheres to the creed of subsidized credit for the poor. In fact, they lend at market-based interest rates, charging around 30 per cent interest p.a., plus an up-front service charge of about 1 per cent. They are also aware that they should cover at least part of their operating costs. Credit screening and loan appraisal techniques were found to be sound.

Collateral substitutes such as joint liability, peer pressure and pledged group savings were found to be adequate, resulting in loan repayment rates in the order of 95 per cent. Forced savings were used as an emergency loan fund and at the same time as collateral. One MFI offers a rebate of 5 per cent for timely repayment and adds a penalty of 2 per cent on past-due loans. At the same time, NGO banking with the poor is expensive. Only one of the MFIs has a cost ratio per Peso of loan outstanding below 0.20; four have ratios between 0.29 and 0.71; one has costs of one Peso for every Peso of loan outstanding; and one MFI spends P1.30 on every Peso outstanding (Table 9.9). It is concluded that the MFIs are generally inefficient and not cost-effective, with high management and overhead expenses relative to the number of clients served and the volume of business generated. The only exception in the sample is the co-operative rural bank, which was found efficient and cost-effective.

There are serious shortcomings in financial reporting and monitoring,

Table 9.9 Viability Indicators of Seven Sample MFIs in the Philippines, 1995

MFI	Cost per Average Peso of loan outstanding	Degree of Operational Self-sufficiency %	Degree of Financial Self-sufficiency in %
A	1.30	21	19
B	1.00	8	7
C	0.71	51	42
D	0.48	67	48
E*	0.19	134	118
F	0.29	113	93
G	0.34	66	N.A.

E* = the CRBLI, singled out for more elaborate presentation in this chapter.

which make it difficult to calculate arrears ratios and to determine portfolio quality. What is lacking in particular is a financial monitoring system that tracks arrears and loan delinquencies as they occur, and then use them as an input into a management information system. Instead, repayment ratios and default rates are calculated at the year's end. This was found to encourage laxity on the part of management, which fails to take immediate remedial action on delinquency. The absence of accounting and quality standards also makes it difficult to accurately measure the performance of MFIs. This may turn out to be a major obstacle for donors or commercial banks that might otherwise be willing to invest in promising MFIs. It is concluded that internal financial policies and practices need a lot of improvement, particularly in the installation of sound financial reporting and monitoring systems, portfolio management, assessment and management of risks, product packaging and pricing, management of loan arrears and strategic business planning.

On the whole the MFIs are not operationally self-sufficient, and much less financially so. Their delivery of financial services to the poor continues to be contingent upon the availability of grants and concessional loans. If such funds dry up, it is feared that the survival of the MFIs is endangered. Again, an exception in the sample is the co-operative rural bank, which does not suffer from the constraints faced by the NGOs as non-formal financial institutions. It is difficult to avoid the conclusion that the most promising avenue of reversing the trend leading to their financial collapse would be their transformation into a financial institution of appropriate legal status, such as a co-operative rural bank, including the adoption of sound financial practices.

To make MFIs viable and self-sustained, it is recommended: to build up their equity base through capital infusion from existing owners and new investors; to diversify credit, savings and other financial products in response to demand; to maximize savings mobilization opportunities; to provide training in financial management, resource mobilization, portfolio management, risk management, product packaging and pricing, and strategic business planning; and to improve operating systems and procedures, including the institutionalization of performance standards, the installation of a standardized accounting and reporting system, and the adoption of internal auditing.

Over the three-year period 1993–5, the CRBLI has been profitable, and so has its KPP Grameen replication scheme. During that period, the CRBLI's gross earnings averaged about US$220,077 and its costs US$162,162, yielding an annual average net income of over US$57,000. Revenues increased at a slightly faster rate than expenses. While loan interest charges were the principal source of income, earnings from service charges and other receipts have become increasingly significant.

Salaries paid to personnel were the biggest expense item, comprising about half of total expenses. Thirty per cent went to interest payments on borrowings mainly from other banks and government agencies, comprising 1.5 per cent of loans outstanding in 1993 and jumping to 5.2 per cent in 1994 and 6.0 per cent in 1995. Interest paid on deposits consisted of 6 per cent of the CRBLI's expenses.

The CRBLI makes a profit from its KPP Grameen scheme, but at 6 per cent of gross revenues and 7 per cent of net revenues only on a minimal scale. Salaries eat up more than half of the bank's aggregate expenses for this activity (Table 9.10).

Costs calculated per Peso of total financial services (credit and savings) in 1995 were P0.17 for the entire bank operations and P0.15 for the KPP Grameen scheme (Table 9.11). In both cases there was a slight increase in costs since 1993 by P0.01. Total salaries spent for every Peso of financial services by the entire bank were P0.06. KPP operations were slightly more personnel-intensive, costing P0.07. Total costs per average loan outstanding were identical at P0.19. With a debt-equity ratio of 1.64 in 1995 (substantially down from 2.59 in 1994), borrowings of the bank appear adequately backed up by equity. The total income of the bank per Peso of loan given out was an identical P0.26 for both the KPP Grameen and the entire bank operations. However, there is a substantial difference in

Table 9.10 Revenues and Costs in the CRBLI, KPP vs. Entire Bank Operation, 1995 (in US dollars)

	KPP (Grameen)	Entire Bank Operations
Total revenues	22,934	262,587
Interest on loans	22,548	208,533
Other loan service charges and receipts	386	54,054
Total costs	17,220	193,320
Interest paid on deposits	4,633	10,734
Interest on borrowings	0	61,853
Salaries	11,467	88,957
Other operating costs	1,120	31,776
Net revenues	5,714	69,267

Exchange rate: US$1 = P25.90.

Table 9.11 Efficiency Measures in the CRBLI, KPP vs. Entire Bank Operation, 1995 (Amounts in '000 pesos)

	KPP (Grameen)	Entire Bank Operations
Total costs (Peso '000)	446	5,007
Total costs (US dollars)*	17,220	193,320
Total Peso costs per one Peso of total financial services	0.15	0.17
Salaries as % of total financial services	7.32%	6.03%
Ratio of salaries/Total assets	6.57	5.97
Ratio of administrative costs/Total assets	6.81	9.21
Total peso cost per One Peso Loan	0.19	0.19
Debt-Equity ratio		1.64
Return on performing assets	0.33%	0.56%
Gross return per Peso of Loan outstanding	0.26	0.26

* Exchange rate: US$1 = P25.90.

Table 9.12 Degree of Operational and Full Financial Self-sufficiency in the CRBLI, KPP vs. Entire Bank Operation, 1995 (amounts in US dollars)

	KPP (Grameen)	Entire Bank Operations
Interest rate to borrowers	25%	25%
Repayment rate	97%	89%
Default rate	7%	18%
Interest and fees from clients ($)	22,934	255,212
Degree of operational self-sufficiency	1.34	1.34
Savings for on-lending ($)	5,830	193,590
Bank lending rate + 2%	27%	27%
Adjusted total costs ($)	19,498	293,552
Degree of full financial self-sufficiency	1.18	0.87

Exchange rate: US$1 = P25.90.

magnitude and trend of net operating income over total performing assets, which is 0.33% for the KPP Grameen scheme (down from 0.46% in 1993) and 0.56% for the entire bank operations (up from 0.39% in 1993).

Default rates resulting from bankwide operations appear within manageable limits but could be substantially improved. In the last three years, the ratio of past due loans to total loans outstanding was steady at 17–18 per cent. Collections on matured loans improved slightly from 85 per cent to 89 per cent. The recovery performance of the KPP Grameen scheme was substantially better, with a repayment rate of 97 per cent in 1995 (down from a high of 99 per cent in 1993). The CRBLI's earnings from interest income and fees covers more than its costs, with a degree of operational self-sufficiency (defined as the ratio of said earnings to total costs less depreciation) of 134 per cent of the entire bank operations as well as the KPP Grameen scheme (Table 9.12).

Adjusting the costs by taking into account the costs of financial services and borrowings and other costs, the proportion of the CRBLI's interest earnings and fees are higher than the standard ratio of 80 per cent, though not much. With a yield of P0.87 (a slight increase over a ratio of 0.84 in 1993) in income for every Peso of adjusted cost, the bank as a whole is reasonably close to financial self-sufficiency. In contrast, the KPP Grameen scheme, with a ratio of 1.18, has attained more than full financial self-sufficiency to which the government has contributed with free training and funding assistance.

Concluding Observations

The CRBLI has demonstrated the profitability of microfinance in two respects: both its own original operations with poor and non-poor members and its more recent operations with very poor women under a Grameen-type replication scheme cover their costs and yield a profit.

The CRBLI has faced three constraints: a limitation in outreach, a not quite satisfactory repayment rate, and a weakness in savings mobilization. It has attempted to solve the first constraint by adopting the KPP Grameen replication scheme, which has more than doubled its outreach in terms of numbers of clients. As the repayment rate in the KPP scheme has been far better than that of its co-operative clients, this has also contributed to a solution of its second constraint, but given the small size of the KPP loan portfolio, only to an insignificant measure. Its management may also feel that an overall repayment rate of 89 per cent is an excellent performance compared to other co-operatives in the country which have been undermined by a tradition of preferential loan channelling and un-penalized defaulting; and that it might be difficult in such a culture to do much better. No solution is in sight for its third constraint, weak savings mobilization. This is due, on the one hand, to zero or negative real returns on savings which could of course be remedied by increasing the rates of interest on both savings and loans which is optional for any institution. On the other hand, there seems to be little pressure on the bank to mobilize more savings as long as it has access to governmental sources of easy money which are liberally replenished by international donors.

In terms of most performance indicators, the CRBLI's Grameen-type scheme with poor women organized in groups of five has been a success. Local out-reach has been substantially increased; repayment rates are high; and the bank makes a profit from the operation. Yet, the bank's management is not enthusias-tic. In quantitative terms, the volume of savings mobilized and loans disbursed to poor women is only an insignificant share of the bank's overall business, and so is the volume of profit derived from the KPP Grameen replication scheme. The management does not see enough potential in this market segment of poor women to argue that in the long run the bank will contribute to the growth of their microenterprises and that these in turn will contribute to the growth of the bank. Such is perhaps not the logical inclination of a co-operative bank with a governance and incentive structure quite different from a privately owned bank such as BSD in Indonesia. The management therefore considers terminating the KPP scheme, which it finds profitable in relative but not in absolute terms. As there are less than 1500 participants in the KPP scheme and the bank seems to be close to its perceived limits of capacity, costly efforts of convincing the management of its social mission may be difficult to justify.

Notes

1 Exchange rates, $US1.00 = (1991) P27.48; (1992) P25.51; (1993) P26.99; (1994) P26.45 and (1995) P25.90.
2 As there are no borrowers without a savings account but there are savers without active loan portfolios, the total number of clients of an institution equals the number of savers.

10
Microfinance in the Pacific Islands: Adjusting to Aid Dependence and the Dutch Disease

Joe Remenyi

Introduction

The South Pacific island economies (PIEs) are a collection of 'poor little rich countries'. Rich in scenery, area of fisheries, sunshine and cultural heritage, the PIEs are also burdened, more than any other with the twin tyranny of distance and fragmented markets. The sovereign territories of the South Pacific consist of collections of islands and atolls, often separated by treacherous reefs and vast areas of ocean. Even in the most populous of the PIEs, Fiji and Papua New Guinea, there are no domestic markets of any scale or the resource base to envisage self-sufficiency in many of the commonest of the artefacts of modernity. Local aspirations to gain access to complicated manufactures, commonplace electro-chemical products, the latest communications or transport technologies and many of the services related to modern medicine or higher education are tied to the ability to import or emigrate for overseas employment. To pay for these imports, almost all PIEs are chronically dependent on foreign aid. Although PIEs account for only one-tenth of one per cent of the population of the Third World, in 1995 they received three per cent of total ODA flows to all developing countries. In no other way have the PIEs been able to sustain the chronic foreign trade deficits on which virtually all the PIEs, with few exceptions, have become dependent.

Economic dependence on persistent trade deficits has spread like a

Table 10.1 GDP Growth in Selected PIEs

	GNP per head:		Exports as % Imports 1994	ODA Receipts, 1995:		Debt Service Ratio '94 %
	1994 US$	Growth 1985–94 % p.a.		Total Millions US$	As % GNP	
Nauru	16,400	N.A.	N.A.	2	N.A.	N.A.
Cook Islands	3,784	N.A.	0.05	13	17	N.A.
Fiji	2,320	2.4	1.02	43	2	7.1
Micronesia	1,764	N.A.	N.A.	77	N.A.	N.A.
Tonga	1,640	0.3	0.20	38	14	3.3
Papua New Guinea	1,240	2.2	N.A.	372	6	N.A.
Vanuatu	1,150	−0.3	0.73	46	19	1.5
Tuvalu	1,050	N.A.	0.06	8	40	N.A.
Western Samoa	970	−0.3	0.09	43	15	10.5
Solomon Islands	800	2.2	N.A.	47	15	5.6
Kiribati	730	N.A.	0.20	15	43	N.A.

Sources: Development Assistance Committee, 1996; World Bank, 1996b, 1993c; South Pacific Forum Secretariat, 1996.

pandemic across the South Pacific. With the possible exception of Fiji and Papua New Guinea, exchange rates have become a poor measure of the strength of the domestic economy. Aid inflows support exchange rates that are overvalued relative to the productivity of the local economy and the level of export-related economic activity. The result is that imports are artificially cheap and the capacity of local producers to compete with imported foods, clothes and other wage goods is seriously undermined if not wholly compromised. This is a classic 'Dutch disease' scenario, which continuously undermines local self-reliance as well as efforts to stimulate domestic economic growth and higher levels of domestic employment. It is not surprising, therefore, that the economic growth record of the PIEs is less than impressive. Consider the data in Table 10.1.

Where data are available (not all PIEs produce annual national accounts), these revealed a record that the World Bank, 1993c described as a 'paradox': i.e. despite a relatively favourable resource endowment, reasonably prudent macroeconomic management in the 1980s and high levels of foreign aid, there has been little or no growth in real income per head. As we will see, however, the record is not inconsistent with a region that has a very limited 'extent of the market', to use Adam Smith's famous phrase to describe what limits the wealth of nations, and where consumer aspirations are so intimately tied to imports.

In the 1980s, despite the long-term ramifications of the energy crisis of the 1970s, the PIEs had reasonably good economic management, as evidenced by low inflation, generally low fiscal deficits, modest growth in money supply and reasonably stable exchange rates. This delivered macroeconomic stability but little in the way of economic growth, employment generation or rural development. In the 1990s, however, there has been a deterioration in macroeconomic performance in a number of countries. In Papua New Guinea, budget deficits increased significantly, ending in a fiscal trauma in 1994, further complicated by continuing political unrest in Bougainville and the Fly river areas that disrupted the flow of financial returns from two of the country's largest mining ventures. The Papua New Guinea government sought assistance from the World Bank and the International Monetary Fund (IMF), which resulted in the reluctant acceptance of a structural adjustment package.

Similar fiscal indiscipline in the Cook Islands led to an economic crisis in 1996, with a major restructuring of the economy needed there too. In the Solomon Islands, allegations of gross corruption involving illegal logging and flaunting of conservation regulations by persons at the highest level of government were also very disruptive, fuelling uncertainty and a hostile investment environment. In Fiji, too, there was political unrest associated with the collapse of democratic due process, institution of constitutional reforms to establish a republic, and mass emigration of significant numbers of ethnic Indian-Fijians and their capital. Hence, even in PIEs where the economic growth record over the past decade has been positive 'on average', this average hides the roller-coaster ride that political events and associated macroeconomic management have delivered to the people of the region. In this unstable and largely negative environment it is very difficult for newly launched microfinance and microenterprise initiatives to survive unaided.

The apparent ineffectiveness of government policies in ensuring sustainable economic growth has focused attention on the need for accelerated private-sector development, including informal-sector and microenterprise development for income and employment generation at the household level. In 1991, out of an economically active population of 1.8 million, there were not more than 400,000 formal-sector jobs throughout the region. Most of the remaining labour force was engaged in subsistence agriculture, with a small number of people working in the urban informal sector. This situation has come about because the labour force in almost all PIEs has expanded much more rapidly than the number of jobs in the formal sector. This continues to be the case in almost all PIEs. Hence, there is an important role for private-sector-based self-help programmes and policies to promote opportunities for self-employment, family employment and growth in microenterprise economic activity, all of which has contributed to increased awareness of and interest by policymakers and development agencies in the South Pacific in the potential benefits of greater support for microfinance for poorer households.

Demographic and Infrastructure Constraints to Delivery of Microfinance Services

A major obstacle to be overcome in successfully implementing microfinance and microenterprise development programmes in the South Pacific is the

Table 10.2 Population Distribution in PIEs

	Population		
	1995 ('000)	Density per sq. km.	Percentage Urban
Papua New Guinea	3951.5	9	15
Fiji	777.7	42	39
Solomon Islands	385.2	13	13
Vanuatu	168.4	13	18
Western Samoa	159.9	56	21
Micronesia	105.9	56	21
Tonga	98.3	132	23
Kiribati	78.4	97	35
Cook Islands	19.1	81	59
Nauru	10.5	N.A.	N.A.
Tuvalu	9.5	365	43

Sources: South Pacific Forum Secretariat, 1996; Economist's Intelligence Unit, 1996.

fragmented market that characterize the PIEs. Fragmented markets are the direct result of the geography of the region. Consider the data in Table 10.2. Not only are the absolute population numbers relatively small compared to the populous nations of Asia, where the microfinance models being emulated were developed, but the critical mass of consumers and producers is further stretched by the vast areas over which these small population totals are spread. The six million or so people in the area covered by the PIEs are spread over a massive 14 million square kilometres, with almost three-quarters of the total population in one country – Papua New Guinea. Yet, even in Papua New Guinea the population density figures are small and geography ensures that the population centres are anything but contiguous. Only in the atoll economies of Tuvalu and Tonga do the population density figures bear some comparison to those for Malaysia, the Philippines, Pakistan or Indonesia. But in the South Pacific, the most disadvantaged and vulnerable people tend to be concentrated on the outer islands or in the more isolated areas of the main islands, making the realization of economies of scale especially difficult. (See Getu, 1996.)

Indeed, with the exception of Western Samoa, all the PIEs are archipelagos with a number of remote outer islands located some distance from the capital. However, these problems are perhaps greatest for Kiribati (with a population of 78,300 living on 28 main islands spread over 3,550,000 square kilometres, an area larger than India), the Cook Islands and Tuvalu, with populations of 19,100 and 9500 respectively, also spread over very large areas of ocean.

Low population densities and the unique physical geography of the South Pacific also reduce the scope for meeting the transport and communications needs of widely separated communities in many parts of the Pacific. Consequently there is a common lack of transport and communications infrastructure throughout the Pacific. In Papua New Guinea and Solomon Islands, roads are extremely limited and many villages are accessible only by long and arduous journeys on foot. While some main roads exist, the lack of feeder roads hinders access to areas away from the main population centres. In almost all PIEs there are many outlying islands accessible only by sea or air services. Typically inter-island communications and transport services are known for their irregularity, infrequency, costly delays and lack of reliability.

Another related constraint is the subsistence base of much of the economic activity. While no official data are available, the vast bulk, upwards of 70 per cent, of the labour force in the South Pacific is engaged primarily in subsistence agriculture in relatively isolated rural areas. There is limited production of goods and services for the market, either because there is no surplus to market or because there is no market to supply. Hence, the establishment of microenterprises involves a transition from producing for home consumption to producing for the market, and this is unlikely until monetization has burrowed more deeply into the local needs of households.

Although parts of Asia share some of these constraints, the PIEs have them in abundance. It may well be, therefore, that expectations as to what is achievable in the PIEs through the spread of microfinance should be more modest than in more densely populated countries such as Bangladesh, India, Indonesia or the Philippines.

Incidence of Poverty

There is great reluctance among policymakers and civil servants from the PIEs to admit that there is a poverty problem in the South Pacific. The concept of 'poverty' is treated as a highly sensitive issue, with frequent assertions that in the PIEs there is no poverty, but 'subsistence affluence', with the vast majority of the population having ready access to land for subsistence agriculture or the sea for fishing. While people may have low cash incomes, their ties to the subsistence economy is supposed to insure that everyone can maintain a decent standard of living. Moreover, communal obligations mean that nobody goes without. It is not surprising, therefore, that for none of the PIEs is there an official poverty line, nor do they have any endorsed estimates of the number of people living in poverty.

The UNDP has recently undertaken a study of income distribution and poverty in Fiji (reported in Hussein, 1996), which estimated poverty lines based on minimum requirements for food, housing and clothing, with separate poverty lines depending on whether or not vegetables and staples were home grown. Using data from the 1990–1 household income and expenditure survey, it found that around 25 per cent of the population in Fiji were living below the poverty line. The results of the study have been presented in public seminars, but the report has not been released or endorsed by the Fiji Government (McGuire, 1996). However, given that Fiji has one of the higher per capita incomes in the region, it is likely that this finding for Fiji is indicative of significant poverty in other PIEs also. This surmise is supported by the Pacific Human Development Report for 1994, also produced by the UNDP, which analysed human development in the South Pacific. The study showed that a number of countries, most notably Papua New Guinea and Solomon Islands but also Vanuatu and Kiribati, had low levels of human development in terms of indicators such as life expectancy at birth, literacy, and educational attainment. This is evident from the trends in human capital indicators shown in Table 10.3.

Why there is a reluctance to acknowledge the existence of widespread poverty in many PIEs is not a matter we explore here, but it is a factor that undermines the commitment of officials to poverty-alleviation programmes, microfinance included. Also, there is resistance to close targeting of poor households, based on the view that rural development in the South Pacific is not about poverty reduction but about modernization and income growth for all households. Yet, if one studies the evidence it is clear that there are large numbers of people living in poverty in the South Pacific. There is every probability that their poverty persists in part because they lack access to even the most rudimentary services. This conclusion is supported by the data in Table 10.3.

Compared to other developing economies in the same lower-middle income group, PIEs have a high age dependency ratio, low female participation rates in paid employment, and declining food production per head of population. In most PIEs the average life expectancy is less than 60 years and mortality rates for infants and pregnant mothers are well in excess of the median. The most populous country, Papua New Guinea, ranks especially poorly on these grounds, with infant and maternal mortality rates excessively high by any standards. Similarly, fertility rates are often twice those common in even the poorest economies of Asia, and the proportion of rural communities with access to potable water is as low as one in five.

There are also disturbing signs that poverty and basic needs deprivation are increasing in many areas of the South Pacific. A number of countries are experiencing rapid population growth. Lack of land in the rural areas is encouraging rural-urban migration, giving rise to health, sanitation and housing problems in urban areas. In addition, the social support mechanisms that have limited poverty in the past are beginning to break down, especially in the urban areas. It is essential that there be official acknowledgement that there is a poverty problem. Without this as a policy prior, it is difficult to see how an explicit focus on poverty reduction in the development programmes of the PIEs can be implemented.

In summary, the evidence that is available suggests that there are significant numbers of disadvantaged and vulnerable people in the Pacific. To the extent that this poverty persists because of a lack of access to financial services by poor households, there is a role for increased attention to the microfinance needs of poor households in the South Pacific. Happily, some prominent central banks in the region have recently begun to give

Table 10.3 Human Capital Trends, Selected PIEs

	Life Expectancy (Years)	Mortality Rates: (per '000 live births)			% GDP Spent on Basic Social Services	Enrolment Ratios Primary Schools		Female Literacy Rate %	Total Fertility Rate %	People per Nurse	% with Access to Clean Water, Urban: Rural
		Infant	Under 5 Years	Maternal		Male	Female				
Fiji	72	27	22	0.9	10.6*	128	127	89	2.8	490	100:48
Micronesia	63*	37	N.A.	N.A.	N.A.	N.A.	N.A.	N.A.	5.1	N.A.	N.A.
Tonga	69	19	24	N.A.	N.A.	133	N.A.	84	3.4	546*	92:98
Papua New Guinea	57	65	95	7.0	N.A.	80	67	63	4.9	1164	94:20
Vanuatu	60	47	N.A.	N.A.	N.A.	105	107	80	5.1	469*	100:64
Western Samoa	69	23	N.A.	N.A.	2.8	136	N.A.	76	4.3	406*	100:77
Solomon Is.	62	42	52	N.A.	N.A.	102	87	N.A.	5.2	N.A.	82:58
Kiribati	57	65	N.A.	N.A.	N.A.	84*	N.A.	N.A.	3.8	190	91:62
Comparisons:											
East Asia	68	35	51	N.A.	N.A.	119	115	76	2.2	1490	84:61
All LDCs in same income group	67	47	36	N.A.	N.A.	105	101	N.A.	2.7	N.A.	N.A.
Next higher income group	69	36	43	N.A.	N.A.	107	N.A.	85	2.8	N.A.	94:65

Notes:
Data are the most recent available, typically for the early 1990s.
* estimated average.
Sources: Development Assistance Committee, 1996; World Bank, 1996b, 1993c; South Pacific Forum Secretariat, 1996.

microfinance greater attention. For instance, in June 1996 (see Belloni, 1996), a number of PIEs central bankers attended an ESCAP workshop on informal financial systems, held in Fiji. As a follow-up, the Reserve Bank of Fiji organized a national conference on microfinance in 1997. There is also a move in Papua New Guinea to revitalize and redevelop the savings and loan society movement, but much more is needed in Papua New Guinea and in the other PIEs.

Financial Institutions and their Outreach to the Poor

McGuire, 1996, in a significant regional survey of the financial institutions that operate in nine PIEs, reported that there is very limited financial sector outreach to poor households irrespective where they are located in the South Pacific. Moreover, what experience the modern banking sector has had in reaching out (whether on their own account or as an agent of government or an aid agency), to small business, women's groups, NGOs working with disadvantaged groups, or rural and urban clients seeking very small loans, has not enamoured them to this market place. The lessons they learnt were not about how to serve these markets profitably, but that these markets are a quicksand of poor repayment rates, high transaction costs and the hand-out mentality. Almost without exception, the only contact that the commercial banking sector now has with poor households is a readiness to accept savings deposits, but these are not recycled as loans into the communities from which depositors from poor households hail.

Outreach to poor households by credit unions in the South Pacific is only a little better than it is among the commercial and development banks. McGuire, 1996, confirmed in Getu, 1996, found that with the notable exception of some outreach in Kiribati, Solomon Islands, Tonga and Vanuatu, there is no significant outreach to the rural poor by credit unions in the other PIEs. In the main credit unions in the South Pacific serve wage-earning urban residents and in not one instance do membership numbers climb to more than 10 per cent of households. As a share of the number of poor households this figure is unlikely to exceed 1 or 2 per cent, even in Solomon Islands where the credit union is strongest and rural outreach most well developed. In 1996 Solomon Islands could claim 133 registered and active credit unions with 15,115 members, 6802 of whom were from rural areas, out of a total rural population of around 320,000. The IFAD has provided the local Credit Union League with significant assistance to expand their outreach to these rural people, but there has been little targeting on vulnerable or economically disadvantaged households on the grounds that all rural people in Solomon Islands fall within the IFAD's target population. Similarly in Vanuatu, Kiribati and Tonga, there are rural credit unions, but the total membership is small relative to the total population. If one were to conjecture on the basis of where donors have put their resources, the reasons for the limited outreach would seem to be tied to inadequate training and the problems of overcoming the logistical constraints of a vast geography and isolated pockets of potential clients. As incomplete as they might be, what data surfaced from the regional survey reported in McGuire, 1996, on the work of credit unions as microfinance providers in the South Pacific, is presented in Table 10.4.

In addition to the limited outreach of the credit unions, there is an increasing level of activity in the microfinance area in the South Pacific by donors and NGOs. Information on the initiatives currently being implemented or mooted was gathered by McGuire, 1996, and these have also been incorporated into Tables 10.5 and 10.6. These show a rising level of activity, with particular interest in revolving funds and the replication of minimalist Grameen-Bank-style lending programmes, using small groups and regular weekly or monthly repayment arrangements. Collateral substitutes in the Grameen replications in Fiji, Papua New Guinea and Western Samoa are closely tied to group formation and group activity. Revolving funds, on the other hand, which appear to be the preferred model among donors and local authorities working for rural development, typically provide loans to individuals (predominantly women), and there is a move in some countries, notably Kiribati and Papua New Guinea, to nurture these into village banks. However, overall the repayment track record of the many revolving funds that have been established throughout the PIEs is more often poor than robust.

All the microfinance programmes in the PIEs, (including the very small, very recently established and very nascent Grameen replications in Fiji, Papua New Guinea and Western Samoa), are heavily dependent on donor subsidies and lack the support base of a strong tradition of savings. They struggle to distance themselves from the handout mentality that has characterised so much of what has gone for modernization and relief-work in the South Pacific. None of the microfinance providers active in the South Pacific appear to have adopted a strategy of financial independence from donor support and few provide more than a limited range of financial services to households, sometime not including even compulsory savings as a form of in-built loan guarantee or insurance. Also, if training activities are included in their range of project components, these are typically not for the edification of clients, but represent a concern to improve the skills of MFI staff. The lack of access to a pool of personnel with the skills needed to bring microfinance to poor households in the villages of the South Pacific is counted as one of the most urgent needs holding back outreach. Another priority constraint is the absolute level of funding available.

Consider the summary shown in Table 10.5. If indeed the number of poor households in the South Pacific is around 25 per cent of the total, and if one makes the highly conservative assumption that the summary statistics 'understate' the resources currently devoted to microfinance by one-half (which is most unlikely), then the level of funding currently given to

Table 10.4 Financial Services Providers to the Poor in the South Pacific

Institution	Dates	No. of Loans to:		Average Total*	Collateral Loan US$	Interest Needed	Rate %	Loan Repayment		Revolving	Funding Source
		Males	Females					Rate %	Frequency		
Cook Islands											
CIDBRF	1995–6	118	47	165	500	No	10	Good	Monthly	10,260	NZODA
NRF	1988–91		291	126	275			94		6,840	SPC
Sub-totals									17,100		
Fiji											
FDBRWLS					2,800	Yes		60			NZODA
FDBSLS					14,000			77			GoF
FDBAL					7,000	Yes		87			GoF
FCUL				11,565							
CCSLA				4239							
WOSED	1993–6		184	184	400		15		Weekly	76,805	SPC, NZODA
HAF	1992–				300		10	70			FDB
Sub-totals			15,988					76,805			
Kiribati											
30 CUs						Yes					
OIDP	1992–3				232			54		46,412	UNDP
23 VB	1995–							n.a.		309,400	OIDP, UNDP
Sub-totals								354,812			
Papua New Guinea											
WMLS	1994–5		533	533	945		8	46	Monthly	503,000	RBPNG
YMLS	1994–5			245	1,175		8	22	Monthly	288,000	RBPNG
NSRDP	1996–2004			58,885						155,800	RBPNG, IFAD
21 CUs											
LDAT	1993–6		334	334	230		20	91	Weekly	256,906	UNDP, AusAID, GoPNG
PNGWCP	1988–6			500	350				Monthly	175,000	APDC, SPC, NZODA, GoPNG
Sub-totals										1,560,000	
BEST	1997– 1996										
DCS	1997–				150		30			389	HRDF
PNKP	1997–										LDS

Table 10.4 cont.

Institution	Dates	No. of Loans to:		Average Total*	Collateral Loan US$	Interest Needed	Rate %	Loan Repayment		Revolving	Funding Source
		Males	Females					Rate %	Frequency		
BPWCMP	1997–										EU, GoPNG
Sub-totals			60,497							2,783,295	
Solomon Islands											
DBSI	1970–85				280	No		5			GoSI
	1985–96				1,400	Yes					GoSI
RTCLS	1994–6			73							EU
133 CUs	1995			15,115	32	No	10	79		217,000**	SICUL, CUFA, HSF
RFSP	1991–8			46	140		12	92	Monthly	168,800	IFAD, AusAID, NZODA
WCP	1987–93		46		120	No	0	58		3,910	SPC, NZODA
CBRS					140						SCF
PBSI	1997?										GoSI
Sub-totals			15,234							389,710	
Tonga											
OICP	1990–5			189	800			Good		151,200	NZODA
	1993–5			2,943	800			Good		2,354,400	IFAD
	1996–8			1,957	800			Good		1,565,600	IFAD
34 CUs				2,000			12				
TCUL	1991–5										HSF, CUFA
WCP	1995–				410		8	95		5,000	SPC
NCW					400		8	95		4,194	SPC
TNYCS	1993–6			125	820		10	Poor		14,760	
S&LC											10% population
Sub-totals			7,214							4,095,154	
Tuvalu											
DBTSBL	1992–5	11	21	32	2,525		5			83,349	NZODA
TIRDF	1997–			619	225					61,880	SPFS, NZODA
NCW	1997–										NZODA
Sub-totals			651							145,229	

Vanuatu										
35 CUs										
VCUL (15)	1996–		5,000							British ODA
VWDS	1990–3		2,899	130				Weekly	30,000	UNDP
VWCS	1993–		7	450		54			7,920	SPC
PVTCW				140						VWC
Sub-totals			7,906						37,920	
Western Samoa										
DBSBL	1996–	133	4,460	1,400	Guarantor	13			205,000	IFAD
19CUs	1995–									
WESAP	1996–								30,000	UNDP
ADBMCP										ADB
WASLS	1992–		25	110	Guarantor	20	Poor	Monthly	4,928	SPC
WBF	1994–			200			Poor		2,875	UNDP
Sub-totals			4,485						242,803	

Notes:
* Total shows number of loans made or number of members, whichever figure was available. Wherever there are no data shown, this should not be taken as indicating that no loans were made by that programme to members or clients.
** All figures are based on total loans outstanding among the 15,115 members of the 133 registered credit unions (CUs) as at the end of 1995.
Source: Assembled from data in McGuire, 1996.

Table 10.5 Summary: Microfinance Providers in the South Pacific, 1996

	No. of Loans or Members	No. of Borrowers by Type of Provider, 1996				Revolving Loan Funds Capital Base US$	Total Population mid-1995 '000
		Development Bank	Credit Union	Grameen Replication	Revolving Fund		
Cook Islands	291	0			291	17,100	19.1
Fiji	15,988	0	1,719	184	0	76,805	777.7
Kiribati	n.a.	0	n.a.	n.a.	n.a.	354,812*	78.4
Papua New Guinea	60,497	0	1,000	334	500	2,783,295*	3,951.5
Solomon Islands	15,234	73	6,802	0	0	389,710	385.2
Tonga	7,214	1,957	2,000	0	125	4,095,154*	98.3
Tuvalu	651	0	0	0	651	145,229	9.5
Vanuatu	7,906	0	2,000	0	10	37,920	168.4
Western Samoa	4,485	158	4,000	20	10	242,803*	159.9
Total	112,266	2,188	17,521	538	1,587	8,142,828*	5,648.0

* Includes amounts indicated as 'planned' or 'programmed' for implementation in 1997–8. May also include project funds intended for project activities other than lending, such as training and administration.

Source: Assembled from data in McGuire, 1996 and EIU, 1996.

microfinance for poor households in the South Pacific is only $US10 per poor person. It is difficult to believe that this figure could not be significantly higher (at whatever opportunity cost of funds one might want to apply to the allocation of scarce aid funds), or that the absorptive capacity of the sector and of poor households in the PIEs is not similarly very much higher.

Microfinance Capacity Assessment

In the main, development banks in the South Pacific lack the extensive branch networks that go with serving a farflung market and do not claim microfinance as their area of comparative advantage. Moreover, there is an air of contradiction about government-owned banks in the charge of civil servants taking their brief from potential users of microfinance. The tradition among these banks has been as a conduit of funds for government-approved development projects, not household-level lending for financially viable purposes on a financially viable basis. Where small loan programmes have been administered, typically they have been allowed to deteriorate into relief-type hand-out programmes with poor repayments and little human or institutional capital accumulation. If the development banks of the region are to become more active as microfinance providers, they will have to undergo a radical change of procedure and attitude before one could confidently resource them to the level needed for significant outreach to the urban poor and rural communities.

Having voiced this note of caution, it is instructive in assessing the capacity for outreach and the constraints to be overcome to look more closely at four examples of microfinance delivery programmes in the South Pacific, and to contrast their respective performance records. We begin with the Tonga Development Bank's Outer Islands Credit Project (OICP), which has been in operation since 1993; followed by the Rural Financial Services Project (RFSP) of Solomon Islands Credit Union League, 1991–8; the Women's Social and Economic Development Programme (WOSED) in Fiji, which also began in 1993; and, finally, the NGO-based Grameen Bank replication, the Liklik Dinau Abitore Trust (LDAT) in Papua New Guinea, that made its first loans in 1994.

The OICP (Tonga)

The OICP of the Tonga Development Bank is a five-year $US6 million IFAD-funded project, 1993–8, in which two-thirds of the budget is for the provision of financial services to disadvantaged and vulnerable groups, including credit and savings mobilization, and one-third is for infrastructure development to facilitate the use of the branch network of the Tonga Development Bank. The Bank has a head office in Nuku'alofa, and branch offices on the outer islands of Vava'u, Ha'apai, 'Eua, Niuatoputapu and

Niuafo'ou, to ensure coverage of all the main island groups of Tonga. These branches are responsible for implementing the project as part of their normal operations, assisted by administrative and financial services provided by head office.

Under the OICP, loans are given to both groups and individuals, but the criteria for successful application is not rigorously applied. Security is meant to be tendered, but normally a guarantor is accepted as a collateral substitute and where collateral is identified it is often not easily sold or converted to cash to cover delinquent loan repayments. Moreover, the means test specified for the project is complex and not easily applied as it specifies a level of cash income that is not easily confirmed. It is likely, however, that the lax attitude to applicant selection reported in McGuire, 1996, is directly related to the view that very few outer island households do not meet the project's means test, so there may be little to be gained from being too diligent in implementing this aspect of the project specifications.

Distribution of Loans Disbursed

The target market for the OICP includes both individuals and groups, organized into five categories of borrower: smallholder farmers; rural women; small-scale fishing; women's groups; and small rural enterprises. All borrowers require a co-borrower, who in effect guarantees the loan, but no business plan is needed. McGuire, 1996, notes: 'Bank staff commented that in general, borrowers will be able to qualify for the loan so long as they have a realistic project, not too much other debt and do not have a previous history of default' (p. 115). Group loans are not intended for 'relending' within the group, but for group projects. The distribution of loans outstanding by category of borrower at the end of 1995 is summarized in Table 10.6.

Loans are given for not more than 24 months, with monthly repayments, at the same interest rate that the bank uses in its general lending activities. No allowance is made to recoup higher transaction costs, a risk or insurance

Table 10.6   OICP Outstanding Loan Portfolio by Category of Borrower, 1995

	Loans Outstanding		Average Loan	
	Total US$	%	US$	As % of GDP/head
Rural women	380,159	41.7	532	25.9
Smallholder farmers	269,617	29.6	630	30.7
Small rural enterprises	192,105	21.1	568	27.7
Small-scale fishing	41,388	4.5	511	24.9
Women's groups	28,371	3.1	834	40.7
Total	911,640	100.0	572	27.9

Source: McGuire, 1996

premium. The terms of the project envisage that approximately 1000 loans will be made annually at an average loan size of about US$500. This goal has been achieved, with 2943 loans being made in the three years 1993–5. Moreover, the project appears to adhere to specific gender goals with nearly half of all loans going to female borrowers, even though only 4 of the 24 loans officers attached to the project are female. Women's groups received the largest absolute loans, but smallholder farmers the largest average individual loans.

Performance Indicators and Management Constraints

No category of client is offered follow-up services by the OICP, unless the borrower falls into arrears, in which case counselling and arrears management workshops are arranged. This suggests that the project strategy implemented is to deal with problems after they arise and not on a preventative basis. The result is that on-time repayment rates for the OICP have remained poor. Consider the data on repayment performance in Table 10.7. Only in the case of individual loans to rural women and microenterprises are the repayment rates or 1995 reasonably respectable at 80 per cent or above. While it is true that drought affected the repayment record of farmers in that year, it will not do to excuse the performance record on this basis. If the project is to be financially viable and economically defensible, it must demonstrate robustness. However, it may be that as the OICP expands to provide complementary financial services, such as savings, in the remainder of its projected plan of action, its repayment record will improve and exhibit the robustness needed to weather changes in the economic landscape. The IFAD plan of action included significant attention to the importance of savings for the successful implementation of microfinance on sustainable lines (along the lines recommended in Yaron, 1991, 1994, Getubig, *et al.* 1997, and Hulme and Mosely, 1996), but this has clearly not been a priority of the implementers in the first few years of the project cycle.

The lack of attention given to savings mobilization may well be indicative of a deeper and more general management and personnel constraint facing

Table 10.7 OICP On-time Repayment Rates, 1995

Category of Borrower	On-time Repayment Rate
Smallholder farmers	27.6
Women's groups	58.2
Small-scale fishing	60.6
Small rural enterprises	79.9
Rural women	87.2
Average	68.3

Source: McGuire, 1996.

microfinance expansion in Tonga and the South Pacific generally. The OICP design includes significant but time-consuming monitoring and evaluation provisions, based on detailed continuous sampling of around 50 clients to ascertain how household consumption, expenses and asset holdings are changing. The results of this data collection should be a valuable resource to the OICP managers, yet there is no evidence that this data is utilized by managers responsible for the project. While one might question whether such detailed monitoring and evaluation is necessary or useful to the implementation of a microfinance project in a financially viable manner, it is indicative of the importance that must be attached to having project staff that are both competent, committed and confident in their own ability.

There are other reasons, however, to highlight the importance of the management constraint. First, the Tonga Development Bank makes no effort to separately monitor the cost of implementing the OICP. In order to obtain an estimate of the extent to which the OICP covers costs, McGuire, 1996 had to dig these figures out based on some rough but reasonable assumptions about how overhead and operational costs might be shared between the IFAD-funded clients and the Tonga Development Bank's normal operations. The results revealed a level of subsidy to the OICP in excess of 80 per cent of the full cost of the service delivery, including only the actual cost of funds for the line of credit from the IFAD (i.e. 3 per cent p.a.), not the full opportunity cost (which might well be at least 10 per cent p.a.). This is clearly not sustainable. At this level of subsidy, the OICP is operating with a subsidy-dependence index not less than five times that which Yaron, 1994 calculated for Grameen Bank. It is difficult to imagine how the mere act of giving the Tonga Development Bank greater access to additional funds for outreach would help it to overcome this fundamental, structural, problem.

Need for Regulatory Reform

An important component of the OICP 'structural' problem is the regulation of interest rates that the National Reserve Bank of Tonga controls at the 'general' level for normal Tonga Development Bank transactions. This limitation clearly prevents the Tonga Development Bank from setting rates that are related to true costs of microfinance service delivery. However, if the Tonga Development Bank were free to set rates at full-cost recovery levels, it is clear that there would be borrower resistance, and that borrower resistance would further shrink what is already a very small market. There are less than 10,000 households resident on the outer islands of the kingdom of Tonga. Of this number, there will be a significant proportion that do not want or do not need access to poverty-alleviation-targeted microfinance. These include households that have lost their economically active members to work opportunities overseas or in the capital, Nuku'alofa. These households tend to have access to remittances, received regularly through the post.

Concluding Observations on the OICP

The problem of small and geographically scattered markets is not unique to Tonga, but in Tonga the realities of a dispersed geography underlie the problem of serving what will always be a small and fragmented market in the South Pacific. Hence, another necessary if not sufficient condition for successful microfinance outreach in the South Pacific is the choice of service delivery mechanisms and stratagems that are suited to a market place that is characterized by the diseconomies of smallness and the tyranny of distance. Among the options available, those that seem to commend themselves are:

- closer collaboration with complementary groups or NGOs;
- formal linkages to existing commercial entities serving the region;
- cost saving through use of computers and satellite-based modern communications systems to facilitate money transfers, other banking transactions and documentation; and
- investment in appropriate performance rewards and training for personnel charged with delivery of microfinance services.

The RFSP (Solomon Islands)

Credit unions have been active in Solomon Islands since the early 1980s, but it is only in the 1990s that they have seen broad-based growth, reaching out to both rural and urban communities, and have attracted significant support from external donors, including the IFAD, AusAID (Australian Agency for International Development) and NZODA (New Zealand Overseas Development Agency). As at the end of 1995 there were 133 registered members of the Solomon Islands Credit Union League, the industry peak body.

Regulation of the sector comes under the Governor of the Reserve Bank who is also the Registrar of Credit Unions, but the role of the registrar has essentially been restricted to prudential matters and has not imposed any obviously restrictive limits on credit union policies or programmes. In the main, government and its regulatory arms have been supportive of the credit union movement in its efforts to be the financial service provider to the whole of the Solomon Islands population. Currently the Solomon Islands Credit Union League is reaching around one in five households, but the goal is to more than double this figure before the close of the present millennium (at the time of writing).

Each credit union has an average of 113 members in Solomon Islands, but regulations specify that each new entity must have no less than fifteen members. This small number removes any restrictions that may have applied to the formation of new credit unions in the remoter and least populated parts of the island group. Nonetheless, each separate entity, no matter how small, must establish a governing board of directors, a credit committee of not less than three members, and a supervisory committee, also of not less than three members. The directors and committee members are normally volunteers, though some honoraria may be paid in some instances. The Solomon Islands Credit Union League provides assistance with training and entity establishment. The board is required by regulation to meet twice monthly, but the meeting of the credit union members or its committees are at the behest of local needs or desires. In many instances regular meetings are scheduled to help promote local community development or the achievement of group activities to which members have made a commitment.

The goals of credit unions in Solomon Islands are summarized in the Credit Union Act of 1986 as: to promote thrift among its members, to create a source of credit at a fair and reasonable rate of interest for provident and productive purposes, to issue member's shares and certificates of deposit, and to provide an opportunity for members to use and control their own money in order to improve their economic and social well-being. These goals are wholly consistent with the broader development policy goal that poverty reduction should amount to more than temporary 'relief', but also establish the conditions for sustained improvements in the economic welfare of poor households.

The Role of the Credit Union League in the RFSP

It is into this environment that the IFAD-funded RFSP was launched in 1991 through the Solomon Islands Credit Union League, with a revolving fund of US$168, 800 for on-lending to individual credit unions at a cost of funds of only 1 per cent p.a., with the stated aim of becoming the major provider of financial services in all the rural areas of Solomon Islands by the end of 1998.

Under the RFSP the duties of the Credit Union League are to organize rural credit unions, ensure their proper conduct, provide leadership training and management assistance, exercise general supervision, and provide policy guidance to member credit unions. As at the close of 1995, there were 97 rural credit unions in existence, founded around the community attached to a village, a tribe or a school. In addition there is a large number of local savings clubs which do not need to be registered, but which are commonly regarded as a step in the evolution to formal credit union status.

RFSP Performance

The IFAD projected that by the end of 1998, there would be a minimum of 300 registered credit unions with 45,000 members, equal to around 19 per cent of the adult population, consisting of 29,000 rural members, and 16,000 urban members. By the end of 1995 the aim was to have reached out to 13,000 rural members and 10,800 in the urban areas, but achievements have fallen short of these goals, having registered 6802 rural members and 8313 urban members at that time. Nonetheless, the credit union movement is well established in Isabel, Temotu and Malaita provinces, with the other provinces less well served. In the absence of hard data, one can only presume that the great bulk of these rural members are from poor households that meet the IFAD poverty brief, though the greater proportion of urban members are likely to be wage earners with incomes above the average for the country as a whole. The IFAD appraisal report for the RFSP (September 1991), noted that:

> The average per capita income in the rural areas was around US$230 in 1988, which is less than two-thirds of the income per capita for the nation as a whole. In view of the generally low level of development in the rural areas, there are only a few communities who through timber concessions or baitfish rights, stand out from the rest in terms of income. Given the social framework, differentiation of income within communities is generally not marked. Thus, the vast majority of the population in the rural areas would fall within the IFAD target group, a group that is best approached ... through the strengthening of the credit union movement.

Lending criteria for credit unions in Solomon Islands are normally tied in one way or another to the savings record of the member, with a minimum three-month no-loan probationary period upon taking out membership. In the case of rural credit unions, the first loan is generally limited to US$140 or twice the member's share balance, whichever is the lesser amount, but in practice loans tend to be below this level. Repeat loans can be for increasing amounts, up to a maximum of US$1,400. The interest rate is set by the board of the Credit Union League, and has stood at around 12 per cent p.a. in 1995–6. Loan duration is not normally in excess of twelve months and repayments are on a monthly schedule. As of 31 December 1995, total loans outstanding by all rural credit unions was US$217,000, an average of US$32 per member, compared to savings deposits of US$365,000, an average of US$53 per member. Why this excess is not put to work as loan capital is unclear, but it suggests that the availability of loan funds is not a constraint on further extending outreach to rural households by Credit Union League members.

It is difficult to assemble a detailed picture of the client base of Credit Union League members, but it is clear that women, who account for almost one-half of all members but fill less than one in ten of the committee positions in the credit union structure, are under-represented. The role of women, both in village life and in the rural credit union movement, remains overshadowed by men. Nonetheless, from the limited information available about the primary purposes to which borrowed money is used, it may well be that women and children are significant beneficiaries of microfinance. In the course of his interviews with credit union staff, McGuire, 1996, was told that most loans were for 'provident' purposes, such as facilitating the education of village children through loans for school fees, uniforms and transport to school. Also, staff indicated that there is a trend towards small loans for income-generating activities, such as the development of vegetable gardens, with production that is surplus to household needs being sold for cash.

Alas, no specific information could be had on the effective on-time repayment rate of borrowers by type, whether new borrowers or repeat borrowers, though staff claimed an overall repayment rate for rural credit unions of 92 per cent. If this is true then this is an excellent result, but the non-availability of such fundamental management data from auditors or regular programme monitoring is disturbing. It again highlights the training of personnel and the scarcity of management skills as a major constraint on greatly expanded outreach. This constraint is further highlighted by the observation made by the RFSP project manager in the project report for 1995, that even though there is a statutory requirement to do so, only 23 of the 133 registered credit unions had provided audited financial statements for the year, and 53 credit unions had not provided any reports at all. While money for on-lending might be had from the savings deposits of members, funding for training and management development is not easy to access, and cannot readily be funded from levies on members' funds or members' deposits.

Concluding Observation on RFSP

Despite difficult conditions, the credit union movement in Solomon Islands is making substantial progress in providing financial services in rural areas. The supply of members deposits for on-lending is running ahead of growth in the loan portfolio. Whether this is because demand for loans is slack or capacity to disperse loans is limited is not clear, but the Credit Union League does appear to have mobilized the credit union sector to service the rural areas in an impressive way. A good beginning has been achieved. Further success will depend upon the ability of the Credit Union League to wean itself from dependence on donor subsidies, and its member credit unions to contain costs, increase revenues and service the market with products that are appropriate to the needs of rural households in Solomon Islands.

The WOSED (Fiji)

The WOSED is a government-run programme within the Department of Women and Culture, with primary funding from the South Pacific Commission and other assistance from NZODA and Women's World Banking. The WOSED is overseen by the head of the Department, who was directly responsible for establishing the programme and takes a strong personal interest in it. Day-to-day project management is delegated to four female departmental officers, each of whom is a WOSED co-ordinator for, respectively, the Eastern, Western, Central and Northern divisions of Fiji. These supervisors have other responsibilities within the Department, but they spend around 80 per cent of their time working on the WOSED. They are assisted by three US Peace Corps volunteers, who act as 'small business advisers', plus a number of field-based WOSED facilitators who, in turn, are responsible for borrowers in their assigned locality. All WOSED staff are women.

The WOSED is more than a microcredit programme. It also includes activities to support women's income-earning activities, promote savings, improve the living standards in participating households, support those women seeking to become self-employed, and prepare women for integration into the commercial banking system. As a unifying theme to all these activities, the WOSED has social development objectives based on promoting women's sense of independence, dignity and confidence that they have the means and the ability to take charge of their own futures. Gender in development is an integral part of the WOSED's philosophical foundations.

The WOSED has organized its microcredit programme on the Grameen Bank model, but there are important differences. Borrowers organize themselves into groups of three to seven members, headed by an elected leader. The WOSED provides newly formed groups with familiarity training about the programmes goals and activities. Once this is completed, group members are eligible for a WOSED unsecured loan. All members of a group receive their loan simultaneously, and group responsibility exists on individual loans to group members. All loans are for eighteen months, normally repaid weekly at an effective interest rate of around 10 per cent p.a. The WOSED made its first loans in April 1993, and by the end of June 1996 it had 137 borrowers with an average loan of US$132. A further 47 women were approved for their first loans and would have received them but for lack of funds for on-lending.

Programme Targeting and Outreach

The WOSED is meant to be targeted at disadvantaged women in poor circumstances, but there is no formal targeting mechanism employed in selecting participants. Instead, the WOSED was launched on a pilot basis in 1993 in three areas known for chronic poverty. Two of these areas are in Suva and a third is in a cluster of rural villages. When prospective clients from these target areas expressed an interest in the programme, fieldstaff visited them to make a subjective judgement as to whether or not the applicant falls within the target group for the programme. Beyond this no other checks are undertaken. Eventually, 27 borrowers were selected for the pilot project, and the number expanded to 110 borrowers in nine districts in 1994, and a further 27 borrowers in the year after. On a geographic basis the WOSED is, therefore, very thinly spread, making for a dispersed and logistically expensive programme.

In the course of interviews with WOSED officials, McGuire, 1996 reported that there was some concern expressed that as news of the WOSED has spread the demand to participate has grown to include women from outside the original three locations. The WOSED has not been inclined to turn these applicants away, with the danger that new clients may not always be from among the most disadvantaged women. This has prompted the Director for Women and Culture to consider introducing a means test into the programme in the near-future. However, given the political sensitivity attached to the topic of poverty, and resources that would be needed to further train staff in the administration and assessment of means tests, the self-interest of a resource-poor and hard-pressed civil servant will be not to rush to implement closer programme targeting. One can only hope that any leakage that might come to the attention of WOSED officials, remains insignificant and, therefore, not a constraint on further outreach to poor households.

Client Training

Clients of the WOSED must undertake considerable training before being permitted to borrow. The training period is four hours per day for around eight days, spread over two to three weeks. The training covers group development (including lending policies), business training and social development. During the last week, participants prepare their business plans. Hence a considerable commitment of time is required to participate in the programme; time that the poorest women may not have. If a member needs to miss a session, the group leader is responsible for passing the information on to the member, and a report is given at the next session.

The facilitator conducts training according to guidelines in the WOSED facilitator's training manual. The preparation of a business plan serves as a *de facto* test of the borrowers' understanding of the business training. However, unlike the general practice of the Grameen approach, there is no group recognition test administered by a programme supervisor to test whether group members fully understand the nature of the programme and their responsibilities as participants and borrowers. After receiving their loans, group meetings are held weekly or fortnightly, depending on whether the group has elected to make weekly or fortnightly repayments. Meetings focus on making loan repayments, collecting savings contributions, and discussing problems or issues of interest to group members.

Financial Management and Policy

All WOSED borrowers are required to save a minimum of one Fiji dollar per week. In addition, the WOSED has a voluntary savings programme, but as with the compulsory savings component no withdrawals are permitted while a member has a loan outstanding. Effectively, therefore, the programme uses savings as a crude form of loan guarantee or default insurance. Even so, the on-time repayment rate of 71.6 per cent as at June 1996 was relatively low compared to 90 per cent plus achieved by Grameen Bank and most Grameen replications.

Although the WOSED has a voluntary savings programme, members receive no interest on amounts saved and deposits are frozen while a member has a loan that is outstanding. The penalty that these policies imposed on members for making voluntary savings deposits would appear to be counter-productive to the goals of the programme and the important role that those savings could play as a source of loan funds. If the WOSED is to attract an increasing flow of savings as a basis for growth in its lending programme, a set of interest rate policies that provide members with rewards for saving instead of penalties would seem to be in order. Why the WOSED has not seized this option must remain a mystery, but it does draw a cloud over the soundness and consistency of policies adopted by project management.

The potential importance of savings mobilization to the WOSED's capacity to reach out to poor Fijians is all the more urgent because the WOSED faces an excess demand for loans from its members. At the close of the 1995–6 financial year, the WOSED had a queue of 47 qualified first-time loan applicants awaiting the availability of loan funds and another growing queue of second- and third-time borrowers from among the 37 first-time borrowers who had already repaid their loans and are wanting to borrow again to sustain their initial investments. Instead of looking to savings mobilization to meet this demand, the WOSED has approached bilateral donors for increased aid money. The logic of this approach to meeting these demands is opaque, at best, because at the very time the WOSED was seeking additional aid money, it had US$30,746 on deposit as cash at bank, consisting largely of loan repayments. It is possible that this money was not being re-lent because the WOSED management thought it more important to build up reserve funds as some sort of nest-egg. While such a decision may well reflect a commendably prudent attitude, it is not clear why the money could not have been re-lent. This would simply replace one asset (cash at bank) with another (loans outstanding). While loans outstanding are a less liquid asset than cash at bank, the sacrifice of some liquidity to maintain the momentum of the project seems to be a relatively small price to pay for a programme that is meant to operate at the risky end of the finance market.

Each of the above examples would be enough on their own to undermine one's confidence in the management capacity to efficiently implement a significantly expanded programme without major investments in manage-ment training, procedural and policy reforms. The discovery that WOSED revenues and costs are subsumed into the costs of the Department of Women and Culture, making it almost impossible to monitor WOSED costs and revenues heighten the urgency of reform by programme component.

Programme management is forced to assume that the costs of individual programme activities are under control and according to plan. There is an air of *déjà vu* about the WOSED that seems to confirm the worst fears of a generation of microcredit specialists about the inappropriateness of government departments as a vehicle for the delivery of microfinance.

In McGuire, 1996 the author reported on his effort to obtain sufficient accounting and financial data to at least allow for an estimate of the operational self-sufficiency of the WOSED. Based on the figures he was able to obtain, plus some assumptions about the amount of time departmental personnel devote to the WOSED, interest on cash at bank and interest from loan repayments, he determined that the WOSED's operational self-sufficiency ratio is no higher than 2 per cent. It is difficult to disagree with McGuire's conclusion that, 'WOSED is essentially operating as a social welfare programme, with very little emphasis on cost recovery'.

Concluding Observations on the WOSED

The WOSED is an infant programme with as much potential as it has problems to overcome. Many of these problems are likely to persist so long as the WOSED remains a programme of a government department. That the Department of Women and Culture comes with a remit in an area of social welfare does not make it easy to transform the WOSED into a cost-effective microfinance programme. Nonetheless, the direction in which reforms need to move if the WOSED is to become the Grameen Bank of Fiji is clear. Without reform the WOSED will remain a social welfare programme instead of a vibrant and financially viable MFI. Nonetheless, the reputation of the WOSED among donors for integrity and quality staffing is an asset; one that has brought to the WOSED resource commitments in excess of $75,000 in the four years 1993–6.

The LDAT (Papua New Guinea)

The LDAT is an NGO modelled on Grameen Bank, established in 1993 and headquartered in the Eastern Highlands city of Goroka, to manage a UNDP-funded and inspired microfinance project in Papua New Guinea, targeted at women in the informal sector. A United Nations Volunteer technical adviser manages it. The first LDAT loans were made in August 1994. The LDAT or Liklik, as it is commonly called, is governed by a seven-member board of trustees, chaired by a representative from the Papua New Guinea Banking Corporation, and with representatives from the UNDP, the Department of the Prime Minister, the Department of Village Services and Provincial Affairs, the Department of Home Affairs, the Foundation for Law, Order and Justice, and the National Council of Women. Unlike Grameen Bank, there are no board positions reserved for representatives of borrowers from the trust,

Table 10.8 LDAT Microfinance Activity, 1994–5

	No. of Clients	Average US$	Total US$	Interest % p.a.
Loans	216	71	15, 374	29.4
Savings	224	46	10, 380	4.0

but the group-based operating procedures of Grameen have been followed fairly closely, including group responsibility for loans and compulsory savings by group members.

By the end of 1995 Liklik had established 45 groups of five members and delivered 216 loans at an average of US$71 per loan. (See Table 10.8.) Growth in the following six months was rapid, propelling the number of borrowers to 334 by the end of June 1996, but if the target of 5000 borrowers by the end of the UNDP's five-year plan of support is to be achieved growth will need to be at least double this number.

Programme Targeting

The Liklik programme takes targeting very seriously. Not only is the programme exclusively for disadvantaged women, but a means test is used in participant selection, based on a housing index, an income index and an asset index. At current settings borrowers cannot have a monthly income in excess of $12 per month and the asset index is set at a total value of not more than US$400. In an independent test based on an assessment of the quality of housing available to borrowers, McGuire, 1996 found that for the sample of households examined, all of whom came from an area not especially noted for its poverty, Liklik successfully selected-out disadvantaged women for programme participation.

Client Training

True to its roots as a Grameen Bank replication, Liklik client training is rigorously programmed and focused on ensuring that potential borrowers have a clear understanding of what it means to be a member of Liklik rather than on training for productive investment. Prospective members are required to participate in a seven-day training programme of approximately one hour per day before they are admitted into the programme. Training covers principles of the loan scheme, functioning of groups and centres, procedures for loan applications, and loan utilization and repayment. Group members must satisfy the trust staff as to their integrity, commitment and understanding of the principles of the programme.

A condition of entry into Liklik is that members must attend weekly 'centre' meetings, where reinforcement training and motivation for borrowers are the principal topics, and where there is also an opportunity for existing and potential borrowers to raise issues of concern. However, in April 1996 Liklik was forced into the courts to recover loans made to 32 so-called 'wilful' defaulters (i.e. those who had ceased making repayments and had ceased attending 'centre' meetings). Liklik won all 32 cases, and the defaulters were made to promise to pay back their loans during the next coffee season. Nonetheless, court proceedings are an expensive way of maintaining borrower discipline, which the tried and tested group processes of the Grameen model are meant to contain if not avoid when well implemented.

In addition to Liklik focused training, Liklik also co-ordinates member access to technical training by the Department of Primary Industry on poultry raising, garden cultivation and general assistance with agricultural production.

Savings Mobilization and Financial Viability

Liklik has both a voluntary and a compulsory savings programme. The compulsory savings programme includes contributions to a default fund as a form of loans repayment insurance, plus a similar amount (1 Kina or US$0.78 per week) to the Liklik mutual aid fund. Group members also deposit 1 Kina per week towards the group-administered group fund. Liklik contributes a further 5 per cent of the loan principal of loans granted to the group into this group fund. When the balance reaches K100 (US$78), the group may loan up to 50 per cent of the amount to one of its members on whatever terms the group members see fit.

The voluntary savings programme is based on a savings book, in which individual deposits and withdrawals are recorded. A depositor can access their savings at any time. The LDAT pays an interest of 4 per cent p.a. on the minimum quarterly balance, which is the same rate as that paid by the Papua New Guinea Banking Corporation. The savings facility has proved to be very popular among members, and is all the more important because of the lack of access to savings facilities in the area where Liklik operates.

It is particularly encouraging to see the success that Liklik has had in mobilizing savings, especially at this early stage in Liklik's development. By the end of 1995, savings deposits represented almost two-thirds of the outstanding loan portfolio. The margin between the effective loan rate and the deposit rate is around 25 percentage points, which indicates that there may well be considerable scope for offering savers greater incentives to save than the current 4 per cent p.a. offered. The potential for considerably improving savings mobilization bodes well for future financial viability of Liklik and the prospect that it can become independent of donor support more rapidly than otherwise would be the case. Nonetheless, the task ahead is substantial, with operational financial self-sufficiency being less than 20 per cent at the end of 1995.

Impact and Efficiency of the LDAT

It is too early to assess the impact that Liklik is having on poverty in its areas of operation or even in the households of borrowers. Nonetheless, it is clear that in addition to being a microfinance programme, Liklik is also a microenterprise development programme. In this respect there is some concern that two-thirds of loans have been devoted to only three areas of income-generating enterprise: poultry raising, vegetable cultivation and small trade stores. Given the isolation of many villages and small size of the market, this lack of diversity may create problems should there be a downturn in cash income at village level and the limited opportunity that village women have to sell their produce outside the village economy. Unless greater attention is paid to further diversifying the investment opportunities open to borrowers, it may be difficult to sustain the on-time repayment rate at its current level of 89 per cent as at June 1996. This rate is already lower than it was in 1995 and is well below the norm for Grameen Bank replications elsewhere in Asia.

In April-May 1996, a UNDP review mission examined the administrative and management competence of Liklik. The review reported that there is significant room for improvement. Liklik has a financial operating procedure manual that is a comprehensive document. However, actual practices were found to significantly differ from those prescribed in the manual. At the time of the review Liklik had no financial manager, and none of the staff had formal training in accounts or bookkeeping. In the view of the review members, Liklik held excessive cash balances, was not using double-entry accounting procedures as required, and was vulnerable to losses and cost increases because of inadequate financial control systems. Management capacity and human resource development are among Liklik's most serious constraints on growth and performance.

Concluding Observations on the LDAT

The Liklik programme is small, with only a very recent track record that is still to be tested for robustness and capacity to manage both rapid and extensive growth in microfinance business. Liklik has been very successful at attracting donor support. In the three years since the first loans were made, Liklik has attracted more than US$300,000 in donor funds, only 5 per cent of which has found its way into the loan programme. In addition, significant savings deposits have been generated, amounting to almost two-thirds of the outstanding loan portfolio. This indicates that there is great potential for funding growth in the loan programme from growth in members' deposits, but the amounts involved, relative to the total operational costs, are small. On the basis of current earnings, Liklik is grossly dependent on donor funds to meet both its programme costs and infrastructure investments. These are at levels that are not sustainable in the long term.

Government policies in Papua New Guinea are supportive of the work of microfinance institutions like the LDAT. There are no government-imposed restrictions on pricing policies, interest rates or member operations at village level. MFIs are not subject to any regulation at all, not even in the setting of prudential requirements that non-member depositors may demand. However, if MFIs like Liklik are to mobilize savings from non-members they will need government approval and some regulatory reform.

Constraints to Microfinance Expansion in the South Pacific

Financial Viability

Financial viability is the number one issue for MFIs in the South Pacific. None have operational self-sufficiency ratios that are any higher than 40 per cent and most have ratios that are less than half this level. Sustainability or expansion of MFI programmes is deeply dependent on the availability of donor funds, which has allowed Pacific island MFIs to avoid the hard issues that need to be addressed for institutional independence and rapid shift to full financial self-sufficiency.

Liklik excepted, none of the MFIs operating in the PIEs separates-out all income and expenses of their MFI programme, with the result that estimates of levels of financial viability are based on assumptions or 'guesstimates', where possible, with the strong possibility that the data reported are overestimates rather than the reverse. This unacceptable state of affairs is indicative of an urgent need for improvements in management and MFI information systems, which must precede any possibility that MFIs in the South Pacific will begin to move to achieve financial viability status. To date, all programmes have been concerned primarily with service delivery rather than cost-effectiveness. As they expand their outreach and become more experienced, they can be expected to increase their productivity and become more self-sufficient, but it is clear that achieving financial self-sufficiency will be an enormous task. For some South Pacific MFIs full financial self-sufficiency may never be a realistic option, given the dispersed and thin markets that characterize many of the PIEs.

Resource Mobilization

In the past five years around US$9 million has been contributed by bilateral donors, local governments, NGOs and multilateral agencies to the support of MFIs in the South Pacific. Less successful has been the extent of savings mobilization by MFIs or the generation of fees for services rendered. Consequently, one is justified in claiming that the greater part of MFI activity in the South Pacific has operated as though it was part of a social welfare 'relief' programme rather than an income generation and micro-enterprise support programme for sustainable development and poverty reduction. Serious doubt must exist over the capacity of MFIs in the South Pacific to absorb additional donor funds for an expanded programme of MFI lending activity effectively and efficiently. The role of donors must be to assist MFIs in the South Pacific to improve their absorptive capacity and overcome the human resource and infrastructure obstacles to less costly and more targeted financial intermediation to an expanded client base.

Policy and Regulation

MFIs have received significant support from the governments of the PIEs. In most economies there are few restrictions, though interest-rate ceilings do exist in some countries. For the protection of depositors it may be essential for governments to take a more active interest in setting prudential guidelines and in nurturing industry-wide commitments to documentation and accountability that protect the interests of borrowers, depositors and donors. Most central banks in the region have recently taken a closer interest in microfinance, including attendance at an ESCAP workshop on informal financial systems, held in June 1996. It is important that central banks maintain the momentum of MFI expansion in a manner that is consistent with declining aid dependence, increased savings mobilization, and transparent administrative guidelines to minimize losses to moral hazard, outright fraud or leakage to households that are not 'poor'.

Concluding Observation

It is tragic that the progress of microfinance in Pacific Island countries appears to be mired in issues and strategies for outreach that are inimical to successfully helping those who need access to financial intermediation services in a financially viable and sustainable manner. Existing practice appears to fly directly against the weight of the evidence built up through the experiences of others in other countries, as recorded in previous chapters of this book. A misplaced and false sense of pride comes at a heavy price that is directly borne by the poor and those who would want to see the poor in the South Pacific escape the net of chronic dependence.

Acknowledgement

The author is most grateful to Paul McGuire for comments made on an earlier draft of this chapter and for permission to use data gathered by him.

IV

Conclusions:
Learning from Experience

11
Microfinance For and By the Poor: Lessons from Experience

David Gibbons, Ben Quiñones, Joe Remenyi
and H. Dieter Seibel

Introduction

After having studied the MFIs reported on in the foregoing chapters, what can we say about whether 'banking with the poor' is poor banking? This question deserves a serious answer. For those of us who want to contribute to the alleviation of poverty and believe that microfinance is a useful tool to this end, a convincing answer to this question is at the heart of the matter. The case studies presented in this book, covering more than 40 individual microfinance programmes, provide us with that answer, which is an unequivocal and resounding 'no'. The case studies are a source of the insights and evidence needed to see that 'banking with the poor' can be successful banking, useful banking and profitable banking, if done properly. The case studies document a track record for microfinance providers that are not uniformly impressive. But, on the whole the contribution of microfinance providers to poverty reduction has been consistently positive and lasting. There is supporting evidence for this view in an ever-growing list of respected publications, including recently published works by Harper, 1998, Johnson and Rogaly, 1997, Schneider, 1997, Wood and Sharif, 1997, Bennett and Cuevas, 1996, Counts, 1996, Hulme and Mosely, 1996, and Todd, 1996a and 1996b.

Our knowledge of the impact of microfinance on poverty reduction has graduated from the anecdotal to the general. There are now too many success cases and too many microfinance providers who are reaching significant numbers of genuinely poor households to ignore. If microfinance is not a panacea for all the ills associated with systemic poverty, microfinance is addressing a number of important constraints to escape from poverty for many poor households in the Asia-Pacific region. Sceptics will remain, but to the millions of clients of microfinance who have used their access to financial intermediation services to pull themselves out of poverty, microfinance has provided the building blocks to freedom from chronic under-employment, recurrent periods of hunger, gender bias in past modernization strategies, fear of the future, lingering uncertainty, and lack of control over their own circumstances.

The case studies in this book also allow us to comment in a more informed way on the complex business of fostering the development of a financially viable microfinance industry while at the same time assisting the poor, without dependence on ongoing subsidies, to help themselves escape from poverty. An important obstacle to microfinance has been the conventional wisdom about poverty and the poor. The received wisdom is 'welfare-biased' and has largely blinkered our view to the fact that poor people are not only able to pay market rates for financial services, but are very willing to do so and will protect their access to ongoing financial services by ensuring that they are among the best debt repayers. In the past, there has been much incredulity and resistance directed at this lesson with the result that history has seen many microfinance programmes launched and supported on the basis of practices that encouraged dependence on financially non-sustainable subsidies. There are still many donor groups, especially in the NGO sector, which resist the implications and importance of the financial viability lesson for the design and management of microfinance provider programmes.

The answer to our opening question – Is banking with the poor banking? – is unequivocally in the negative, but with several important caveats. First, microfinance is likely to be only one of several instruments, albeit a very important one needed to secure a permanent reduction in poverty. Profitable, well-managed and financially viable MFIs will not only work with the poor but also with an increasing number of those of its clients who have graduated above the poverty line. As it serves these clients, it is likely to find it profitable to also serve the finance needs of others in the community that are also not poor. As a healthy 'business' a microfinance provider cannot and should not eschew the commercial opportunities associated with serving these its 'best clients'. As we have seen from the case studies examined in this book, this does not mean that MFIs can eschew poverty targeting. On the contrary, if the focus on reaching out to an ever-more inclusive circle of poor households is not to be lost, a firm commitment by MFIs and their financial supporters to growth through greatly expanded outreach to the genuinely poor is essential.

The importance of financial viability aside, the key role that poverty targeting must play in microfinance outreach is a core lesson of the capacity assessment case studies. It is also the only way of ensuring that poverty reduction is combined with good business practice. In the remainder of this chapter we will review those lessons that our studies and the data presented in this book supports.

Lessons Learnt

Financial viability is a choice: money does not follow outreach

Project Dungganon is a Grameen Bank replication of the Negros Women for Tomorrow Foundation in the Philippines. It is a member of the CASHPOR Inc. network of Grameen Bank replications, and is the largest programme of its sort in the Philippines, serving over 10,000 poor women. In the course of its history, Project Dungganon is described by its founders and its CASHPOR Inc. advisers as having lurched from financial crisis to repayment crisis to financial crisis again, largely because its growth had not been based on the establishment of financially viable branches, but on the unfounded belief that 'if you reach and benefit large numbers of the poor, the money will be forthcoming'. But this strategy is clearly not sustainable and history has proved this to be so. Demand can always be expected to be in excess when things of value are being given away or distributed at well below what users would be willing to pay. As aid fatigue bites ever deeper and the flow of development assistance funds slows, donors willing to pay the bill for such profligacy cannot be so easily called forth.

Financial viability in poverty-alleviation projects has been a hard lesson to learn; one that flew in the face of the signals that donors were giving pioneers in the microfinance business in the 1970s and 1980s. In those early days, any amount of funding appeared to be available to any microfinance provider able to show that they could disburse loan funds to the poor in substantial amounts rapidly and with good documentation. There is no easier way to do this than to encourage potential clients to borrow by offering them funds at heavily subsidized interest rates. However, as donor funds dried up and official aid flows declined in both relative and absolute amounts in the 1990s, microfinance programmes that were expanding on the basis that donor funds would continue to be forthcoming to fund expansion and outreach to the poor fell on hard times.

Project Dungganon is one of many NGOs involved in microfinance that has been forced to reconsider its growth strategy. In place of dependence on donor funds Project Dungganon has embraced the goal of financial viability and switched to growth through the development of a network of financially viable branches. This has slowed their outreach to the poor, but it is being achieved on a more sustainable foundation, which is essential for lasting poverty reduction. The Project Dungganon team describes their conversion in the following terms:

It took us, members of a diverse team, a while to arrive at that conclusion. We started asking ourselves whether and how microfinance can help alleviate poverty. We ended asking ourselves whether and how microfinance institutions may become self-reliant and viable. Outreach to the poor was thus our first concern. In the context of this question we examined the issue of resource mobilisation from a purely instrumental viewpoint: where to find the resources for poverty lending. It appeared to go without asking that most of these sources had to be found externally, especially in the form of donor money. There seemed to be little chance that commercial banks would engage in poverty lending. This was in line with the view expounded in documents released in preparation for the MicroCredit Summit of February 1997.

However, funds given by governments and donors are not hard-earned by the beneficiaries. Easy money is not taken seriously, i.e. it is frequently not paid back, or not repaid on time. This, we realised, had disastrous consequences for outreach. Microfinance providers which fail to mobilise their own resources and whose capital base is eroded by heavy losses will decrease, rather than increase, their outreach, until they eventually go out of business altogether. Wasting precious resources, they contribute to financial shallowing rather than deepening and financial narrowing rather than widening. Savings are a pillar of sustainability. A sustainable institution is one, which is viable and does not depend on donor grants but on resources generated through market-oriented instruments.

Private correspondence to BankPoor '96, October 1996, David Gibbons, CEO Cashpor Inc. and Consultant to Project Dungganon

The importance of targeting the poor

If 30 years of targeted subsidized agricultural credit for poor farmers in developing countries has taught us anything, it is how not to target the poor. The development landscape is littered with rural credit programmes that failed to deliver to the poor, but which did disburse substantial resources to the not-poor. As 'outreach', these programmes failed miserably. Why should we expect microfinance providers to be any more successful?

Past experience is a wonderful source of wisdom and 20:20 hindsight, if only we will learn. We know why so many rural credit programmes failed to target the poor and the case studies examined for this book have demonstrated that by avoiding some clearly identified pitfalls, outreach to the poor can be effectively targeted. The first pitfall to be avoided is the use of delivery systems that are not suited to the circumstances of the poor. In the past, providing credit access to targeted poor groups was an argument for the creation of specialized finance institutions focusing on agriculture and rural clients. These institutions typically did not involve their clients in the activity of loan disbursal, loan repayment or savings mobilization. In addition, the procedures used were best suited to relatively well-educated clients with literacy and numeric skills well beyond those of poor rural farmers. Poverty targeting removes these obstacles to the involvement of poor clients, substituting procedures that tap local knowledge, social capital and skills of its client-beneficiaries. Even so, quality control demands that microfinance providers retain due vigilance to prevent the growth of resource leakage to not-poor households in the bid to meet outreach benchmarks.

Successful microfinance providers will have an increasing number of clients who graduate above the poverty line and begin to make demands on resources that might otherwise flow to outreach to new poor clients. This is a difficult tightrope to walk. One cannot expect a microfinance provider to turn its back on its best customers just because they have managed to achieve what was expected of them when the first financial service was extended to them as a poor household. Moreover, an important aspect of sustainability is the capacity of the institution to continue to meet the financial needs of all its customers, not just its most recent and most vulnerable. Nonetheless, this 'happy dilemma' does need careful management to ensure that adequate funding is allocated to outreach to poor households still without adequate access to microfinance services.

The evidence from the case studies is that the balance between services offered for outreach and services extended to established but not-poor clients can be so managed as to be complementary and not competing. Microfinance providers that serve both poor and not-poor clients have a track record that demonstrates significant success in resource mobilization. This is so because not-poor clients, with their larger equity base, save more often. This can bring to the microfinance programme the resources needed to also make larger loans at higher profit margins. Outreach to the poor only suffers where management fails to be vigilant and allows the programme to grow more from services extended to the not-poor than services to the poor. This is not an argument for excluding the microfinance provider from the benefits that can come from having clients who are near poor or clearly not poor. It is an argument for ensuring that the products that the microfinance provider offers are tailored to the needs of the poor rather than the not-poor, and that management takes seriously its responsibility to ensure that significant growth in the new client base is from outreach to the poor. Only in this way can the microfinance programme ensure that it is serving the poor and contributing to meeting the financial needs of those households that would otherwise slip back below the poverty line.

In a significant number of microfinance programmes examined for the case studies in Part II of this book, the efficacy of poverty targeting has been well established. Even so, this does not divert us from the far more important observation that outreach to the poor ultimately depends on governance and source of funds. One-third of the programmes in the case studies, most of them NGOs, depend on grants and soft loans as the major source of funds for on-lending and overhead expenses. As a result, donors have an influence on MFI governance and outreach growth strategies that tends to displace the interests of the poor in favour of external administration, reporting and documentation pressures. It is not surprising, therefore, that for donor-dependent MFIs, outreach targets are typically conservative and lacking in boldness. The outreach track record of donor-dependent programmes is only one-fifth of that achieved by a similar number of non-donor-dependent programmes studied. The latter included 15 programmes with almost 125,000 poor clients in 1995, while the latter group, covering 14 programmes, had almost 700,000 poor clients at the end of the same year.

Two ways of increasing outreach

In general, the conventional wisdom is that a microfinance provider needs to amass a client base of 20,000 or more to ensure an adequate foundation for financial viability. In the case of microfinance programmes that seek, in time, to achieve the status of a bank of one sort or another, this conventional wisdom has merit. The case studies clearly show that there are substantial economies of scale in finance services delivery. However, there are many private-sector-based, not-for-profit programmes operating in almost every Asia Pacific country that do not seek to become a bank or to remain in business forever and a day. Typically these microfinance providers are small and often relatively informal organizations, established and run by their members for their members. The reasons why these small location-specific programmes come into being are a complex matter. Often it is linked to the geographic isolation of many poor rural communities or to ethnic affiliations. In other cases a RoSCA or savings group has formed for a specific purpose and the minimalist overhead, administrative and legal needs of remaining small are an advantage, especially if there is no intention of offering members the full range of financial services.

In many developing countries, therefore, we see outreach happening in two forms. On the one hand there are comprehensive microfinance provider institutions that achieve outreach to the poor by increasing the number of poor clients participating in their savings, loan and services programmes. On the other hand there is the proliferation of small 'boutique' microfinance service providers that operate largely to facilitate access to one product. These 'boutique' providers can take any number of institutional forms, including a formally constituted NGO, an informal SHG or a specialist activity of a community development programme. Consider, for example, the case of Nepal. The five Grameen Bikas Banks in Nepal had a total membership of 32,000 in December 1995, which rose to almost 48,400 by the middle of 1996. But Nepal also has 12,000 registered and unregistered savings and credit organizations and co-operatives with a total of 792,000 members. These 12,000 savings and credit organizations represent outreach through increases in the number of institutions, while the Grameen Bikas Banks represent outreach through increases in the number of clients.

Hence, while there are economies of scale in the delivery of microfinance, there can be no best practice concerning the manner in which outreach is achieved. Much depends on circumstantial factors such as population density, settlement patterns and the institutional preferences of the local people. Many markets remain relatively secluded and isolated. Microfinance provider institutions may have to devise special products and instruments to effectively serve these markets. Local markets may be so special that only local, rather than national, financial institutions are effective. In the fragmented financial markets that characterize the financial landscapes in developing countries, there is much to commend outreach through the proliferation of small, purpose-built institutions owned and managed by local people.

There are 'best practices' that lead to microfinance provider viability

Unsound financial practices find their way into the operations of microfinance providers in a number of ways, none more seductive than access to donor-proffered 'easy money'. There is an important role for donor-based grants and soft loans, but not without strict conditionality and well-articulated enterprise goals that commit management and staff of the microfinance provider to achieving financial viability within a reasonable timeframe. In the past governments and donors have provided support for the operations of microfinance providers with a minimum of conditions so long as funds were dispersed and accounted for. Little or no attention was given to applying the same standards of the market place to the microfinance provider as were routinely applied to potential borrowers. Easy money of this sort did not establish the incentives needed for microfinance providers to make financial viability for their programmes a priority. In too many cases this resulted in welfare-oriented microfinance dispersal procedures and pricing policies that could only be maintained so long as donor funds remained available. As donor funds became less readily available, microfinance providers were forced to confront the sustainability of their own activities. Many were found to have adopted operating procedures that involved unsound financial practices, including the use of pricing policies for loans and services supplied that bore little or no relation to profit goals or the cost of funds lent. The absence of rigour and fiduciary standards in programme budgetary and management details was exhibited as inordinately long loan periods, inappropriate instalments and repayment schedules, excessive loan sizes, lack of insistence on timely repayment and heavily subsidized interest rates. These are the characteristics of a welfare programme and not a financially viable vehicle for the long-term delivery of services. As the case studies show, poor people are more than willing to pay the full cost for the microfinance products that they need and can use, including a profit margin sufficient to keep the microfinance provider in business.

Many donor-dependent microfinance operators wrongly assume that donor funds are cheaper than client-generated savings or profit-supported equity funds. In fact, donors typically insist on documentation and monitoring requirements that are specific to their own funds, with the result that the administrative burden of a grant or a soft loan increases disproportionately. One small microfinance provider in Nepal was found to have 72 different ledgers: one for each loan programme, differentiated by donor and the loan purpose specified by the donor! There can be little to commend such practices or to justify any claim that grants and soft loans from donors are 'cheap' money, although the need for donors to insist that the programmes they support should meet accountability requirements are not disputed. Management of the dispersal of own-savings to borrowers is far easier and the practices available to ensure compliance are relatively easily defined as performance guidelines which double as management tools. Typically, therefore, financial viability leads to management demands that are focused on serving poor people instead of donors, with every possibility that the administrative requirements are significantly less complex than those needed to meet the documentation required for donor accountability and reporting. In Indonesia's P4K, for example, BRI excludes villages and sub-districts from access to further credit if arrears exceed 10 per cent of repayments due. As a result, management at branch level has a powerful reason to make timely repayment of loans to groups a priority in their monitoring and evaluation routines. The effect is that all the right financial viability signals are sent: P4K branches have an excellent on-time repayment rate, and they also mobilize their own resources.

Subsidized credit-driven growth of microfinance programmes keep the poor from saving

In 1984 a book appeared on rural credit for poor farmers in developing countries with the title *Undermining Rural Development with Cheap Credit*. This message from the book's authors, Adams, Graham and Von Pischke, now needs repeating in the case of microfinance and poverty reduction. Contrary to popular belief, the practice of providing subsidized credit, whether by government, the agents of government or microfinance providers, has hurt the poor by depriving them of access to savings deposit facilities. It is only quite recently that many development banks, the major providers of subsidized credit, have recognized the importance of savings facilities for the poor and begun to make them available. Most donor-supported credit programmes do include a savings component, but these have typically involved compulsory savings to the exclusion of a vigorous promotion of a range of savings products designed to meet the unique needs of poor households. In effect the compulsory savings component of the typical microfinance provider was little more than a form of loan guarantee insurance. It has not been uncommon for providers to handle these savings as though they were 'equity capital', and to deny the borrower any access to their contributions to compulsory savings, even when repayment default was imminent. In these circumstances, which until quite recently prevailed at Grameen Bank as much as they still do with most smaller programmes in the Asia Pacific, compulsory savings were an added cost of capital to borrowers, hidden from scrutiny because of the way they were described and handled within the accounting systems of providers.

In credit programmes with a compulsory savings component there is invariably a much closer match of the number of savers and borrowers than in institutions which offer unbiased savings and credit services. In the latter, the number of savers exceeds the number of borrowers by a wide margin, as the few examples in Table 11.1 show.

BRI is a bank for the near-poor and not-poor while the BPD was set up with church funds as a commercial bank for the poor. The contrast in saver-to-borrower ratios for these two 'banks' is indicative of the fact that both the poor and the not-poor have savings and will use deposit facilities when they are offered (see Table 11.1).

Table 11.1 Ratio of the Number of Savers to Borrowers, Selected MFIs, 1995

Institutions/Country	Number of Savers	Borrowers	Number of Savers per Borrower	Nature of Savings Programme*
GPU, Sri Lanka	47,954	4,392	10.92	V
BPD, Indonesia	11,893	1,322	9.0	V
RRDB, Sri Lanka	24,902	3,136	7.94	V
BRI	16,174,000	2,488,000	6.50	V
TCCS, Sri Lanka	24,600	6,900	3.56	V & C
Navajiban Co-operative Society Ltd, Nepal	195	67	2.91	V & C
SEWA, India	56,541	20,840	2.71	V & C
TSPI, Philippines	1,958	764	2.56	V & C
BSD, Indonesia	30,340	12,656	2.40	V
RDRS, Bangladesh	18,308	7,877	2.32	V & C
P4K, Indonesia	328,670	203,790	1.61	C
BRAC, Bangladesh	1,510,802	1,059,199	1.43	C
ASA, Bangladesh	404,218	326,255	1.24	C & V
Grameen Bank, Bangladesh	2,065,661	1,870,371	1.10	C
PRDA, Sri Lanka	3,549	3,250	1.09	C
Grameen Bikas Bank, Nepal	26,296	25,028	1.05	C
LLDAT, Papua New Guinea	224	216	1.04	C
CARD, Philippines	3,980	3,980	1.00	C
Project Dungganon, Philippines	1,941	1,993	0.97	C

* C = compulsory, V = voluntary. Since 1995, several of the above institutions have initiated vigorous voluntary savings programmes, including Grameen Bank and most CASHPOR Inc. members.

Internal resources are the essence of sustainable self-help and self-reliance, and voluntary savings are by far the most flexible and important growth factor available to microfinance providers. The delivery of savings products also opens opportunities for the microfinance provider to involve its client base in its operations in a whole new range of activities, reinforcing the philosophy that the client base should feel a sense of 'ownership' of the programme. Increasing the liability of the provider to its client base through growth in the value of deposit liabilities is a traditional way to achieve this, long since used by credit unions and RoSCAs.

Over time an established microfinance provider that seeks to ensure long-term financial viability will fund a rising proportion of the loan portfolio from internally generated voluntary savings. The microfinance providers examined in the case studies clearly demonstrate that the key to so doing is imposition of the right incentives: i.e. positive real returns, frequent and convenient collection services, easy withdrawal procedures, and offer of tailored saving products, including passbook savings, time deposits, long-term contractual savings with special provisions for microloans, short-term regular savings, rotating savings, lottery savings and many others.

A large number of providers have found it very useful to tie savings collection procedures to loan instalment collection. In some of the poorest communities in Bangladesh, for example, poor women have been prepared to pay a fee for these collection services. (See Rutherford, 1996.) In other instances the offer of insurance products to protect against the death of a key member of the household, provide for health services or simply save to prepare against the occurrence of a specific but unscheduled future event (such as a funeral, multiple birth, school costs, major equipment repairs, a wedding, etc.) have proved to be effective vehicles for grassroots resource mobilization. However, the offer of such financial products at a profit normally requires financial and management skills that are of a different order from those needed for the operation of a one-stop MicroCredit programme. Few of the smaller microfinance providers in the Asia Pacific region have adequate access to these skills, but donors are in a strategic position to rectify this situation by making available the resources needed to gain access to the technical expertise and training required.

The role of linkage programmes

It would be wrong to suggest that institutional innovation, in the form of distinct microfinance providers, is the only way to bring financial intermediation services to poor people. It is a fact that MFIs complement the list of existing financial service providers in developing countries, but this does not mean that existing mainstream institutions cannot reform what they do in order to also become important microfinance providers. There is even a plausible line of argument that in the fullness of time current clients of microfinance will outgrow microfinance providers and will graduate into the banking mainstreams. There is likely to be an element of truth to this view, but underlying it is the possibility that banks and other financial institutions that have not previously served the poor might be brought to do so. Moreover, is it possible that microfinance delivery mechanisms could be designed in ways that facilitate the graduation of poor households to a status where commercial sectors of developing countries, banks especially, are able to meet the needs of the poor for credit, savings services, insurance, money management advice and financial planning? Linkage programmes are intended to achieve these goals.

Many NGOs, including World Vision, Oxfam, CARE, and Opportunity Foundation, have tried to incorporate commercial-sector linkages into their poverty-alleviation and microenterprise-promotion programmes. Few of these have been as successful as one might have hoped, but they have not been without their achievements. However, for almost a decade now, the APRACA in co-operation with financial and technical support from GTZ, has been promoting a programme to link banks and credit unions in the financial mainstreams in poor countries to SHGs of poor households. Similarly, in more recent years the Brisbane-based FDC, with support from the UNDP and several bilateral donors, has been operating a linkage programme involving networking between banks seeking to use linkage devices to reach out to the poor. Both the APRACA and FDC programmes seek to promote linkage in various ways, especially by sharing between network members institutional experiences that highlight what has worked and what has not. While both programmes have had their problems, they have made participants more keenly aware of difficulties to be overcome in successfully banking with the poor. Both the APRACA and FDC experience is that 'linkage' can be an effective way of promoting outreach to the poor. Typically, however, success demands the creation of a dedicated 'finance window for the poor', which many banks cannot achieve without the assistance of a third party, normally a facilitating NGO or an SHG.

The resources that mainstream financial institutions can bring to these linkage programmes loosens the resource constraints facing many small informal and semi-formal microfinance providers as they seek to meet the financial needs of their mature and new customers. The APRACA supports linkage programmes in six Asian countries, the two largest national projects being in India and Indonesia. The FDC, on the other hand, facilitates the growth of a network of linkage programmes with Nepal, the Philippines and the PIEs as key members. In all developing countries microfinance represents a minute portion of total financial intermediation. It is inconceivable, therefore, that the commercial banks and other mainstream financial institutions in developing countries should not collaborate with microfinance providers in bringing greater access to microfinance services to the poor. Linkage programmes and the role of the banks in microfinance is an important topic that deserves to be placed high on the poverty reduction agenda of developing country governments. Part of that agenda is rightly devoted to collaboration with multinational agencies, bilateral donors and local financial institutions, especially central banks, in the mobilization of adequate resources for outreach.

Is financial viability feasible for all microfinance providers?

The overwhelming majority of more than 40 microfinance providers included in the regional case studies presented in Part II of this book have yet to achieve financial viability. Many have yet to adopt financial viability as a corporate policy. Is this because financial viability is not a feasible objective for most microfinance providers, or is there some other reason? The case studies show that any suggestion that financial viability is not feasible for some microfinance providers is unfounded.

Most microfinance programmes created and supported by donors do not cover their costs. A further but much smaller number does make a profit, but it is insufficient to remain in business and grow without continuing access to subsidized external funds. The sample of providers included in the case studies reflects this dichotomy. However, there are a few microfinance providers in our sample which have demonstrated that financial viability is a choice and not the result of chance or serendipity. The guidelines that must be embraced in order to give effect to this choice are clear from their experiences. These guidelines can be summarized as follows:

Guidelines for being a financially viable microfinance provider
(i)   Vision:
   • be a service-oriented commercial institution by knowing your market intimately.
(ii)   Strategic planning:
   • corporate commitment to viability expressed as clear performance goals and growth objectives.
(iii)   Sustainable pricing policies:
   • cover costs, especially the cost of funds, administrative overheads, loan losses, and
   • profit margin needed to remain in business;
   • take inflation into account in determining pricing policies;
   • offer depositors attractive real returns on their savings.
(iv)   Trend to financial independence:
   • fund a rising share of the loan portfolio from internally generated resources, especially voluntary, withdrawal savings of borrowers.
(v)   Poverty targeting:
   • concentrate on sources of growth that favour expanding outreach to poor households;

- adopt operating procedures that are tailored to the needs of the poor, including:
  - gender bias favouring poor women;
  - use of collateral substitutes;
  - frequent doorstep collection and repayment services;
  - offer of suitable loan and savings products;
  - set loan sizes and repayment schedules appropriate to the circumstances of the borrower.

(vi) Management benchmarking:
  - strict cost control;
  - standardize and computerize;
  - establish the programme as a separate accounting entity;
  - decentralize and localize operations to the greatest possible extent;
  - realize economies of scale by increasing the number of poor customers;
  - keep it simple and transparent;
  - reward performance by staff at branch level;
  - insist on business standards and reject welfare or charity initiatives;
  - insist on honesty, but use procedures that minimize opportunities for moral hazard.

(vii) Risk management:
  - maximize recovery by insisting and rewarding timely repayment;
  - offer good clients repeat loans of increasing size;
  - use appropriate collateral substitutes;
  - build credit discipline by mobilizing peer group discipline.

(viii) Invest in your staff:
  - recruit good staff
  - provide orientation, promotional and refresher training;
  - schedule skill and motivation training;
  - insist on exposure training for management.

(ix) Strategic alliances
  - share client-support services with other agencies;
  - co-operate with local institutions, SHGs and locally operating NGOs to provide add-on services;
  - establish service centres as financially independent subsidiaries.

In almost all case study countries there was a need for government-policy reform and finance-sector deregulation to enable the above guidelines to be followed. Since the Asian financial meltdown of 1997–8, the danger is that attempts to respond to the crisis in formal-sector banking will mean more inappropriate financial regulation and control over the microfinance sector as well. The case studies clearly show that MFIs do not function very well under conditions of repressive policies that prevent them from pursuing financial viability. However, this said, it must also be noted that freedom to set interest rates and charges does not preclude the usefulness of sensitive prudential regulation and supervision by the central bank or some other arm of government. The crucial need is that microfinance providers should be free to:

— set their own interest rates on deposits and loans so that costs can be covered and the savings of borrowers mobilized;
— establish branch networking to facilitate outreach to the poor in even the most remote communities and villages;
— apply for a banking licence, if judged necessary, that is specific to the needs of expanded outreach to poor households;
— compete vigorously for clients and resources;
— access guidance and supervisory services in prudential matters from the regulatory agencies, possibly a purpose-specific and separate second-tier regulatory authority, such as the Rural Bankers Association in the Philippines.

Governments can do more to facilitate microfinance outreach to the poor

It is important to recognize the ways in which government intervention in savings mobilization, rural credit, the establishment and spread of co-operatives and other areas of institutional innovation in development have gone awry and left the poor no better off and, at times, worse off. The lesson from these experiences is not to reject any role for the public sector, but to avoid the source of the failure. The tragedy is that all too often the source of the failure is well known; i.e. inappropriate and excessive public-sector interference in programme implementation, lack of trust of the poor and their ability to manage their own affairs, and inability to actively listen to the client group to clearly ascertain their needs.

There is a universal tendency on the part of public-sector officials to assume that they know what the poor need, and to seek control over how these needs will be met so as to satisfy their own need to meet documentation and accountability requirements. The result is invariably a welfare-biased approach to poverty alleviation that disenfranchises the poor and establishes new dependency relations. If the agents of government are to have a constructive role in microfinance it will be because these traps have been avoided.

Instructive examples of ways in which government can effectively promote and nurture the outreach of microfinance providers can be found in several Asia Pacific countries. None are more instructive than the history of the AIM in Malaysia or the contribution that the PSKF in Bangladesh has had on the ASA, the BRAC and other microfinance providers in that country. Similarly P4K in Indonesia, the network of Grameen Bank replications in

Nepal and, Philippine Business for Social Progress (PBSP) and TSPI in the Philippines have received public-sector support that has not seriously compromised their independence or the active involvement of their clients in management and member services. In each of these cases funding has been made available at subsidized rates in quantities that have enabled outreach to proceed beyond what would otherwise have been the case. These examples are demonstrations of the very positive impact that government funding for microfinance can have on outreach and sustainable poverty reduction.

In no area of public-sector activity, however, is the role of government more important than in the creation of a policy and regulatory environment that is supportive of the outreach work of microfinance providers to poor households. The wake of the Asian meltdown will bring calls for financial-sector reforms that must not be applied insensitively across the board. MFIs do not need the same sorts of prudential controls as do commercial enterprises in the mainstreams of competitive banking. Interest rate controls, liquidity requirements, reporting requirements and licences to practise or offer particular services are matters that must be tailored to the realities of working with very poor clients. The Asian financial crisis, especially as it has unfolded in Indonesia, Thailand, Malaysia and the Philippines, has undone much of the good work that had been achieved in poverty reduction over the past twenty years. Access to microfinance services must not be unduly constrained by the policy reforms introduced to shore up and rebuild the commercial finance sector. Governments will need to be conscious of the special needs of microfinance providers and ensure that legislation is suitably drafted with the necessary caveats and exclusions. In addition, it will be essential for governments to take whatever steps are needed to ensure that the loss of resource flows from the commercial sector into microfinance that was expected prior to the financial crisis is recovered and made up. One way in which this might be done is for a share of the international 'bailout' funds secured from the World Bank, the IMF and bilateral donors to be directed into the microfinance sector as part of the effort to protect the vulnerable and assist the near-poor from sliding back into poverty.

Impact of microfinance outreach on the incidence of poverty

The case studies confirm what an increasing number of researchers have found: i.e. that the services that microfinance providers bring to poor households can make a significant contribution to poverty reduction, economic welfare, and the capacity for household-level self-reliance. There is now no doubt that microfinance does benefit the poor. The replication of similar findings over a number of years for individual programmes, such as the AIM, Grameen, P4K and the BRAC, is reason to be confident that this positive impact can be sustained. In a major study of microfinance providers in Asia, Africa and Latin America, Hulme and Mosley, 1996 were drawn to

Table 11.2   Impact of MicroCredit on Income and the Incidence of Poverty, Selected Countries

	Annual Average Rise in Income % 1988–92: Borrowers	Annual Average Rise in Income % 1988–92: Control Group	Borrowers as a Ratio of Control Group	Sample Size: No. of Borrowers: '000	
Indonesia	12.9	3.1	3.80	2,500	
Bangladesh	29.3	22.2	1.34	608	
Sri Lanka	15.6	9.9	1.57	700	
India	46.0	24.0	1.91	25	
	% Change in Monthly Income of AIM Borrowers	% Change in Monthly Income of Control Group			Change in % Borrowers Below Poverty line
Malaysia, 1990	90.0	N.A.	N.A.	N.A.	N.A.
Malaysia, 1991	124.0	80.0	1.0	N.A.	−66
Malaysia, 1991	134.0	N.A.	N.A.	396	−63
Malaysia, 1992–3	139.0	N.A.	N.A.	N.A.	N.A.
Malaysia, 1995	272.0	56.0*	3.05	367	−86
Malaysia, 1996	182.0			310	−53

* % of control group that crossed the poverty line.
Sources: AIM, 1993; Chamhuri, 1996; Gibbons and Kassim, 1990; Gibbons, 1994; Hulme and Mosley, 1996, p. 88.

conclude: 'our study confirms the emerging consensus that well designed credit schemes can raise the incomes of significant numbers of poor people' (p.114). Six separate evaluations of the AIM conducted over the period 1990–5 all arrive at similar findings, in each case confirmed by the increase in the clients' quality of life in terms of value of assets accumulated and the quality of housing. The data are summarized in Table 11.2.

Improving the working of financial institutions and expanding access to financial intermediation by the poor is not enough for sustained poverty reduction. Economists are agreed that an environment of economic growth is essential for sustained poverty reduction. In a recent study of 114 World Bank-supported poverty-reduction structural adjustment programmes implemented in the period 1980–93, Jayarajah, Branson and Sen, 1996 reported that, 'in no country where growth was negative did poverty decrease'. (p. 2). Creating the conditions for macroeconomic growth is not, however, the responsibility of microfinance providers. This is the responsibility of governments and their policy advisers. The fact remains, however, that it is very much harder for microfinance providers to succeed in what they do in the absence of a macroeconomic environment of economic growth.

How to make microfinance a more effective tool for poverty reduction

It is in the ken of microfinance advocates to consider what needs to be done to make microfinance-based interventions more effective as a tool for poverty reduction. It is clear, for example, that microfinance providers will always remain marginal to the big picture so long as they remain small and insignificant in their outreach to poor households. Since 1980, outreach in Bangladesh, Indonesia and Malaysia has been extended to one-third or more of poor households in those countries. It is also in these three countries where the situation of the poor has improved the most over the 20-year period to the close of 1995. If outreach can be similarly increased in all developing countries, the likely impact on the incidence of poverty can be expected to be similarly positive.

In recent years there have been at least eight major studies of the impact of MicroCredit on the incomes of poor households. Without exception these studies confirm that household income of families with access to credit is significantly higher than for comparable households without access to credit. Poor households that have had access to microfinance services also show significant increases in asset accumulation, providing them with both a safety net against misadventure and resources for self-help investments. Jones, 1995 reports that the multiplier effects of greater credit outreach combined with reduced hoarding are not trivial. There is also an important 'competition' dividend of expanded outreach that is observed as lower informal-sector interest rates and increases in the quantity and variety of finance products offered to poor households. These benefits are in addition to the increase in productivity associated with higher levels of investment and less hoarding.

The cost-effectiveness of outreach ought to be sensitive to where in the poverty pyramid one focuses the greatest attention. If new clients can be recruited from among households that are below the poverty line but not the most vulnerable, the poorest of the poor, there may well be a larger and more sustained 'trickle-down effect' that is of benefit to the ultra poor. Is it possible that because outreach to the poorest of the poor is especially difficult and costly, concentration of effort on the higher strata of the poverty pyramid can result in a more cost-effective and sustainable fall in the incidence of poverty? There is no firm evidence on which to decide this question, but it is an important issue for many microfinance providers, and especially those for which microenterprise promotion is also a goal. Until more evidence is available, this issue must represent fertile ground for further research.

Bibliography

References

Acharya, Meena, Bishnu P. Shrestha and Hans Dieter Seibel (1988) Self-help groups in Nepal, *Asia Pacific Rural Finance* (Bangkok), **1**(1), 3-6.

Adams, D.W. and D.A. Fitchett (eds) (1992) *Informal Finance in Low-Income Countries,* Westview, Boulder.

Adams, D.W. and J.D. Von Pischke (1992) Microenterprise credit programmes: déjà vu, *World Development,* **20**(10), 1463–70.

Adams, D.W. and R.C. Vogel (1986) Rural financial markets in low-income countries: Recent controversies and lessons, *World Development,* **14**(4), 477–87.

Adams, D.W., C. Gonzales-Vega and J.D. Von Pischke (eds) (1986) *Agricultural Credit and Rural Development,* Ohio State UP, Ohio.

Adams, D.W., D. Graham and J.D. Von Pischke (1984) *Undermining Rural Development with Cheap Credit,* Westview Press, Boulder.

Adams, Dale W. and G.I. Nehman (1979) Borrowing cost and the demand for rural credit, *Journal of Development Studies,* **15**, 165–76.

ADB (1993) *Asian Development Outlook – 1993,* Oxford University Press, NY.

ADB (1991) *The Urban Poor and Basic Infrastructure Services in Asia and the Pacific Basin,* Manila.

ADB (1997) *Microenterprise Development: Not by Credit Alone,* Manila.

ADB and NRB (1994) *Nepal Rural Credit Review: Final Report,* 4 vols, Nepal Rastra Bank, Kathmandu.

Afshar, H, (ed.) (1991) *Women, Development and Survival in the Third World,* Longman, London.

Ahmed, Anwar and John Kennedy (1994) The effect on the viability of Bangladeshi farm households of permitting multipurpose institutional credit, *Savings and Development,* **18**(4), 473–95.

Ahmed, Nizam Uddin (1997) *Report on the Socio-Economic Impact of MSFSCIP,* GTZ, Dhaka.

Ahmed, Salehuddin (1997) *The Microfinance Technology of Palli Karma Sahayak Foundation (PKSF),* Dhaka.

Ahmed, Zia U. (1989) Effective costs of rural loans in Bangladesh, *World Development,* **17**(3), 357–63.

AIDAB (1995) *Papua New Guinea: Improving the Investment Climate,* International Development Issues No. 39, November, AIDAB, Canberra.

AIM (1989–94) *Annual Reports,* AIM, Penang.

Alamgir, Dewan A.H. (1997) *Flexible Financial Services for the Poor: The Bangladesh Unemployed Rehabilitation Organisation-Tangail (BURO-Tangail) in Bangladesh,* CDF, Dhaka.

Albe, Alana and Nandasiri Gamage (1996) *Our Money, Our Movement – Building a Poor People's Credit Union,* ITP, London.

Aleem, I. (1990) Imperfect information, screening, and the costs of informal lending: A study of a rural credit market in Pakistan, *World Bank Economic Review,* **4**(3), 329–50.

Amenomori, Takayoshi (1993) Grameen Bank in the Philippines: TSPI & CARD, CASHPOR Inc. Reprint, Seremban, Malaysia.

Anderson, D. and F. Khambata (1985) Financing small scale industry and agriculture in developing Countries: the merits and limitations of commercial policies, *Economic Development and Cultural Change*, **33**, 349–71.

Anderson, R.T. (1966) Rotating credit associations in India, *Economic Development and Cultural Change*, **14**, 334–39.

APRACA (1983) *Agricultural Credit Policies and Programmes for Small Farmers Development in Asian and Pacific Countries, Country Profiles 1982 and Strategy for Recovery of Loans*, APRACA Report No. 9, FAO, Regional Office for Asia and Pacific, March, Bangkok.

Ardener, S. (1964) The comparative study of rotating credit associations, *Journal of the Royal Anthropological Society of Great Britain and Ireland*, **94**(2), 201–29.

Ardener, S. and S. Burman (1995) *Money-Go-Round, The Importance of RoSCAs for Women*, Berg, Oxford.

ARTI (1994) *Statistical Abstract, 1994–95*, Data Bank, ARTI, Colombo.

ARTI (1990) *Food Security – Discussion Paper on Food Policy Issues, Marketing and Food*, Policy Division, ARTI, Colombo (mimeo), 1–19.

ASA (1996) *ASA Financial Services*, ASA, Dhaka.

Ashe, Jeffrey and Christopher E. Cosslett (1989) Credit the Poor: Past Activities and Future Directions for the UNDP, *UNDP Policy Discussion Paper*, UNDP, New York.

AusAID (1996) *Papua New Guinea Private Sector Development Study – Final Report*, May, AusAID, Canberra.

Bailey, F.G. (1958) *Caste, Class and Economic Frontier*, Oxford UP, Oxford.

Baker, Judy L. and Grosh, Margaret E. (1994) Poverty reduction through geographic targeting: how well does it work?, *World Development*, **22**(7), 983–95.

Balicasan, A. (1992) Rural poverty in the Philippines: incidence, determinants and policies, *Asian Development Review*, **10**(1), 125–63.

Balicasan, A. (1994) Urban poverty in the Philippines: nature, causes and policy measures', *Asian Development Review*, **12**(1), 117–52.

Balkenhol, Bernd (1995) Collateral substitutes – adoption and performance, paper presented at the *Finance Against Poverty* conference, University of Reading, 27–28 March, mimeo.

Banerjee, A.T. Besley and T. Guinnane (1994) Thy neighbour's keeper: The design of a credit co-operative with theory and a test, *Quarterly Journal of Economics*, May, 491–515.

BASIX (1996) *A New Generation Rural Livelihood Promotion Institution, Feasibility Report*, Hyderabad.

Basu, Santonu (1997) Why institutional credit agencies are reluctant to lend to the rural poor: a theoretical analysis of the Indian rural credit market, *World Development*, **25**(2), 267–80.

Bechtel, P.K. and R. Zender (1994) *Providing Financial Services to the Poor: IFAD's Experience, Challenges & Evolving Approaches*, IFAD, Rome.

Bedard, Guy (ed.) 1989 *Fighting Poverty Through Self-Help*, proceedings of the Feldafing Conference, Germany, 29 September – 5 October, 1988, German Foundation for International Development (DSE), Bonn.

Begashaw, G.E. (1978) The economic role of traditional savings institutions in Ethiopia, *Savings and Development*, **2**, 249–62.

Behrman, Jere and T.N. Srinivasan (eds) (1995) *Handbook of Development Economics*, Vol. III A and B, Elsevier, Amsterdam.

Bell, C. (1990) Interactions between institutional and informal credit agencies in rural India, *World Bank Economic Review*, **4**, 297–328.

Belloni, Serge (1995) *Solomon Islands: Evaluation of a Survey on Informal Financial Systems Conducted by The Central Bank of the Solomon Islands*, April, ESCAP Pacific Operations Centre, Port Vila.

Belloni, Serge (1996) *Overview of Projects for the Development of Informal and semi-Informal Financial Systems in Papua New Guinea*, March, ESCAP Pacific Operations Centre, Port Vila.

Bencevinga, V.R. and B.D. Smith (1991) Financial intermediation and endogenous growth, *Review of Economic Studies*, **58**(2), 195–210.

Bennett, L. and C.E. Cuevas (1996) Sustainable banking with the poor, *Journal of International Development*, **8**(2), 145–52.

Berger, Marguerite (1989) Giving women credit: the strengths and limitations of credit as a tool for alleviating poverty, *World Development*, **17**(7), July, 1017–32.

Besley, Timothy (1994) How do market failure arguments justify interventions in rural credit markets?, *World Bank Research Observer*, **9**(1), 27–47.

Besley, Timothy (1995) Credit, Savings and Insurance, chapter 36 in Behrman and Srinivasan (eds) (1995), 2123–2207.

Besley, Timothy (1997) Political economy of alleviating poverty: theory and institutions, in Bruno and Pleskovic (eds) (1997) *Annual World Bank Conference on Development Economics*, Washington, DC, 117–134.

Besley, T. and S. Coate (1995) Group lending, repayment incentives and social collateral, *Journal of Development Economics*.

Besley, T.S. Coate and G. Loury (1993) The economics of rotating savings and credit associations, *American Economic Review*, **83**(4), 792–810.

Bester, H. (1985) Screening vs rationing in credit markets with imperfect information, *American Economic Review*, **74**(4), 850–5.

Biggs, Tyler S. Donald R. Snodgrass and Pradeep Srivastava (1991) On minimalist credit programmes, *Savings and Development*, **15**(1), 39–52.

Binhadi, Bp. (1995) *Financial Sector Deregulation, Banking Development and Monetary Policy: the Indonesian Experience, 1983–93*, Institut Bankir Indonesia, Jakarta.

BKI (1990) *Kupedes Development Impact Survey*, BRI Planning, Research and Development Department, Jakarta.

Blackwood, D.L. and R.G. Lynch (1994) The measurement of inequality and poverty: a policy maker's guide to the literature, *World Development*, **22**(4), 567–78.

BNM (1995) *Annual Report*, BNM, Kuala Lumpur.

Bouman, F.J.A. (1995) RoSCA: on the origin of the species, *Savings and Development*, **19**(2), 117–48.

Bouman, F.J.A. and O. Hospes (eds) (1994) *Financial Landscapes Reconstructed: the Fine Art of Mapping Development*, Westview Press, Boulder.

Bouman, F.J.A. (1977) Indigenous savings and credit societies in the third world: a message, *Savings and Development*, **1**, 181–220.

Bouman, F.J.A. (1982) Informal saving and credit arrangements in developing countries: observations from Sri Lanka, Discussion Paper No. 4, Colloquium on Rural Finance, Economic Development Institute, World Bank, Washington, DC.

Bouman, F.J.A. (1984) Informal credit and savings arrangements in developing countries: observations from Sri Lanka, in Adams, Graham and Von Pischke (1984), 232–76.

Bouman, F.J.A. (1989) *Small, Short and Unsecured: Informal Rural Finance in India*, Oxford UP, Delhi.

BPM (1995) *Annual Report*, BPM, Kuala Lumpur.

BRAC *RDP Phase II and RCP Mid-term Evaluation Report*, Dhaka.

Braverman, A. and J.L. Guasch (1986) Rural credit markets and institutions in developing countries: lessons for policy analysis from practice and modern theory, *World Development*, **14**, 1253–67.

Braverman, A. and M. Huppi (1991) Improving rural finance in developing countries, *Finance and Development*, March, 42–4.

Bruno, Michael and Boris Pleskovic (eds) (1997) *Annual World Bank Conference on Development Economics*, World Bank, Washington, DC.

Burkett, P. (1991) Group lending programmes and rural finance in developing countries, *Savings and Development*, 401–19.

Carter, M.R. and K.D. Weibe (1990) Access to capital and its impact on agrarian structure and productivity in Kenya, *American Journal of Agricultural Economics*, December, 1146–50.

CDF (1996) *Savings and Credit Information of NGOs*, CDF, Dhaka.

Central Bank of Ceylon (1979) *Report of the Consumer Finance and Socio-Economic Survey of Sri Lanka – 1978/79, Part I & II*, Central Bank Press, Colombo.

Central Bank of Ceylon (1982) *Report of the Consumer Finance and Socio-Economic Survey of Sri Lanka – 1980/81, Part I & II*, Central Bank Press, Colombo.

Central Bank of Sri Lanka (1960–94) *Annual Reports*, Central Bank Press, Colombo.

Central Bank of Sri Lanka (1984–94) *Statistical Bulletins*, Central Bank Press, Colombo.

Central Bank of Sri Lanka (1988–94) *Economic and Social Statistics of Sri Lanka*, Central Bank Press, Colombo.

Central Bank of Sri Lanka (1995) *Review of the Economy – 1995*, Central Bank Press, Colombo.

CGAP (1995) *Micro and Small Enterprise Finance: Guiding Principles or Selecting and Supporting Intermediaries*, mimeo, originally published by CGAP predecessors, Committee of Donor Agencies for Small Enterprise Development and Donor's Working Group on Financial Sector Development, Washington, DC.

CGAP (1996) *Format for Appraisal of Microfinance Institutions*, World Bank/CGAP, Washington, DC.

Chambers, Robert (1995) Poverty and livelihoods: whose reality counts?, IDS Discussion Paper No. 347, IDS, Brighton, Sussex.

Chamhuri, Siwar (1996) *Microfinance Capacity Assessment: Malaysia Country Report*, background paper prepared for Bank Poor '96, December, APDC, Kuala Lumpur, mimeo.

Chan, Julius (1996) *Launching of The Papua New Guinea Women's Credit Project*, speech by the Prime Minister and Minister for Foreign Affairs & Trade, 29 March, Port Moresby.

Chandrasiri, J.K.M.D. (1993) Poverty and land, *Sri Lankan Journal of Agrarian Studies*, 8(1/2), 45–61.

Chenery, H. and T.N. Srinivasan (eds) (1988) *Handbook of Development Economics*, Vol. 1, North Holland, Amsterdam.

Christen, R.P. (1990) *Financial Management of Micro-Credit Programmes*, ACCION International, Cambridge, M.A.

Christen, R.P. (1996) *Executive Summary*, Maximising the outreach of microenterprise finance: an analysis of successful microfinance programmes, by Christen, R.P., E. Rhyne and R.C. Vogel (1995), USAID Programmes and Operations Assessment Report No. 10, Washington, DC.

Committee of Donor Agencies for Small Enterprise Development and Working Group on Financial Sector Development, 1995, *Micro and Small Enterprise Finance: Guiding Principles For Selecting and Supporting Intermediaries*, October, CGAP, Washington, DC.

Chua, Ronald, and Gilberto M. Llanto (1995), *Assessing the Efficiency and Outreach of Microfinance Schemes*, ILO, Geneva

Coate, S. and M. Ravallion (1993) Reciprocity without commitment: characterisation and performance of informal insurance arrangements, *Journal of Development Economics*, 40, 1–24.

Collier, Paul and Deepak Lal, (1984) Why poor people get rich: Kenya 1960-79, *World Development*, **12**(10), 1007–18.

Conroy, J.D., K.W. Taylor and G.B. Thapa (1995) *Best Practice of Banking with the Poor*, FDC, Brisbane.

Copestake, James G. (1995) Poverty oriented financial service programmes: room for improvement?, *Savings and Development*, **19**(4), 417–36.

Colter, Jusuf M. and Pandu Suharto (1993) Grameen Bank in Indonesia: impact on Karya Usaha Mandiri, report prepared for the Indonesian Banking Development institution, Jakarta, CASHPOR Inc. Reprint, Seremban, Malaysia.

Counts, Alexander M. (1996) *Give Us Credit*, Research Press, New Delhi.

Cuevas, C.E. (1988) Savings and loan co-operatives in rural areas of developing countries: recent performance and potential, *Savings and Development*, 5–17.

Cuevas, C.E. (1996) Enabling environment and microfinance institutions: lessons from Latin America, *Journal of International Development*, **8**(2), March/April.

CWR (1995) *Facets of Change: Women in Sri Lanka 1986–95*, CWR, Colombo.

CWR (1993) *Women and Credit in Sri Lanka*, CWR, Colombo.

Darling, Malcolm (1924) *The Punjab Peasant in Prosperity and Debt*, Oxford UP, Oxford.

Deaton, A.S. (1990) Saving in developing countries: theory and review, *World Bank Economic Review*, Proceedings of the 1989 World Bank Annual conference on Development Economics, 61–96.

Deaton, A.S. (1991) Saving and liquidity constraints, *Econometrica*, **59**, 1221-48.

Department of Census and Statistics (1950–94) *Statistical Abstracts*, Government Press, Colombo.

Desai, B.M. (1984) Group based savings and credit programmes in rural India, in ILO (1984).

Desai, B.M. and J.W. Mellor (1993) *Institutional Finance for Agricultural Development: An Analytical Survey of Critical Issues*, IFPRI, Washington, DC.

deAghion, Beatriz Armendariz (1995) On the design of a credit agreement with peer monitoring, paper presented at the *Finance against Poverty* conference, University of Reading, 27–28 March, mimeo.

deSoto, Hernando (1986) Constraints on people: the origins of underground economies and limits to their growth', a book review of *El Otro Sendero*, (The Other Path), 1986, Instituto Libertad y Democracia (ILD), Lima, Peru.

Devas, Charles (1991) Financing mechanisms, constraints and future options, in ADB (1991.

Development Assistance Committee (1990–6) *Development Co-operation*, OECD, Paris.

Devereux, Stephen and Henry Pares (1987) *A Manual of Credit and Savings for the Poor of Developing Countries*, Oxfam, Oxford.

Dev-Pant, Harihar and Dhungel, Dipak (1996) An assessment of the capacity and financial performance of microfinance institutions: the Nepal case, background paper for Bank Poor '96, December, APDC, Kuala Lumpur.

Drake, Deborah and Maria Otero (1992) *Alchemists to the Poor: NGOs as Financial Institutions*, ACCION, Cambridge, MA.

Drake, P.J. (1980) *Money, Finance and Development*, Robertson, Oxford.

EIU (1996) *Country Profile: Pacific Islands 1996–97*, EIU, London.

Egger, Philippe (1986) Banking for the rural poor: lessons from some innovative savings and credit schemes, *International Labour Review*, **125**, 447–62.

ESCAP (1993) *Non-Farm Employment for Rural Poverty Alleviation*, United Nations, New York.

Eugenio, Ofelia C. (1995) *A Study of the Credit Programmes and Schemes Benefiting Disadvantaged Groups in Fiji*, September, Pacific Regional Equitable and Sustainable Human Development Programme, United Nations Development Programme, Suva.

Eugenio, Ofelia C. (1996) *Evaluation of the Tonga National Youth Credit Scheme: A Report*,

Pacific Regional Equitable and Sustainable Human Development Programme, May, UNDP, Suva.

Everett, J. and M. Savara (1991) Institutional credit as a strategy towards self-reliance for petty commodity producers in India: a critical evaluation, in Afshar (1991), 239–59.

Fairbairn-Dunlop, Peggy (1995) *A Review of Some of the Loan Schemes Available for Western Samoan Women*, Pacific Regional Equitable and Sustainable Human Development Programme, July, UNDP, Suva, Fiji.

FDC, 1992 *Banking With the Poor*, FDC, Brisbane.

Feder, Gershon *et al.* (1990) The relationship between credit and productivity in Chinese agriculture: A micromodel of disequilibrium, *American Journal of Agricultural Economics*, **72**(5), 1151–7.

Fernando, E. (1986) Informal savings and credit organisations in Sri Lanka: the Cheetu system, *Savings and Development*, **10**(3), 253–63.

Fernando, Nimal, A. (1989) *Informal Finance in Papua New Guinea: An Overview*, Paper, presented at the Seminar on Informal Financial Markets in Development, Washington, DC, 18–20 October 1989.

Fernando, Nimal A. (1991a) Determinants of rural savings in Papua New Guinea, *Savings and Development*, **15**(4).

Fernando, Nimal A. (1991b) Mobilising rural savings in Papua New Guinea: myths, realities, and needed policy reforms, *The Developing Economies*, March, **29**(1).

Fernando, Nimal A. (1991c) *Reaching Small Borrowers in Developing Countries: Problems, Innovations and Unresolved Issues*, Islands/Australia Working Paper No. 91/8, National Centre for Development Studies – Research School of Pacific Studies, Australian National University, Canberra.

Fernando, Sunimal (1996) *Microfinance Capacity Assessment, Sri Lanka Research Report*, background paper prepared for Bank Poor '96, Asian and Pacific Development Centre, December.

Fiji Senate Report (1994) *Report of the Senate Select Committee on the Desirability of Setting Up a Rural Bank to Serve the Rural Areas of Fiji*, September, Parliamentary paper No. 27, Parliament of Fiji.

Firth, Raymond and B.S. Yamey (1964) *Capital, Saving and Credit in Peasant Societies*, George Allen & Unwin, London.

Fisher, Bernhard (1988) Rural financial savings mobilisation in Sri Lanka: bottlenecks and reform proposals, *Savings and Development*, **12**(1), 35–62.

Fleischer, Rebecca (1996) *Replicating Grameen in Papua New Guinea*, AusAID, May, Canberra.

Food Commissioner's Department (1970–94) *Annual Reports*, Government Press, Colombo.

Forum Secretariat (1996) *Pacific Island Countries: Regional Economic Policy Overview*, Economic Development Division Working Paper 96/2, September, Suva.

Friedmann, J. (1992) *Empowerment: The Politics of Alternative Development*, Basil Blackwell, Oxford.

Friends of Women's World Banking (1996) *Building linkages – people's institutions and financial sector*. Proceedings of national workshop, Ahmedabad, India.

Fuglesang, A. and D. Chandler (1986) *Participation as Process: What We Can Learn from the Grameen Bank, Bangladesh*, Norwegian Ministry of Development Co-operation, Oslo.

Gadgil, M.V. (1986) Agricultural credit in India: a review of performance and policies, *Indian Journal of Agricultural Economics*, **III**(2), 33–56.

Galbraith, John Kenneth (1979) *The Nature of Mass Poverty*, Harvard University Press, Cambridge, MA.

Garson, Jose (1996) *Microfinance and Anti-Poverty Strategies: A Donor Perspective*, UNCDF, New York.

Geddes, Bill, Jenny Hughes and Joe Remenyi (1994) *Anthropology and Third World Development*, Deakin UP, Geelong.

Gee, Alan Edric (1993) *Kiribati Financial System, ESCAP Pacific Operations Centre*, May, Port Vila, Vanuatu.

Geertz, C. (1962) The rotating credit association: A 'middle rung' in development, *Economic Development and Cultural Change*, **10**, 241–63.

Gersovitz, M. (1988) Savings and development, chapter 10 in Chenery and Srinivasan (1988).

Getu, Makonen (ed.) (1996) *Microenterprise Development in Theory and Practice*, Issues in Global Development, No. 8, World Vision Australia, Melbourne.

Getubig, I.J. Remenyi and B. Quiñones (eds) (1997) *Creating the Vision: Microfinancing the poor in Asia-Pacific: Issues Constraints and Capacity Building*, Asia Pacific Development Centre, Kuala Lumpur.

Getubig, I. (ed.) (1993) *Overcoming Poverty Through Credit: The Asian Experience in Replicating the Grameen Bank Approach*, APDC, Kuala Lumpur.

Ghate, Prabhu (1988) Informal credit markets in Asian DCs, *Asian Development Review*, **6**(1), p. 64–85.

Ghate, Prabhu (1992a) *Informal Finance: Some findings from Asia*, Oxford UP for ADB, Manila and Hong Kong.

Ghate, Prabhu (1992b) Interaction between the formal and informal financial sectors: the Asian experience, *World Development*, **20**(6).

Ghate, P.E. Ballon and V. Manalo (1996) Poverty alleviation and enterprise development differentiated approach, *Journal of International Development*, **8**(2).

Gibbons, D. (ed.) (1994) *The Grameen Reader*, 2nd ed., Grameen Bank, Dhaka.

Gibbons, David S. (1996a) Outreach to the Poor with Financial Services, *Issues paper No. 1, Bank Poor '96*, background paper prepared on behalf of APDC for Bank Poor '96, 10–12 December, APDC, Kuala Lumpur, mimeo.

Gibbons, David S. (1996b) Financially-sustainable microfinance institutions for the poor', Issues paper No. 2, Bank Poor '96, background paper prepared on behalf of APDC for Bank Poor '96, 10–12 December, APDC, Kuala Lumpur, mimeo.

Gibbons, David S. (1996c) Resource mobilisation for maximising MFI outreach and financial self sufficiency, *Issues paper No. 3, Bank Poor '96*, background paper prepared on behalf of APDC for Bank Poor '96, 10–12 December, APDC, Kuala Lumpur, mimeo.

Gibbons, David S. (1996d) Supportive policy and regulation for microfinance institutions working with the poor, *Issues paper No. 4, Bank Poor '96*, background paper prepared on behalf of APDC for Bank Poor '96, 10–12 December, APDC, Kuala Lumpur, mimeo.

Gibbons, David S. and Sukor Kasim (1990). *Banking on the Rural Poor in Peninsular Malaysia, final report of project Amanah Ikhtiar Malaysia*, APDC and University Science Malaysia, Kuala Lumpur.

Goodwin-Groen, R. (1998) *The Role of Commercial Banks in Microfinance: Asia-Pacific Region*, The Foundation for Development Cooperation, Brisbane.

Goonaratne W. and P.J. Gunawardene (1983). Poverty and inequality in Rural Sri Lanka, in Khan, Azizur Rahman and Eddy Lee (eds) (1983), *Poverty in Rural Asia*, ILO, Bangkok. 82–119.

Government of India (1996) *Economic Survey, 1995–1996*, Ministry of Finance, Government of India, New Delhi.

Government of India (1993) *Report of the Expert Group on Estimation of Proportion and Number of Poor*, Planning Commission, Government of India, New Delhi.

Government of Malaysia (1991) *Sixth Malaysia Plan (1991–1995)*, Government Printers, Kuala Lumpur.

Government of Malaysia (1996) *Seventh Malaysia Plan (1996–2000)*, Government Printers, Kuala Lumpur.

Government of Malaysia and Asian Development Bank (1987) *Agro-Industries Credit Project-Malaysia*, Final Report, TA No. 743-MAL, Kuala Lumpur and Manila.

Government of Sri Lanka (1988) *Report by the High Level Committee of Officials on Poverty Alleviation Through People Based Development*, Government Press, Colombo.

Greeley, M. (1994) Measurement of poverty and poverty of measurement, *IDS Bulletin*, **25**(2), 50–8.

Groetz, A.M. and R. Sen Gupta (1996) Who takes the credit? gender, power and control over loan use in rural credit programmes in Bangladesh', *World Development*, **24**(1), January, 24–64.

Groh, Barbara and Gloria Somolekoe (1996) Mighty oaks from little acorns: can Microenterprise serve as the seedbed of industrialisation, *World Development*, **24**(2), 1879–90.

Gugler, Josef (ed.) (1988) *The Urbanisation of the Third World*, Oxford UP, New York.

Gulli, H. (1998) *Microfinance and Poverty*, Inter-American Development Bank, Washington, D.C.

Gurgland, M., G. Pederson and J. Yaron (1994) Outreach and sustainability of six rural financial institutions in sub-Saharan Africa, World Bank Discussion Paper, No. 248, Washington, DC.

Gunting, R.S. and F. Rantau (1993) *Projek Usahamaju: From Action Research to Institutionalisation – Problems and Prospects*, in I.P. Getubig et al. (eds), *Overcoming Poverty through Credit*, APDC and IDS, Kuala Lumpur.

Gurung, Harka (1997) *Flying Geese and Sitting Ducks: Patterns of Economic Growth in Asia*, United Nations Association of Nepal, Kathmandu.

Hansen, Jeef and Hans Hofmeijer (1993) *Small-Scale Credit in the Pacific*, ILO, October, Geneva.

Harper, Malcolm (1998) *Profit for the Poor: Cases in Microfinance*, Intermediate Technology Publications, London.

Hashemi, Sayed M., Ruth Schuler Sidney and Ann P. Riley (1996) Rural credit programmes and women's empowerment in Bangladesh, *World Development*, **24**(4), 635–53.

Hayami, Y. and V.W. Ruttan (1971) *Agricultural Development in International Perspective*, Johns Hopkins, Baltimore.

Henderson, Dennis and Farida Khambata (1985) Financing small-scale industry and agriculture in developing countries: the merits and limitations of 'commercial' policies, *Economic Development and Cultural Change*, **33**, 349–73.

Herath, Gamini (1994) Rural credit markets and institutional reform in developing countries: potential and problems, *Savings and Development*, **18**(2), 169–91.

Herath, Gamini (1996) Rural credit markets and imperfect information: a new perspective, *Savings and Development*, **20**(2), 241–53.

Hoff, K., A. Braverman and J.E. Stiglitz (eds) (1993) *The Economics of Rural Organisation: Theory, Practice and Policy*, Oxford UP, New York.

Hoff, K. and J. Stiglitz (1990) Imperfect information and rural credit markets: puzzles and policy perspectives, *World Bank Economic Review*, **4**, 235–50.

Holcombe, Susan (1995) *Managing to Empower: The Grameen Bank's Experience of Poverty Alleviation*, Zed Books, London.

Holdcroft, L.E. (1982) The rise and fall of community development in developing countries 1950–65: a critical analysis and implications, in Jones, G.E. and R. Rolls, (1982).

Holt, Sharon L. and Helena Ribe (1991) Developing financial institutions for the poor and reducing barriers to access for women, World Bank Discussion Paper No. 117, World Bank, Washington, DC.

Hospes, O. (1992) People that count: the forgotten faces of rotating savings and credit associations in Indonesia, *Savings and Development*, **16**(4), 371–402.

Hossain, Iftekhar and Sakhawat, Javed (1996) Microfinance capacity assessment, Bangladesh Country Report, APDC, Kuala Lumpur.

Hossain, Mahabub (1988) *Credit for the Alleviation of Rural Poverty: the Grameen Bank in Bangladesh*, IFPRI and BIDS, Washington, DC and Dhaka.

Howell, John (ed.) (1980) *Borrowers and Lenders: Rural Financial Markets and Institution in Developing Countries*, ODI, London.

Hulme, D. (1990) Can the Grameen Bank be replicated? Recent experiments in Malaysia, Malawi and Sri Lanka, *Development Policy Review*, **8**(3), 287–300.

Hulme, David (1995) Finance for the poor, poorer or poorest? Financial innovation, poverty and vulnerability, paper presented at the Finance against Poverty conference, University of Reading, 27–28 March, mimeo.

Hulme, David, Richard Montgomery and Debapriya Bhattacharya (1996) Mutual finance and the poor: a study of the thrift and credit co-operatives in Sri Lanka, in Hulme and Mosely (1996), 177–245.

Hulme, David and Richard Montgomery (1994) Co-operatives, credit and the poor: private interest, public choice and collective action in Sri Lanka, *Savings and Development*, **18**(3), 359–82.

Hulme, David and Paul Mosley (eds) (1996) *Finance Against Poverty*, 2 vols, Routledge, London.

Hunte, Kenrick C. (1996) Controlling loan default and improving the lending technology in credit institutions, *Savings and Development*, **20**(1), 45–59.

Huppi, Monika and Gershon Feder (1990) The role of groups and credit co-operatives in rural lending, *World Bank Research Observer*, **5**(2), July, 187–204.

Hussein, Bernadette (1996) The poor among us – report reveals startling statistics on poverty', *Fiji Times*, Monday, 29 January.

Hussi, Pekka *et al.* (1993) *The Development of Co-operatives and Other Rural Organisations – The Role of the World Bank*, Technical Paper No. 199, The World Bank, Washington, DC.

IDS (1991) *Evaluation of Project Usahamaju*, IDS, Sabah.

IDS (1993) *Evaluation of Project Usahamaju II*, IDS, Sabah.

IDS (1994) *Evaluation of Project Usahamaju III*, IDS, Sabah.

IFAD (1985) *The Role of Special Projects in Reaching the Poor: IFAD's Experience*, International Fund for Agricultural Development Special Studies Series, Tycooly Publishing, Oxford.

IFAD (1992) *Annual Report*, Rome.

IFAD (1995a) *India: National Women's Development and Empowerment Project, Formulation Report, Annex 6 – Self-Help Groups*, Rome.

IFAD (1995b) *Solomon Islands Rural Finance Services Report: IFAD Loan 224-SM, UNOPS Project No. SOI/87/FO1 – Mid Term Review Report*, June, IFAD, Asia Division – Programme Management Department, Rome.

IFAD and Tonga Development Bank (1993a) *Outer Islands Credit Project: IFAD Loan 327-TA; OPS Project TON/92/FO1 – Full Supervision Mission Aide Memoir*, July, IFAD, Rome.

IFAD and Tonga Development Bank (1993b) *Outer Islands Credit Project: Project Brief*, August, IFAD, Rome.

ILO (1984) *Group Based Savings and Credit for the Rural Poor*, ILO, Geneva.

ISACPA/SAARC (1992) *Report of the Independent South Asian Commission on Poverty Alleviation – Meeting the Challenge*, SAARC Secretariat, Colombo.

Jacklen, Henry R. and Elisabeth Rhyne (1992) Toward a more market oriented approach to credit and savings for the poor, *Small Enterprise Development*, **2**(4), 4–20.

Jain, Pankaj S. (1996) Managing credit for the rural poor: lessons from the Grameen Bank, *World Development*, **24**(1), January, 79–89.

Jayarajah, Carl, William Branson and Binayak Sen (1996) *Social Dimensions of Adjustment: World Bank Experience, 1980–93*, World Bank, Washington, DC.

Johnson, Susan and Ben Rogaly (1997) *Microfinance and Poverty Reduction*, ITP, London.
Jones, G.E. and R. Rolls (eds) (1982) *Progress in Rural Extension and Community Development*, Vol. 1, John Wiley & Sons, Chichester.
Jones, J.H.M. (1995) Women's access to formal and informal finance in a Rajasthan village, paper presented to the Finance against Poverty conference, University of Reading, 27–28 March, mimeo.
Jones J.H.M. (1994) A changing financial landscape in India: macro-level and micro-level perspectives, in Bouman and Hospes (1994), 375–94.
Kannapiran, C. (1991) *Agricultural Credit and Rural Savings*, Proceedings of the Seminar on Agricultural Development in Papua New Guinea: Policies and Issues, 4–5 December, Papua New Guinea by the Department of Agriculture and Livestock and the Asian Development Bank, Port Moresby.
Kannapiran, C. (1994) Sustainable Rural Credit for Agricultural Development In Papua New Guinea, *Papua New Guinea Journal of Agriculture, Forestry and Fisheries*, **37**(1), May, Department of Agriculture and Livestock, Port Moresby, Papua New Guinea.
Kannapiran, C. (1995a) Institutional Rural Finance: Lessons From the Past and Reforms for the Future, *Pacific Economic Bulletin*, **10**(1), July.
Kannapiran, C. (1995b) *Institutional Rural Finance in Papua New Guinea: Lessons from the Failure and the Need for Reform*, NRI Discussion Paper No. 86, November, National Research Institute, Boroko, Papua New Guinea.
Khalily, B. and Richard Meyer (1993) Factors influencing the demand for rural deposits in Bangladesh: a test for functional form, *Journal of Developing Areas*, **26**, 371–82.
Khan, A.Z.M. Obaidullah (1993) Rural Development in South Asia, *Sri Lanka Journal of Agrarian Studies*, **8**, (1 & 2), 1–8.
Khandker, Shahidur R. and Baqui Khalily (1996) The Bangladesh Rural Advancement Committee's Credit Programmes: Performance and Sustainability, World Bank Discussion Paper No. 324, IBRD, Washington, DC.
Khandker, Shahidur, Baqui Khalily and Zahed Khan (1995) Grameen Bank: performance and sustainability, World Bank Discussion Paper No. 306, IBRD, Washington, DC.
King, R. and R. Levine (1993) Finance and growth: Schumpeter might be right, *Quarterly Journal of Economics*, **108**(3), 717–37.
Kiribati Government (1995) *Village Banks*, Paper for Presentation to the Workshop on Integrated Rural Development, November, Tarawa, Kiribati.
Kropp, Erhard, M.T. Marx, B. Pramod, B.R. Quiñones and H.D. Seibel (1989) *Linking Self-Help Groups and Banks in Developing Countries*, GTZ and APRACA, Eschborn and Bangkok.
Lacson, Gil V. and Cecille C. Satirizes (1996) *Micro Credit and Saving Project* (PNG/93/001), May, UNDP, Papua New Guinea.
Lamberte, Mario and Gilberto M. Llanto (1995) A study of financial sector policies: the Philippine Case, in Zahid, S. (ed.), *Financial Sector Development in Asia*, Asian Development Bank, Manila.
Land Bank of the Philippines (1995) *Annual Report*, Manila.
Ledgerwood, J. (1999) *Microfinance Handbook: An Institutional and Financial Perspective*, The World Bank, Washington, DC.
Levitsky, Jacob, (ed.) (1989) *Microenterprises in Developing Countries*, ITP, London.
Lewis, John P. (ed.) (1988) *Strengthening the Poor: What Have We Learned?*, Transaction Books, New Brunswick.
Lipton, M. (1976) Agricultural finance and rural credit in poor countries, *World Development*, **4**, 543–53.
Lipton, Michael and Martin Ravallion (1995) Poverty and Policy, in *Handbook of Development Economics*, Vol. 3, ed. Behrman, Jere and T.N. Srinivasan, Elsevier,

Amsterdam, 2551–7; first published as World Bank Policy Research Working Paper, WPS1130, Washington, DC, 1993.

Lipton, Michael and J. van der Gaag (eds) (1993) *Including the Poor*, World Bank, Washington, DC.

Llanto, G. (1990) Asymmetric information in rural financial markets and interlinking of transactions through self-help groups, *Savings and Development*, 137–51.

Llanto, Gilberto, Bernd Balkenhol and Noor Zulkifli (1996) *Breaking Barriers to Formal Credit: Asian Experiences on Collateral Substitutes*, ILO, Geneva, and APRACA, Bangkok, 1996.

Llanto, Gilberto M. and Ronald Chua (1996) *Transaction Costs of Lending to the Poor*, Foundation for Development Co-operation, Brisbane.

Llanto, Gilberto M, Edgardo Garcia and Ruth Callanta (1996) *An Assessment of the Capacity and Financial Performance of Microfinance Institutions: The Philippine Case*, background paper prepared for Bank Poor '96, December, APDC, Kuala Lumpur, mimeo.

Lovell, Catherine H. (1992) *Breaking the Cycle of Poverty: The BRAC Strategy*, Kumarian Press, Connecticut.

Lyon, J. (1991) Money and power: evaluating income generating projects for women', in Redclift and Sinclair (1991), 172–96.

Malhotra, M. (1992) Poverty lending and microenterprise development, GEMINI Working Paper No. 30, GEMINI, Bethesda, M.D.

Marx, Michael T. (1994) Grameen Bank in Philippines: DUNGGANON & CARD, Report prepared for Deutsche Gesellschaft fur Technische (GTZ), Germany, CASHPOR Inc. Reprint, Seremban, Malaysia.

McGuire, Paul (1996) *Microfinance in the Pacific Island Countries*, report prepared for Bank Poor '96 on behalf of APDC, Foundation or Development Co-operation, Brisbane.

McKee, K. (1989) Micro level strategies for supporting livelihoods, employment and income generation by poor women in the Third World: the challenge of significance, *World Development*, **17**(7) 993–1006.

McKinnon, R.I. (1973) *Money and Capital in Economic Development*, Brookings Institute, Washington, DC.

Mel, Ronnie de (1988) The Pro-Poor Policies: The Keynote Address, in Central Bank of Sri Lanka 1988, *The Symposium on Poverty Alleviation*, Central Bank Press, Colombo, Sri Lanka, 15–23.

Mellor, John W. (1970) *The Economics of Agricultural Development*, Cornell University Press, Ithaca.

Ministry of Foreign Affairs and Trade (1993) *Papua New Guinea Women's Credit Project: An Appraisal of a Papua New Guinea Government Proposal Appraisal* (Draft Report), December, Evaluation and Analytical Support Unit, Development Co-operation Division, Ministry of Foreign Affairs and Trade, Wellington, NZ.

Misra and Puri (1995) *Indian Economy, 1995*, Himalaya Publishing House, Bombay.

Morduck, J. (1997) *The Microfinance Revolution*, Harvard Institute for International Development and Department of Economics, Harvard University.

Morrison, Christian, Henri-Bernard Solignac and Xavier Oudin (1994) *Micro-enterprises and the Institutional Framework in Developing Countries*, OECD, Paris.

Moser, Caroline O.N. (1996) *Confronting Crisis: A Comparative Study of Household Responses in Four Poor Urban Communities*, Environmentally Sustainable Development Studies and Monographs Series No. 8, World Bank, Washington, DC.

Mosher, A.T. (1966) *Getting Agriculture Moving: Essentials for Development and Modernisation*, Praeger, New York.

Mosley, P. (1995) Optimal incentives to repay in institutions lending to low income groups: an Indonesian case study, *Savings and Development*, **19**(3), 257–78.

Mosley, P. (1996) Risk insurance and small farm credit in developing countries: a policy proposal, *Public Administration and Development*, **6**, 309–19.

Mosley, P. and R.P. Dahal (1987) Credit for the rural poor: a comparison of policy experiments in Nepal and Bangladesh, *Manchester Papers in Development*, **3**(2), 45–59.

MPI (1990) *Strategies for Poverty Alleviation: The Sri Lanka Experience*, working paper presented at the Fifth SAARC Meeting of Planners, March 1990, SAARC Secretariat, Colombo.

MPPI (1990) *An Appraisal of Food Subsidy Scheme in Sri Lanka*, Colombo, (mimeo), 1–26.

NABARD (1989) *Studies on Self-Help Groups of the Rural Poor*, Bombay.

NABARD (1995) *Linking Self-Help Groups with Banks – An Indian Experience*, Bombay.

NABARD (1996) *NGOs as Intermediaries in Microfinance – An Indian Experience*, Bombay.

Nagrajan, G., C.C. David and R.L. Myers (1992) Informal finance through land pawning contracts: Evidence from the Philippines, *Journal of Development Studies*, **29**(1), 93–107.

Nayar, C.P.S. (1986) Can traditional financial technologies co-exist with modern technologies? The Indian experience, *Savings and Development*, **10**(1), 31–56.

O'Donohue, Jane and Vaine Wichman (1995) *Review of the SPC Women's Credit Scheme in Melanesia* (Papua New Guinea, Solomon Islands, Vanuatu), South Pacific Commission, Noumea, New Caledonia.

Osner, Karl (1991) *Development Has Got A Face: Interpretation of Life-stories of Thirteen Women in Bangladesh*, German Commission of Justice and Peace, Bonn.

Otero, M. and E. Rhyne (1994) *The New World of Microenterprise Finance*, Kumarian Press, W. Hartford, CT.

Otter, Mark (1996) *Banking with the Poor in the South Pacific*, The Foundation for Development Co-operation, October, Brisbane.

Padmanabhan, K.P. (1988) *Rural Credit: Lessons for Rural Bankers and Policy Makers*, ITP, London.

Paeniu, Bikenibeu (1995) *Final Report on the Evaluation of the North Tarawa Integrated Rural Development Project*, Funafuti, Tuvalu.

Parhusip, Uben (1996) *Microfinance Capacity Assessment: Indonesia Country Report*, background paper prepared for Bank Poor '96, December, APDC, Kuala Lumpur, mimeo.

Patten, R.H. and J.K. Rosengard (1991) *Progress With Profits: The Development of Rural Banking in Indonesia*, ICS Press, San Francisco, CA.

Peiris, W.A.A.S. and Dixon Nilaweera (1985) *Rural Poverty Alleviation in Sri Lanka*, UN/FAO, Rome.

Pestelos, Nestor M. (1992) *Practical Lessons from the Successes and Failures of Revolving Loan Fund Schemes*, IADP Occasional Paper No. 11, March, UNDP Integrated Atoll Development Project, Suva, Fiji.

Pitt, Mark M. and Shahidur R. Khandker (1996) Household and intrahousehold impact of the Grameen Bank and similar targeted credit programmes in Bangladesh, World Bank Discussion Paper No. 320, IBRD, Washington, DC

Poudyal, Ramesh (1994) Grameen Bank in Nepal: Grameen Bank Nepal Biratnagar, CASHPOR Inc. Reprint, Seremban, Malaysia.

Pulley, R.V. (1989) Making the poor creditworthy: a case study of the Integrated Rural Development Programme in India, World Bank Discussion Papers No. 58, World Bank, Washington, DC.

Quiñones, B.R. Jr. (ed.) (1991a) *Group Lending Approach to Rural Finance in Asian Countries*, APRACA, Bangkok, Thailand.

Quiñones, B.R. Jr. (1991b) Financial Instruments for Small Enterprises, *Asia Pacific Rural Finance*, Bangkok, Thailand.

Quiñones, B.R. Jr. and Bernd Balkenhol (1992) *Collateral Substitutes for Small Entrepreneurs*, APRACA, Bangkok, Thailand.

Quiñones, B R. Jr. & Erhard Kropp (1992) *Financial Intermediation System in Support of the People's Economy*, APRACA, Bangkok, Thailand.

Raiffeisen, F.W. (1866, reprinted 1951) *The Credit Associations* (Die Darlehnskasses-Vereine), Neuweid, Verlag der Raiffeisendruckerei G.m.b.H.

Rajasekhar, D. (1996) Problems and prospect of group lending in NGO credit programmes in India, *Savings and Development*, **20**(1), 79–104.

Rashid, Mansoora and Robert M. Townsend (1994) Targeting credit and insurance: efficiency, mechanism design and programme evaluation, ESP Discussion Paper No. 47, World Bank, Washington, DC.

Ratnapala, Nandasena (1989) *Rural Poverty in Sri Lanka*, Sarvodaya Press, Ratmalana, Colombo.

Ravallion, M. (1992) Poverty comparisons: a guide to concepts and methods, Living Standards Measurement Study Working Paper No. 88, World Bank, Washington, DC.

Ravallion, M. (1994). Measuring social welfare with and without poverty lines, *American Economic Review*, **84**(2), 359–64.

Ravallion, M., G. Datt and D. van de Walle (1991) Quantifying absolute poverty in the developing world, *Review of Income and Wealth*, **37**, 345–61.

RBI (1996). *Expert Committee on Integrated Rural Development Programme – Interim Report*, RBI Bombay.

Redclift, N. and M.T. Sinclair (eds) (1991) *Working Women*, Routledge, London.

Reichel, Richard (1995) Development aid, saving and growth in the 1980s: a cross-section analysis, *Savings and Development*, **19**(3), 279–96.

Reidinger, Jeffrey M. (1994) Innovations in rural finance: Indonesia's Badan Kredit Kecamatan Programme, *World Development*, **22**(3), 301–13.

Remenyi, Joe (1991) *Where Credit is Due: Income Generating Programmes for the Poor in Developing Countries*, ITP, London.

Remenyi, Joe (1992) Community development through poverty alleviation, paper prepared for the *International Workshop on Poverty Alleviation in China in the 1990s*, Beijing, 28–30 October, for the World Bank, the United Nations Development Programme, and the China Leading Group for Economic Development in Poor Areas, Office of Poverty Alleviation, Beijing.

Remenyi, Joe (1993) The role of credit in a holistic strategy for sustainable poverty alleviation in Southwest China, *World Bank Consulting Report*, prepared for the 2nd Southwest China Poverty Mission, July-August 1993, Washington, DC, and Centre for Applied Social Research, Deakin University, Geelong.

Remenyi, Joe (1994b) The role of credit in the Qinghai Community Development Project, Pingan, Haidong County, Qinghai, PRC, *Consulting Report*, prepared for CARE Australia, Hassall & Associates and the Australian International Development Assistance Bureau, Canberra. (Also available in Chinese from CARE Australia, translated by Dachang Liu, Southwest College for Forestry, Kunming, PRC.)

Remenyi, Joe (1994a) Poverty targeting, in Geddes, Bill, Jenny Hughes and Joe Remenyi (1994), *Anthropology and Third World Development*, 261–93, Deakin UP, Geelong.

Remenyi, Joe (1995) Monitoring and evaluation in the Mongolian national poverty alleviation programme, *World Bank Consulting Report*, prepared for the East Asia Office, Vulnerable Groups in Mongolia Project, World Bank, Washington, DC, by Remedy Research, Torquay.

Remenyi, Joe (1996) *Microfinance for Poverty Reduction*, Rapporteur General's Report on Bank Poor '96, an Asia-Pacific Conference sponsored by the Asia Pacific Development Centre, 10–12 December, APDC, Kuala Lumpur.

Robertson, A.F. (1984) *People and the State*, Cambridge UP, Cambridge.

Rutherford, Stuart (1995) *ASA: The Biography of an NGO*, Association of Social Advancement, Dhaka.

Rutherford, Stuart (1996) *A Critical Typology of Financial Services for the Poor*, ActionAid, London.

Sanderatne, N. (1986) The political economy of small farmer loan delinquency, *Savings and Development*, **10**, 343–54.

Schmidt, Reinhard H. and Claus Peter Zeitinger (1996) The efficiency of credit-granting NGOs in Latin America, *Savings and Development*, **20**(3), 353–84.

Schmit, L. Th. (1991) *Rural Credit between Subsidy and Market: Adjustments of the Village Units of Bank Rakyat Indonesia in Sociological Perspective*, Leiden University, Leiden.

Schneider, Hartmut (ed.) (1997) *Microfinance for the Poor?*, OECD, Paris.

Schoeffel, Penelope (1996) *Socio-cultural Issues and Economic Development in the Pacific Islands*, Pacific Studies Series, April, Asian Development Bank, Manila.

Schreurs, Stijnte and Arleen Richmond (1991) *Opening the Marketplace to Small Enterprise: Where Magic Ends and Development Begins*, ITP, London.

Schultz, T.W. (1964) *Transforming Traditional Agriculture*, Yale University Press, New Haven, Connecticut.

Schultz, T.W. (1979) Nobel lecture: The economics of being poor, *Journal of Political Economy* **88**(4), 639–51.

Seibel, Hans Dieter (1985) Saving for development: a linkage model for informal and formal financial markets, *Quarterly Journal of International Agriculture*, **24**(4), 390–8.

Seibel, Hans Dieter (1988) Financial innovations for micro-enterprises: linking informal and formal financial institutions in Africa and Asia, paper presented at the World Conference on 'Support of microenterprises', of *Committee of Donor Agencies for Small Enterprise Development*, 6–9 June, Washington, DC.

Seibel, Hans Dieter (1989) Finance with the poor, by the poor, for the poor: financial technologies for the informal sector with case studies from Indonesia, *Social Strategies* (Basel) **3**(2).

Seibel, Hans Dieter (1992) *Self-Help Groups as Financial Intermediaries: A Training Manual for Self-Help Groups, Banks and NGOs*, Verlag fuer Entwicklungspolitik, Saarbruecken (Germany).

Seibel, Hans Dieter (1995) Credit guarantee schemes in small and microenterprise finance: do they really do more good than harm? The case of the Philippines, *Quarterly Journal of International Agriculture*, (Berlin) **34**(2), 171–9.

Seibel, Hans Dieter (1996a) *Financial Systems Development and Microfinance*, Deutsche Gesellschaft fur Technische Zusammenarbeit (GTZ), G.m.b.H., Technical monograph No. 258, Rossdorf, Eschborn.

Seibel, Hans Dieter (1996b) Indonesia, in H.D. Seibel, *Financial Systems Development and Microfinance*, 17–23, GTZ, Eschborn, and TZ-Verlagsgesellschaft, Rossdorf.

Seibel, Hans Dieter (1996c) Nepal in H.D. Seibel, *Financial Systems Development and Microfinance*, 23–8, GTZ, Eschborn, and TZ-Verlagsgesellschaft, Rossdorf.

Seibel, Hans Dieter (1996d) Philippines, in H.D. Seibel, *Financial Systems Development and Microfinance*, 28–34, GTZ, Eschborn, and TZ-Verlagsgesellschaft, Rossdorf.

Seibel, Hans Dieter and Uttam Dhakhwa (1997) From informal to formal microfinance: the transformation of Dhikuti in Nepal, *Asia Pacific Rural Finance* (Bangkok).

Seibel, Hans Dieter and Uben Parhusip (1992) Linking formal and informal finance: an Indonesian example, in Dale W. Adams and A.A. Fitchett (eds), *Informal Finance in Low-Income Countries*, 239–48, Westview Press, Boulder.

Seibel, Hans Dieter and Bishnu P. Shrestha (1988) Dhikuti: the small businessman's informal self-help bank in Nepal, *Savings and Development* (Milan), **12**(2), 183–200.

Shanmugam, B. (1989) Development strategy and mobilising savings through RoSCAs: the case of Malaysia, *Savings and Development*, **13**(4), 351–66.

Siamwalla, A., C. Pinthong, N. Poapongsakorn, P. Sarsanguan, P. Nettayarak, W. Mingmaneenakin and Y. Tubpin (1990) The Thai rural credit system: public subsidies, private information and segmented markets, *World Bank Economic Review*, **4**(3), 271–96.

Simillie, Ian (1995) *The Alms Bazaar: Altruism Under Fire – Non-Profit Organisations and International Development*, ITP, London.

Sinnapan, P. (1995) *Activating Community Participation through Development Enterprise: Case Study of Koperasi Kredit Rakyat Bhd*, Jakarta, mimeo.

Snowden, Mary Lou (1995) *Report on Community Training Workshop on Implementing a Micro-Credit Scheme for Women in Western Samoa*, Workshop held at Apia on August 24 – September 1, UNDP, Suva, Fiji.

South Pacific Forum Secretariat (1996) *Annual Report*, Suva, Fiji.

Southwold-Llewellyn, Sarah (1991) Some explanations for the lack of borrower commitment to specialised farm credit institutions: a case study of the role of rural Sri Lankan Traders in meeting credit needs, *Savings and Development*, **15**(3), p. 285–313.

Srinivas, Hari and Yoichiro Higuchi (1996) A continuum of informality of credit: what can informal lenders teach us?', *Savings and Development*, **20**(2), 203–20.

Stiglitz, J.E. (1990) Peer monitoring and credit markets, *World Bank Economic Review*, **4**(3), 351–66.

Taumoepeau, Paula M. (1996) *Informal Financial Systems in Tonga*, Paper presented at the Workshop on Informal Financial Systems, 10–13 June 1996, Noumea, New Caledonia.

Teabo, Alex (1993) *Assessment Report on OIDPIMP (Outer Island Development Plan Implementation Management Programme)*, September, Ministry of Home Affairs and Rural Development, Kiribati.

Tendler, Judith and Monica Alves Amorim (1996) Small firms and their helpers: lessons on demand, *World Development*, **24**(3), 407–26.

Tengdui, Mary (1996) *Papua New Guinea Women's Credit Project: Operations Manual*, March, Department of Home Affairs, Port Moresby, Papua New Guinea.

Todd, Helen (ed.) (1996a) *Cloning Grameen Bank: Replicating a Poverty Reduction Model in India, Nepal and Vietnam*, ITP, London.

Todd, Helen (1996b) *Women at the Centre: Grameen Bank Borrowers after one Decade*, Westview Press, Boulder.

Tomlinson, Wayne (ed.) (1994) *Draft Training Manual on Targeting, Identification and Motivation for Credit and Savings Programmes of the Poor*, CASHPOR Inc., Kuala Lumpur, July.

Torres, Carmela I. (1995) Social security in the Philippines: a country study, in *Towards Social Security for the Poor in the Asia-Pacific Region*, UN-ESCAP, New York, 1996.

Townsend, P. (1993) *The International Analysis of Poverty*, Harvester Wheatsheaf, London.

Tuvalu Government Comprehensive Report: Second Phase of Tuvalu Rural Development Management Programme – Island Development Revolving Fund, Funafuti, Tuvalu.

U, Tan Wai (1977) A revisit to interest rates outside the organised money markets of underdeveloped countries, *Banco Nazionale del Lavoro Quarterly Review*, 122, September, 291–312.

Udry, C. (1990) Credit markets in Northern Nigeria: credit as insurance in a rural economy, *World Bank Economic Review*, **4**(3), 265–93.

UNDP (1993) *Micro Credit and Savings Project PNG/93/001-UNDP/ILO* Project Formulation Document, Port Moresby, Papua New Guinea.

UNDP (1994) *Pacific Human Development Report*, UNDP, July, Suva, Fiji.

UNDP (1995) *Tripartite Review Report on The Micro Credit and Savings Scheme PNG/93/001 in Eastern Highland Province*, UNDP, March, Port Moresby, Papua New Guinea.

UNDP (1990–7) *Human Development Report*, Oxford University Press, New York.

UNIFEM (1996) *Village Banking*, UNIFEM and SLEEP Network, New York.

Varian, H. (1990) Monitoring agents with other agents, *Journal of Institutional and Theoretical Economics*, **146**, 153–74.

Versluysen, E. (1999) *Defying the Odds: Banking for the Poor*, Kumarian Press, West Hartford, CT.

Vogel, Robert C. (1986) Savings mobilisation: the forgotten half of rural finances, in Adams, Gonzales-Vega and Von Pischke (1986).

Von Pischke, J.D. (1980) The political economy of specialised farm credit institutions in Howell (1980).

Von Pischke, J.D. (1991) *Finance at the Frontier*, EDI, World Bank, Washington, DC.

Von Pischke, J.D. Dale Adams and Gordon Donald (eds) (1983) *Rural Financial Markets in Developing Countries*, Johns Hopkins UP, Baltimore.

Von Pischke, J.D., in consultation with Peter J. Heffernan and Dale W. Adams (1981) The political economy of specialised farm credit institutions in low-income countries, Staff Working Paper No. 446, World Bank, Washington, DC.

Wahid, Abu (ed.) (1993) *The Grameen Bank: Poverty Relief in Bangladesh*, Westview, Boulder.

Webster, Leila (1989) *World Bank Lending for Small and Medium Enterprises: Fifteen Years of Experience*, World Bank Industry Development Division, World Bank, Washington, DC. (Also published in *Small Enterprise Development*, **1**(1), 17–25.

Wichman, Vaine (1993) *From Words to Wheelbarrows: The Nukuroa Revolving Fund*, Information Document No. 59, March, Case Studies of Rural Development Experiences in the Pacific-Case Study No. 3, South Pacific Commission, Noumea, New Caledonia.

Wigg, David (1993) *The Quiet Revolution*, World Bank Development Essay No. 2, World Bank, Washington, DC.

Women's Business Unit (1988) *A Study of Women in Micro Business: Their Resources and Their Needs*, Department of Co-operative & Rural Business Development in co-operation with the Statistics Office, Republic of Vanuatu.

Wood, Geoffrey D. and Iffath A. Sharif (1997) *Who Needs Credit? Poverty and Finance in Bangladesh*, Zed Books, 1997.

World Bank (1979) *Aspects of Relative Poverty in Sri Lanka*, Working Paper No. 5, Washington, DC.

World Bank (1980) *The Incident of Absolute Poverty in Sri Lanka: 1969–70*, Working Paper No. 6, Washington, DC.

World Bank (1984) *Agricultural Credit: Sector Policy Paper*, 2nd ed., Washington, DC.

World Bank (1988) *Some Aspects of Relative Poverty in Sri Lanka*, Staff Working Paper No. 461, Washington, DC.

World Bank (1989a) *India: Financial Sector Issues and Reforms*, Sector Report No. 8264-IN, Washington, DC.

World Bank (1989b) *Women in Development: Issues for Economic and Sector Analysis*, Policy Planning and Research Working Paper No. 269, Washington, DC.

World Bank (1990a) *World Development Report (Poverty)*, Oxford University Press, New York.

World Bank (1990b) *Indonesia: Second BRI-KUPEDES Small Credit Project*, Staff Appraisal Report No. 8644-IND, Washington, DC.

World Bank (1993a) *The East Asian Miracle: Economic Growth and Public Policy*, Oxford U Press, N.Y.

World Bank (1993b) *A Review of Bank Lending for Agricultural Credit and Rural Finances, 1948–92*, Operations Evaluations Department Report No. 12143, Washington, DC.

World Bank (1993c) *Pacific Island Economies: Toward Efficient & Sustainable Growth*, Vol. 1 Country Department III – East Asia and Pacific Region, March, Washington, DC.

World Bank (1982–95) *World Tables*, World Bank, Washington, DC.

World Bank (1996a) *Poverty Reduction and the World Bank: Progress and Challenges in the 1990s*, World Bank, Washington, DC.

World Bank (1996b) *Pacific Island Economies: Building a Resilient Economic Base for the Twenty-First Century*, World Bank, Washington, DC.

World Bank (1996c) *Bangladesh Rural Finance Report No. 15485-BD*, Agricultural and Natural Resources Division, World Bank, Washington, DC.

World Bank (1996d) *From Plan to Market. World Development Report 1996*, World Bank, Washington, DC.

World Bank (1990–7) *World Development Report*, Oxford University Press, New York.

World Bank (1997) *Conflict and Structural Adjustment in Sri Lanka*, Operations Evaluation Department Précis No. 133, World Bank, Washington, DC.

WOSED (1996) *The Women's Social & Economic Development Programme (WOSED) 1993–95*, Department of Women and Culture, Suva, Fiji.

Yaron, Jacob (1991) *Successful Rural Finance Institutions*, 2 vols, Agriculture Policies Division, World Bank, Washington, DC.

Yaron, Jacob (1994) What makes rural finance institutions successful?, *World Bank Research Observer*, **9**(1), January, 49–70.

Yunus, Muhammad (1983) If you can't beat them join them; or, how to operate your own financial institution, in Mattis, Ann (ed.) (1984) *A Society for International Development Prospectus*, Duke UP for Society for International Development, Durham, NC, 79–90.

Yunus, Mahammad (1988) Credit for self-employment: a fundamental human right, in Central Bank of Sri Lanka (1988) *The Symposium on Poverty Alleviation*, Central Bank Press, Colombo, 31–6.

Yunus, Muhammad (1991) *The Grameen Bank: Experiences and Reflections*, Grameen Bank, Dhaka.

Zander, R. (1992) Financial self-help organisation in rural Sri Lanka, paper presented to the 8th World Congress of Rural Sociology, Penn. State University, 11 August, mimeo.

Further Reading

Anon (1996a) Action towards poverty alleviation in Asia & Pacific. Descriptors: Asia Pacific, China, India, Indonesia, Nepal, Philippines, Thailand, Vietnam, and Poverty Alleviation, Income generation. *Social Development Newsletter* (Bangkok), Oct., No. 35, 2–7.

Anon (1996b) *Economic Liberalisation and Rural Poor. A Study on the Effects of Price Liberalisation & Market Reformism in Asian Developing Countries.* ESCAP (Bangkok) Descriptors: Poverty, Agricultural prices – Asia; China, India, Malaysia, Thailand, Vietnam, Rural Poor.

Anon (1996c) *Mongolia poverty assessment in transition economy IBRD.* World Bank. Washington, DC., 27 June report No. 15723 – MOG.

Anon (1996d) Netherlands funded success case replication project in Vietnam brings new hope for effective rural employment among poor households *Poverty Alleviation Initiatives* (PAI), Oct.–Dec., **6**(4).

Big reduction in poverty in Thailand (1996) *Poverty Alleviation Initiatives* (PAI). United Nations Interagency Subcommittee on Poverty Alleviation for Asia & the Pacific. Oct.–Dec., **6**(4).

Burmeister, Larry L. (1990) South Korea's rural development dilemma. *Asian Survey* (Berkeley), July, **20**(7), 711–23.

de Haan, Arjan (ed.) (1997) Assessing & responding to urban poverty: lessons from Pakistan, Urban Poverty: A New Research Agenda. *IDS Bulletin*, April, **28**(2), entire issue. Descriptors: Poverty: poverty alleviation; rural-urban migration – case studies; India; Pakistan; United Kingdom.

Eor Myong-Keun and Kim Jeong Youn (1994) A review of Korean rural development planning *Journal of Rural Development* (Seoul), **17**(2), 219–234.

Goldberg, Mike (1998) China's emerging microfinance industry. CGAP Secretariat No. 5, January,

Harper, Caroline (1994) *An Assessment of Vulnerable Groups in Mongolia: Strategies for Social Policy Planning*, IBRD. World Bank. Washington, DC. 74 pp.

Johansen, Frida (1993) Poverty reduction in East Asia: the silent revolution, August, World Bank Discussion Paper No. 203.

McGuire, Paul B., John D. Conroy, and Ganesh B. Thapa (1996) *Getting the Framework Right: Policy & Regulation for Microfinance in Asia*. Foundation for Development Corporation, Brisbane. May. 306pp.

Mukherjee, Joyita (1998) Strengthening Asian MFIs, CGAP Secretariat, No. 5, January.

Øyen, Else, S.M. Miller, and Syed Abdus Samad (eds) (1996) *Poverty: A Global View, Handbook on International Poverty Research*. Scandinavian University Press.

Prescott, Nicholas (1997a) Poverty, Social Services, Safety Nets in Vietnam. October, World Bank Discussion Paper No. 376.

Prescott, Nicholas and Menno Pradhan (1997b) A poverty profile of Cambodia, World Bank Discussion Paper No. 373.

Quibria, M.G. (ed.) (1996) *Rural Poverty in Developing Asia*. Indonesia, Republic of Korea, Philippines and Thailand ADB Manila, Philippines, vol. 2.

Todd, Helen (ed.) (1996) *Cloning Grameen Bank: Replicating Poverty Reduction Model in India, Nepal and Vietnam*. Intermediate Technology Publications, London. (Chapter 4, 77–97, Tau Yew Mai, Vietnam.)

Vinod, Ahuya *et al.* (1997) Everyone's miracle? Revisiting poverty and inequality in East Asia. *Directions in Development* IBRD, World Bank, Washington, DC. Descriptors: Poverty, Income distribution, Economic policy – Case Studies East Asia; Thailand.

Wignaraja, Ponna (1996) Poverty eradication: lessons from China and South Korea in the 1950s and 1960s, *International Social Science Journal* (Oxford), June, No. 148, 191–205.

Index